contents

preface

Despite the computer—or perhaps because of it—society in the 21st century is difficult to envisage. Technological developments occur so rapidly that the job of the planner has become little more than imaginative logic.

Let me give you an example in terms of the realities of the world of this decade. Developed only a few years ago, the transistor, a substitute for the vacuum tube, was adapted to thousands of uses in electronic devices. Because of the skyrocketing demand for the pea-sized economical device, one of the largest manufacturers in the world planned a huge new plant, expecting to employ about 8,000 people, to produce in tremendous quantities numerous varieties of this new electronic component.

By the time the plant was finished (about a year), its total nature had to be changed: a substitute device had been perfected which, using specialized photographic technology, made it possible to incorporate into the same pea size dozens of transistor-like items, *plus* even greater numbers of the other components which make up an electronic circuit. In addition, these new Integrated Circuit (I. C.) devices incorporated the multitude of connections needed. While the transistor is still valuable for many specialized uses, the I. C. has replaced it in thousands of products.

Moreover, less than ten thousand years ago, the only power source available to man was his own muscle. In a forward step of enormous magnitude, the domestication of animals in about 7,000 B. C. added the strength of animal power. Except for the utilization of wind and water, no sizeable advance was made for almost nine thousand years—until the invention of the steam engine in the nineteenth century.

The pace of discovery increased. The nineteenth century added electricity and the internal combustion engine; in the first half of the twentieth, the power of the atom. Before the twenty-first, solar power? Use of earth-core heat?

Each successive advance freed mankind from the more onerous chores of everyday existence. From a day spent entirely in providing for bare survival only nine millenia ago, man—in the industrialized nations, at least—has been able to shorten "work" time to less than eight hours per day. And efforts continue toward lowering that figure.

Technologically speaking, progress in other areas has spurted ahead at a phenomenal rate, particularly since World War II. It is estimated that human knowledge doubled in the two decades between 1945 and 1965, and that it will double again in each following decade. To synthetic muscle power we have added the brain-assist faculties of the computer, a device whose potential (for both good and bad) has barely been estimated. Some socio-economists anticipate that in the early 21st century it will be feasible to replace most muscle power with machines, most mental efforts with computers, and that only 2% of the members of industrialized society will *ever* be engaged in producing goods and services. They also predict that we will enjoy the highest standard of living we have ever experienced.

This potential is both exciting and threatening. We are presently totally unprepared for developments of this nature—psychologically and philosophically. Most of the tenets which guide our conduct today would become obsolete. "Man must live by the sweat of his brow"—the work ethic on which most of our religious, political, economic, sociological and educational mores are based—could become an archaic bromide. The word "leisure" will need a new definition; the meaning of "human," a much broader connotation. Tensions between the "have" and "have-not" nations could reach unbearable heights. A soaring world population could multiply the difficulties.

But at least we are aware of these problems and recognize that they will have to be faced. There exists, however, a far more serious threat to a possible glorious future for mankind. It is the fact that psychologically we are unprepared for a leisure society. Our educational institutions are doing little or nothing to prepare students for the flexibility that will be demanded of them. Courses in humanities continue to be oriented to the past in the assumption that history will provide the answers to questions that never existed before. A recent revision of a college economics textbook included the usual chapter on the law of supply and demand but relegated only two pages to a discussion of the effect of the computer! Philosophers discuss Plato's intellectual ideas but take no position on the promise of geneticists that the intellectual level of all men may be raised to exceptionally high levels. Students do research papers on the economic causes of the War between the States, but pay little or no attention to conditions that may exist when economic pressures are nonexistent. Communications experts devote much of their energy to exciting desires for industry's products, giving little thought to the fact that minority and student unrest may well be caused by bringing both war and luxury (in living color) into the living rooms of all but a tiny fraction of this country's homes.

A group of most capable students at Phoenix College, in a course called Advanced Critical and Evaluative Reading, undertook a research program into the thinking of a number of authorities on the changes these next decades may bring. These students do not profess to be prophetic; they do agree with Alvin Toffler, a social critic, when he says that "the new education must shift its accent from today to tomorrow. The only way to cushion individuals against future shock is to prepare them for the future, to offer them in advance some idea of what they may expect as tomorrow unrolls."

Most of us are optimists, and believe that there *will be* a society in the 21st century, developed from the cultures of today rather than from the devastation a third world war would wreak. "Brush wars," civil rights tensions, the restlessness prevalent today are stages in the accelerating movement of man toward a better life—for all men. Differing vigorously in our approach to the various aspects of the future discussed in this book, the majority thinks that, given the right set of circumstances, man is inherently capable of good rather than evil, action governed by intelligence rather than by emotion.

Others cannot accept the above premises. In general, they feel that the triple threats of war, pollution and over-population have gone beyond the controlling point, and that our present policies are inadequate and too late. They conclude that man is, by nature, so self-seeking that he cannot restructure priorities and is incapable of overcoming his fear of the different, the all-pervading motif of today's society. They argue that a society which provides huge sums for moon-shots, supersonic transport research and anti-ballistic weapons while paying only token attention to the poor, the underprivileged, the mentally ill and the elderly is incapable of the changes in attitude demanded by the accelerating rate of change. Several of their ideas, in proportion to their number, are to be found in the chapters that follow.

We all take heart, however, from the fact that the upcoming generation is far more aware of critical problems than was any preceding generation. We are however, most aware that to reach the year 2001 we must live through 1984.

It was with these considerations in mind that these students and I decided to collaborate in producing a book of readings. In your discussions of the various issues raised, we think you will find, as we did, that there is a powerful inter-relationship between all of these issues and that no single one can be evaluated by itself.

Maxwell H. Norman, *Senior Editor*

I.
the computer goes round and round: cybernetics

ELECTRONICS, COMPUTERS, AUTOMATION, AND INFORMATION PROCESSING

herman kahn & anthony wiener

THE CYBERNETIC AGE: AN OPTIMIST'S VIEW

glenn t. seaborg

Introduction and comment by jerry l. campbell

One of the newest "sciences," cybernetics, deals with the control of complex machines and communications as an extension of man's mental and physical powers. The instrument that has made this innovation possible is the computer.

Of all the probable advancements foreseen in the next 30 years, the continual growth of computer technology is the most certain and the most basic. Just as the steam engine ushered in the industrial revolution, the computer has set our course for a cybernated society.

Computers are already essential to our way of life. To an extent that most people do not comprehend, our lives are already irreversibly entwined with the circuits of a hundred computers. There is a new industrial revolution at hand and its by-words are cybernation and automation.

At Tyler, Texas, the Texas Eastern Transmission Corporation operates an oil refinery covering 360 acres. A master control panel records data from all sections of the plant and instructs three technicians as to what adjustments are necessary and where. This large complex, capable of processing 17,000 barrels of crude oil a day, is run solely by these three men. To qualify for such work, they need only a high school education. In more advanced plants, the three technicians are replaced by computers.

The world's largest computer is at your fingertips. The coast-to-coast direct dialing network of the Bell Telephone Company is a complex example of automation and computerization. When a number is dialed, the system automatically sets to work, locating the desired number—only one among 115 million telephones (Jan. 71) in the United States. It explores the myriad of available lines until it finds one open; in a matter of seconds or less a call across the country is complete. As many as 100,000 moving parts may be involved in a single call. Looking to the future, Bell engineers are hard at work replacing those moving parts with electronic devices less prone to breakdowns. They are also installing computers to make repairs when necessary.

Automation has even overtaken the kitchen. The kitchens of Sara Lee are now run by a Honeywell 610 computer capable of 62,500 computations a second. Each day, this computer turns some 36,000 pounds of milk, 66,000 pounds of eggs, 90,000 pounds of butter and other ingredients into countless cakes of about twelve varieties, storing them automatically on the shelves of a warehouse which is as big as a football field.

Our space technology is almost totally dependent on computers for its existence. The Apollo journeys would have been impossible without the aid of computers; their calculations are simply too many and too complex to be handled any other way. The Real-Time Computer Complex at the manned spacecraft center near Houston computes the operational activities of an Apollo spacecraft so fast that virtually no time lapses between receiving and solving a navigational problem.

These are just a few of the present applications of computers. By the time this book reaches print computers will be capable of even more fantastic operations. By the year 2000 the scope of usage of the computer will be so immense it cannot even be imagined. Computers will do jobs and coordinate other machines much better, much faster, and much cheaper than human labor. Quite possibly by the year 2000, 98 percent of the world's population will never have any job or wage responsibility, but will be required merely to serve as full-time consumers for what society's machines produce.

To a large extent, the scientific knowledge necessary for computer advancement is already at hand. No one really knows what the next major breakthrough will be. The major scientific activity in this field will be toward miniaturization and specialization along with more efficient methods of input and output. The impact of the computer will not be felt as a sudden development. Rather it will be gradual, as the computer slowly but surely invades every aspect of life. As scientific problems crop up, they will be easily overcome. Before long man will probably no longer have to design computers; computers will design each other much more efficiently.

What must be realized when considering the complications of our cybernated society is that most of the pressing problems are moral rather than scientific. We are confronted with questions such as: What is man's role in a society controlled by computers? What are the boundaries of human freedom? At what point is privacy being invaded? What is there for man to do when he no longer needs to work? At what point does the machine turn from slave to ruler and man from ruler to slave? These questions must be answered—and not by a computer.

In the excerpts that follow, three well-known authors describe a number of aspects of automation.

j.l.c.

ELECTRONICS, COMPUTERS, AUTOMATION, AND INFORMATION PROCESSING

Herman Kahn—mathematician, physicist, master strategist—is the Director of the Hudson Institute, a policy research organization which he joined in 1961. Previously he was with the Rand Corporation as senior physicist (1948 to 1961). He has been a consultant to the Atomic Energy Commission, Office of the Secretary of Defense, as well as to various private firms. His works include: On Thermonuclear War, *1960;* Thinking About the Unthinkable, *1962;* Metaphors and Scenarios, *1965; and numerous articles in scientific journals.*

Anthony Wiener is associated with Dr. Kahn at the Hudson Institute, where he is chairman of the Research Management Council.

We turn now to what may be—at least as far as the postindustrial world in the last third of the twentieth century is concerned—the most important, exciting, and salient aspect of modern technology. If the middle third of the twentieth century is known as the nuclear era, and if past times have been known as the age of steam, iron, power, or the automobile, then the next thirty-three years may well be known as the age of electronics, computers, automation, cybernation, data processing, or some related idea.

This whole area is currently about the most dynamic and volatile of our technologies. As a result, when one specialist declares that "the computer gives signs of becoming the contemporary counterpart of the steam engine that brought on the industrial revolu-

Reprinted from Herman Kahn and Anthony Wiener, The Year 2000: A Framework for Speculation *by permission of the authors and publisher. Copyright © 1967 by the MacMillan Company.*

tion,"[1] and another argues that the computer represents "an advance in man's thinking process as radical as the invention of writing,"[2] one is not irritated by the grandiosity of the claim, but only by what has become its obviousness. The capacity of the computer ultimately to effect a dramatic extension of man's power over his environment, as well as many other social and economic changes, is by now obvious to all.

electronics

Let us consider first the basic electronic technology. In the last decade this has progressed spectacularly, and the changes foreseeable for the next decade—much less the next thirty-three years—are equally impressive.

The pace of change in electronics—and the accelerating tempo—is shown by these dates: vacuum tubes, around 1900; first practical transistor, 1948; transistor use and invention of the integrated circuit, 1958; development of integrated circuits, 1960–1963; and now invention of a fourth generation of change, called large-scale integration or LSI, 1967. LSI is basically an extension of integrated circuit technology involving the wiring of complete circuits on a silicon chip, instead of tying components together. Military systems and commercial applications using LSI techniques should begin to appear in a year or two. Another aspect of LSI devices is that they will not only be used to build better computers, but will also be the product of computers: computers are used to design, interconnect, and produce the circuits.

As a result of these innovations the cost of complex circuits is dropping, from about eighty cents now (compared to three dollars for equivalent transistor circuits) to predictions of a few cents per chip in the next decade. This reduction in cost of about 100 accompanies an increase in reliability of a factor of 100 to 1,000 over what was achieved a decade ago and a 10,000-fold reduction, in the last two decades, in the volume required for a complex electronic package. Present technology permits the manufacture of 100-500 integrated circuits on a silicon wafer an inch in diameter and less than one-hundredth of an inch thick, or complete computer and communications subsystems containing more than 1,000 circuits, each with more than 400 transistors, on half-dollar-size silicon chips less than one-eighth inch thick. The accelerating rate of

[1] From "Information" by John McCarthy, Copyright © 1966 by Scientific American, Inc. All rights reserved. September 1966, p. 65.
[2] Herbert A. Simon, quoted in *Time,* April 2, 1965, p. 88.

change in electronics technology makes it almost impossible to say much that is interesting about the electronics technology of the year 2000. Almost all of the possible developments that one can explicitly formulate seem likely to be realized much sooner.

electronic computers

Let us first consider the basic computer. Without elaborate input-output devices or sophisticated programs, a computer is really little more than a very large, very fast, and very complex abacus, but even so stripped, it has amazing potentialities. It has also had an amazing record of increase in potentiality over the last fifteen years. If one uses as a standard of measurement the size of the memory space divided by the basic "add time" of the computer (which measures roughly a computer's ability both to hold and to process information), then over the past fifteen years this basic criterion of computer performance has increased by a factor of ten every two or three years (this is a conservative estimate).

While some will argue that we will not duplicate this performance in the future because we are beginning to reach limits set by basic physical constraints, such as the speed of light, this may not be true, especially when one considers new techniques in time-sharing, segmentation of programs to add flexibility, and parallel-processing computers. The experimental parallel-processing ILLIAC IV to be developed for ARPA by Burroughs Corporation, using LSI circuit arrays and extremely high-speed thin-film memory storage, will provide a data processing speed 500-700 times that of existing computer systems and more than 100 times faster than any computer known to be in development.[3] The parallel-processing concept permits various elements of a complex problem to be solved simultaneously, rather than serially as in present systems. Other means of continuing the increase in computer capabilities by a factor of ten every several years may include using basic computational units that operate on the basis of matrices rather than single numbers; large-scale improvement in the present "soft-ware crisis" in programming language, treating complex operations as single units and combining them in both parallel and hierarchical operations, and so on. Thus even excluding the impact of new input-output devices and new concepts for programming and problem formulation, but just considering the basic capacity of the computer as a large and fast abacus has still meant that any doctrine about capabilities and

[3] See *Technology Week* and the *New York Times,* February 11, 1967.

limitations has had to be revised extensively every two or three years. But these exclusions are also important. About nine years ago, a program containing five thousand instructions was considered quite large. Now with the present capacities of computers and new programming languages such as FORTRAN, ALGOL, or MAD for scientific problems, JOVIAL for military applications, or COBOL, LISP or CPL for other problem-solving uses, an individual can handle programs about ten times larger and a team may easily produce a program still larger by a factor of five to ten. These programs that used to take an hour or two to run now take a few seconds.

If computer capacities were to continue to increase by a factor of ten every two or three years until the end of the century (a factor between a hundred billion and ten quadrillion), then all current concepts about computer limitations will have to be reconsidered. Even if the trend continues for only the next decade or two, the improvements over current computers would be factors of thousands to millions. If we add the likely enormous improvements in input-output devices, programming and problem formulation, and better understanding of the basic phenomena being studied, manipulated, or simulated, these estimates of improvement may be wildly conservative. And even if the rate of change slows down by several factors, there would still be room in the next thirty-three years for an overall improvement of some five to ten orders of magnitude. Therefore, it is necessary to be skeptical of any sweeping but often meaningless or nonrigorous statements such as "a computer is limited by the designer—it cannot create anything he does not put in," or that "a computer cannot be truly creative or original." By the year 2000, computers are likely to match, simulate, or surpass some of man's most "human-like" intellectual abilities, including perhaps some of his aesthetic and creative capacities, in addition to having some new kinds of capabilities that human beings do not have. These computer capacities are not certain; however, it is an open question what inherent limitations computers have. If it turns out that they cannot duplicate or exceed certain characteristically human capabilities, that will be one of the most important discoveries of the twentieth century.

Existing programs for such near human functions as recognizing analogies between geometric figures, taken from a well-known college-admissions examination, can score at about the tenth-grade level; a second, checker-playing program uses information gained in previous attempts—its experience—to improve its analysis; a third called Student "probably surpasses the average person in its ability to handle algebra problems," using a limited range of ordinary English. "When it runs into difficulty, it asks usually pertinent questions . . . often it resolves the difficulty by referring to the knowledge in its files." [4] If this is where we are now, then the future possibilities—particularly as improvements of many orders of magnitude are realized—may well include something that might reasonably be described as "artificial intelligence"—something much more than just a very fast abacus.

This idea of computer "intelligence" is a sensitive point with many people. The claim is not that computers will resemble the structure of the human brain, but that their functional output will equal or exceed that of the human brain in many functions that we have been used to thinking of as aspects of intelligence, and even as uniquely human. Still a computer will presumably not become "humanoid" and probably will not use similar processes, but it may have properties which are analogous to or operationally indistinguishable from self-generated purposes, ideas, and emotional responses to new inputs or its own productions. In particular, as computers become more self-programming they will increasingly tend to perform activities that amount to "learning" from experience and training. Thus they will eventually evolve subtle methods and processes that may defy the understanding of the human designer.

In addition to this possibility of independent intelligent activities, computers are being used increasingly as a helpful flexible tool for more or less individual needs—at times in such close cooperation that one can speak in terms of a man-machine symbiosis. Eventually there will probably be computer consoles in every home, perhaps linked to public utility computers and permitting each user his private file space in a central computer, for uses such as consulting the Library of Congress, keeping individual records, preparing income tax returns from these records, obtaining consumer information, and so on.

Computers will also presumably be used as teaching aids, with one computer giving simultaneous individual instruction to hundreds of students, each at his own console and topic, at any level from elementary to graduate school; eventually the system will probably be designed to maximize the individuality of the learning process. Presumably there will also be such things as:

1. A single national information file containing all tax, legal, security, credit, educational, medical, employment, and other

information about each citizen. (One problem here is the creation of acceptable rules concerning access to such a file, and then as discussed below the later problem of how to prevent erosion of these rules after one or two decades of increased operation have made the concept generally acceptable, as discussed below.)

2. Time-sharing of large computers by research centers in every field, providing national and international pools of knowledge and skill.

3. Use of computers to test trial configurations in scientific work, allowing the experimenter to concentrate on his creativity, judgment, and intuition, while the computer carries out the detailed computation and "horse work." A similar symbiotic relationship will prevail in engineering and other technological design. Using the synergism of newer "problem-oriented" computer language, time-sharing, and new input-output techniques, engineer-designers linked to a large computer complex will use computers as experienced pattern-makers, mathematical analysts of optimum design, sources of catalogs on engineering standards and parts data, and often substitutes for mechanical drawings.

4. Use of real-time large computers for an enormous range of business information and control activity, including most trading and financial transactions; the flow of inventories within companies and between suppliers and users; immediate analysis and display of company information about availability of products, prices, sales statistics, cash flow, credit, bank accounts and interests on funds, market analysis and consumer tastes, advanced projections, and so on.

5. Vast use of computers to reduce and punish crime, including the capacity of police to check immediately the identification and record of any person stopped for questioning.

6. Computerized processes for instantaneous exchange of money, using central computer-bank-and-store-computer networks for debiting and crediting accounts.

In addition, there will be uses of computers for worldwide communications, medical diagnostics, traffic and transportation control, automatic chemical analyses, weather prediction and control, and so on.

The sum of all these uses suggests that the computer utility industry will become as fundamental as the power industry, and that the computer can be viewed as the most basic tool of the last third of the twentieth century. Individual computers (or at least consoles or other remote input devices) will become essential equipment for home, school, business, and profession, and the ability to use a computer skillfully and flexibly may become more widespread than the ability to play bridge or drive a car (and presumably much easier).

automation and cybernation

We now turn to one of the most widely misunderstood aspects of modern technology. Perhaps it would therefore be best to start with a few simple definitions.

Historically, the first use of mechanization was to increase the usefulness of human or animal muscles in a more or less direct fashion, such as by gaining "mechanical advantage." Thus primitive man learned to use such simple machines as levers in order to lift objects which he could not otherwise lift. The use of an inclined plane is really an advanced form of a lever. A wheelbarrow enables a less primitive man to carry things more conveniently and easier than he could without one. And so on to quite complex machines, such as plows and boats. Later, other sources of energy—principally windmills and waterwheels—were added.

With the impact of industrialization two new things were added: (1) better organization of work—particularly by increased specialization, and (2) the increased mechanization and even automation of production. In the first case, the work is reorganized or broken up into small, specialized pieces, each of which can be done more expeditiously or with less skill. In the second, a sequence of operations was carried out automatically by using simple control devices or more complex machines. The first process is often a forerunner of the second process because simplification or reorganization of the work is often a necessary prerequisite to mechanization and automation.

Very early in this process of the use of complex mechanization and automation there was use of so-called cybernetic techniques. In a cybernetic system there is some method of looking at the output of a system, comparing it with a desired norm and then using this difference to actuate some control mechanism that attempts to adjust the system to the desired norm. A thermostat in a house or a governor on an engine are typical examples of cybernetic systems. Donald Michael has coined the term "cybernation" to describe the situation in which a computer is used to cybernate some automatic system so as basically to eliminate the role of man as a supervisor and use him only as a monitor who can if necessary "override" the system. There is today much concern about the supposedly large, or imminently large, degree of mechanization, automation, and cybernation in the United States.

Thus manufacturers of automation equipment have estimated that automation is eliminating 40,000–50,000 jobs a week, or between 2–2.5 million jobs a year. Limited automation in the steel industry is estimated to have eliminated 80,000 jobs out of a total of 600,000 in the industry between 1953 and 1966, with a minimum of 100,000 more job losses estimated for the next decade. Yet despite the fewer employees needed to turn out increased steel production, mills find it difficult to recruit enough help of the type they need, one reason being that many skilled workers let go in earlier years have moved into other fields.[5] Despite the job losses due to automation, and the influx of about three and a half million young people into the labor market yearly, our present unemployment rate is undeniably low. The economy today is able to supply jobs to replace those lost to automation and to accommodate an expansion of the total working population, with the exception of an official unemployment rate of 4–5 percent. Moreover, a study by Columbia's Bureau of Applied Social Research found no correlation between mechanizing industries and a better educated work force in 1960, compared to 1950. It concluded that there are "plenty" of jobs in the economy which high school dropouts are capable of handling, even in automated industries, and that the higher unemployment rate among dropouts is probably due to employee selectivity in a too-large labor force. Thus the present problem of automation may not be one of education and retraining, but simply of generating more jobs.

Indeed, as some skeptics are fond of pointing out one has only to go to any construction site, store, or house to see that it is hard to replace the human being in many kinds of relatively lowly labor. In fact, in some ways this low-quality labor with its erratic and sporadic demands is more difficult to replace than some branch of much more skilled labor which, however, has much more predictable demands and requirements. In any case it is important to note that despite all the publicity and controversy there are almost no cybernated industrial plants in the United States today and that even automation has not progressed as far as many publicists, enthusiastics, or viewers with alarm would have us believe. (This is an almost unbelievable statement when one con-

[5] *Wall Street Journal,* September 16, 1966.

siders all the publicity, but it seems to be true. For this reason more than any other the impact of cybernation and automation, particularly on employment, has been much exaggerated.) [6]

This seems to be one of those quite common situations in which early in the innovation period many exaggerated claims are made, then there is disillusionment and a swing to overconservative prediction and a general pessimism and skepticism, then finally when a reasonable degree of development has been obtained and a learning period navigated, many—if not all—of the early "ridiculous" exaggerations and expectations are greatly exceeded. It is particularly clear that if, as suggested in the last section, computers improve by five, ten, or more orders of magnitude over the next thirty-three years this is almost certain to happen.

For the near future, automation and cybernation are likely to create as many jobs as they eliminate, by contributing to the increase of productivity and economic growth. The creation of new jobs is a subtle and undramatic process, and it is difficult to chart how and to what extent increases in productivity causes investment which leads to new jobs, whereas the direct elimination of jobs is both noticeable and dramatic.

The net effects on employment, hours worked, and productivity are difficult to predict, particularly because the rate at which industrial processes are automated may increase and the tradeoff between increased production and leisure that society may choose are both quite uncertain.

Nevertheless it is quite clear that in the next ten years automation will begin to impinge on or to increase its foothold in many areas of activity. Thus to reach its goal of "next day" delivery anywhere in the United States, the Post Office has several companies intensively studying the design of electronic optical scanners to recognize zip code addresses on letters at the rate of six envelopes a second, to be combined with automatic face-cancelers, and letter sorting machines. The twenty-three million dollars to be spent this year by the Post Office on automation equipment is a small part

[6] For a very good discussion of the issues in this section, one might see *The Shape of Automation* by Herbert Simon (New York: Harper and Row, 1965) or *The Myths of Automation* by Charles E. Silberman (New York: Harper and Row, 1966). These are probably the two best popular books on the subject, though they have a difficulty: both authors are so concerned to give a proper perspective on the subject by debunking the exaggerated claims of various enthusiasts and alarmists that the reader may come away with an underestimate of the long-term impact of automation, even if he has achieved a reasonable perspective on the short-term issues.

of the investment that will be required to meet the mail "crisis." Other industries will soon have to do much the same thing. Automation and cybernation may be extended to the home also. The idea of moderately priced robots doing most of the housework by the year 2000 may be difficult to accept at first. According to an enthusiast, Meredith Wooldridge Thring, professor of mechanical engineering at Queen Mary College in London, "within 10 to 20 years' time we could have a robot that will completely eliminate all routine operations around the house and remove the drudgery from human life."

> The great majority of the housewives will wish to be relieved completely from the routine operations of the home such as scrubbing the floors or the bath or the cooker, or washing the clothes or washing up, or dusting or sweeping, or making beds.
> By far the most logical step to allow this variety of human homes and still relieve the housewife of routine, is to provide a robot slave which can be trained to the requirements of a particular home and can be programmed to carry out half a dozen or more standard operations (for example, scrubbing, sweeping and dusting, washing-up, laying tables, making beds), when so switched by the housewife. It will be a machine having no more emotions than a car, but having a memory for instructions and a limited degree of instructed or built-in adaptability according to the positions in which it finds various types of objects. It will operate other more specialized machines, for example, the vacuum cleaner or clothes-washing machine.
> There are no problems in the production of such a domestic robot to which we do not have already the glimmering of a solution. It is therefore likely that, with a strong programme of research, such a robot could be produced in ten years. If we assume that it also takes ten years before industry and government are sufficiently interested to find the sum required for such development (which is of the order of £1 million), then we could still have it by 1984.[7]

His description of robot household capacities and widespread use seems most reasonable by the year 2000. We shall have to ponder the *double* impact within the next thirty-three years of widespread industrial and household automation.

[7] M. W. Thring, "A Robot in the House," in Nigel Calder (ed.), *The World in 1984* (Baltimore, Md.: Penguin Books, 1964), Vol. 2, p. 38.

information processing

The next step in automation is to apply it to information rather than machines. This application is, of course, very closely related to computers as just discussed, but is perhaps best perceived as examining various ways for acquiring, processing, storing, retrieving, and using information.

The problems of putting something like the Library of Congress conveniently at the fingertips of any user anywhere are dependent on our understanding and simulation of the ways in which people make associations and value judgments. One sticking point is the analysis and comparison of records or documents. Of seven stages in information storage, requesting, machine search, retrieval, and print-out, the first two currently require human judgment. Humans must identify those records that deal with a common area of interest, and must analyze each record or document to decide what specific topics it covers, and the other areas with which it should be associated. The process is accomplished by specialization; limiting the records in scope and purpose; analyzing and organizing a collection with great precision in anticipating questions, usually by means of indexing; or permitting a record-by-record search of the whole collection. Technological advances, particularly automatic data-processing equipment in association with computers and new microrecording mediums, are reducing the cost of operating a large information storage and retrieval system, but currently the human labor involved in collecting and analyzing records is still enormous.

However, computers can even now index documents by all the major words in their titles, though they will only select synonymous words for indexing according to their machine language dictionary. The need to improve computer capacities for making associations is therefore critical to real-time search and retrieval of the literature on a subject with many subsidiary facets.

It is impossible to predict how far along we will be by the year 2000 in simulating in computers analytical abilities that require decades and vast amounts of experience for humans to acquire, but thirty-three years of continuing work should be enough to surpass any current expectations that have been seriously and explicitly formulated. We should keep in mind that we have been discussing the most difficult problem of information storage and retrieval. For storage and retrieval of categories of information than can be described in a straightforward way, adequate systems exist now and will continue to grow rapidly.

Fully automatic systems have been developed for detecting index codes of various types (optical film reels, film cards, magnetic cards and paper cards) and for retrieving or displaying records on demand. . . . Records that are already in machine-readable form can be transmitted easily over wires and microwave channels to printing devices, recording devices or computers. Records not in machine-readable form can be scanned by optical-electric devices and then transmitted, to be reconstituted at the receiving end. . . . Second, the capability of controlling the transmitting process . . . can be given to the human or the machine at the receiving end. . . . With such developments, the geographic boundaries of traditional information storage and retrieval systems are beginning to evaporate. In their place are beginning to emerge vast networks of compatible communication devices linking users with many specialized and overlapping collections. Data-transmission costs are still sufficiently high, however, to keep the dissolution of traditional systems from becoming a runaway revolutionary process.[8]

Within about fifteen years, data-transmission costs are likely to be reduced so much that information storage and retrieval will become a runaway revolutionary process.

The current proposal for a National Data Center being debated in Congress, in which the records of some twenty or more government organizations will be amalgamated in one place is an example of things to come. In this case it is proposed that records be kept in the form of individual files so that the information will be as detailed and useful as possible. There is also concern, as we have said, about the possible abuses of such systems. Much of the discussion and debate is focused on methods of preventing such abuse, but almost all agree that the system or one like it will soon be operating.[9]

Similarly, there are likely to be great strides in real-time credit, auditing and banking systems, and in the real-time collection and processing of economic and social information generally.

If all this information is made available to the government, this should give it the ability to assess various current programs and situations, to rapidly initiate new programs or modify old ones, and

[8] Ben-Ami Lipetz, "Information Storage and Retrieval," *Scientific American,* September 1966, p. 238.
[9] See the story on the current IBM study on computer pooling of all files for the city of New Haven, *New York Times,* March 29, 1967.

then to study the short-run results of these actions almost immediately and continuously. Indeed the government might interact with short-term changes in the economic and social system in much the same way as the pilot with a plane, or the driver with an automobile. In terms of research in economics, sociology, medicine, and so on, these detailed personal, social, economic, and biological records should make possible some startling advances. Even with current techniques we should be able to process this information and find out all sorts of subtle correlations or cause and effect relationships as the state of the art of data-processing improves. And as we get some experience in monitoring and manipulating and develop new techniques and theories there should be some most impressive increases in our understanding and control of various aspects of our society.

Of course, the possibility of a serious invasion of privacy by the government (or private individuals) is raised by the rapid progress toward centralized data processing for government, business, and personal record-keeping. This is clearly a serious problem, and while some discussion has involved apocalyptic language, the authors would agree that without adequate safeguards some of these warnings may prove justified.[10] Indeed it is possible that such problems will be raised not as a by-product of normal commercial and government operations, but because there has been special design and procurement of systems for the surveillance, monitoring, and control of individuals.

Thus a future President of the United States might easily have command and control systems that involve having many television cameras in a future "Vietnam" or domestic trouble spot. Since he would be likely to have multiple screens, he would be able to scan many TV cameras simultaneously. In order to save space, some of the screens would be quite small and would be used only for gross surveillance, while others might be very large, in order to allow examination of detail. Paul Nitze, the present Secretary of the Navy, has made the suggestion that similar capabilities might be made available to the public media or even the public directly. This would certainly be a mixed blessing. Obviously such capability can give a misleading psychological impression of a greater awareness, knowledge, and sensitivity to local conditions and issues than really exists. This in turn could lead to an excessive degree of central control. This last may be an important problem for executives generally.

[10] See our discussion of Social Control in Chap. VIII, and the related discussion on pp. 389–91.

There are also important possibilities in the field of law enforcement. New York State has already tried an experiment in which the police read the license plates of cars going over a bridge into Manhattan and had a computer check these licenses against its files of scofflaws. The police were able to arrest a number of surprised drivers before they got to the other side of the bridge. (Some of the drivers seem to feel that this was like shooting quail on the ground.)

Such systems could be made completely automatic. Indeed it would be no trick at all, if the license plates were written in some suitable computer alphabet, to have them read by a television camera that was mounted on an automatic scanner. We can almost assume that toll booths or other convenient spots will be so equipped at some future date. It would then not be difficult to place these records of automobile movements in a computer memory or permanent file as an aid to traffic-flow planning, crime detection, or other investigations (as is done with taxicab trip reports in many cities today). One can even imagine fairly large-scale records of all license plates (or other identification) passing various checkpoints being kept for many streets and routes.

Let us take an even more extreme example. A capability for listening and recording temporarily (or even permanently) can be made very inexpensive. One can imagine the legal or illegal magnetic or other recording of an appreciable percentage of the telephone conversations that take place. (For that matter, the same techniques could be applied to "bugged" conversations in bars, restaurants, offices, and so on.) It would then be feasible to scan these conversations rapidly by means of a high speed computer—at least for key phrases—and then record any conversations that meet some criteria for justifying special interest or placement in a more permanent file for further investigation—or just to keep a record. For simple computers, the criteria could be certain words—underworld jargon, obscenities, or words such as "bet," "horserace," "kill," "subvert," "revolution," "infiltrate," "Black Power," "organize," "oppose"—or more sophisticated combinations. Indeed future computers and programs should be able to carry out much more complex operations—possibly responding to nonverbal information, such as an unusually angry or threatening tone in a voice. Such computers may also be able to apply a great deal of inferential logic on their own—they may become a sort of transistorized Sherlock Holmes making hypotheses and investigating leads in a more or less autonomous or self-motivated manner, all the while improving their techniques as they accumulate information about patterns of criminal behavior—or any other kind of behavior that authorities decide ought to be observed. New legal doctrines will need to be developed to regulate these new possibilities for "just looking." [11]

[11] See the special issue on "Privacy" in *Law and Contemporary Problems,* XXXI, No. 2 (Spring, 1966), for several interesting discussions of problems that have *already* arisen.

THE CYBERNETIC AGE:
AN OPTIMIST'S VIEW

Glenn T. Seaborg was educated at the University of California, Los Angeles and received his Ph.D. in Chemistry at the University of California, Berkeley. Honorary science doctorates were awarded by the University of Denver, 1951, Northwestern, 1954, and Notre Dame, 1961. During World War II he collaborated in discoveries of radioactive isotopes and headed a group at Metallurgical Laboratories. He was associated with the Radiation Laboratory at Berkeley, where he became Chancellor in 1958. He was co-recipient of the Nobel Peace Prize in 1951, as well as recipient of countless other honors and awards here and abroad. He served as Chairman of the Atomic Energy Commission until the middle of 1971.

Dr. Seaborg is the author of Nuclear Properties of the Heavy Elements, *1964, and other books and journal articles.*

What we need is a computer that will tell us where all other computers are leading us. We have computers that make up corporation payrolls, review a nation's tax returns, diagnose diseases, help design, produce, and market new products, control air and auto traffic, operate bakeries, hire and fire, read and write, learn and teach, and even play Cupid—though fortunately not yet to other computers, just among people. But the ultimate computer that can assess the significance of all this has yet to be built and programed. This task is still left to humans.

And it is an incredibly difficult task. Why? Because the ultimate potential of the computer puts us to the test as human beings. It brings up questions we have lived with for centuries, but never have been asked to answer fully or act upon if we believed we knew the answers. It gives us new freedom and yet tremendous responsibilities which, if not acted upon, could result in a loss of almost all freedom. It presents us with choices and decisions of enormous consequences. It offers man a remarkable new chance to shape his own destiny, but asks him to be God-like enough to select that destiny without much margin for error.

Let me project a few thoughts on how the computer may forge our future—and, more important, on some of the ideas and alternatives with which we must come to grips if we are going to control the direction of that future.

To begin with, I believe that cybernation—the complete adaptation of computer-like equipment to industrial, economic, and social activity—will represent a quantum jump in the extension of man. The Industrial Revolution amplified (and to a large extent replaced) man's muscle as a productive force. Still, a large percentage of our production resulted from the energies of man and beast. Today in the United States, only a fraction of 1 per cent of our productive power results from the physical energy of human beings or animals.

Springing from our Scientific Revolution of recent decades is what is being called a "Cybernetic Revolution." This revolution, which, comparatively speaking, is only in its infancy, amplifies (and will to a large extent replace) man's nervous system. Actually, this is an understatement because computers amplify the collective intelligence of men—the intelligence of society—and, while the effect of the sum of men's physicial energies may be calculated, a totally different and compounded effect results from combining facts and ideas—the knowledge generated within a society or civilization. Add this effect to the productive capacity of the machine driven by an almost limitless energy source like the nucleus of the atom, and the resulting system can perform feats almost staggering to our imagination. With the fullest development of cybernation we could be faced with prospects that challenge our very relationships to such basic concepts as freedom and the nature of work and leisure.

Let me suggest a few random scenes from the coming Cybernetic Age which contain some significant implications. I will not vouch for the accuracy of these forecasts or try to predict the year they might occur, but perhaps you can imagine yourself in one of these three situations:

Situation No. 1: You have flown out of town on a business trip and upon arrival at your destination have a few spare hours in which to visit an old friend. At the airport you rent a car, or some other type of ground vehicle. The procedure for putting you in the driver's seat is simple and efficient. You place an identifying card containing your bank account number and a microfiche of your fingerprints in a slot, and the fingers of your free hand over a flat, innocent-looking plate. Within seconds you have been identified as the owner of the card and your credit rating has been checked. The keys to your rented car are released to you and you are on your way.

Driving through town you encounter a minimum of delay at the busiest hour because the traffic lights are controlled by computers. But, anxious to see your old friend, you step up your speed once you are on the outskirts of town and, without realizing it, you exceed the speed limit by a few miles an hour. You remain unaware of this violation until you return home, at which time you receive a notice of it and learn that the violation calls for a fine, which, you also learn, has already been charged to your bank account.

How did this happen? It was almost as simple as renting the car. An inconspicuous device clocked your speed and recorded your auto tags. It reported the violation to the owner of the vehicle whose own computer had your records at hand and instantly "turned you in." The computer operated by the long arm of the law had no difficulty in tracking down both you and your bank account, so justice was swift and complete.

You are fairly well conditioned to this sort of situation by now, but sometimes you have moments of doubt and anxiety about what happened. If someone, or something, was watching you that closely on the road, where else might they be watching you? What if the system was in error—if someone, somewhere, was "adjusting" it so as to create more violators and bring in a little more revenue? But paying the fine was far easier than trying to investigate that possibility, so you give up what you once considered a legitimate right. Furthermore, you've heard that next year they're installing systems which will automatically regulate your speed on those roads, so you won't have to worry about exceeding the limit. You won't have that worry—or choice.

I will not belabor the implications of this situation. I believe they speak for themselves. Let me move on to situation No. 2:

For several days you have not been feeling well, and you call your local health center for an appointment. You can remember when you used to call your doctor, but it's been many years since he's bothered with initial diagnoses, and he would be the first to admit he could not be as thorough or accurate as the health center.

At the center you give all the necessary information to a medical secretary, whose typewriter feeds it into a computer system. First comes your identification number, which automatically supplies the system with your previous medical history, then all your new complaints and symptoms. On the basis of the information given so far and a comparison with your previous history, the computer may venture an immediate diagnosis, but if it has any doubts—and it is a highly conservative computer—it recommends one or several diagnostic tests. The tests are conducted simply and efficiently with the aid of one or two capable medical technicians and a battery of equipment.

The battery of diagnostic equipment programs its findings into the central computer which already has your previous medical history and your current complaints. Within seconds, after the tests are completed, the system presents its full diagnosis. At the same time it also makes recommendation for treatment, perhaps printing out a prescription which can be filled before you leave the center.

Does your doctor ever see patients? The computer refers a few cases to him because of their unusual interest. The high level of medicine he practices now enables him to help these patients. Their cases also help him in his work with engineers to improve the design of diagnostic and treatment systems and to train the many medical technicians who are needed to handle the increased population.

As in the first situation, there are a multitude of implications in this project. But let me proceed to situation No. 3:

You are a key man in a company that produces certain products for the home. You feel quite fortunate because you have a creative job in a highly automated plant. Market surveys analyzed by computers tell the company of the need for a new product. You sit at a desk containing a large fluorescent screen and with an electronic "lightpen" draw your conception of the new product. As you design the product you "tell" the computerized screen what materials you want the product to be made of. The system coordinates the information from the lightpen with your other instructions. As you work, it guides you in your design by making recommendations, by showing you on command the stress and strain in various points of your design, by correcting your errors, by recommending alternatives and improvements.

When both you and the system are satisfied with your handiwork, you release the design for manufacture. The system has theoretically tested the product so that no initial sample or test model is necessary. It turns the design over to another department —probably other computers—which calculates and orders the materials necessary to produce it, sets up the required manufacturing equipment, and prepares the production schedule. You never see the product, but you know it has been turned out just the way you envisioned it. And how long will it be before the computer will make it without you?

To some people these three examples sound like science fiction. Others will refer to them as "windy futurism." But they are far from being either. Some of the devices and methods mentioned are already in existence and in practical use. Others are in the development stages. And many more are not only technically feasible but may someday become economically and socially acceptable.

What are some of the implications in these examples, and what bearing will they have on our future? Running through all three examples were many common features: depersonalization, a separation of man and product, a collapse of time, a further reduction of human work, and a shift of needs and skills. All of these offer both threats and promises. I believe that the promises will eventually override the threats, but not before they have made us face and solve a great many problems we have not had to face before. This in itself is going to account for a great deal of human growth.

There is no doubt that the Cybernetic Revolution is going to make us reexamine the relationship between our freedoms and our responsibilities within the framework of society and find ways to guarantee a maximum of freedom for the individual within a highly organized society.

Another way in which the Cybernetic Revolution is going to force considerable human growth is in making us take a more rational, long-range approach in handling our affairs—our relationships with our fellow man and with nature. We are beginning to learn that the crisis-to-crisis approach that we have been using to carry on will no longer work. Science and technology have shrunk time by increasing the rate of change and have forged the world into a global civilization capable of exerting tremendous forces in a highly interrelated sphere of activity. We must make the fullest use of tools like the computer to help us prevent chaos and self-annihilation in such a complex world.

Looking at the most positive aspects of the computer, and projecting how its growing applications might control and multiply the forces of science and technology, one can foresee some remarkable "alternative futures." The most promising among these would be an era of abundance for all mankind—one in which most goods and services are provided by cybernated systems. And this brings us to the most striking aspect of human growth that could take place as a result of the Cybernetic Revolution—the change in our relationship to labor and leisure.

in my opinion...

It is very hard to comprehend how thoroughly computers will change our lives. Of necessity, government will change. With the computer as prevalent as it no doubt will be, the possibility arises that millions of people could be effectively repressed and controlled by a very few. A new method for a more efficient delegation of power must be devised to protect the public or we might unfortunately find a Brave New World evolving out of the computer age.

By the year 2000 there may be many ways in which computers may impinge upon our personal freedoms. Computers will probably never rise up in revolt and overthrow their human counterparts; but if, as computers are installed, they become operative in the philosophical purpose of simply maintaining social stability, the result could be a structured society akin to an authoritarian state. The computer is capable of many superb activities, but it must never be allowed to make a value-judgment. The place of the computer in a court of law is dubious; certainly it should never occupy the judge's seat. Value-judgments must be left to man or we may find "human-ness" slowly leaving our culture.

A National Data Center is already in the making. Bills have been introduced into Congress and the possibilities here are both encouraging and frightening. What kind of information will be involved? Who will have access to such information? (Do the memory banks of Washington computers already contain lists of political "dissidents"?) In how much depth will information be recorded?

A story here might point up one aspect of the problem. While travelling at sea, the first mate of a respectable vessel celebrated his birthday. In honor of the event a party was held and the mate became very drunk. At the end of the day the Captain took it upon himself to record in the ship's log with no explanation these words: "First mate was drunk today." The mate, not thinking that this was entirely fair, tried to prevail upon the Captain to remove it from the log, but the Captain refused. The next day, when it was the mate's turn to keep the log, he blithely recorded these words: "Captain sober today," and refused the Captain's plea to have it struck from the record. Not only *what* information is used, but *how* it will be interpreted and the importance placed on it is vital.

The eventual takeover of much of industry by computerized mechanization is inevitable. It seems likely that businesses will continue to operate under the axiom of making the greatest possible profit, and to accomplish this, the greatest possible production by the cheapest means is necessary. As long as production is the goal, cybernation is the key. The human laborer will no longer be needed in the industrial labor force. There simply will be nothing for him to do.

For generations, our societal mores have centered around work. Staying alive demanded hard work from sunrise to sunset. The American hero has always been the poor boy with a few bucks who through diligence and hard work made his million. This will probably still be possible in the year 2000 but to most people making money will seem quite senseless.

Most people may never hold a job. Through some system, possibly a negative income tax or a guaranteed annual income, a man may be paid weekly or monthly by the government and may have no other responsibility than to consume. Education may become a lifetime occupation. The computer will make it possible.

For many people this concept is totally incomprehensible. For the American, work has an intrinsic and inherent value. The man who doesn't work is shunned. The fact that he is a human being entitles him to nothing unless he works for a living. Even the accepted Puritan ethic declares that "man shall live by the sweat of his brow." Anything less is sinful.

Of necessity this attitude will change. If the majority are to prosper in the year 2000, people will need to accept a whole new set of values. There will have to be a new estimation of human worth and its position of value in the social context.

The computer is a source of great promise. If it can be seen in perspective and used wisely and carefully, if it can function as an extension of man's mind, it will also create an extension to his humanity. Hopefully, the computer will free man to function at his solely human tasks without economic and physical restraints.

The computer has brought with it a new epoch. The age of affluence and the unlimited expansion of man's consciousness is at hand. We must meet it wisely—and soon—to survive the change.

jerry l. campbell

questions

1. In the year 1811, English craftsmen known as the "Luddites" organized in the industrial areas of England to destroy the machines which were replacing home weaving with powered manufacturing of cloth. What factors which exist today might lead to 20th century activities of the same kind, this time in an effort to destroy computers?

2. In what ways is a National Data Center of value to the nation? In what ways can it be dangerous?

3. "By the year 2000, computers are likely to match, simulate, or surpass some of man's most 'human-like' intellectual abilities, including perhaps some of his aesthetic and creative capacities . . ." write Kahn and Wiener. If computers do indeed reach this level, what characteristics might man then call the most essentially human?

4. What are some of the factors which exist today that limit the amount of automation of existing plants? Some factors that make it necessary?

5. In what ways will automation contribute to the quality of life in the next three decades?

2.
the economics of affluence: a philosophy

POLICY FORMATION FOR NEW GOALS

robert theobald

introduction and comment by rae r. hanson

The subject of this chapter is, as its title suggests, concerned with a philosophy of future economics rather than an attempt to define any definite economic structure for the future. Economics is an integral part of any society, both determining its structure and determined by it. As college students we are part of the generation which will determine the philosophy of the future and shape the structures with which to implement that philosophy. The decisions that we make now will shape the course of history for many generations to come. At this point in history it is even conceivable that our decisions could bring mankind's story to a close in fifty to a hundred years. It is my feeling that simply by failing to act at all we may insure this latter possibility. The reason for this life or death alternative to our actions comes from more than just nuclear arms; it is due in great part to a present social philosophy which is no longer viable. We must, I believe, have a new one soon or suffer the ultimate consequences of our lethargy.

The present obsolete philosophy of which I speak has its roots far back in man's past. Since his beginnings as a small tribe of wandering hunters, man has lived by the biblical injunction "go forth and multiply." To see that we have been successful in our attempts to do just that requires only a quick look at a world population of better than three billion —and rising. Upon this simple premise are built some of the most potentially lethal doctrines for our modern world. Unlimited growth, whether it be in the number of human beings or the U.S. gross national product (G.N.P.) requires that we assume an unlimited supply of resources to support such growth. There is, however, no such unlimited supply, as we are now becoming aware. Even the air we breathe is part of an ecological equilibrium that our numbers and activities threaten to destroy. The possibility of an arid wasteland is not a prospect for millions of years from now; we may reach it, as previously stated, in the next fifty to one hundred years —simply by following our present undisciplined course of growth for the sake of growth.

In addition to these physical realities, there are also social realities which we have not adequately recognized and with which our present philosophy cannot cope. The old saying that "the world gets a little smaller every day" was never so true as it is now, for twentieth-century man. Increasing numbers, decreasing usable space, mass communications and rapid transit place a higher premium on "getting along" with our neighbors than ever before. The trend towards nationalism and self-interest which has again become the rule for most of the world is not a sane approach in terms of our survival. Helping one's fellow man, not holding him at arm's length, is the key. A starving man cannot be kept from food by threatening his life: a bomb won't keep a desperately poor and underdeveloped nation from grasping for what it needs to survive. If for no other reason than enlightened self-interest, we must help overcome poverty and ignorance among the poor of the world.

While we are trying to help our fellow men, we need also to help ourselves. We find it too easy to tell ourselves that because the scientists and sociologists were wrong in the past about the coming of the judgment day, they are still wrong now. This is no longer the case; the way it was and the way it is, is not the way it shall ever be. The human race is rapidly approaching the time when childlike faith in things "taking care of themselves" just won't work. We must come to the adult realization that nothing is forever or for free. If this earth is to support us much longer we need to learn to nourish and conserve its resources rather than to squander them. To become a race of responsible adults capable of doing the things that need doing, we need a new concept of ourselves. That concept is one which sees each member of humanity as having individual worth and dignity. By pursuing our own self-development and understanding we will be led to a new understanding of others.

The new philosophy is actually nothing more than a mature attitude which sees the world and our place in it as it really is. The form of a new philosophy and the part economics will play in it is the subject of the following article by Robert Theobald.

r.r.h.

POLICY FORMATION FOR NEW GOALS

Robert Theobald, now residing in Arizona, is an India-born British socioeconomist with a Master's degree in Economics from Cambridge University. He is also a futurist—a scholar, social scientist or writer who attempts to chart ways for man to move successfully into the 21st century—who originated the idea of a guaranteed annual income.

Theobald has lived in England and France, and for the past 13 years in the United States, during which time he has written many books on the effects of the new technologies, wealth, and man's adjustment to coming social and economic changes. These works include The Guaranteed Income, Free Men and Free Markets, The Challenge of Abundance, The Rich and the Poor, *and* An Alternative Future for America— *required reading for participants in Hawaii's 1970 Governor's Conference on the Year 2000.*

* * *

In our present situation, it is now clear that any analysis of methods of policy formation start from a logically prior level of analysis: how does one determine which goals are appropriate in today's conditions?

This question is not normally asked for it is generally assumed that present goals of nationalism and economic growth are valid—or at least necessary. This acceptance of the validity of present goals by those in the political and philosophical mainstream ensures that discussion is normally confined to examining how to reach accepted goals. Policies are therefore sought that will ensure the continuance of a viable national state and bring

Reprinted from Robert Theobald, ed., Social Policies for America in the Seventies *by permission of the author and publisher. Copyright © 1968 by Doubleday & Company, Inc.*

about the maximum rate of economic growth. Thus, for example, one of the present debates is whether a faster rate of economic growth will be achieved by providing additional financial resources to those people who will increase investment, or to those who will spend the money on consumer goods. The course of this argument has determined the shape of much recent legislation. Similarly, the space program has been examined in terms of its impact on national power and technological competence.

Debate on any significant legislation, however, must inevitably be complex, for it will be conducted on different levels and many of the participants will fail to be aware of the vital differences in these levels. There will be those who agree both with the analysis of the causative chains—for example, how economic growth occurs—and also with the policies proposed to affect these causative chains in order to reach the goal of higher levels of economic growth. Then there will be those who agree with the analysis of causative chains but who believe that the policies proposed will not have the maximally favorable effect. Then there will be those who claim that the analysis of the causative chains is incorrect and that the legislation must therefore, *necessarily,* be ill-designed. There may also be those who argue that the structuring of goal *priorities* is inappropriate—that it would be more important, for example, to concentrate on achieving greater military capacity in an attempt to defend the country rather than to increase the rate of economic growth. And finally there may be some who see economic growth as a means rather than an end or even deny its necessary continuing utility in increasing the range of human freedom within a functioning society.

We are therefore involved in a hierarchy of debates, and an ordering of the level of the debates is essential if clarity is to be achieved and appropriate decisions taken. First, we must decide on our goals or purposes. Second, we must decide what priorities we wish to accord to these goals and purposes. Third, we must decide what causative chains exist. Fourth, we must determine what particular policies, if any, will most effectively improve our chances of achieving our goals and purposes. Finally, if we discover that our desired goals and purposes are out of our effective reach, we must re-evaluate the possibilities actually open to us and, if it is still clear that we cannot achieve the desired goals, re-examine what feasible goals we do wish to pursue.

It is, of course, obvious that it would be impossible to examine fundamental goals and purposes in every debate over a proposed policy. The operation of any society is possible only because there is rather general acceptance of certain goals and purposes. Similarly, we cannot re-examine priorities or even causative chains every time we have to re-examine policies. Nevertheless, it must be clear that if it can be shown *at any time* that the present set of goals is no longer valid, it then becomes necessary to undertake an immediate, profound re-examination of the structuring of the whole socioeconomic system. It will be the object of this essay to show that our present central goals are no longer appropriate and that we must therefore find new ways to define goals and purposes for the coming cybernated era.

nationalism

The present national state system can be traced back to the desire to extend territorial dominance over an ever wider geographical area. Thus England was united by kings who broke the power of the individual lords and barons. America was created by a relatively few individuals who took risks to develop the widest possible contiguous land area. In the nineteenth century, the colonial powers tried to dominate the world and it appeared to many nineteenth-century commentators that most of the world would enter one or other European empire. After the Second World War, however, the tide was reversed: new national states gained their independence in great numbers.

The viability of the national state depends upon its ability to defend itself against any potential enemy. Most attention has so far been given to the implications of this situation for total nuclear war among the rich countries: this led Herbert York and Jerome Wiesner, both of whom held high office in recent administrations, to declare that today each country destroys its own security in the very attempt to achieve it. Escalation of weaponry continues despite increasing efforts to avoid it: the development of new war technologies effectively forces all countries to deploy them for fear that the use of the same technology by their enemy or potential enemy would make them helpless. For example, attempts are being made to avoid the necessity of constructing an anti-missile missile system, but there are few who hope that such a development can be avoided without a fundamental change in goals.

But the national state system also has highly unfavorable consequences in the poor countries, for it involves the waste of a substantial portion of the budget in developing and training armed forces. Such a waste of resources is tragic at a time when all the meager resources of the poor countries are clearly insufficient to deal with the immediate, crucial policy problems being created by excessive rates of population growth, by excessive tides of migration to the cities, and by the continuing "revolution of rising expectations."

The key to the economic problems of the poor countries does not lie within them but rather in improved relations between rich and poor countries. The vast majority of the poor countries cannot hope to achieve necessary levels of economic development without major aid from the rich countries. Such aid appears impossible of achievement without an end to nationalism. This is partly because of economic pressure: expenditures on arms by the rich countries are felt by policy makers to be so great that meaningful aid to the poor countries appears impossible. The ending of the ideal of nationalism and the international arms race would free well over $100 billion in resources; the rich countries would then be driven by the economic necessity to preserve production levels and led by new moral attitudes into a recognition of the value of sharing more fully with the poor countries.

Failure to achieve this aid will lead to a far more dangerous situation than during the now defunct cold war. For hidden below the cold-war rhetoric, there remained common interests between America and Russia. The consequences of failure to deal imaginatively with a split between the rich and the poor countries, the white and the non-white nations will not be so palliated. In effect, the world would be divided between those with everything to lose and those with nothing to lose: such a situation would clearly be profoundly unstable.

Despite the fact that more and more people believe that the development of a profound split between the rich and the poor countries is inevitable, many "realists" are not concerned. "What can the poor countries do to the rich?," they ask. This assumption of invulnerability is based on a belief that the only truly destructive weapons systems are nuclear, and that the nuclear weapons not only are, but will remain, confined to the rich countries. (China, while sometimes seen as a long-run threat in this pattern, is largely ignored because of lack of immediate power.) In reality, however, bacteriological and chemical weapons are just as effective against mass populations as nuclear weapons, particularly in complex, technological societies, and weapons of this type are cheap and easy to produce.

When further arguments of this type are advanced to practitioners of *Realpolitik* they fall back to another level of argument.

Let us look, they say, at the ability to preserve the peace that has existed during the cold war. But this experience cannot be generalized, as has already been pointed out—not only because there were real underlying compatibilities between the interests of Russia and America, but also because the sophistication and stability of leadership in the rich countries must inevitably greatly exceed that of the poor countries in coming years. Indeed, the problem of instability must inevitably worsen if the threatened split between the rich and the poor countries should occur, for the ability of the leaders of the poor countries to bring about real improvement in the position of their people would be almost eliminated.

A further disturbing consequence of such instability can already be perceived. One of the oldest political tricks used to shore up a group or nation whose morale becomes shaky is to discover an external enemy. It can be anticipated, therefore, that many poor countries would whip up hatred against the rich; the rich would react in kind and a new downward spiral into conflict would begin.

The theoretical over-all solution to these problems is, of course, known. We must develop a world order in which force is outlawed as a way of settling disputes, and in which the rich countries accept their responsibilities to help the rest of the world. This process parallels what has occurred within countries: the progressive elimination of the right to use violence and the progressive increase in obligations that rich people have accepted within their country. Unfortunately, however, little imaginative research has been devoted to discovering appropriate policies for such a changed purpose; almost all of the effort is devoted to devising policies that will preserve an outmoded national state system.

economic growth

Sometime during the Middle Ages, Western man came to believe that he could increase his ability to produce material goods and that this increase would add to his satisfaction. The ever growing emphasis on economic growth as a goal effectively revolutionized philosophical and religious assumptions about where blame should be ascribed when the individual failed to be able to gain enough resources. We have forgotten that during the Middle Ages, it was believed that the individual who failed was entitled to not only economic but also psychological support from his society. In other words, it was assumed that society was basically responsible for individual failures. Today, of course, we have come to believe the opposite.

In addition, concentration upon the benefits of economic growth came to disguise its very real costs. Indeed, some economists still see economic growth as essentially costless: they argue that economic growth provides the benefits of increased production without any offsetting factors. But in recent years, most economists have come to agree that the peculiarities of national-income accounting have permitted us to ignore the public costs of private production. Our view of this issue is continuing to evolve with great rapidity—the debates on polluted air and water as well as highway deaths are perhaps primarily responsible. Furthermore, many psychologists and psychiatrists now argue that the damage to man *himself* has been even greater than the damage to his external environment—they believe that man was forced to narrow his perceptions before he was prepared to toil efficiently and willingly within the limited possibilities of the industrial system.

* * *

Economic growth effectively involves both benefits and costs. As the standard of living rises and further increases in material production therefore become less urgent, the priority accorded to economic growth declines. It will decline still further: we will come to try to achieve an environment in which man can develop himself to the full. (It is interesting to see how the economists' very patterns of assumptions support their biases. Thus housewives working in the home are not considered part of the Gross National Product. An increase in the female work force is therefore seen as a clear economic gain, although many would agree that the value of the individual's work in the home is greater than the value of her work outside it. It is interesting to speculate about the effect that a shift in this convention would have on policy formation.)

But while it is true that the standard of living in the United States is so high that attitudes are already shifting from a desire for further increases in wealth to a desire for self-realization, we must recognize that the situation of the poor countries is different, for they urgently require economic growth, that is, a larger quantity of goods and services. But their route toward economic growth must be very different from the route taken by the countries that are now rich.

The growth process in the presently rich countries during the nineteenth century and the first half of the twentieth needed the services of all the members of the society—there was a place for the educated and for those with no education, for those with skills and for those without them. It is true that the rewards for the educated and the successful entrepreneur were far greater than they were for the laborer, but it is equally true that the labor of all the members of the society was essential.

The truth of this statement can be seen by examining the situation in the early years of the nineteenth century before the Protestant ethic was inculcated in the workingman. It was impossible to get many people to stay steadily on the job; they would leave just as soon as they had earned what they considered enough money. This situation had to change if the industrial revolution were to be successful. The needed result was achieved by getting people to see a job as required for their dignity.

The Protestant ethic, which was necessary in the nineteenth century, is proving highly undesirable in the second half of the twentieth. Today both structured manual labor and structured mental labor are being taken over by machines.[1] It is unjust and dangerous to socialize an individual to believe that he can achieve satisfaction in a job and then deny him the possibility of finding a job.

It is therefore no longer desirable that the socialization system should concentrate on the goal of jobs for all since an increasingly large proportion of the population will be excluded from the need or even the possibility of holding a job. This is true in both the rich countries and the poor countries, but the problem of unemployability is most crucial and urgent in the latter.

Because our value systems are still dominated by the views of economists, there is an assumption that if a man is not forced to toil he will necessarily fall into idleness. This appears to be

[1] This point is no longer really controversial among those who have studied the impact of automation and cybernation. Even those who most vigorously deny the importance of the immediate impact of automation and cybernation, accept that its long-run effect will be to replace people by machines. For example, Charles Silberman in his book *The Myths of Automation,* which was designed to debunk the significance of the development, stated: "Sooner or later, of course, we will have the technical capability to substitute machines for men in most of the functions men now perform." The debate has been narrowed to a question of the time span involved: there is no longer any real question about the reality of the development.

unrealistic in the light of current psychological knowledge which increasingly believes that man moves toward achieving self-realization when his lower, bodily needs have been satisfied. It is interesting to note that this insight is applied to a considerable extent by those directing business and governmental research who give free rein to their creative personnel in the belief that they will produce more in this way than they would under tight supervision. Application of the same theory to the total society would suggest that allowing people to follow their own bent rather than forcing them to act within a given structured situation might be expected to maximize imaginative developments.

An additional structural problem arises when individuals cannot be expected to find jobs, for this means that most of them will be unable to obtain adequate income. Our present social system limits the receipt of adequate incomes in most cases to those with jobs—the only major exception is those with substantial capital. Thus it is not only necessary to provide the individual with the internal depth to develop his own life pattern, it will also be necessary to find different ways to provide funds.[2]

In effect, therefore, the position of the rich and poor countries is very different despite the fact that in both cases enough jobs will not be available. The rich countries both can, and should, place a lower priority on economic growth than in the past because the goal of economic growth is already so heavily built into the system that its continuance can be made almost automatic so long as they continue to recognize the necessity for productive efficiency even while they develop new criteria for evaluating human development. In the poor countries, on the other hand, the goal of economic growth must still be seen as critically important.[3] However, it must be recognized that economic growth is only a means to the end of greater human fulfillment, and also that our present assumptions about how to achieve economic growth are based on beliefs about socioeconomic relationships that are no longer valid.

[2] For a further discussion of this subject see, Robert Theobald, *Free Men and Free Markets* (Clarkson N. Potter, 1963; also published in paperback by Doubleday Anchor) and *The Guaranteed Income,* ed. Robert Theobald (Doubleday, 1966; also published in paperback by Doubleday Anchor).

[3] For a discussion of appropriate patterns of economic growth in the poor countries, see Robert Theobald, "New Possibilities in Modern Technology," in *Economic Growth in World Perspective,* ed. Dennis Munby (Association Press, 1966); also in *World Outlook* (July 1966).

the development of alternative goals

It may be helpful to recapitulate briefly here the reasons why present goals, which represent continuations of past desires, must now be changed. Nationalism was the latest step in the lengthy historical process that extended control over wider and wider geographical areas as methods of transportation became more and more rapid. It is now essential to abolish national barriers and to institute a worldwide socioeconomic system if survival is to be ensured. Second, the desire for economic growth grew out of the belief that we could and should provide adequate resources for all men. We now have the technical means to provide a reasonable standard to all within a limited period of time, but we have not developed the necessary will. The goal of economic growth in the rich countries and the poor must be subordinated to that of social justice if it is not to be totally destructive.

If our past goals are no longer valid, to what ends must man devote himself in the coming decades? Because we are now gaining the power to do what we wish, we can no longer find adequate purpose in continuing our drive toward the domination of our environment. Mankind must ask a far more fundamental question: What does it *desire?* In the past, we have argued that we must accept the world as we found it for we did not have the power to change it. The situation has now changed; we can now say that man has the power, within the limits imposed by his own nature and the environment, to change the structure of the world in ways that seem favorable to him.

It is essential to spell out the exact meaning of this statement because a rapidly growing body of literature, sparked by Jacques Ellul's book *The Technological Society,* argues that man is trapped in the technology he himself has created. This is, however, to mistake the present position for inevitability: to argue that because the present social system does indeed force man to obey the dictates of technology, he is unable to bring about change in the system to free himself from the present tyranny. It is the maintenance of the present operational goals that forces man to accept technology. The need of each country to defend itself against any potential attackers forces it to accept any form of weaponry, however dreadful it may be. The need for each firm to be able to make a profit, and the need for each country to be able to export enough to pay for its imports, forces each to accept any new machine-systems that will increase productivity, whatever the effect on the labor force. The insistence that each man be able to find a job forces society to find ways to consume all that can be produced. Finally, society finds it extremely difficult to evaluate the benefits and costs of technology because so many people simply assume that all uses of technology will inevitably serve to increase not only man's control over his environment but also his happiness.

Man *can* set up a social system in which he will control decisions; the last part of this essay will be concerned with some preliminary steps in this direction. But there are formal conditions if he is to achieve such control: these are determined by cybernetics—the science of communication and control. First, in any system, whether mechanical, human, or social, there must be actors—switches, mechanisms, or people as the case may be—willing and able to take the necessary steps to ensure that necessary actions occur as the system-state changes. Second, there must be correct information so that the "actors" have the required data to be able to act intelligently in seeking changes.

It is these formal limits that disturb many people today. Rather than being gratified by man's capacity to change the world to eliminate toil and to provide adequate resources, it appears that a deep fear of the new potential is presently developing. It is argued that the development of technological potential will *necessarily* lead to dull uniformity and the elimination of difference. This, however, totally misunderstands the potential. We know from anthropology that different groups created widely divergent cultures in similar natural environments. Our technological potential will further increase our freedom; it will permit each group to create its own technological-natural environment, thus providing it with a suitable set of conditions to foster its desired activities and relationships.

Those raised in the industrial age find it difficult to accept this conclusion, for they have seen men and institutions forced into patterns of dull uniformity without understanding the reason. They have therefore come to believe that the cybernated era must necessarily continue in this direction. The industrial age, however, involved the mass production of goods and services at a profit and their transportation throughout the world. Methods of production, transportation, and sale had to be standardized. This required, in turn, that the people within institutions as well as the institutions themselves be standardized because differences reduced efficiency. The cybernated era, on the other hand, depends on the movement of information; it contains none of the inherent necessities for standardization required by the industrial age.

It is interesting to speculate about the techniques and institutions that will survive into the cybernated era. If the aim has been to reduce complex reality to uniformity, the survival potential of the institution or technique will usually be very low. Thus one must scrutinize the future of bureaucracy, of modern legal systems, of schools and universities as we know them, of the whole statistical apparatus of the present day.

changing values

These speculations lead us directly into the question of how to discover a new operational goal for mankind. Up to the present time, we have been able to assume that our basic environment was fixed. Today, we have it in our power to change the world. If we are to use this power wisely, we must understand the nature and limits of this power, and we must decide the direction in which we desire to go. Man has chosen to take charge of his own evolution; his survival requires that he carry out this task successfully.

The discussion of a hierarchy of goals earlier in this essay suggests what must be done. First, we must discover what purposes and goals are desirable and feasible. Second, we must understand the existing socioeconomic system sufficiently well to be able to determine our *present* course and the changes that have to be made in order to achieve the type of socioeconomic system desired. Third, we have to work out the new policies that are suitable to achieve the desired goals and that are capable of being adopted.

There is one formal rule about achieving innovation that must be understood and observed if successful cultural change is to occur. This was stated by Conrad Arensberg, an anthropologist at Columbia University: "The first effect of a successfully adaptive . . . innovation of any kind is to hold onto something tried and true, to conserve the old in the face of change. In paleontology, this conservative first effect of evolutionary advance is called Romer's rule, it could well be called that in cultural and social advance too. . . . The second effect of a successfully adaptive innovation of any kind, biological or social, is quite other than conservative: indeed, it is the opening of a vast new door, a splendid serendipity. But the evolutionary gain comes next: the first step, it is clear, is indeed conservative. Evolutionary advance it turns out, is at least a two step process, conservative and trail blazing at once, and in that order." [4] In effect, then, proposals that fail to appear conservative of existing values have no opportunity of success, and proposals that will not be trail-blazing have no relevance. The task is to discover those measures that appear conservative and will be trail-blazing.

Unfortunately, it is difficult to perceive present situations and possibilities with sufficient clarity to determine what should be done. Indeed, it is now certain that determination of appropriate steps cannot be achieved while using existing tools of analysis, because our present perception of the world around us is essentially determined by the value structures we currently accept. Thus in the words of the dialogue-focuser on technology: "Most 'facts' are not single events but rather relate to overall patternings of behavior and relationships. The ways in which we perceive patterns of behavior and relationships are themselves heavily structured by the environment in which we live—thus societally perceived facts tend to support the existing socioeconomic order." [5] One example of this pattern has already been cited in this essay: the decision of the economist to exclude work done in the home from calculations of total production biases both his perception of events and his suggestions about the most appropriate policy measures.

Gregory Bateson, an anthropologist and psychologist at the University of Hawaii, has provided a theoretical explanation of the nature of the dilemma. He has pointed out that in effect our patterns of knowledge are self-validating: they are designed in such a way that they call forth patterns of action that confirm us in our beliefs. Thus he points out, for example, that the belief in positive and negative sanctions on which most psychologists presently operate is based on experiments that make it effectively impossible to react in any way *except* in response to the positive and negative sanctions. Imagination and creativity have no place to show themselves within the experimental format; the experiment excludes what it does not wish to perceive. A science-fiction writer made this point vividly when he examined the plight of a psychologist who was caught by aliens and placed in

[4] Conrad Arensberg, "Cultural Change and Guaranteed Income," in *The Guaranteed Income,* pp. 211–12.

[5] The dialogue-focuser is a new form of document designed to clarify the agreements and disagreements on a particular topic. In *Dialogue on Technology,* ed. Robert Theobald (Bobbs-Merrill, 1967).

an experimental situation designed by the alien race similar to the experimental situation in which he had placed rats. He desired to show his human intelligence, but discovered that the design of the cage made the display of "intelligence" impossible without killing himself.

It is the fundamental nature of this point that makes it difficult to comprehend. The most critical reason why a social system has worked is that people believed it would work. Inevitably most people within the system have not examined why they believe that the system will work. Thus the real sanctions, constraints, and rewards first appear automatic and later invisible—a point made by Marshall McLuhan in much of his writing.

But McLuhan has failed to point out that what is now invisible *must* be made visible. At this point in man's history, when he has decided to control his own evolution, he must find ways to ensure that he will understand the nature of the existing socioeconomy. The fundamental question, therefore, is what route can be taken to ensure that assumptions that are presently hidden be made visible and then examined to discover their validity. This requires that we break through the present systems of analysis, which were formed by the very assumptions we now desire to examine.

Present evidence suggests that the technique most likely to succeed is a common attack on existing problems. If the problems are sufficiently real and immediate, it has often proved possible to abandon philosophical and disciplinary presuppositions to reach a common stance. But this is not the end of the potential benefits of the technique. Attempts to solve real problems with people from different backgrounds, forces each person to examine how much of the values he/she presently holds must be preserved in any particular situation. It also forces her/him to understand the different sets of values and assumptions that motivate the other individuals in the thinking and/or decision-making group. Progress toward solutions can be made only through genuine striving to understand the causes of disagreements and to discover the maximum area of possible understanding through the use of personal and interpersonal dialogue.[6]

Successful dialogue occurs when those involved are willing to strive to achieve rapport with others in the group, and when they are also willing to strive to understand their own presuppositions and biases. Many people believe that an ever larger proportion of

[6] For information on techniques being developed to achieve these purposes write Room 758, 475 Riverside Drive, New York 10027, N.Y.

the population will be willing to act in these ways in coming years. This belief is based on the new psychological theorizing, which postulates a struggle toward self-realization. In effect, choices begin to be based on an internal understanding of what is and what ought to be; people cease to rely on authority and cease to need to be pushed into action by the use of external sanctions.

The view that man can be responsible is still a minority one. The majority view, which presently determines national and international policies, is based on the belief that man must be forced into action by external sanctions applied by others, and that unless men are forced they will inevitably fail to perform any sort of useful action. It is argued that there can be no successful activities where man is not constrained by authority. This belief determines attitudes in schools and universities, in labor-management bargaining, in international politics, and in every other field.

* * *

The opposite position, which is the one I have advanced here, argues that it is the need to hold a job that prevents man from developing his own uniqueness to the full, and that the guaranteed income is the first step down the road that will encourage each individual to develop himself and his society. In this view the availability of the guaranteed income will set free a burst of. creativity that will not only ensure that the necessary toil of the society is accomplished, but also that solutions to the most vexing problems of the present world will be more easily found for people will be free to work on the issues that seem most crucial to them rather than for their employers. This will necessarily occur because many of the priorities in research today are determined either by the need for profit, or by the need to maintain military dominance; the meshing of the priorities for these purposes and the real needs of the world is clearly low. In addition, it is clear that the real breakthroughs occur when individuals are set free to carry out the types of study and research that seem most immediately relevant to them.

Despite the profound psychological and indeed philosophical disagreements, divergencies in opinions about immediate practical steps are limited. (That this is inevitable can be determined by re-examining Conrad Arensberg's insight stated above. Because all steps must necessarily be seen as conservative, there is relatively little margin for variation in immediate policy proposals if they are to have any chance of success.) Both groups agree that it is necessary for each individual to be provided with an income and with meaningful activity. Those who believe in the necessity of sanctions see the desirability of forcing as many as possible to hold jobs, and discouraging as many as possible from taking advantage of the availability of the guaranteed income. They also apparently see no need for fundamental shifts in the educational pattern, although this should not be taken to mean that they are not interested in improving education; their concern, however, is with better education rather than different education.

Those who believe in the possibility of self-realization reverse this order of priorities. They believe that we should encourage people to set their own patterns of life and see the guaranteed income as a necessary means to this end. Many of them believe that we must provide sufficiently high income levels to make it psychologically feasible for those now in the socioeconomic system to leave it and to develop their own interests.[7] Above all, they claim that the most urgent necessity is to change the educational system so that it will be possible to ensure that an ever rising proportion of those leaving schools and universities will have the interior resources to set their own life styles. But this group does not minimize the reality that there will be many who cannot find meaningful activity for themselves and that steps must be taken to find activity for them—indeed, they argue that one of the most crucial social tasks will be to develop enough ways to provide meaning for those who are convinced that life consists of spending eight hours a day in a factory.

This latter view is based on the belief that the fundamental problem of the present period does not lie in the failure of the socioeconomic system but rather in our fundamental need for a new vision of man. I believe that it is now clear that poverty, inequality, and powerlessness are inevitable parts of the industrial-age socioeconomy, and that they can be eliminated only on the basis of the totally new socioeconomic system required by present developments.

The critical problem of our time is that of powerlessness. This is common to the condition of the poor, the student, the Negro, the aged, those in the poor countries. But the elimination of powerlessness will be a far more complicated task than is generally realized. Most strategies that have so far been developed

---

[7] It appears necessary, as a transition measure, to provide an income floor and an income maintenance plan for those who have had high incomes in the past. For an explanation of the reasons and some suggestions as to techniques, see *Free Men and Free Markets*.

aim at the provision of power to a previously powerless group. Such a strategy must, however, inevitably fail to solve the overall problems because the mere transfer of power from one group to another will not eliminate the problem of differential power but will simply shift its locus.

I am convinced that the issue is how to achieve a society in which power has been eliminated. I am aware that the whole of human history speaks against this possibility, but no alternative seems visible—at least to me. We now know that power distorts the movement of information, for the serving individual inevitably feeds information to his superiors that will meet their preconceptions and thus present him in a favorable light. On the other hand, we know that a functioning system of any type requires that information be transmitted without distortion so that appropriate decisions can be made. It therefore appears essential to eliminate the concept of power and to substitute the concept of leadership.

*   *   *

I am convinced that nothing but a fundamental rethinking of our values and goals will be adequate today. It is worthwhile to quote John Maynard Keynes, the British economist who has quite unjustly been made the apostle of growthmanship: "When the accumulation of wealth is no longer of high social importance, there will be great changes in the code of morals. We shall be able to rid ourselves of many of the pseudo-moral principles which have hag-ridden us for two hundred years, by which we have exalted some of the most distasteful of human qualities into the position of the highest values. We shall be able to afford to dare to assess the money-motive at its true value. . . . All kinds of social customs and economic practices affecting the distribution of wealth which we now maintain at all costs, however distasteful and unjust they may be in themselves . . . we shall then be free, at last, to discard." [8] This time has now come; the question is whether we are willing to take the steps that would lead to our recognition of the immorality of the present system.

[8] J. M. Keynes, *Essays in Persuasion* (New York: Harcourt, Brace and Company, 1936), pp. 369–70.

in my opinion...

As a college student confronted with many of society's present problems, I agree completely with the ideas expressed by Mr. Theobald. There are many more facts that justify his point of view than he has chosen to present. Today, as I look around me, I see a world where the rich countries develop their technologies at a rate that allows no time to correlate the data already accumulated. Barring a major national breakdown, this technological development will continue to increase in rate as well as in amount. The distance between what we *can* do and what we *are doing* grows larger daily. As this gulf between capability and performance grows, it becomes harder to tolerate the lack of solutions to many of these countries' most pressing problems. We need to set new goals now, and then work to accomplish them.

Theobald has mentioned several goals in his article. Replacing nationalism as we now know it with internationalism is one. The U.S. today faces a prospect of a twenty-hour (or less) work week while productivity and usable income continue to increase. By practicing even a minimal level of birth control, we could achieve a level of abundance for every person in this country such as the world has never seen before. But what of the have-not nations who grow poorer in real as well as by comparative terms? How long will they stand for this inequity in distribution of wealth? The answer, I think, is not long in coming. To avoid some kind of global confrontation, we must set a goal of developing the poor nations' capability of helping themselves.

Nationalism presents an internal problem also. The short work week may soon become no work week at all for many, as automation replaces jobs, and lack of skill—and to put it brutally —a plain lack of intelligence keep people from filling the new jobs that will appear. The current goal of this country is a continued increase in the G.N.P. and in the job market in order to maintain low unemployment levels. Automation, technology and the limits placed on growth by nature itself will make this an impossible and unrealistic aim for the future.

Our own technology and these archaic goals threaten to destroy us if they are not brought into line with nature's delicate balance. The waste products of a modern technology are proving to be harmful and difficult to dispose of. Yet we need not give up our technology, for we have the means—or can develop them— for using or disposing of those wastes.

Modern technology threatens to destroy us in another way, however. Our resources are, as I have said, limited and it takes a great amount of those resources to maintain our present standard of living. As our numbers grow so does the drain on our resources. To maintain the present standard of life we must limit our numbers and limit waste in the economy. If we fail to realize this, our end will be the same as that of any other species whose numbers have outrun the land's ability to support it.

To sum up, then, we are faced with some very basic problems created by the old philosophy of self-concern and continued growth. These are: destruction of our world's ecology from modern civilization's growth and its waste products; a toppled world order as the gulf between rich and poor grows; the population problem; and, finally, if we survive by solving these problems, the question of what to do with the large numbers of unemployed and unemployable.

Theobald's socio-economic philosophy is a suggested answer to all of these things. By changing our economic policy from one of continued internal development to a steady output concept and by initiating a meaningful birth control program, we could solve many of our problems. Such a finite system would conserve resources and allow the profit that has been freed by halted expansion to be used in cleaning up our present industries. The economic system should also provide an income for those who are no longer employable in present terms, without regard to the Puritan work ethic. Our energy and wealth could then be lent to the have-not countries in an effort to bring them up to the same levels of wealth and education. We could also devote the suddenly released human time and resources to improving the race of man. Through a lifelong process of education and growing self-knowledge, we have the possibility of coming as close to Eden as we ever will. The frightening and yet wonderful part of this is that we will have to create Eden or our children will inherit Hell. To me, it appears there is little choice. You and I stand at the gates of the greatest opportunity anyone has ever seen; it's our choice—whether we will die just outside those gates, or make the effort, enter, and begin the second half of the epic story of man.

rae r. hanson

questions

1.   Mr. Theobald cites the need for a redefinition of our goals as human beings. If we assume this is a valid need, what goals do you feel should be considered at this point in time? If you can, give them an order of priority.

2.   If the idea of an automated society is viable, what methods might be used to raise the standards of the have-not nations?

3.   What trends have affected nationalism since the end of World War II?

4.   What are the several reasons worth considering for the down-rating of our Gross National Product as a measurement of progress?

5.   Do you agree with Theobald that "a guaranteed income will set forth a burst of creativity"? Explain why you agree or disagree.

3.
full employment: the carrier pigeon of economics

CONSUMERS OF ABUNDANCE

gerard piel

introduction and comment by thomas r. fritts

Projecting the economic future of man has proved to be next to impossible. Even Karl Marx, one of the greatest economic thinkers of all time, was not able to accurately anticipate the economics of the 20th century. To try to forecast what lies ahead in the next three decades with any accuracy demands even greater gifts of prophecy, for we must include not only hypotheses which will guide the usual activities of the economic planner, but others which will, of necessity, have to deal with every phase of human existence. Theories of economics based on scarcity seem hardly able to cope with the products of abundance.

It is somewhat of a paradox, perhaps, to focus on the problems of "too much" in discussing the economics of the highly industrialized nations of the world today. Even in the United States, the most technologically advanced nation of the world, one-third of our families live below the "normal comfort" standard suggested by government agencies, and in parts of the world, people are literally starving to death. We must question, then, the meaning of "abundance" in the economic sense, and attempt to envisage the effect of the capacity to produce more than we can consume on generations to come.

Many economic "laws" may be shattered in the process. The argument that what is produced is determined by the demands of the consumer, for example, can hardly be taken seriously in light of the advertising techniques of today. Clearly, a major problem of tomorrow will be finding a realistic way to determine what production serves man—and what does not.

We have found no economist willing to delineate an ordered program for the next century. The questions are impossible to solve even if limited to one discipline. Every area of human existence is involved: the nature of man; his ability to adapt; changes in human values; new methods of distribution: in short, a revamped relationship between men.

But regardless of the complexities of our socioeconomic problems, we dare not continue to fumble with past-oriented measures that are little more than temporary expedients. Not only do we need a presidential Council of Economic Advisors to deal with immediate questions, but we should be marshalling our finest minds in a variety of disciplines to prepare workable hypotheses for forthcoming developments. This, too, is a many-faceted activity.

A "Committee on Future Economics" must be free of political pressures, and should be selected from a wide-range group of the most competent thinkers in a variety of fields, regardless of the political platforms of the party in control of the government. It must be able to predict desired goals for our society three decades in advance and to prepare a program that will allow us to move toward those goals with a minimum of social chaos. It must be inordinately flexible and ever-prepared to re-evaluate both goals and programs, should new information become available—sociological as well as technological. Of necessity, it must be able to "sell" its product, as well as to train teachers who can persuade a reluctant populace that the goals are desirable as well as possible. And it must be able to withstand the attacks of the multitude of vested interests which will unquestionably fight any change in the status quo.

Perhaps we are asking too much. The ultimate question is—do we have any choice? If we accept the logic of Gerard Piel in the monograph that follows, we must either attempt to destroy mechanization in a futile and unacceptable move back to the full employment myth, face economic anarchy, or use our full facilities in an attempt to benefit all mankind by accepting the demise of the work ethic.

Goals, means—education to achieve them: we choose to accept the chance for Utopia.

t.r.f.

CONSUMERS OF ABUNDANCE

Gerard Piel, graduated with honors from Harvard, and also received his Doctor of Science from Laurence College. He was Science Editor of Life *from 1939 to 1945, and was associated with the Kaiser Company until he launched the new* Scientific American *in 1948. Holder of three honorary degrees, he was a director of the American Civil Liberties Union and is also a Fellow at the American Academy of Arts and Sciences.*

The advance of science has for many years been undermining the two pillars of our economy—property and work. Each at length has fallen from its place. Property is no longer the primary source of economic power, and ownership no longer establishes the significant, functioning connection between people and the things they consume. Work occupies fewer hours and years in the lives of everyone; what work there is grows less like work every year, and the less the people work, the more their product grows. In the place of work and property, illusions and old habits and compulsions now support the social edifice. Public understanding must eventually overtake this transformation in the relationship of modern man to his physical environment. Fundamental changes in the social order—in man's relationship to man—are therefore in prospect and are already in process.

It is difficult and perhaps dangerous to forecast where these changes may lead. Full employment, for example, now seems to be not only an unattainable but an out-moded objective of economic policy. What takes the place of wages in a workless society? If such a question must be asked, then others follow. Does profit remain a useful standard of accounting in a propertyless society?

But these questions are not only too big; they are premature. Before they can even be asked, the scientific revolution that occasions them must be more closely examined.

As the withering of these institutions from the life of society suggests, property and work are artifacts of civilization. In the kinship economies of pre-agricultural societies they have no place whatever or appear only in the faintest analogues. The wampum hoard that confers prestige in one culture becomes the potlatch of another. Hunting and food-gathering are not work, but adventure, assertion of manhood, magic, and craft.

Property and work make their appearance with the agricultural revolution. They are devices for gathering and impounding the surplus that four families at work upon the land can now produce to support a fifth family off the land. Property is the institution by which the church, the state, and their individual agents assert their control over the land as one of the two primary factors of production. Work is the institution by which they assert their control over the other primary factor of production—the energy of human muscle. The word "work" signifies toil and at the same time the product of toil; it is the measure ("according to his works") of the portion of the product that may be allocated to the unpropertied worker. The two institutions together furnished the rationale for the compulsions necessary to assure the removal of the surplus from the land. Thanks to these arrangements, even fairly primitive agricultural technologies were capable of supporting substantial urban civilizations, as in Mexico.

In the feudal societies identified with agricultural technology, land was the only economically significant property. It was typically inalienable, except by order of the suzerain; it was cherished and maintained from generation to generation, physically occupied by its possessors, who enjoyed all the rights of usufruct as well as the power to exploit. In medieval Europe the land so completely dominated economic life that the taking of interest was synonymous with usury, a crime as well as a sin. It took a religious revolution to establish the practice of selling things for more than they cost and to secure propriety for profit in the worldly virtue of thrift.

Profit, thrift, and the accumulation of capital brought an entirely new kind of property into ascendance in economic affairs. This was the machine. At first the machine had the same immemorial look of permanence as the land. It embodied a high ratio of brute material to design and was built for depreciation over at least one generation of ownership. Through such time periods, ownership of the machine carried the same stability of power and place as ownership of the mine or plantation.

It was not long, however, before the ratio of design to material in the machine began to rise and then reverse. As the machine became ever less substantial, its lifetime grew shorter. Today the economically significant industrial property is not the machine, but the design, and not so much the design as the capacity to innovate design in process and product. This is scarcely property at all, but is rather a capacity inhering in an organization. To have that capacity encumbered by a gigantic plant can be hazardous. This is what the steel industry has found in the present technological free-for-all that has brought steel into competition with materials—glass, ceramics, reconstructed wood, plastics, and exotic new metals—that no self-respecting steelmaker ever heard of fifteen years ago. The most profitable manufacturing enterprises are those that show a shrinking ratio of plant to output and a rising ratio of instrumentation to plant. Not only the plant but the product and the very industry in which the company is engaged may be subject to obsolescence. The decisive factor of production is research and development.

As the nature of property, in the sense of the thing that is owned, has changed, so has the nature of the social institution of property. Property was subverted by another social institution, the corporation. With ownership represented by stock certificates, the proprietor ceased to occupy the premises. The right of property vested in the stockholder, as A. A. Berle, Jr., and Gardiner C. Means made clear more than a generation ago in *The Modern Corporation and Private Property,* was reduced to the right to vote for the directors of the corporation (if the stockholder bothers to return the proxy statement) and to a claim on earnings (if the directors declare them out in dividends on his class of stock). Even these vestiges of power are delegated today to a third party for the increasing percentage of the voting equities in American industrial enterprise that is held by insurance companies, pension funds, and mutual investment companies.

The puissance in research and development that determines the fortunes of a corporate enterprise is commonly valued at one dollar on the balance sheet. This accounting fiction hypothecates the talents of the men who make up the organization, and the common-stock certificate is a thrice-removed share in that hypothecation. Under the circumstances, it is hard to see how the stockholder could be vested with a larger claim. The instrumentalities of ownership have become as insubstantial as the decisive factor of production itself.

Against this statement of the terms on which the present owners of the American industrial system hold their property, it may be argued that the really giant new fortunes are being made in the old-fashioned kind of property; that is, land and the mineral riches underneath it. But even the discovery of mineral resources has moved into the realm of invention. It is *par excellence* a yield on instrumentation, implemented by an equally intangible talent for politics. As a result, most of the prospecting is carried on by large corporations, and ownership stands at the same remove as in other activities of the industrial system.

With the emergence of two to five corporations in control of assets and sales in all but a few realms of industrial activity, economic power has become highly concentrated in our society. But it is no longer attached to property. The power is vested in self-perpetuating managements. How they derive their legitimacy is a question that troubles a great many people, including those who exercise the power as well as those who are critical of the power-holders.

Edward S. Mason, of the Harvard economics faculty, has astutely asked what difference, if any, this transfer of power has made. It is true that the profit margin—the yield to ownership—remains the ruling discipline of corporate management. And it is also true that operation under this discipline chronically fails to realize the full potential of industrial technology. That failure is the measure of the present business recession: with the gross national product holding steady at an all-time high, fully one third of the steel plant and comparable percentages of capacity in other industries lie idle. As the self-appointed management contemplates the troubling question of the legitimacy of its power, it must also face increasingly insistent questions about its stewardship of power.

The same transformation of the nature of property is to be seen again in the relationship of the owner to property as usufruct. There are more home-owners today in the United States than ever before in this century, more than 60 per cent of the occupiers of dwelling places compared with less than 50 per cent in 1900. But whereas 30 per cent of the homes were mortgaged to 40 per cent of their aggregate value in 1900, more than 60 per cent are mortgaged to more than half their aggregate value today. The builders and bankers of the new surburbs will tell you that the ownership of one out of six homes there turns over every year.

Plainly, the so-called home-owner is buying not a home but a housing service, much as he buys transportation, not a car, from the auto industry. His equity in these two utilities rarely controls before he turns in the old house or car for the new model. By the same token, the total installment debt represents, from one year to the next, by far the major property interest in all of the other consumer durable goods in use in the country. The householder is correct in regarding these transactions as the purchase of a service rather than property. For the objects themselves are self-consuming, designed for depreciation to desuetude in 1,000 hours of service.

In sum, the typical American consumer owns no property in the classical meaning of the term. Out of current income he pays for services currently rendered. Through income set aside in social security taxes and in pension and insurance funds, he reserves a claim on services to be rendered in the future.

Mention of the social security now provided for the overwhelming number of United States citizens brings this discussion to the topic of work. Social security is one of the devices evolved in the recent history of our industrial economy to help solve the problem of "distribution." This, as is well known, is the last frontier of economics. Viewed from the vantage of the economy as a whole, it is the problem of finding people qualified to consume the increasing abundance of goods produced by a declining number of workers. From the point of view of the individual citizen, it is the problem of finding work in a shrinking labor market in order to qualify as a consumer of that abundance. Thus, as we shall see, the primary function of work is the distribution of goods. This is clearly a different situation from that which prevailed in the valleys of the Tigris and Euphrates 7,000 years ago, when the surplus had to be extracted from scarcity by coercion.

Modern industrial technology produces a vast material surplus of goods, many times greater than the need of the workers engaged in producing it. That surplus goes begging for consumers because technology has subverted the social institution of work. The subversion of work began, of course, with the displacement of the biologically generated energy of human muscle by the mechanically generated energy of steam engines. The reciprocal steam engine gave way after little more than half a century to the steam turbine, the generator of electrical energy in the huge quantities that are measured in kilowatts. Studies conducted many years ago, when muscles were yielding a day's work to steam, showed that one man can put out about 48 kilowatt-hours in useful work in a year. On that basis, the 750 billion kilowatt-hours of electricity generated in the United States puts the equivalent of eighty-five slaves at the disposal of each man, woman, and child in the population.

But this is an old story. The new story is the disemployment of the human nervous system. In industrial production the function of the human worker has been to set the tool, start up the machine, supervise its performance, correct its error, and keep its parts in working order. The machine has been doing all the work, including work that exceeds human physical capacity. But, for lack of a nervous system, it has had to depend upon human beings to regulate its operations.

The robot, or artificial nervous system, is the steam engine of the present phase of the industrial revolution. Unlike the steam engine, it does not announce its presence by huffing and puffing, and it has no easily recognized anatomical structure. But it does have a single underlying principle, which is as clear-cut and universal as the idea of converting heat into mechanical energy. This essential idea is known to engineers as feedback.

Feedback is the principle that underlies all self-regulating systems, including living organisms. The nearest and simplest example of feedback in action is the household thermostat: A mechanical sense organ absorbs a little of the heat generated by the household heating plant and thereby makes a measurement of its output. This small fraction of the output is fed back in the form of a signal to correct the input of fuel to the heating unit. By this feeding-back of output to input, the household heating plant is made to regulate itself.

Now, the principle of converting heat to mechanical energy is embodied in about half a dozen economically important heat engines—including the steam turbine, the internal combustion engine, the gas turbine, and the rocket engine. The feedback control systems in our economy, on the other hand, appear in a host of species and varieties—electrical, electronic, pneumatic, hydraulic, mechanical—and in such diversity of design and appearance that they have only the essential feedback principle in common.

An accurate census of these robots has not been made. But the evidence is strong that they now out-number the human workers employed in industry. Our entire energy economy—from the steam plant out across the high-tension lines to the rotating machinery of industry—is now subject to automatic control. The new technology of atomic energy is critically dependent upon automatic control; dozens of feedback circuits in the depths of a nuclear reactor control the dreadful flux of atomic particles in which no living things could survive. Our petroleum refineries and almost all of our chemical process plants are today so highly robotized that their entire operations are controlled by one or two human operators stationed at the central push-button control panel.

It is only a few steps from here to the fully automatic factory. In the petroleum industry, such a factory would make use of an instrument—such as the nuclear resonance spectrometer, which has only recently graduated from the laboratory—to analyze the output stream of a refinery. The spectrometer would feed back its reading to a mechanical computer, one of the "giant brain" variety. These machines are already equal to doing the work of the human operator at the control panel; they need merely to be equipped with instructions covering all possible contingencies in the operation of the plant. Comparing the spectrometer report on the output of the refinery with the instructions stored in its memory, the computer would check and correct the performance of the robot valves at all points on the process stream. In fact, the first full-scale refineries incorporating the principal elements of the self-regulating robot factory are now "on stream."

Obviously, the purpose in designing the automatic petroleum refinery is not to replace the one or two human operators who still remain on the payroll. This was the naïve idea of a Middle Eastern petroleum prince for whom an American oil company was building a refinery not long ago. Out of consideration for the under-employed *fellaheen* who were to squat in the sand outside the refinery fence, he asked whether jobs might not be created by disengaging the robots from the valves. The engineers took him seriously enough to re-examine the entire control system. They had to conclude that no team of human beings could be trained and coordinated to do its work.

So, also, the dial telephone, with the ramifications of direct long-distance and direct inward dialing, is designed not to save the wages of human female telephone operators, but to make the operation of the modern telephone system possible. The heart of that system is not the dial on the telephone but a computer in the central station known in the telephone company as the "line marker." Its self-regulating internal circuitry is so complex that its designers cannot tell at any given moment just which elements in it are performing the work at hand. The American Telephone and

Telegraph Company estimates that, at the present rate of traffic, it would have to employ all of the women in the labor force, plus 20 per cent more, to do the work of its line markers. The task of coordinating the output of that many human nervous systems in a single telephone system is quite impracticable.

To engage the robot in functions of this kind takes some doing. The control system must be furnished with receptor organs, like the spectrometer or the dial on the telephone, to supply it with inputs from the world outside. And it must be linked with the world on its output side by means of effector organs, the hands that carry out its instructions. These may take the form of the electrical and pneumatic motors that drive the valves on a refinery or the relays that close connections in the telephone system.

Since the computer's function is to handle information, the easiest way to hook it up to the world outside it is by typewriter. Equipped with typewriters, it becomes a white-collar worker.

Thus far the impact of the automatic control revolution upon the industrial payroll has been felt most acutely by the production worker. Until about twenty-five years ago, the ranks of skilled and semi-skilled factory hands were the growing element in the labor force, absorbing the inward migration from farm to city. In the last ten years, however, as the index of manufacturing output has climbed from 75 to 110, the number of production workers has hovered around 12,000,000. It is evident that the number is now due to decline. In the electrical industry, for example, production employment shrank by 10 per cent in the six-year period from 1953 to 1959; during that same period production in this industry increased by 20 per cent. Even more striking records have been made by the larger units of the industry. In three years, from 1956 to 1959, the General Electric Company increased its output by 8 per cent and at the same time reduced its production payroll by 25 per cent. Its non-production workers now outnumber those on the factory payroll proper. Corresponding trends are to be observed in other industries. After the last retooling, the auto industry produced more units than ever before, and yet the auto cities of Michigan were rated as distress unemployment areas throughout the year of peak production. Projection of these trends into the future shows factory workers becoming as scarce as farmers toward the end of the century.

Vocal union organizations imbued with the Luddite spirit have made the public uncomfortably aware of these developments in recent years. Less is heard of what must be the already considerable impact of the white-collar computer. This movement has only just begun. Since typewriters furnish all the necessary linkage, it is clear that the liberation of white-collar workers from their routine tasks is due to proceed at a much faster rate. Again it should be emphasized that the object is not labor-saving alone. With a computer to do the job, all the many records kept by a corporation become a deck of punched cards or a length of magnetic tape that serves as the single record for every function from inventory control to the computing of a salesman's bonus. Herbert A. Simon, of the Carnegie Institute of Technology, has pointed out that the computer so programed is not merely a clerk but stands ready to assume a large portion of the functions of middle and top management. As a decision-maker, the computer can subject much larger masses of data to more sophisticated analysis in much shorter periods of time. Not only does it know the theory of linear programing better than most of our highest-paid executives; it can also learn from experience to improve its performance in the managerial function.

From decade to decade, the American economy has adjusted to the subversion of the social institution of work with flexibility and something of the same inventiveness with which it has absorbed the consequences of the subversion of property. One man-hour of work today produces what it took three man-hours to produce sixty years ago. This means that we could be producing the same national product as in 1900 with one third of the 1900 labor force. That would leave 58,000,000 members of the present labor force unemployed. But, of course, the American people have elected to apply their rising productivity to the production of a much larger volume of goods, about six times as much as in 1900. A major part of this vast increase in output is represented by products not dreamed of in 1900. In other words, the workers disemployed by rising productivity in the old industries have been absorbed in new ones to produce an expanding variety of goods or in entirely new functions created by the flow of abundance.

They could be producing goods in even greater volume if not variety today, but they have chosen to take a substantial portion of the gain in leisure. With the work week shortened from around sixty hours to forty hours, the much larger 1960 labor force is putting in a total number of man-hours that is only 40 per cent larger than that worked by the 1900 labor force. If the sixty-hour work week still prevailed, only 40,000,000 workers would be needed to produce the 1961 national product and some 27,000,000 workers would be unemployed.

This invention—the spreading of the same amount of work over the larger labor force by giving everyone less work to do—constitutes only one of the measures so far evolved to handle the problem of distribution. Moreover, it should be distinguished from the desperate share-the-work measures taken in the Great Depression, because it does not involve sharing the wage.

On the contrary, the portion of the national income going to the labor factor—that is, compensation of employees as against profit, interest, rent, and so on—has risen slowly from 53 to 73 per cent since 1900. Some substantial portion of this shift must be attributed to the decline in the number of proprietors, large and small, especially in agriculture. That the shift also reflects a gain on the problem of distribution becomes clear, however, when it is considered in connection with the way the total income is shared among the income groups. Since 1929 the share of the national income going to the most fortunate fifth of the nation's families has shrunk from 55 to 45 per cent. Almost the entire 10 per cent subtracted from the income of the top fifth has gone to the three middle fifths, improving their relative position by about 25 per cent.

This redistribution of purchasing power is another important factor in reducing the amount of work people do in the course of their lives. It makes it possible for young people to postpone their entrance into the labor market through high-school and even college age, and it takes workers out of the labor market by voluntary retirement at the other end of their careers.

But the shortening of the work week and the working life still leaves untold the real story of how work has been spread in order to secure the spread of purchasing power. If work is defined with any sort of strictness to mean productive work—that is, the extraction of raw materials and the making of consumable goods from them (farming, mining, manufacturing, building, and transportation)—then less than half of the labor force, only 25,000,000 people, are really at work.

The distribution of the abundance they produce is secured in large part by employing people in the task of distribution. This is not to say that the distributors do not serve a valid economic function. But selling and distribution costs commonly mark up the manufacturing cost of durable goods by 250 per cent. The major portion of the profit on the sales price therefore comes from the distribution process. Since gimmickry is thus made to grow by what it feeds upon, the distribution system pays a premium on waste. Its principal economic justification is that it does provide "work" and so increases the number of consumers.

To the 12,000,000 employed in distribution should be added another 12,000,000 who qualify as consumers by virtue of their employment in financial, clerical, and service functions—necessary but again not productive work even as it is formally defined in our national bookkeeping. Another large group of consumers are qualified by their enrollment on government payrolls. Certain members of the community will stoutly deny that these people ever do a day's work. Not counting the armed forces, their number now exceeds 5,500,000. If the figure looks too big, it is because we usually forget local and state governments in these calculations. The figure comes back into scale when we recognize that $132,000,000,000, nearly 30 per cent of the gross national product, turned over in government budgets in 1959. Those expenditures not only set up 5,500,000 consumers for the goods made by those more productively employed; the money also made substantial direct purchases of goods and so generated millions of the jobs in the production sector.

Our roll-call ends with the approximately 2,000,000 household employees and the 2,000,000 or more who are employed in teaching or self-employed in the learned professions. Those whom we have here classified as non-productive workers constituted only 30 per cent of the labor force of 1900; they make up 60 per cent of it today. Compared with the day's work that confronts most of mankind every morning, most American citizens are not engaged in work at all.

Thus, up to the present, the American society has managed to handle the subversion of the institution of work without undue stress upon the system of distribution that has carried over from the days of scarcity. Work, the illusion of work, and pleasant substitutes for work furnish an expanding population with the purchasing power to consume an even more rapidly expanding volume of production. For most of the past twenty years employment has been "full."

It now appears, however, that the advance of technology has begun to outstrip our capacity for social invention. Before the second World War, in the flux of technological change and the oscillations of the business cycle, the system chronically fell 5 or 10 per cent below full employment and fell as far as 25 per cent below in 1933. It is instructive to compare this experience with the present. During the past several years, despite a steady rise in gross national product, unemployment has been rising. Each wavelet in the now well-damped business cycle has left a larger number of workers high and dry on the beach. Unemployment now approaches 6,000,000, or nearly 10 per cent of the labor force. But this figure seriously understates the gap between the jobs available in the production and distribution of goods in the economy and the number of people who need employment in order to be able to purchase their share of those goods.

That gap has been filled for the past fifteen years by the war economy that has grown up alongside the consumer economy in our country. The rolls of the employed include today the 2,500,000 in the armed forces; they are certainly not employed in the production and distribution of goods. To their numbers should be added the 1,000,000 civilian employees of the Department of Defense, whose principal employment is that of housekeeping and procurement for those in uniform. Finally, we must add the 2,500,-000 workers in industry engaged in filling the procurement orders of the military. The total of those unemployed or employed outside the civilian economy thus comes to 12,000,000, close to 20 per cent of the labor force, only 5 per cent below the unemployment peak of 1933—and this at a time when the gross national product has reached an all-time high.

Wassily Leontief, of Harvard University, has recently adapted his "input-output" technique to permit detailed analysis of the prospective economic consequences of disarmament. Study of his tables indicates that even if the gross national product is maintained at peak levels through the transition period following an agreement to disarm, the civilian economy would very likely fall short of re-employing all of those who would be disemployed by the cut in military expenditure. The same study indicates that by 1965 technological disemployment will, in any case, eliminate about one fifth of the jobs in industry now generated by the procurement of arms (unless progress in the technology of armament continues to generate new starts on new weapons systems). In other industries, in the same period, technological progress promises to reduce employment by an average of close to 10 per cent.

The evidence that full employment is no longer an attainable objective seems to be growing. Of course, the arms budget can be arbitrarily increased, and the size of the armed forces along with it, to offset technological disemployment in the armament industries. But no one really wants to contemplate an indefinite continuation of the arms race. Alternatively, or concurrently, some of the slack can be taken up by a thirty-hour work week, a measure advocated by both presidential candidates as long ago as 1956. After that, the work week could be reduced to twenty-five, then twenty hours—and the inefficiencies inherent in such a short work week would help to create more jobs. At that point the nation will have come really close to being a workless society.

No reasonably predictable rate of growth in the productive sectors of the economy seems equal to overtaking the current rate of technological disemployment. Every step of progress in automatic control reduces the capital investment as well as the employment per unit of output. As the cost of investment goes down, the rate of technological progress must increase and with it disemployment. Even an expanding economy must employ progressively fewer workers in its productive sectors. At some point the terminus of full investment will be reached; even at the present level of opulence, the consumer economy shows signs of surfeit. There is, of course, a vast untapped market in the income groups at the bottom third of the economic pyramid. But how are their wants to be implemented with purchasing power when that bottom third already counts the disemployed among its members?

In the long run, larger questions must be asked and answered. If a fraction of the labor force is capable of supplying an abundance of everything the population needs and wants, then why should the rest of the population have to work for a living? Preposterous alternatives come forward: give-away programs on television suggest that television might be employed to give the abundance away instead of trying to sell it. If production cannot be maintained at a profit under such circumstances, then why should a profit be made? Some other standard of accounting might serve even better to reduce waste and inefficiency.

These questions are put in a deliberately extreme form. They suggest the kind of overturn in the values of our society which is already quaking the ground beneath our feet. The virtues of hard work and profit are rooted in scarcity. They have no relevance to the economics or the sociology of abundance.

Any hard work that a machine can do is better done by a machine; "hard" these days means mostly boring and repetitive, whether in the factory or in the office. But the instinct for workmanship, the need to feel needed, the will to achieve, are deeply felt in every human heart. They are not universally fulfilled by the kind of employment most people find. Full employment in the kind of employment that is commonly available, whether blue-collar or white-collar, has been plainly outmoded by technology. The liberation of people from tasks unworthy of human capacity should free that capacity for a host of activities now neglected in our civilization: teaching and learning, fundamental scientific investigation, the performing arts and the graphic arts, letters, the crafts, politics, and social service. Characteristically these activities involve the interaction of people with people rather than with things. They are admittedly not productive activities; nor are they profitable in the strict sense. But they are highly rewarding to the individuals involved and add greatly to the wealth of the nation. There is no question that our population numbers increasing millions of people qualified for such functions; our institutions of higher learning will have an enrollment of 6,000,000 before the decade is out. The nation's principal economic problem has become that of certifying its citizens as consumers of the abundance available to sustain them in tasks worthy of their time.

What disturbs the scarcity economist, of course, is that such certification is likely to be provided by the public payroll. It must be recognized, however, that these activities—along with urban rapid transit, the enhancement and conservation of natural resources, public works, the best kind of medicine, the operation of museums, and so on—have never been or can no longer be conducted at a profit. Most of these activities and institutions are now short-changed. With abundance to support the expanding portion of the population engaged in them, we may anticipate that they will assume a higher priority in our civilization.

In any event, so long as the institutions of work and property preside over our economic activities, it is clear that the distribution of material goods will be achieved as it has been in the past, by expansion of the "non-productive" payroll in both the public and the private sectors of the economy. The "peace corps" and the revival of the conservation corps proposed by the Kennedy administration are the latest steps in this direction. There is plenty of need, if not demand, for labor of this kind. A really adequate program of assistance to the under-developed countries might engage large numbers of disemployed factory workers in teaching their skills to people now entering on their industrial revolution. For some time to come, we can be sure, the real work that remains to be done in the world will stave off the specter of universal leisure.

As for profit, considerations other than profit are already being pressed upon the great corporations by society through governmental regulatory agencies. The self-perpetuating management is understandably wary of such invasion of its prerogatives. In the present ascendance of its reputation, however, it should be more concerned about its performance than its prerogatives. What is most to be asked of the corporate enterprise system is the vigorous promotion of technological progress. This, in fact, is the primary purpose served by profit in the industrial system today; as a kind of involuntary savings, extracted beforehand from the thriftless consumer, retained corporate earnings have furnished the principal capital for industrial expansion throughout the past fifty years. In the future, the "economic republic" of A. A. Berle envisions the insistent intrusion of the public interest in the councils of the private governments that operate our economy, especially when it comes to the deployment of investment funds.

Our society is probably closer to being propertyless than workless today. But the rate of technological progress is speeding up. It appears now to be moving faster than even the responsive and resilient American social order can evolve. Some of the changes may have to come in quantum jumps. For these we need economic and political leadership whose perception and judgment are not compromised in any fashion by commitments to the past.

in my opinion...

Mr. Piel's conclusion that we are moving rapidly toward a "propertyless, perhaps workless" society is a profound one. And as he so rightly points out, the American social order seems unable to respond to this change. What is needed is unfettered imagination and the determination to accept the possibility of a new century where only a minute portion of our populace participate in the production process.

With a little thought, it becomes clear that the drastic changes which are taking place present enormous problems, not actually in the fields of economics or production, but in persuading a society based on a work ethic to accept the blessings of abundance. If we are now close to being "propertyless" and moving in giant strides towards an era of "worklessness," then society's attitudes towards the processes of production, distribution, centralized controls, total planning, and the end of the competitive system will be subjected to earth-shaking strain.

The first uneasy step has been made. Acting on the reports of a half-dozen federal committees over a period of a decade, a recommendation advocating a guaranteed annual wage was made to Congress. The minimum figure, in terms of living costs, is brutal; the word "wage" carefully protects the public from the possibility of a threat to the work ethic, but it is a step. (In this respect, more than 80 experts of the Rand Corporation have anticipated a guaranteed *international* annual *income* by the year 2000. The italics are mine!)

Mortimer Adler, talking of the future of man, startled an audience by acclaiming the introduction of slavery in prehistoric times, pointing out that man, who, up to that time had been totally preoccupied with staying alive, was given his first opportunity to meditate, to reason and to dream. For ten thousand years, these privileges had been restricted to the few. As technology improves, more men, perhaps all mankind, may have that opportunity.

But men do not become philosophers simply because the wherewithal for survival is made available at little expense of energy or time. And many men who lack flexibility, men who have an inbred need for material success, may find themselves incapable of accepting the gratuity of abundance—indeed they may fight its advent with the endless stock of obsolete aphorisms which directed their efforts from infancy. Of what value the "penny saved"?

It is in the area of inflexibility that the dangers lie. If abundance is to mean only more time to fish, bowl and hunt, more hours to be wafted off into never-never land by means of the tele-heara-smellovision sets of the future, then nature's great experiment with a thinking, reasoning, rational animal has failed.

If man is truly rational, he will not fail. Indeed, if he proves incapable of reason, man will never reach the twenty-first century. Without question, man's "humaneness" will face its greatest test in every area of human endeavor in the next three decades. And despite the headlines, the angry belching of uncomprehending politicians, the prevalence of dying lakes and angry outcries against population control, rational man will prevail. We are betting our lives on it.

thomas r. fritts

questions

1. If computers have already had a substantial effect on the production worker, and are, as Piel suggests, in the process of making inroads into middle and top management decision-making, what changes in education should take place?

2. "Compared with the day's work that confronts most of mankind every morning, most American citizens are not engaged in work at all." Explain.

3. A major goal of most candidates for high office in the United States has been "full employment." If this concept is no longer valid, what are the political implications?

4. What problems face a political leader in the U.S. if the directions of the economy toward nonemployment (as suggested by Piel) are accurate?

5. What complications would develop if people in the highly industrialized nations of the world become work-free?

4.
whatever happened to the work ethic? the onslaught of leisure

OF TIME, WORK AND LEISURE

sebastian de grazia

introduction and comment by douglas o. snyder

In many different time periods and in many different cultures men have attempted to define and obtain leisure. From Greece to Rome to Medieval Europe to Renaissance Italy to twentieth century America, the search has continued. The problem of obtaining leisure is a technological question which seems about to be answered by modern methods of production and distribution, but the philosophical problem of determining exactly what it is we are about to obtain is as perplexing as ever. Since it is apparent that leisure is at least in some part the absence of work, let us first examine briefly what is meant by this seemingly simple term.

Work is first of all labor, the manual, sweating kind of toil that produces backaches and callouses. Secondly, work may be thought of as the activity one engages in to sustain life—that is, to produce the necessities: food, shelter, clothing. But even in these simple concepts of work there are pitfalls and ambiguities. When a man plays a strenuous game of tennis, he definitely perspires, physically exerts himself, and may even develop a few sore and painful muscles. Yet he does not consider this activity work. To obtain the essentials for survival all that is needed is a place on the welfare rolls. While this method of surviving may not provide any of the qualities of the "good life," it does allow the possibility of life without work. However, the idea of simply sitting back and receiving sustenance without producing anything useful in return is abhorrent to most Americans and would be largely rejected on the basis that one who does not work serves no purpose. Perhaps we have stumbled upon yet another quality of work: it has a concrete and useful purpose. To work is to accomplish some predetermined goal. But our tennis player was certainly seeking a goal—in fact, he was probably accomplishing several purposes. The distinction that makes his activity not work seems to be that he did not *have* to do it. Work can be defined then as an activity one pursues out of necessity or obligation and which has a purpose or goal aside from itself. In this context it becomes increasingly difficult to think of anything one does as other than work. The recreations, hobbies, and pastimes of America are all engaged in for the purpose of obtaining a respite from the everyday job. Moreover, they are carried on to fulfill our obligation to "do something." What American can truthfully and without a twinge of guilt reply to the question, "What are you doing"? with an answer such as "Just thinking," or worse yet, "Nothing"?

We are a nation of doers and makers and a large part of our preoccupation with activity stems from our notions and emotions concerning time. If a man is not involved in some form of activity we say he is wasting time. We tend to see time as a commodity to be rationed, spent, used, and measured. It is the measuring which is the root of the problem. Because we are so concerned with the exact amount of time involved in all our living, we segment time and compartmentalize it and then try to match our lives to this contrived rhythm. The result is that far too often our lives become segmented and our thought neatly boxed in, and we lose sight of the fact that both time and our act of living must be experienced, not measured. The proper question is not "What are you doing"? but rather "What is happening to you"?

And so, once again, what is meant by work, leisure, time? It appears that the answer is not easily found. We are rapidly approaching the time when not only a few men of questing mind, but the great masses of our country will have to wrestle with the dilemma of leisure. The tragedy is not that we are nearing this crossroad, but that we are doing so little to prepare ourselves and the next generation for its coming.

The following pages contain excerpts from the book *Of Time, Work and Leisure* by Sebastian de Grazia. This in-depth examination of man's concept of time, his search for meaning in his everyday activity, and his great consternation at finally realizing his age-old dream of freedom from toil, is thorough and exacting. The passages included here attempt to provide some background for an understanding of the situation with which we are faced at the present time, a situation which involves widespread changes in our social, political, economic and personal lives. When only two out of every one hundred people are engaged in producing the necessities of life, what will the rest of us do? Perhaps we will do nothing and enjoy it. Perhaps we will discover how to turn free time into leisure. Perhaps we will discover our full humanity.

d.o.s.

OF TIME, WORK
AND LEISURE

*Sebastian de Grazia received his Ph.D. in Political Philosophy
from the University of Chicago. From 1941 to 1943 he was a
member of the research staff of the Federal Communications
Commission, and was research director of the Twentieth Century
Fund until 1962. At present he is Director of Research for the
Twentieth Century Fund in addition to his post as Professor of
Political Philosophy at Eagleton Institute, Rutgers University.
A member of the American Political Science Association,
Professor de Grazia is associated with the American Council of
Learned Sciences and was with the Office of Strategic Services
(1943–1945). His published work includes* Of Time, Work and
Leisure *(published by the Twentieth Century Fund in 1962),
and two scholarly texts:* The Political Community, *1948, and*
Errors of Psychotherapy, *1952.*

The Greeks took the question of leisure seriously. Their ideas
are worth attention for they not only examined many of the
problems confronting us today but asked questions we have not
dared to ask ourselves. Who today would say that a nation could
collapse because it didn't know how to use its leisure? Who today
so predicts the downfall of the United States or of China? But
Aristotle not only lived in but was preceded by a century interested
in leisure. His Greece, his Athens, pulled back the curtains to offer
the West an ideal.

The etymological root of *scholē* meant to halt or cease, hence
to have quiet or peace. Later it meant to have time to spare or,
specially, time for oneself. Of the great Greeks, Aristotle was the
one who most often used the word *scholē*. For him life could be

Reprinted from Sebastian de Grazia, Of Time, Work and Leisure *by
permission of The Twentieth Century Fund, New York, 1962.*

divided into different parts—action and leisure, war and peace. Citizens must be capable of a life of action and war, but even more able to lead a life of leisure and peace. Warlike states are safe only while they are fighting. A sword resting unused in the scabbard loses its temper. In any case it never had a temper for peace. Courage in battle is a virtue of limited use in peacetime. The legislator is to blame if he does not educate citizens to those other virtues needed for the proper use of leisure. A greater emphasis on temperance and justice should be taught them for times when they are faring exceptionally well and enjoying all that the world holds to be happiness. In war the virtues of men come forth for a united effort; in peace and prosperity men lose their temperance and justice toward one another and become overbearing. The greater the abundance of blessings that fall to men, the greater will be their need for wisdom, and wisdom is the virtue that cannot appear except in leisure.

So, the dangerous period is peace. Yet for Aristotle it was self-evident that just as a person would not want to be fighting all his life, so a state would not want to make war all the time. The end could never be war. It had to be peace. The good thing about peace was that it allowed leisure. But what was this precious leisure? If the legislator was to provide for it, he had to know what it was. Or how was he to keep leisure in mind with regard not only to what wars are fought for, but to all problems pertaining to the state?

In some cases it seems that leisure is another word for spare or free time. For example the well-to-do, says Aristotle, if they must attend to their private affairs have little leisure for politics and absent themselves from the assembly and the courts. In common usage _scholē_ seems to have had this meaning. Aristotle apparently uses the same sense when he says the Spartans used their leisure to prepare for war. But one senses a different element, an ethical note, a hint that spare time when misused is not leisure. The case of the Helots who lived for one day only, the day on which they would massacre their masters, reveals that free time if shot through with fear is not leisure. Yet the clearest of the charges against Sparta is that against the women, whose time, though all free, became not leisure but license. Obviously time on one's hands is not enough to make leisure.

At one point Aristotle gives a rough equivalent of leisure. He speaks of it and then adds, "or in other words, freedom from the necessity of labor." This at a glance seems similar to the modern idea of free time—time off the job—but we would be well advised to go slowly here. The differences, though mainly in the nuances of words, reflect a different world. We can note to start that free time accentuates time; it sets aside a unit of time free of the job. In Aristotle's short definition time has no role. Leisure is a condition or a state—the state of being free from the necessity of labor.

Elsewhere Aristotle mentioned not labor but action as a contrast to leisure. He spoke of the life of leisure versus the life of action. By action here he intended activities toward other persons or objects in order to effect some purpose. He was using "action" in a common meaning, but, as he often makes clear, for himself a living being can hardly be anything but active. The gods live and therefore they too are active. Though invisible, even thought moves, even pure speculation, and so does contemplation, the activity of the gods. Indeed, thoughts and those who hold them are active in the fullest measure since it is they that move persons and things to the outward, visible kind of activity.

Leisure is active, then, though not necessarily a highly visible kind of activity. But what had Aristotle against labor that he made it almost the contrary of leisure? In Greek there are two common words for labor or work. One is *ponos,* which has the connotations of toil in our sense, that is, the sense of fatiguing, sweating, almost painful, manual effort. The other is *ascholia,* which is more like our idea of work or occupation in that it has less of the painful physical element. In origin the word really denotes the absence of leisure for its root is *scholē,* before which an *a-* is placed to signify a want or a lack. It thus means un-leisure or the state of being busy or occupied. This being at unleisure, though it seems a roundabout way of putting things, may be the closest to our phrase of being occupied or at work. The Spartan women, however, were free of the necessity of working, and still they had no true leisure.

The idea of occupation here is somewhat different from ours. We come closer to it when we speak of being occupied or busy, for the noun forms, both occupation and business (originally busyness), are further away from the idea, having come to be associated with work and the job. We can now rewrite the original definition thus: Leisure is freedom from the necessity of being occupied. This includes freedom from the necessity to labor, but it could also embrace any activity one finds necessary to perform, but would fain be free of. Here again we seem to be near a modern notion of leisure, as time in which a person can do as he pleases, time, perhaps, for amusement or recreation.

We would still do well to proceed cautiously. When Aristotle uses the word occupation, he cuts out the idea of "do as one pleases." An occupation is activity pursued for a purpose. If the purpose were not necessary, the activity would not occur. Therefore no occupation can be leisure, not even the self-employer's, whose purpose is self-chosen. Nor can leisure be anything related to an occupation. Amusement (*paidia*) and recreation (*anapausis*) are necessary because of work. They are not ends in themselves. Happiness does not lie in amusements, the things children do. In the *Ethics,* Aristotle says, "To exert oneself and work for the sake of amusement seems silly and utterly childish." Rather is it the reverse, that we take to amusements as relaxation. We need relaxation, for we cannot work constantly. We need amusements and recreation to restore, to re-create ourselves for our occupation. But the goal of being occupied should only be to attain leisure.

The distinguishing mark now begins to appear. Leisure is a state of being in which activity is performed for its own sake or as its own end. What Aristotle means by an end in itself or a final end he himself has demonstrated in the *Ethics:* clearly not all goals are final goals, though the chief good evidently is. Therefore, if there is only one final goal, this will be what we seek; if there are more than one, what we shall seek is the most final among them. Now that which is in itself worthy of pursuit we call more final than that pursued for the sake of something else, and that which is desirable not for the sake of something else we should say is more final than things that are desired partly for themselves and partly for the sake of some other thing. And we call final without reservation that which is always desirable in itself and never for the sake of something else.

Leisure stands in the last class by itself. It is not exaggerating to say that, as Aristotle is a philosopher of happiness, he is also a philosopher of leisure. Happiness can appear only in leisure. The capacity to use leisure rightly, he repeats, is the basis of the free man's whole life.

We can better see the logic of this conception if we ask, What is one to do in leisure? To play would be impossible. Play—at least for adults—belongs to the side of occupation: it relaxes the worker. It produces not happiness but the pleasant feeling of relief from exertion and tension. "Leisure is a different matter,"

Aristotle holds in the *Politics.* "We think of it as having in itself intrinsic pleasure, intrinsic happiness, intrinsic felicity. Happiness of that order does not belong to occupation: it belongs to those who have leisure." Occupations aim at some end as yet unattained; felicity is a present end and is attained by leisure in its every act and very moment. When Aristotle himself puts the question, it is clear that play is out, for he says, "With what kind of activity should we do (*skolēn agein*) our leisure?" We do not *do* our leisure with play, yet we do not *do* it with work. An occupation is not taken on as an end in itself, and play for adults is needed only to relieve work.

*   *   *

Leisure or *scholē,* believed Newman, the student of Aristotle, meant being occupied in something desirable for its own sake— the hearing of noble music and noble poetry, intercourse with friends chosen for their own worth, and above all the exercise, alone or in company, of the speculative faculty. From what we have learned of those musicians, the Greeks, we would agree with him, though we would make explicit the *playing* of music, the *reciting* of poetry, and the *composing* of both. All these things fit the word Aristotle uses occasionally to describe the activities of leisure, namely, the cultivation of the mind (*diagōgē*). He used the word leisure in at least two senses, as we have seen—one as available time, the other as absence of the necessity of being occupied. It is not immediately clear whether in talking about *diagōgē* he is saying that in leisure you should cultivate your mind or that in the true state of leisure you cannot do anything but cultivate your mind.

So far I have not discussed contemplation, or what Newman described as above all the exercise of the speculative faculty. By going into this idea, we shall get a firmer grasp on what Aristotle meant by the cultivation of the mind and "freedom from necessity" in leisure, and the relation between the two. Contemplation in the Greek sense is so close to leisure that in describing one and the other repetition is inevitable. Plato first developed the idea in the *Republic.* His models were the Ionian philosophers, whose absorption in knowledge for its own sake inspired Plato's academy and Aristotle's Peripatetic school. Thales of Miletus was one of these philosophers. Plato has told us his story, of how gazing at the stars he fell into a well, and of the little maid who, standing by, laughed at the sport. The idea of contemplation itself in those days seemed to be groping for its true meaning.

Our word comes from the Latin but the Latin is a translation from the Greek *theorein,* to behold, to look upon. *Theōria* was also the word for theory, and was used in the phrase "the theoretical life," which in Latin became "the contemplative life," both of which have a fast friendship with the life of leisure.

Contemplation for Plato and Aristotle was the best way of truth-finding. They prized it above all other activities. It was the only activity in which they could picture the gods. The contemplator looks upon the world and man with the calm eye of one who has no design on them. In one sense he feels himself to be close to all nature. He has not the aggressive detachment or unfeeling isolation that comes from scrutinizing men and objects with a will to exploiting them. In another sense he is truly detached because he looks on none of them with intent to manipulate or control or change, on neither man nor beast nor nature. Whoever does look on the world with design, who wishes to subdue or seduce others, to gain money, to win fame, cannot see much beyond the slice he is cutting. His aim on the world puts lenses before his eyes. He doesn't even know his sight is distorted.

When Plato describes the ideal education of those who should be the rulers of the country, he has them passing every test and trial with honors, so that finally they can "lift up the eye of the soul and fix it upon that which gives light to all things." In contemplation they can see the essence of the good and take it for their pattern. They can see things and how they fit together so well because, as rulers, they are free of all necessity to take an oblique view. They do not have the compulsion of those who must make money or win honors. Take the mechanic or anyone who has to work for his living. He is the one who must watch his job and tools and his boss, who must have relief from toil and calculate how best to sell his wares or his services, and who gets caught up in a futile flurry of activities that lead nowhere. How can he see true and carry truth forward to the outer reaches of the cosmos circled by man's eye?

Contemplation, like leisure, or being itself leisure, brings felicity. Aristotle in the *Ethics* contends that happiness extends only so far as contemplation does. Those who can contemplate are the most truly happy. Indeed, happiness must be some form of contemplation. The activity of God, surpassing all others in blessedness, must be contemplative. Those men who most cultivate the mind are most akin to the gods and therefore dearest to them. The man in contemplation is a free man. He needs nothing. Therefore nothing determines or distorts his thought. He does whatever he loves to do, and what he does is done for its own sake.

There is one more Greek philosopher whose influence on the contemplative life was great, Epicurus, but his contribution comes in better at a later stage of our study. Thus far we can see how philosophers, in an interplay of *scholē* and the contemplative life, transformed a word meaning simple spare time into the classical ideal of leisure with all its sense of freedom, superiority, and learning for its own sake.

We begin to grasp how leisure is related to politics. If a man is at leisure only when he is free, the good state must exist to give him leisure. What he does in this leisure can be equated with what we today call the good life. Surprisingly few political philosophers have seen the connection between freedom and leisure as ends of the state. The prevalence of work in modern times, as we shall see, partly explains the oversight. Aristotle took it for granted: the life of leisure was the only life fit for a Greek.

* * *

In Italy, where the Renaissance first appeared, classical learning seemed more essential to the energetic men of Florence. That imaginary dialog between Alberti and Lorenzo the Magnificent fits the classical mood. The fifteenth and sixteenth centuries looked on the gothic ones with contempt. So far had Renaissance men been freed by those prior centuries that they no longer acknowledged their debt, indeed saw their inheritance as chains, and looked to the glories of a remoter past for inspiration. Looked to, but, try as they might, they could never bring themselves to make a copy of their ancient models; so Leonardo, Galileo, Michelangelo, and Brunelleschi stooped to do things with their hands that only a mechanic in Greece would have done. The Renaissance brought forth a new philosophy of work, leaning more on *praxis* than *theoria,* moving away from *scientia contemplativa* to *scientia operativa.* The honorable position the monks gave labor could not be shed so quickly, not even in Italy, any more than could another monkish innovation that went so well with work—the clock.

Perhaps because they sensed that manual work was so unusual a demand to make of monks, the Benedictines worked out a regular system of work and prayer or meditation. To some monks, as to Frère Jacques of the time-honored round, the bed felt good in the cold, early morning. To others, contemplation, which did not die with the Greco-Roman world, seemed to be the more appropriate activity for a religious man. St. Thomas had insisted on it. So bells and clocks were used as never before to pull monks out of bed, to send them off to prayers and then to the fields, to mark off the time for work and prayer and contemplation.

To Luther, himself a monk, certain doctrines of the Church of Rome were dangerous for the soul, but not the praise of work that the monasteries had given to the world. Indeed the prospering monasteries by this time had begun to let manual work out to others. They had their own serfs, whose life, too, was now run by the bells. The original idea, though, was sound—to work is to serve God—sound not alone for Luther, but later for Calvin and Wesley as well.

The Reformation's ideas of work have been examined by many scholars. It was, in fact, one of the most intense areas of historical study in the first half of the twentieth century. Many points of controversy sprang up—whether religious ideas or industrial necessity first created the new idea of work, whether its first flowering was in Catholicism or in Protestantism, whether work is less prominent for the reformers than other doctrines were, and so on. With or without saying so explicitly, however, most students agreed that out of the Reformation came a new atmosphere. Labor commanded a new tone. Once, man worked for a livelihood, to be able to live. Now he worked for something beyond his daily bread. He worked because somehow it was the right or moral thing to do.

It is outside our limits to trace the spread of this work ethic or gospel of work, as it much later came to be called, over Germany, England, Scandinavia and elsewhere in Europe. We are chiefly interested in the fact that it eventually reached the United States, there to obtain the fullest expression. Perhaps the linking of work to God is no longer so clear as it once was, yet we can certainly see that the shadows of the great reformers fell over the idea of work in America. Here, all who can must work, and idleness is bad; too many holidays means nothing gets done, and by steady methodical work alone can we build a great and prosperous nation. Here, too, work is good for you, a remedy for pain, loneliness, the death of a dear one, a disappointment in love, or doubts about the purpose of life.

Today the American without a job is a misfit. To hold a job means to have status, to belong in the way of life. Between the ages of twenty-five and fifty-five, that is, after school age and before retirement age, nearly 95 per cent of all males work, and about 35 per cent of all females. Being without a job in prosperous times is bad enough, but being without one in a depression is worse yet. Then the American without work—or the German or Englishman—is a damned soul. Various studies have portrayed the unemployed man as confused, panicky, prone to suicide, mayhem, and revolt. Totalitarian regimes seem to know what unemployment can mean: they never permit it.

The modern doctrine of work affects all countries that try to solve their problems by industrialization. It has migrated to Russia, to China, India, and will make inroads on every modernizing nation, for work cannot be made methodical, rational or impersonal without the addition of some incentive besides the schoolbook triumvirate of food, clothing, and shelter. After the triumph of the United States in World War II—so heavily attributed to massive industrial productivity—the work ethic along with so many other things American was imported by countries all over the globe at an accelerated pace. In not a few nations new constitutions were drawn up. The very first article of one of these proclaims that the country is "a democratic republic based on work." It is hard to recognize from this definition the same Italy where the fervor of laboring monks had least shaken the Greco-Roman ideal of tranquillity, where Lorenzo and Alberti had agreed that the contemplative life must take an active life by the hand, where Thomas Aquinas had raised contemplation again to the skies, and where Venice had become the queen of serenity. Other countries have made similar constitutional provisions, as though the saying would make it so. The American influence was indirect; the more direct pressure for a work clause usually came from the communists or socialists. In Italy today even the newest recruits to an industrial life, unskilled workers coming up from the south to cluster in and around the big cities, will say almost in unison that what one has to do in this life to make one's way is, "work." The latest version of the bill of rights for mankind, the UNESCO Declaration of Human Rights to which almost all nations have put a signature, proclaims, "Everyone has the right to work."

* * *

When Americans are asked why they would like a few hours, a half day, a day more of free time, they answer typically that they could then get the shopping done, or take the children to the dentist, or replace that worn-out weather stripping on the back door. They mention such unfree things because they assume "free" means "off-the-job." The word leisure has turned into the phrase free time, and the two are now almost interchangeable.

We have slipped backward to the level of ancient Greece before Plato, when *scholē*, too, meant either leisure, time or free time. It was through the efforts of the philosophers that leisure found its identity. Today the benefit of their thinking is largely lost to us. Why should this confusion in terminology continue to exist? Does anyone benefit from it? In a way everyone benefits from it. The confusion helps us to think of our life as the best of existing or possible worlds. Industrialization gives us not only work and many other good things; it gives us the gift of leisure, that is, free time, more free time than ever this hitherto backward old world has seen. It is the signal for a new era, a new way of life, a tribute to freedom and democracy and the fruits they have borne us. Only industrialism and democracy could ever have produced such a marvel. If people somehow feel that this leisure is not passing their way, it is easy to show them how wrong they are. Cite the facts, in leisure hours gained; compare today's leisure with 1850 or 1900. They can go on thinking they have lots of free time and wondering why they do not. Perhaps this makes each person feel petulantly virtuous; he believes all his fellow Americans are having a gay old snap of it while he works like a dog and never has a moment's free time.

We have seen where most of these hours have gone. Free time can perhaps be converted into leisure, but this is only a chance, though an important chance. We should also have pointed out that the country or century or group used for comparison with today's free time makes a lot of difference.

Steelworkers a hundred years ago worked a 12-hour shift, 7 days a week; miners rarely saw the sun in winter. So far we have made our chief comparisons with this one earlier setting. The time was 1850, the place the United States. It was a point from which we had some statistics to go by. Marking a century's distance, it also lent an ample perspective. Moreover, since we were not citing Greece or Rome or some other foreign country, we did not have a patriotic bias to contend with. The only bias we might have had was a progressive one: we might have wanted to show how much progress has taken place since then in these United States. Having skirted that danger, we can now choose other times and places for comparison.

* * *

If instead of to the 1850s we go farther back into the Middle Ages, a long period of ten varied centuries, what do we find? The amount of free time would be even more difficult to estimate than that of a century ago, were it not for the fact that the years typically went by according to a calendar of holidays. It varied from place to place. The number of holidays during the year seems commonly to have been about 115, to which the inviolable 52 Sundays had to be added, making a total of 167 days. Even serfs and slaves had many of the same holidays. One hundred and sixty-seven days a year amounts to over three days a week. Converted to a week with work days 12 hours long, longer even than in the frontier days of 1850, the hours come to 45.6 a week— worked at a tempo closer to that of the 1850s than to the present. The average does not include market days, which usually were also days of no work. Not bad for dark medieval times. And we are talking about peasants, not just about nobles, kings, and patrons.

In Rome working and nonworking days went in the ratio of about 2 to 1. Much depended on the number of public games. At the end of the republican period, there were seven sets of games occuping 65 days. In Greece at about the same time, the late first century B.C., according to Strabo the geographer, the Greek calendar had developed into a complicated catalogue whose fêtes and holidays exceeded its working days. Rome's own calendar within a century or two began to resemble the Greek. By the middle of the second century A.D., Roman games took 135 days, and by the middle of the fourth century as many as 175 days. In republican times the games lasted only part of the day; they gradually began to take up the whole day from early morning onward. At the later period they went on into the night in many cases, requiring artificial illumination.

Apart from exceptional periods of brutal transition, each community weaves its work and nonwork fabric together. Comparisons in our favor are delusive. Since 1850 free time has not appreciably increased. It is greater when compared with the days of Manchesterism or of the sweatshops of New York. Put alongside modern rural Greece or ancient Greece, though, or medieval Europe and ancient Rome, free time today suffers by comparison, and leisure even more.

* * *

Large numbers of persons, it seems, earnestly desire or need more free time, although we may not be able to say whether they would not, if given a choice, prefer something else. Most interview studies tell us about the present moment, and while it interests us, we are also interested in other things. The man whose family is starving will not be much preoccupied with leisure. Lack of food or money is his worry. Restored by food and drink, he begins to think of other things in life. Similarly laborunion leaders may on one day say that the shorter work week will be labor's major battle over the next five years, but six months later, with the onset of a business recession or an inflation, the subject is dropped from the program. Still, if we leave to one side short-run fluctuations like recessions, or the ups and downs of bargaining about the work week, there is the longer-run change that is spanned by at least a generation. Since the turn of the century Americans have pursued time.

One major reason for this change has already been discussed. We have seen that the bonanza of free time that was supposed to be at the American's disposal is legendary. The false image grew out of a punch-clock accounting system. The only entries were time in and time out. Time out was called free time. The economists described the system as one characterized by the free organization of labor, and the phrase free time came into common usage to mean time off the job, as though the company's entrances were not doors to opportunity but the gates of a prison. Perhaps the usage began when work was more unpleasant than it is today, or perhaps, as is more likely, it was picked up by factory workers and pushed by them into the currency it holds today.

No one seems to have noticed this contradiction but it had an important effect on all workers. It allowed a false accounting system to grow up. Instead of counting free time by first figuring out what was free about it and then adding up, the process began upside down: whatever is not time on the job is free. To calculate how much free time you have, take the job's official hours and subtract them from 24; or, to be more exact, take 8 out for sleeping, and subtract the job hours from 16; or another way is to take the work week ten or twenty years ago and from it subtract today's. That also should give a clear gain. In the meantime other processes began insinuating themselves into the worker's life so that he was bearing the cost of added hours without knowing it. If he lived first in one of those concentric circles of the big city characteristic of the early part of the century, his house was fairly near the factory. If the factory moved out to the periphery because of cheaper land or labor, he had to follow it or another factory, or, if not he, his sidekick had to move out there. The factory did not assume the cost of the longer time it might now take him to get to work. And, to make the point, no one counted the loss of time anywhere as part of work time. This is one example of how the American finds himself with fewer on-the-job hours and less free time.

Similarly insidious events took away other hours: the rise of work-pacing, of moonlighting, of women's ranks to become one sixth of the labor force, and so on. It would be wrong to say that American workers have had something put over on them. The same ignorance afflicts office workers and executives as well. They too count their free time by subtracting their work time from something bigger. And then there are days in which they puzzle about where their time has gone.

But is this all? Is the American's chase after time due to this, that he sought to cut down work in only one of its guises, and as it appeared with other faces he did not recognize it? Is free time valued so highly today only because no one has it?

The desire for time we have just considered seems really to be a need for time in which to rest or to get done the many tasks or duties that fall to one's lot after 4:30 or 5:00 or 5:30 P.M. There is more than this alone, it would seem. How else would we explain the important change in our vocabulary over the last fifty or one hundred years, a change in which the "idleness problem" has been supplanted by the "leisure problem," and though idleness was excoriated and leisure is lauded, the problem is still the same—the problem of free time. We have seen there is not so much free time as has been believed and this ought to lessen the fears of those remaining in the anti-idleness class. It is something like saying that, really, workers don't have as much time as we think to get drunk; they are hard at work at numerous chores involving shopping, transportation, housework, repairs and children. The anti-idleness people might reply that the workers have always had enough free time and have more than enough today. If they didn't waste so much of it in frivolous or inane things like TV, they would have time to spare for children and housework. But many people will be disappointed to hear that there is less free time than they had thought. Even were there enough to get all the chores done, they would not be satisfied.

Just as, for some, idleness and leisure like an hourglass have been turned upside down, but remain the same problem of time, so for others, work and leisure have been turned topsy-turvy. For us of the twentieth century the hymns to work are dim memories of infancy. To look for one today is like looking for the dodo. Not even corporation presidents go all out in favor of work. A paean to leisure, though, can be found in almost any magazine one picks up nowadays. Leisure is in the air. Governments now have to promise it, or better yet, write it into the constitution. In Russia after the death of Stalin, his successors reportedly gained favor by reducing working hours. The official work week there is now supposed to be 45 hours. The latest plans for the next seven years call for a reduction to 40 hours, and then a resolute advance on a 32-hour goal. Leisure is one of the fundamental rights of citizens guaranteed by Articles 119 and 122 of the Constitution of the Union of Soviet Socialist Republics (December 5, 1936). The pattern by now seems world wide. In some parts of the globe new regimes, though they have hardly yet managed to build more than two factories with foreign aid, immediately show further signs of their progressive modernity by promising future factory workers that their hours, already hypothetically at 40, will soon stand (hypothetically) at 35.

All this I would call no more than a change in vocabulary. But a change in vocabulary, though subtle, is an event in human history. This change is an important one, for, by turning things upside down, it reveals itself as a revolution. The linguistic evidence is the strongest we have that a change in attitude has taken place, stronger certainly than the data we brought to bear in the beginning of this chapter. Linguistically it is also important that the word leisure has now become a full adjective. It indicates that the word is getting extraordinarily heavy usage. We now have leisure time, leisure rooms, leisure trips to leisure lakes, leisure clothes, leisure equipment, leisure spending on leisure items. This is too great a change, I think, to be explained simply by the fact that the amount of free time the American is supposed to have is more fiction than fact. As in the very phrase free time, there seems lurking here some hostility to the idea of work. Since in American life, work stands high, and since leisure is thought to be the opposite of work, just the pursuit of leisure implies slowing down on the race track of work.

* * *

Since *free time* as a substitute term for *leisure* has its own difficulties, perhaps the moment is right to redefine the terms we have dealt with thus far in this study. Earlier we found leisure as an idea fully explored by the Greeks. Though it had many meanings in common speech, the one that gave it its long life was this: *leisure* is the state of being free of everyday necessity. The man in that state is at leisure and whatever he does is done leisurely. *Play* is what children do, frolic and sport, the lively spraying of wind with water. Adults play too, though their games are less muscular and more intricate. Play has a special relation to leisure. Men may play games in recreation, indeed except for men who work, play is a form of recreation. As far as leisure is concerned, Aristotle had said that we neither work nor play at it. Though this does not describe the exact state of things, play and leisure do have a special relation which we shall want to examine in greater detail later. *Recreation* is activity that rests men from work, often by giving them a change (distraction, diversion), and restores (re-creates) them for work. When adults play—as they do, of course, with persons, things, and symbols—they play for recreation. Like the Romans', our own conception of leisure is mainly recreative. *Work* can be taken in its modern sense as effort or exertion done typically to make a living or keep a house. The activities engaged in while at work all must fall within moral and legal limits, however broadly defined. A man, though a traitor and a spy, may exert himself to earn a living, but he does not work except perhaps in his own eyes or those of his hirer (note that *employer* is not the right word here).

[Earlier, I] distinguished *work time,* that spent in work or on the job, from *work-related time,* that spent in order to appear at work presentably (time spent in journeying to work or in grooming oneself for work) or in doing things that one would not ordinarily do were it not for work, like the husband's doing a share of his working wife's housework. *Free time* we accepted as time off the job that was neither work-related nor *subsistence time.* The last we named after activities like eating, sleeping,.keeping out of the cold and rain, going to the doctor when ill, all presumably performed to maintain the state of a healthy organism, regardless of whether that organism is put to work or leisure.

We did not use any name to designate those activities of free time engaged in because of the influence of the kind of work done, the busman's holiday kind of activity. Obviously activities in recreation may resemble or contrast with work. And recreation may react in the same fashion to family life or religious devotion. Likewise work may be affected by recreative pursuits, drunkenness being the historic example, along with gambling, romance, and adventure. (Were we interested in coining words, the constant and complex flux of relationships, the lack of pertinent physiological knowledge, and the shifting positions of work, free time, subsistence, the family, recreation, and play would enable us to fill a treasury.) The central idea is easy to grasp and accept, however: work and recreation can be affected by each other as well as by other activities, such as taking care of a brood of children. And for this idea a phrase like work-affected recreation or recreation-affected work is not much of a help, being only one syllable shorter than "work affected by recreation."

Leisure, it should be clear, remains unaffected by either work or recreation. It is outside their everyday world. We further would not call work those lifelong pursuits whose scope is not clearly or primarily earning a living. For the clergy, the career ranks of the military and government, the artist and man of letters, the physician, the professor—for all of these we prefer the word *calling*. They don't work, they have a vocation, something they are called to by nature, inclination, God, taste, or the Muses. One will find such persons among the upper ranks of business, also, where the end often is (and often denied to be) not making money but doing good works in the religious or community spirit.

Free time relies on the negative sense of freedom, freedom from something, in this case freedom from the job. I pointed out earlier how it differed from spare time and pastime. Free time, as defined, while reflecting a poor opinion of work, did help in making it seem that the modern world was progressing toward more free time. It left us, however, with serious difficulties. One was deciding whether free time was free from anything else but work. Taking the negative sense in which the idea originated, can it be said that the meaning now has got to the point, or ought to get to the point, where freedom from other things is sought? For instance, every now and then we have had to ask ourselves, what about family pleasures and responsibilities—does free time mean freedom from them too? If so, the man watching TV at home in the midst of his family is not enjoying free time until he picks up his hat and goes out the door. And then, if he wants to be on free time, he should go neither to local party headquarters to lick envelopes for the coming campaign, nor to the church for evening services, nor to the committee meeting on charity. Does free time mean freedom from all these, too? If not, then it is obvious that the pleasures of free time are laced with duties and responsibilities, thereby clouding the whole idea in paradox. Thus even the negative conception of free time is by no means clear.

* * *

To conclude this enigmatic subject: Technology, it seems, is no friend of leisure. The machine, the hero of a dream, the bestower of free time to men, brings a neutralized idea of time that makes it seem free, and then chains it to another machine, the clock. If we but say "free clocked time," the illusion vanishes. Clocked time cannot be free. The phrase connotes, and justly so, that the "clockedness" has a purpose and a collectivity that is at odds with freeness and individuality. Clocked time requires activities and decisions that must always be referred back to (synchronized with) the machine and its ramifications in an industrial culture.

Thus whatever free time we have is unfree from the start. That we oppose it to work really indicates that we still regard work as the dominant obligation. Any time *after* work is finished is "free," but even *that* time, if work must be clocked, is workbound. The difference is that free time in relation to work is indirect; it is tethered with a longer rope. So, through machines, we are bound to the clock. We can break away only a few fragments of a day or a weekend. Really to go off into something new and different is impossible, for at a precise inexorable hour and minute we must answer again to the clock.

Our kind of work, though freer of toil, requires a time-motion that makes our spare time free time and thereby links it inescapably to work. Aristotle was right about recreation. It is related to work, and given and taken so that work can go on. Thus it is with modern free time. If one had been asked earlier where in a list of expenditures the cost of a watch was to be charged, one would have said "To work, obviously." Now one would have to add "To free time, too." Free time has no independence of its own. The most one can do to escape today's time pressure is to "get away from it all," to take a vacation in any place that has a vaguer time sense than our own. We search, then, for places that are as yet freer of the clock than we are—the remote village or shore, the mountains, the woods, the Mediterranean country, the island. A surer solution is to go mad. Otherwise we cannot truly escape, for by now the industrial and scientific Western time crust covers the globe and will soon grow on other planets. The moon may still be the timeless world it has ever seemed for lovers, but it won't remain so for long.

In the picture of the future I have sketched in this chapter, there was no mention of a change in our ideas of time. There are some straws in the wind that lead me to suspect they will eventually change, perhaps after first losing their space-bound character, but not in the near future we have discussed. That no such prospect is in close sight indicates that clock time, as industrial time, will continue to guide our lives. Machines by now have manipulated everyone, their owners and tenders both, into living by the dictates of the clock. An ignorant visitor from a clock-less land might wonder why we reject the tyranny of men while acquiescing to the tyranny of an idol. As long as our basic time concepts remain unchanged, it is useless to look for relief to time-saving gadgets. The story has been told that after the French Revolution a young man asked an old one what life was like in the *ancien régime*. "People had time," said the old man. "Rich and poor alike." *Se non é vera, é ben trovata.*

We have transformed civilization and our lives to win time and find leisure, but have failed. We are not even back where we began. We have lost ground. Worst of all, we have raised a range of Himalayan institutions and habits that block our way forward or backward.

There is no doubt that Americans have reached a new level of life. Whether it is a good life is another matter. This much is clear: it is a life without leisure. Some may say that the sense of abundant unscheduled time is unnecessary, but while pieces of clock-time may be enough for free time, they are not enough for leisure. For leisure is not hours free of work, or even weekends or months of vacation or years in retirement. It has no bearing on time conceived as a flow of evenly paced equal units of which some are free and some are not, and all are on crusade. Indeed, the contemporary phrase "leisure time" is a contradiction in terms. Leisure has no adjectival relation to time. Leisure is a state of being free of everyday necessity, and the activities of leisure are those one would engage in for their own sake. As fact or ideal it is rarely approached in the industrial world.

We see now that in their life with machines people lost not space alone but time too. More subtle than the changes in space, the changes in time went less noticed. They were of capital im-portance. Men were given a reformed time, a reformed calendar, and a reformed cosmology. Time nowadays must be pursued. If pursued, it hides out. It shows itself only when it no longer hears the baying of the hounds. If you have to pursue time, give up the idea of leisure. To transform the lead of free time into the gold of leisure, one must first be free of the clock. And that is just the start.

in my opinion...

In order to transform the free time created by automation and cybernation Into leisure, American society will need all the moral energy it can muster. The change in attitudes toward every phase of life is so tremendous as to stagger the imagination.

The first area which would have to be reconstructed is education. At the present time, the vast majority of our educational institutions are engaged in preparing youth for existing occupations. It is quite possible that by the time today's first-grader reaches college graduation, the area for which he has spent sixteen years preparing will no longer require his services. The rate of change is frightening. Not only are we faced with the extinction of specific areas of employment, but in a period of two "school lifetimes"—we may find no need at all for "jobs" as we now think of them. Educationally, then, we should be aiming our programs at life in an economy of abundance, *now,* not in ten more years. Even if the decision were made today to begin restructuring our school systems, the change would produce results more slowly than necessary.

On an economic level we are perhaps in even deeper water. Can a nation which has always prided itself on its material wealth begin to take that wealth for granted? Can a people who have striven for two hundred years to attain material plenty now be convinced that it is no longer necessary to save and plan and sacrifice for the things they desire? What will become of the tidy little capitalist who has worked hard all his life to provide for a rainy day? Unless some miracle of major proportions can be wrought, he will surely perish. And he exists in numbers which can be stated in millions. The mass of Americans are dependent on their jobs not only for their livelihood but also for their identities. A man defines himself in our society in terms of his income, his possessions, his education, his acquaintances. All these things are dependent largely on his work. We live in a work-oriented culture—it shows vague signs of change, but they may be too little and too late.

What are the alternatives to a rapid transformation to a leisure society? It would be possible simply to continue the present pattern of expanding both the gross national product and the welfare rolls. However, such a policy would have at least two disastrous effects. First, an expanding economy assumes continued growth of the rate of consumption. The only guarantee of such growth as would be necessary to maintain the present rate of employment is continued emphasis on planned obsolesence. We can produce enough refrigerators to replace all that are now in use every three years, but what are we to do with the discarded ones? Waste control is already one of the many facets of pollution of the environment which presents a problem of seemingly desperate proportions. It may be feasible to stabilize the economy by limiting production of consumer goods and channeling more of our energies into service industries. But a stable economy implies stable income and with a stable income a family cannot readily increase its level of services purchased. Perhaps some form of artificial work could be devised to occupy the minds and hands of the nation. But assuming that no shift in values has been accomplished, how satisfying will such pursuits seem? After all, work must have a purpose to fulfill its function as bestower of meaning on life. The choices seem rather unsatisfactory at first glance, but man is an ingenious animal and some workable solution may be found to our greatest challenge.

Although the predictions of an economy of abundance may be both premature and ill-advised, unless cataclysmic circumstances alter the future, such predictions seem to be more reliable than any other view of the twenty-first century. Certainly man is capable of both coping with and revelling in a leisure society, but in order to do so he will have to remove the many layers of tradition and myth that currently obscure his vision. For he will require all the vision he possesses in mind and spirit for the encounter toward which he rushes. As Don Fabun so aptly states in his remarkable book, *The Dynamics of Change,* ". . . if we do not learn to understand and guide the great forces of change at work in our world today, we may find ourselves . . . swallowed up by vast upheavals in our way of life—quite early some morning."

douglas o. snyder

questions

1.   Define leisure in your own words. Do you agree that its meaning must involve the concept of time itself? Explain.

2.   In a section of *Of Time, Work, and Leisure,* not presented in the preceding excerpts, de Grazia characterizes advertising as one the greatest enemies of leisure. Can you explain what his reasoning for this line of thought may have been?

3.   Is it possible that advertising could be used in association with the mass media to help solve "the leisure problem"?

4.   Discuss the following quotation from *Of Time, Work, and Leisure:* "Work, we know, may make a man stoop-shouldered or rich. It may even ennoble him. Leisure perfects him."

5.   As a contrast to the possibility of a leisure society, some authorities believe a "full employment" society, in which jobs in various service industries will replace production-type jobs, should be the goal for the United States economy. Do you think such an economy is workable? What would happen to current notions of status and social class in a "full employment" society?

5.
energy sources and society: a russian viewpoint

THE WORLD OF THE FUTURE

nikolai semenov

introduction and comment by leslie c. czapary

In the recent past most predictions of the future fell far short of the actual discoveries which were made. Rare were the individuals of thirty years ago who anticipated that man would walk on the moon's surface in 1969, or that we would have dispatched exploratory space ships to Mars and Venus. We have become increasingly aware of the fact that in a research-oriented world, dramatic discoveries that can alter our existence may appear suddenly and unexpectedly. Despite the computer's marvelous ability to extrapolate, foreseeing the future seems a more difficult task than ever.

However, if we are moving towards international affluence— it is difficult to believe that a world half-rich, half-poverty-stricken is viable—then thoughtful consideration must be given to the question of energy sources.

For many millenia, man existed solely through the results of his own physical efforts. His total preoccupation was the search for the necessities of life: his sole tool was his own muscle. In a major sense, progress could be represented by the development of other energy sources. Over periods of thousands of years, the domestication of animals, (yes, and slavery), the utilization of wind and water power led to the giant steps of the past few centuries—the use of steam, the internal combustion engine, electricity and atomic power. Each of these in its turn powerfully affected the quality of human life for those peoples of the earth who were in a position to make use of them.

This argument leads us to several disturbing questions. Is there a direct correlation between affluence and the availability of nonhuman energy sources? Should our existing sources of power become exhausted, are we doomed to a return to poverty? Can technology discover new sources of energy, or more efficient use of known sources in sufficient quantity to preserve and improve the quality of living we now have? Should we not be making every effort to provide sufficient energy sources so that all human beings might have the possibility of raising living standards? What would the effect of a nuclear war have on not only energy-utilizing machines but on the raw material that provides the world's energy?

The question is far from academic; already we are feeling a tightening of what only a few years ago was considered lavish energy sources. The problem is aggravated by our new awareness of the dangerous side effects of ruthless, thoughtless exploitation of ordinary power generation. Huge cities are caught in a conflict between urgently needed sources of more power and the threat of pollution. Nuclear power plants generate thermal pollution because of the temperature changes which take place in the rivers that supply the essential water coolants. Each summer, large cities face "brownouts." A huge new coal-fired generator planned in the "four corner" area where Arizona, Utah, Colorado and New Mexico meet has been unable to meet the restrictions demanded by an informed citizenry who are concerned with air pollution. The total acceptance by industrialized societies of the internal combustion engine used in the automobile has changed to vigorous dissent because of the by-products of those engines.

The problems are both enormous and pressing. Professor Nikolai Semenov, in 1964 Chairman of the Soviet Association for the Advancement of Science, adds other dimensions to the energy problem. His eloquently presented vision of a future in which there will be adequate sources of power available to rich and poor countries alike brings into focus the social and humane potentials for a world which could be ours.

l.c.c.

THE WORLD OF
THE FUTURE

*Professor Nikolai Semenov is a noted Russian physical chemist,
a recipient of the Nobel Prize for Chemistry (1956), and was
the chairman and guiding spirit of the Soviet Association for
the Advancement of Science at the time this article was written.
He received an honorary Doctorate of Science degree from
Oxford. In addition, he is the author of* Chain Reactions, *1934,
and* Some Problems of Chemical Kinetics and Reactivity, *1954.*

We are witnessing an unprecedented acceleration of scientific
development. As they master the secrets of nature, scientists
discover great new opportunities for further development of technology, industry, agriculture, and medicine. As Premier Khrushchev said in his speech to the Twenty-second Congress of the
Communist Party of the USSR: "Science is becoming more and
more a direct force of production, and production itself is becoming the technological application of modern science."

On the basis of the rapid development of science and hence
of new technology, the satisfaction, at a very high level, of all the
material and spiritual needs of every man on earth is a real
possibility for the first time in history. The attainment of this great
humanitarian aim is limited neither by the level of science and
technology nor by the resources of labor and materials. It does
demand, however, that the peoples of all the world and their
governments, like the peoples and governments of the socialist
countries, set as their primary aim the full satisfaction of the
material and spiritual needs of their own and all other peoples;
the provision for all people of a happy, creative, and really free
life; the elimination of war as a means of solving disputes between

peoples; general disarmament; and peaceful coexistence between countries of different political systems. This aim is near and dear to all people of goodwill regardless of their political, religious, or philosophical views. What will happen by the end of our century? What now un-imagined level will science and technology reach by that time? What fundamental changes will they bring to world economy? It is impossible to foresee all the new discoveries; but we can predict, with certain probability, that great practical results will develop from present scientific trends. A certain part of my paper will deal with somewhat fantastic topics, such that are not yet substantiated scientifically.

It was at the beginning of the nineteenth century that science and technology began their triumphant progress. The nineteenth century is often called the century of steam and electricity. What shall we call the twentieth century? The century of atomic energy; of the conquest of air and space; of polymers; of radio, television, and electronics; of cybernetics and computors; of chemistry and mechanics in agriculture; or of new medical advances and the prolongation of life? Twentieth-century science is ceaselessly producing new techniques and products, the consequence of what Lenin in 1908 called a revolution in natural science. The twentieth century is characterized not only by the great increase in the volume of scientific knowledge, but by a qualitative change in the character of science itself.

If, in the nineteenth century, scientists were chiefly busy investigating the external characteristics of matter and establishing formal connections between the phenomena of nature, in the twentieth century they went on to investigate the deeply hidden structures and mechanisms accounting for these external characteristics and phenomena. The limit of penetration into the structure of matter in the nineteenth century was atomic and molecular theory. That the question of the internal structure of the atom was not even raised was the result of remnants of scholasticism in science. Atoms were regarded by scientists of the nineteenth century as unchanging building bricks of the universe, as if endowed by God with certain inherent characteristics.

exploring the atom

The attack on the inner regions of the atom began in the first twenty years of the twentieth century and started the revolution in natural science. Atoms proved to be very complicated systems consisting of a compact, positively charged nucleus and a loose shell of electrons rotating around it and neutralizing its charge. The electrons determine the physical and chemical characteristics of an atom except for its weight, while the nucleus plays a passive role.

The laws of electron motion within the atom were found to be very different from the previously known laws of mechanics and electrodynamics. The creation of quantum mechanics, which determined the laws of electron motion both under free conditions and within the atom, was a great achievement, and enabled scientists to establish the nature of chemical forces and valence and to calculate all the characteristics of the simplest atoms and molecules. For heavier atoms and more complicated molecules, these characteristics could be determined only qualitatively. Similarly, it was possible to understand the reasons for some of the physical and chemical characteristics of solid bodies, such as metals, dielectrics, etc.

This understanding of the internal structure of matter made it possible to develop materials with desirable characteristics. In chemistry it led to new methods of synthesis, by which we create new compounds and improve the technology of producing previously known ones. In physics it led to many new discoveries, particularly in the field of solid bodies; for example, the emission of electrons under the influence of heat and light; semiconductors with their astonishing electrical properties; energy transfer in solid bodies and, connected with this, the possibility of producing narrow beams of coherent radiation in the visible region and in the region of radiowaves—the so-called lasers and masers. All these, in turn, have led to the creation of new techniques and new scientific fields, such as short wave technology and electronics.

Study of the atomic nucleus, which plays no active part in chemical reactions, opened up still more new fields in science, with the discoveries of radioactive processes in the atom, artificial transformation of atoms, fission of heavy elements, and isotopic composition of elements. It was found that the nucleus itself is a very complex system. Different nuclei have different numbers of protons and neutrons bound together by powerful nuclear forces. Because of these forces, tremendous energy is liberated when nuclei are formed from their building blocks. According to Einstein's well known equation expressing the equivalence of mass and energy, the energy thus liberated takes away with it some part of the mass. Different nuclei suffer different defects of mass, depending on their original content and structure. The energy released in nuclear reactors increases with the difference between the defect of mass for initial and end-products. According to calculated and experimental data on nuclear reactions, the difference between masses of the initial and final nuclei is greatest in: (1) fission of nuclei of uranium-235, plutonium, etc., into two nuclei of medium mass; and (2) synthesis of helium nuclei from two nuclei of deuterium and particularly from tritium and deuterium. These two findings derived from theoretical investigations of the nucleus are of fundamental importance for science and technology.

The first led to the discovery of the chain reaction in uranium, and thus unfortunately to the atom bomb, and to the peaceful use of atomic energy in atomic power stations. (There have been no previous examples of nuclear chain reactions either in industry or in nature; such reactions probably never occur naturally in the universe. Their discovery and practical realization resulted from purely scientific investigation into the structure of the atomic nucleus.)

The second finding brought about the discovery of the thermonuclear reaction of the light elements—the same reaction that is, as we now know, the source of the energy of the sun and stars. Thermonuclear reactions were used to create the hydrogen bomb, in which the high temperature necessary to start the reaction is created by the explosion of a small atomic bomb, used as detonator. However, the day is not far off when we shall be able to achieve a controlled thermonuclear reaction, promising an unlimited supply of energy to the world.

Nuclear physics is now in a new stage of development because of the discovery, in the last fifteen years, of a great number of new and mostly unstable elementary particles, which appear as a result of nuclear transformations, particularly those caused by cosmic rays or produced in powerful accelerators. These primary particles include neutrinos, all types of mesons, and hyperons, and differ from each other by their mass, charge, magnetic moment, isotopic spin, strangeness, etc. They have a number of surprising properties, pointing to the existence of as yet unknown basic laws of the universe.

Among different elementary particles, there are complementary pairs—particles and antiparticles. Simple examples are the pairs of similar particles with opposite charges, such as the electron and positron, proton and antiproton, etc. In our world, a positron is unstable because, if it encounters an electron, both particles turn into two γ-quanta, the energy of which is equivalent to the total mass of the positron and the electron (annihilation). Similarly, the antiproton disappears on encountering a proton, transforming its mass into the energy of μ-mesons. The energy released in this process is several hundred times greater than in thermonuclear reactions. Electrically neutral particles also have corresponding antiparticles which are annihilated when they encounter each other. Thus a neutron has a corresponding antineutron, which differs from it by an oppositely directed magnetic moment.

Our galaxy consists of substances built of protons and neutrons in the nucleus, and electrons in the shell of an atom. It is possible that other galaxies are made of antisubstances—of antiprotons and antineutrons in the nucleus and positrons in the shell of the atom. In these worlds, antiparticles would be stable and our particles would be unstable. But all other physical and chemical qualities of atoms would be identical in both worlds. There, we could find the same chemical combinations, with the same structures and properties, and it is quite probable that there would exist living beings and even human beings similar to those we have in our world. Imagine a fantastic meeting of a man and an antiman somewhere in space. They would be able to study each other and even become bosom friends, but they would not be able to touch each other. Should they do so, they would both explode with a force considerably greater than that of a thermonuclear bomb.

the research ahead

Scientific speculation brings new delights of understanding and, eventually, new power over nature. Research which may seem very abstract and with no practical application, such as investigating the internal properties of matter, sooner or later leads to revolutionary changes in industry. The research that appeared the most "purely scientific" of all turned out to be the research that produced the greatest practical result—atomic and thermonuclear energy.

Two fundamental problems stand out as major research tasks for science in the next decades. The first is the theory of elementary particles in physics, the interpretation of the *primary* particles of matter. The second, in contrast, deals with the structure and behavior of highly organized matter—living matter. Biologists, physicists, and chemists have started to penetrate the internal physical and chemical bases of life. The great achievements made in biology over the last fifteen years have not yet had serious practical results, but there is no doubt that they will lead to revolutionary changes in medicine and some changes in agriculture.

Thus, cancer will be cured by studies in this branch of biology. And the work clarifying physical and chemical processes in living organisms will produce a new revolution in chemistry. Applying the latter principles to inanimate matter will make it possible to create catalysts of unprecedented power and with specific features, in particular for photochemical processes; and to create new types of machines that will, like muscle, directly transform chemical into mechanical energy with great efficiency.

future energy sources

As another illustration of the gigantic prospects opening before mankind as a result of the further development of science and its practical applications, let us consider the energy sources of the future.

The amount of energy generated in a country plays a decisive role in the development of industry, agriculture, and household services. If people anywhere in the world could have any amount of power, they could raise the well-being of every member of their society to practically any height, even with their present social systems. At present, the average amount of power available to each person in the world is only 0.1 kilowatt. With this low level of electrical supply, especially in underdeveloped countries, hard physical labor is unavoidable. Natural resources will undoubtedly make it possible to increase this number several times over, as witness the Soviet Union where the amount of electricity generated increased more than 160-fold and the power supply about 70-fold in 45 years.

However, modern sources of energy, including coal and oil reserves, uranium and thorium, and water resources are not inexhaustable. The mining and processing of coal, uranium, and thorium, even when highly mechanized, require arduous work. We seek new, more powerful energy sources, almost limitless in amount and easily worked.

At present there are three theoretically possible ways of solving this all-important scientific and technical problem: the achievement of a controlled thermonuclear reaction; the use of solar energy; the use of the underground heat of the magmatic layer.

thermonuclear energy

Unprecedented prospects would unfold before humanity if it could realize a controlled thermonuclear reaction. The very existence of the hydrogen bomb proves that such reactions triggered by an atomic explosion are possible. A continuous, controlled thermo-nuclear reaction, however, is difficult to achieve because the tremendous temperatures characteristic of, and necessary to maintain, such reactions would immediately vaporize the walls of the "thermonuclear furnace." Russian physicists were the first to suggest magnetic isolation, which could reduce the heat radiation to the walls, making the process realizable. They have tested this principle, and managed to briefly heat, by means of a powerful current impulse, substances nearly to the temperature needed to start a thermonuclear reaction. But still higher temperatures are necessary, and there are other difficulties involved in creating an effective magnetic isolation under the conditions of a continuous thermonuclear reaction. This problem, however, will surely be solved in this very century, because modern science has so often shown that what is possible in principle soon becomes possible in practice.

One of the possible thermonuclear reactions is the synthesis of helium from two deuterium nuclei, the resulting transformation of one gram of deuterium giving up to 10 million times more energy than the burning of one gram of coal. Deuterium is extracted by already existing methods from ordinary water, a natural resource in unlimited supply. Two hundred and thirty cubic meters of water contains resources of energy equivalent to the total annual world production of coal.

It appears that there is a limit to the output of power stations once we achieve controlled thermonuclear reactions. This limit will be set by the overheating of the atmosphere and the earth's surface from the release of heat in such reactions. Thus, we are not likely to produce more thermonuclear energy than five or, at the most, ten per cent of the solar energy absorbed by the earth and the atmosphere. But even this is tremendous. It would increase the amount of electrical energy more than by a factor of several tens of thousands and thermal energy several hundred times over the present level, taking into account the amount of energy generated by all types of fuel—wood, coal, peat, oil, gas—and including the amount necessary for household services.

solar energy

The sun sends to earth 4×10^{13} (40 trillion) kilo calories per second. While much of the energy is diffused or partially absorbed by the atmosphere, by clouds in particular, 30 per cent of it on the average does reach the surface. If all this energy could be turned into electricity, we would obtain far more than that gained from maximal use of thermonuclear energy. But this is impossible since it would require covering the entire surface of the earth with photoelements or containers of photosensitive liquid—not to mention the tremendous technical difficulties of assembling such covers on the surface of the ocean. However, even one-tenth of the solar energy falling on the earth's surface would be enough to generate an amount of energy several times greater than that generated at present. Thus, we possess a second large potential of energy that is eternal and that could liberate us from the process of obtaining and wasting fuel. There can be no overheating of the earth if we use solar energy.

The development of photoelectrical, thermoelectrical, and photochemical processes should make it possible within several decades to transform solar energy into electricity with at least 30 or 40 per cent efficiency. Plants and seaweed turn light rays into chemical energy by photosynthesis with more than 20 per cent efficiency because of special catalysts made by nature. Surely the chemists can, with much greater possibilities than nature and with the aim of producing much simpler products, outstrip nature.

The third potential and practically inexhaustible source of energy is the underground heat of the magmatic layers of the earth, distributed on an average of 30 kilometers below the earth's surface and somewhat less than that from the bottom of the ocean. The chief precondition for using this source of energy is the development of economically profitable methods of deep boring.

If these three almost limitless sources are realized, the great amount of electrical energy produced will require completely different methods of transmission. As Academician Kapitza suggests, transmission most probably will be made at high frequencies by the distribution of radiowaves along underground pipelines, which can be made of any material as long as the inside surface is a thin layer of metal. But we should not exclude the possibility of discovering materials that are supersemiconductors at normal temperatures, making it possible to transmit electrical energy without any loss along extremely fine wires. The recently discovered lasers and masers might make it possible to transmit energy through air and through a vacuum in the form of narrow beams of visible light or ultrashort radiowaves.

I believe that, by the end of the century, all three new sources of energy will be exploited, and the first thermonuclear, solar, and underground electric power stations will have been built. In the twenty-first century, electrical energy will be available to man at any place and in any amount. Considering this, only now is the greatness of Lenin's definition becoming clear: Communism is Soviet power plus electrification. And what is Communism if it is not the science of making life happy for all the people in the world?

For complete electrification of all industry, agriculture, transport, and all conditions of life, even if all use of coal, gas, oil, wood, etc., were to cease, the production of electrical energy would not have to be increased by as much as 10,000 times over the modern level. But by having unlimited amounts, mankind would be able to fulfill such magnificent tasks as controlling the climate on earth. Controlled temperature and overhead irrigation could turn the whole world into a flourishing, fruit-bearing paradise.

the conquest of space

Let us consider another problem, fantastic though it is: the possible role of thermonuclear energy in enabling people of earth to live on planets of the solar system, Mars first. Mars is cold, its atmosphere is rarefied, and it has little water and little oxygen. To create an atmosphere and a climate on Mars that would be fit for life for, say, a few decades would require, first of all, the production of some hundreds of trillions of tons of oxygen. Oxygen can be extracted from the water on Mars; if this water is insufficient, the hydrogen obtained from its decomposition could be used to reduce the Mars ores that contain oxygen, simultaneously obtaining water. With thermonuclear power stations built on Mars to provide the electrical energy, enough oxygen could be accumulated within a few decades. I do not know whether mankind will need to conquer Mars; it might find better applications for its surplus energy. But it is interesting to realize what could be done with unlimited sources of energy.

I shall allow myself to dream about a possible, perhaps more practical, use of the moon for earth's energetics. The territory of the moon is 16 times less than that of earth. Because of the absence of atmosphere, one unit of the moon's surface receives three times more solar radiation than one unit of the earth's surface. This means that, in respect to solar energy absorption, the moon's surface is equivalent to one-fifth of the earth's surface, and receives approximately the same amount of energy as falls on the surface of the earth's continents. Thus, if we managed to cover the surface of the moon with semiconductors—photocells of high efficiency for transforming radiant energy into electrical energy—and find means of transmitting this energy to earth (for instance, by directed radio beams), we could use the moon as an electric station with the power of dozens of trillions of kilowatts. (The moon might also become the place for building our atomic and thermonuclear stations to avoid radioactive poisoning of earth.)

in the twenty-first century

Long before the time the amount of electricity generated reaches the enormous figure just mentioned, agriculture and the people's way of living will be radically changed. But before this, scientists and engineers will already have begun using thermonuclear and solar energy. Inorganic chemistry, metallurgy, and the industry of building materials will mostly use reactions at very high temperatures, achieved in electric-arc furnaces or by using the heat, reaching several thousand degrees, of the waste gases from thermonuclear reactors.

Nitrogenous fertilizers will be produced as a result of the synthesis of nitrogen oxides in the atmosphere. People will learn to obtain all the elements of the periodic table, either by electrolysis or by the decomposition of ores at high temperatures using the waste gases of the thermonuclear reactor. They will use any combination of ores, even those formerly unusable because of kinetic inertness.

A practically unlimited amount of cheap electricity will make it possible to produce a practically unlimited amount of organic and inorganic materials. Almost all the resources of gases, oil, and coal—no longer used for electricity—will be used for these purposes. However, despite total electrification, there will still be cars, airplanes, and rockets requiring liquid or gaseous fuel. We could synthesize motor fuels from carbonic acid and hydrogen, or from nitrogen and hydrogen. The hydrogen would be obtained in huge amounts from electrolysis of water, and the carbonic acid from the underground gasification of coal. Or motor fuel would be replaced by a fuel cell fed by hydrogen or carbon oxide and by using electrical engines instead of internal combustion engines. Thus, we could use almost all the resources of natural gas and oil for organic syntheses and for the production of great quantities of polymer materials.

Agriculture and the food industry will be fully electrified and automatized. Irrigation of arid areas with the aid of plastic sheets for retaining water in soil, and soil warming in the north by artificial lighting in large hotbeds and hothouses will result in high yields of crops everywhere and often two crops a year. Enormous sources of energy will permit us to freshen ocean and salt lake water on a large scale. There will be electrical heating and air-conditioning everywhere.

As a result of full automation, working hours will be reduced to three or four hours a day. People will be able to devote all the rest of their time to sport, gardening, art, social activities, people's theaters, literature, and scientific and technical research in public laboratories, which will become centers of scientific development.

Such is my picture of life in the twenty-first century, the century of full electrification. Such is the inheritance we could leave to our children, grandchildren, and great-grandchildren. In the light of these realizable perspectives, we cannot but label as criminals those people who are carrying out a policy of brinksmanship and especially those who are propagating the idea of the inevitable necessity of war, because the use of modern science and technology for war would lead to worldwide catastrophe. It would bring misfortune to all people and death to hundreds of millions, and would completely destroy all material values. Our children, grandchildren, and great-grandchildren would inherit a destroyed, bare earth contaminated with radioactivity. We must avert the senseless, criminal, and thoughtless play with war. We must unite in our fight for peace and complete disarmament. People of all nations must bend every effort toward a development of science and technology which would herald a new and happy future for humanity.

Local and international economic problems will be radically changed, since water, solar energy, and underground heat exist everywhere in excess. The surplus of cheap electrical energy will tremendously increase the amounts of raw materials that will be available any place on earth. The only important thing is that the main goal of society will lie in providing for the welfare of each member of society, of each man living on earth, but not in the gain of some groups of society. When the living standard of all the people is high, there is no sense in gain. These notions of gain, cheap labor power, war, etc., are anachronisms, and their supporters are possessed both of a highly stupid stubbornness and an infantile flippancy.

The ideal of social progress can be approximately formulated as: the maximum happiness for the maximum number of people.

The first precondition for this is full satisfaction of the material and cultural needs of every man on earth. However, the satisfaction of material needs in itself is not enough for a happy life, though it is the chief and necessary precondition for the full spiritual activity of man. But by his nature man is not only a consumer but also a creator of material and spiritual values. The need of creative activity is not only one of the noblest but also one of the deepest, most ineradicable needs of man. Our greatest task is to bring varied creative activities within the reach of the broad mass of people.

Some people may not agree with my understanding of happiness. Many people regard happiness not as a creative activity but as a rest, or as a stormy happiness independent of work. But I personally believe that such an understanding of happiness arises from spiritual poverty or lack of the social conditions that enable the discovery and development of the creative strivings and abilities potentially existing in any normal man.

To demonstrate his creative ability and derive pleasure from doing so, every man must have a certain level of knowledge and development of his mind and feelings, of esthetic taste, and moral attitude toward society and himself. This can be achieved if economic and social conditions are created to ensure the all-round development and creative labor of people.

Under socialism, the main concern of society is people and their material and cultural requirements. Just as the material well being of people determines their spiritual growth, so the creative activity of the masses in turn regulates the material progress of society.

At present our people are confronted with two very important and interrelated problems: to create the high material and technical bases necessary to completely satisfy the people's various needs; and to educate the new man worthy to live in a communist society—to make of every man a person of broad outlook capable of doing individual creative work, a person full of a sense of responsibility and who is inspired by humanistic ideas. These are the main ideas of Communism which were expressed in the classical phrase: "From each according to his abilities and to each according to his needs."

in my opinion...

Disregarding the political references in the article, Professor Semenov envisions the world of the 21st century essentially as do all men who are hoping for peace. However, I feel that the professor tends to oversimplify the problems and the solutions that will have to be faced by man at the turn of the century. Even when the world is producing 10,000 times as much electricity as it does now, most of this unlimited power will probably be utilized in the advanced nations. Even if all this abundance of electrical power is distributed equally throughout the world, what will it be used for? In 30 years, says J. J. Servan-Schreiber, America will be a postindustrial society with a per capita income of $7,500 while over half the world will still be in a preindustrial society stage of development. I think that most people in the world can achieve the industrial society but first they must be educated to become active participating members of such a society. If most of the people in the underdeveloped nations were to become educated, the present rulers of those nations would have to relinquish much of their economic and political power, something that I don't believe they would do peacefully. This is just one obstruction facing Professor Semenov's plan.

Aside from the sociological problems, however, the Russian physicist provides us with two vastly different sources of optimism.

Despite his repeated invocation of Lenin and Communist ideology, there is comparatively little chauvinism included in his paper. He speaks of the vast quantities of electrical power available to all mankind, rather than to the Communist nations alone, and points out that advances in science and technology will contribute to the ". . . material and spiritual needs of every man on earth." In an era of ABM's, MIRV's and multiple brinksmanship, an expression of this kind from a man of his standing provides a note of hope. (And I cannot help but wonder how much of the article's first and last paragraphs were dictated by political necessity rather than by the spirit of the international scientist.) A discussion of this article again emphasized the intricate interrelationships of the various aspects of the total problem of these next three decades. Power sources, yes, but also government, economics, communication and human values.

The second source of optimism was spelled out by the utter reality of the three sources of potential power. Thermonuclear energy is not a scientific hypothesis, *it exists!* Solar energy surrounds us; it is, in fact, used in various parts of the United States as a simple device to heat hot water for domestic use. The underground heat of the earth is there, and to a minor extent has been measured.

I have neither the knowledge nor the desire to minimize the problems that are involved in making practical use of these three energy sources. But there are few scientists alive today who would deny the fact that these problems are incapable of solution within a reasonable period of time. Moreover, the near future may even expand the possibilities of power sources. We are slowly, for example, beginning to understand the mysteries of gravitational force, and a whole new world may open for us when we make headway in this area.

It is my feeling that despite the "brownouts" (due to our exploding demands for power) which occur only too often, we will see solutions by the 21st century, at least in this direction. I must add that I feel that many sociological problems will not be so easily disposed of in the same period.

leslie c. czapary

questions

1.   Professor Semenov believes that the essential factor in the betterment of mankind is an abundance of electrical power. Apply this principle to an industrial nation, an agricultural nation, and to an emerging nation in terms of "quality of life."

2. To the professor, all sources of power—fossil fuels, solar heat, earth-core heat—must be reduced to electrical power for total utilization. What other procedures might be developed?

3. Despite the slant of the article, what evidence do you find in it that indicates agreement with Theobald's economic philosophy? With Kahn and Wiener's automation?

4. What conflicts exist in our accelerating need for power and our ecological plight that the Semenov proposals would increase?

5. Are there finite limits to the amount of fission-produced atomic power that can be produced, based on our present technology? Should we discover the key to producing power by means of nuclear fission, what limits are there?

6.
from here to there: personal transportation

THE NEW URBAN CAR

ken w. purdy

introduction and comment by kyle a. jones

In the past few years America has made great strides nowhere in the fight against air pollution. California, with more (and some of the oldest) anti-pollution laws than any other state, is still suffering from a dangerous increase in air pollution— destructive enough to destroy forests many miles away from any city.

I don't intend to point out once more all the sources of air pollution because they have already been described a thousand different ways and times by many people. I'm concerned only with what I, and many experts, consider the greatest polluter: the automobile.

Numerous sociological studies have been done on the fascination cars hold for people as sex symbols, power symbols, freedom symbols and, of course, status symbols. On the list of reasons for buying a car, convenient transportation, the original purpose, rates the lowest. For a majority of car buyers, practicality has been shoved completely off the list. I personally can't see why it takes $4,000 worth of high performance status to drive half-a-mile for a six-pack or to go four or five miles to work.

Today's automobile may satisfy some psychological demands, but it will cause an ecological crisis which will create an even greater psychological need than that which it now answers—the need to survive.

Not only is the motor car filling our air with unusable garbage, our land area with endless abandoned iron hulks, but it also eats up a great deal of the oxygen that we need to stay alive. If its damaging effects are allowed to continue it will continue doing a great deal of harm to plant life and will seriously decrease our source of oxygen. I don't believe this will go on to the point where human life is greatly threatened, but it could—if people's attitudes about cars (and Detroit's attitudes towards people and cars) aren't drastically changed in the foreseeable future.

Since I can see no promise for pollution control measures for today's cars and even less promise in trying to convince people to give up private transportation, it seems to me that a new type of car is called for: a car that is smaller in order to ease parking space problems and to lessen roadway requirements—a new power plant which produces significantly less or no pollutants. I believe there is also a great need for upgrading public transportation and that some method must be found to make combined public and private transportation feasible.

Innumerable solutions to the problem have been proposed. One suggestion is automated highways which would improve the safety factor immeasurably by eliminating human error in driving. Private transportation in urban areas could be eliminated in favor of such substitutions as moving sidewalks and vacuum tube arrangements, in order to better utilize the land area now used by streets and parking lots.

The following article by Ken Purdy elaborates further on these issues and others, and suggests many different possible solutions to the problem of urban transportation.

k.a.j.

THE NEW URBAN CAR

Ken W. Purdy has been a sports car enthusiast and writer about automobiles since the 1940s. He has been the editor of four major magazines and a free-lance writer since 1954. In 1969 he wrote the following magazine article that represents Detroit's thinking on compact cars.

During the next 12 months, Americans will drive automobiles 900 billion miles. They will suck up a sea of gasoline—well, 75 billion gallons (250,000 filling-station pumps squirting into Main Street!)—they will burn, use up for good, an unimaginable number of tons of oxygen and spread over the land, say, 200,000 tons of pollutants, gases, chemicals and solids (870 tons of solids alone in each 1000-foot-high square mile); and they will do all this, for the most part, in the accomplishment of trivialities, one person (statistically, 1.2) in a 350-horsepower, 4000-pound vehicle, blasting down to the supermart for a carton of cigarettes and a six-pack.

There's a case for outlawing the automobile. The thing is a mad monster that eats our air at one end and spews out unassimilable effluents at the other, whimsically kills or injures 2,105,200 of us a year and, since it lives and functions only on smooth flat surfaces, has taken us well on the way to paving the whole country (1,000,-000 acres a year, and already in existence over one linear mile of road for every square mile—3,600,000—in the country), with consequent destruction of beauty, waterways and essential oxygen-producing flora. Long ago, wise men saw the danger. Winston Churchill, for one: "I have always considered that the substitution of the internal-combustion engine for the horse marked a very gloomy milestone in the progress of mankind." But the Americans love the automobile as they love life; he who helps them have it can grow great, or rich, at least; and he who tried to take it away from them would be ground fine and fed to the dogs. Right. But how about a different *kind* of automobile? At least for the cities, reeling under smog, confrontation, riot, rape, rapine and an 8.5-mph average speed in traffic. The one we've got isn't really right for the job: It makes smog and it's too big. It's so much too big that giving it room to run and places to park uses up half the total downtown area in some jurisdictions, besides blanketing them with exhaust smoke.

For years, everyone who can read without moving his lips has known that smog induces lung cancer and emphysema, bronchitis and asthma, and that automobile exhaust is responsible for 50 to 60 percent of smog; but until really notable inversions over Los Angeles, London, Tokyo and New York triggered deaths both numerous and plainly attributable, there was no action. Then, suddenly, as it is likely to do, the roof fell in. John W. Gardner, Secretary of Health, Education and Welfare in the Johnson Administration, said that he could see "collision in the future of the internal-combustion engine and the interests of the American people." Frank M. Stead, head of Environmental Sanitation for California, proposed a total ban on the internal-combustion engine in that state by 1980. And, for the first time in perhaps 40 years, the notion that only gasoline could move people—a notion that had accumulated the majesty and weight of the law—was shaken out for a hard look.

From the beginning of automobilism until 1920 or so, there did exist what seemed to be viable alternatives to the i.c.e. (internal-combustion engine): the steam engine and the electric motor, both smog-free. So why not bring them, or one of them, back? On the other hand, if they were so great, what happened to them?

In the beginning, the steamers and the electrics looked like the only entrants in the race. They *were* the beginning: The first road vehicle to move under its own power was a steam-powered tricycle run in France by Nicolas Cugnot in 1769. Richard Trevithick ran a steam carriage in London in 1803 and, 30 years later, a fleet of steam buses ran to posted schedules between points as distant as London and Oxford. An electric car set up the first land-speed record—39 miles an hour—in 1898; and another was the first vehicle to do a mile in a minute: 65 mph in 1899.

When the making and running of automobiles grew away from its often dilettante beginnings and got down to business on a standard cutthroat level, the smart money went to the steamers and the electrics. Steam drove the railroads, the ocean liners and the factories and was moving in on the farmer's horse. It seemed logical that it would run the automobiles, if they were to amount to anything. Steam-automobile companies popped up all over the East and the Midwest. Half of them lasted only two years or less. The Twombly, the Binney & Burnham and the Grout were ephemera; but Stanley, Locomobile, White and Doble were cliché words in the public prints.

An antique-car mechanic once said to me, "If you read somewhere that the steam automobile ran on steam, that's true. Anything else you read about it is even money to be a lie." It's an exaggeration but not by much.

The Stanley Steamer—life span in its various reincarnations 1897–1927 (the early Locomobile was a Stanley design)—was an outwardly conventional-looking automobile. A tubed boiler under the hood made steam that ran a two-cylinder engine geared directly to the back axle. To that extent, it was basically simple, and Stanley advertising (of which there was little, since the twin Stanley brothers, F. E. and F. O., did not believe in it) stated, "We use no clutches, nor gearshifts, nor flywheels, nor carburetors, nor magnetos, nor sparkplugs, nor timers, nor distributors, nor self-starters, nor any of the marvelously ingenious complications that inventors have added in order to overcome the difficulties inherent in the internal-explosive engine and adapt it to a use for which it is not normally fitted." All true enough, but the Stanley had complications of its own. To start from dead cold could take up to 30 minutes and involve the use of a blowtorch. Fuel for the fire was kerosene or gasoline or a combination of the two, but the burners of the day were crude and dirt in the jets often shut down the fire, which would stay down until they had been poked out with a bit of wire. The boiler tubes were subject to leakage. The necessity of mixing oil and steam in order to lubricate the cylinders spawned troublesome boiler deposits.

A big teakettle with a roaring fire under it is the image that leaps to mind, but a vehicle steam system isn't that simple. It must make and send to the engine steam as it is needed, a lot of it for going fast, less for going slowly, a lot for uphill, none for going down, and so on. If you drove an early Stanley faster than 40 miles an hour, the boiler pressure dropped quickly, because as boiling water was converted rapidly into steam, cold feed water poured in. Early Stanleys didn't carry a condenser in the system; steam was exhausted to the open air, which meant stopping to refill the water tank every 20 miles or so. Later models did have condensers, which meant they could reuse some of the water.

The great virtue of the steamer, the characteristic that made it worth the trouble, was that it could start itself. The internal-combustion engine couldn't and still can't. Hand-cranking a big engine gummed up with the oils of the day, which went semisolid in cold weather, was beyond the capacity of any but a strong man and was tricky even for him. Doctors, fire chiefs and others subject to emergency liked the steamer.

The steamer's silence and vibration-free running racked up other plus points. Around 1900, all but the very best i.c.-engined automobiles shook, buzzed and rattled and could be heard a block away. The steamer's exhaust made a whuff-whuff sound, passengers were aware of minor roarings and whistlings as the fire came up and down and the pumps worked, but that was all.

The steamer's endearing ability to start against a load, to exert maximum power at its lowest speed, made the gasoline car's clutch-gearbox assembly irrelevant. Aside from the standard steer-stop devices, the Stanley used only a hand throttle and a foot pedal working the cutoff, the device that regulated the amount of steam sent into the cylinders on each stroke, and it didn't require the skill and synchronization needed to handle the gas car's clutch and gear lever expertly. Driving the Stanley was simple, but maintaining it was not, because it was really a miniaturized steam locomotive, a fairly primitive machine. Payment for its silence, smoothness and power ran high. Lighting the fire in a Stanley unnerved some owners: Excess fuel would ignite, producing the dreaded "flashback," a puff of flame that would remove eyebrows and shorten mustaches.

The blow that staggered the Stanley, and probably killed it, fell when Charles Kettering of General Motors popularized the electric self-starter, beginning in 1912. Kettering is usually nominated as inventor of the starter, but, like most basic automotive inventions, it had appeared in Europe some years before it came to America —in this case, in 1896. Kettering's contribution, a massive one, was to make it widely available. In one stroke, the electric starter cut from under the Stanley its main reason for being. It wasn't clinically dead until 1927, but irreversible decline began in 1912. A far better steamer, the best, the Doble, lasted until 1932. Abner Doble, a Californian, laid down his first car in 1914 and was concerned with the steam automobile into the Fifties. He made far fewer cars than the Stanley twins. His final productions were

superb carriages, goodlooking, luxurious, mechanically sophisticated. Steam production was completely automatic; and at −32
degrees Fahrenheit, a Doble would move from dead cold in 40
seconds. It would do 95 mph, would maintain 750 pounds per
square inch of pressure in the boiler under any demand and, like
all steamers, would climb anything on which the back wheels
could find traction. A tankful of water (30 gallons) lasted 750 miles.
Fuel consumption was 8–11 miles to the gallon. An English tester
wrote, in 1920, "Care is necessary, because of the exceptional
acceleration." But the Doble came too late and it ran into simple
bad luck: financial two-timing, war and depression. By mid-
Twenties, the gas car was reasonably quiet, less complicated than
the steamer, easier and cheaper to make.

A folk legend no less viable than the George Washington-cherry-
tree story holds that "the interests" (Detroit and the oil people)
did the steamcar to death. Not true. Detroit didn't have to and the
oil interests didn't want to: The steamers used petroleum. It wasn't
true that hideous danger of boiler explosion was a steamcar characteristic. A boiler of the teakettle type can be destructive in
explosion, but the steam automobiles used fire-tube or flash steam
generators (because they made steam quickly) and these are
relatively safe, since only a small amount of water is being heated
at any one time. The Stanley brothers believed that their boilers
would hold 1600 pounds per square inch, much more than was
normally used. A Stanley could be made to go very fast; a racing
model took the land-speed record at 127 miles an hour in 1906, on
Ormond Beach, Florida, Fred Marriott up. The next year, trying to
break his own record, Marriott was doing 150 when the car hit a
rough spot in the sand, went airborne (it had a flat bottom and a
curved top, like an airplane wing) and smashed itself into junk.
Marriott lived, but the Stanleys never allowed him, nor anyone
else, to run a factory car in competition again, a decision that
cheered the gas-car people, who couldn't come remotely near
150 miles an hour at the time.

So much for the golden years of steam. What now? About two
years ago, the prospects for a revival of the steam automobile
were bright. They are less so now.

William Lear's announcement, in 1968, that he would build a
steam race car and steam passenger vehicles to follow excited the
country, because Lear is a multimillionaire industrialist with a
background of accomplishment—the Lear Jet airplane, for one
example out of many. His plans were ambitious: a team of cars for
Indianapolis, a 130-mph police cruiser, a bus, a passenger auto-

mobile of standard configuration and a $35,000 limousine in limited edition. As of this writing, nothing has come out of his Reno plant.

Lear turned his attention from the steam reciprocating engine to the steam turbine this past summer and, in mid-November 1969, told a University of Michigan audience that he was abandoning the steam turbine as too complex, too expensive, too difficult to maintain for passenger-automobile use. He had spent, he said, $6,600,000 on the steam project and now would concentrate on the gas turbine. Longtime steam specialists, most of whom had been skeptical of Lear from the beginning, were angered at the news and not much mollified by his stated intention to press on with steam applications for trucks and buses.

Lear is not the only runner in the field. Even before the U.S. Senate hearings on steam propulsion in May 1968, steamcars were being built and planned in this country, England, Germany, Italy and Japan. The hearings didn't result in any earth-shaking dicta being issued by Washington, nor had the earlier ones on the electric car; they did startle some segments of the general public by showing them that steamcars were in being, some of very interesting performance, and that intelligent and selfless people had long been earnestly working to bring them forward. There were the Williams brothers, for example, C. J. and C. E., of Ambler, Pennsylvania. With their father, Calvin, the Williams brothers have 30 years in steam-automobile experimentation behind them, and they have a running steam automobile that is almost completely automatic and will do a nearly silent 100 miles an hour. The Williams steam generator and engine system can be dropped into various chassis, and they offered a 250-hp steam Chevrolet Chevelle at $10,500. It would move in 20 seconds from dead cold and show full steam pressure in one minute. It did 50 miles to the gallon of water, 25 to the gallon of kerosene. But the Williams brothers ran out of money last year and, rather than accept outside financing, they closed their doors.

Karl Petersen and Richard Smith of California are successful steam developers of years' standing. They have used Volkswagen chassis and their engines are considerably lighter than the originals: One, built on a four-cylinder Mercury outboard block, weighs 32 pounds, with a 200-hp capability. Steamcar builders have successfully used both methods: cast their own or used proprietary blocks, in some cases V8s or V8s cut in two.

The Williams and Smith-Petersen systems show negligible emissions—unburned hydrocarbons at 20 parts per million, for instance, as against the Federal level of 275. In practical analysis, a modern steamcar would wipe out automotive smog: Because its fuel can be burned externally under controlled conditions, it's nearly pollutant-free. Why not, then? All the major companies have investigated steam and their public reactions have been pessimistic. Technological problems of awesome complexity loom, they have said. Industry-oriented apologists have hinted that difficulties of water-fuel feed alone might require five years of intensive research and development, with no guarantee of success; designing a condenser capable of handling exhaust steam from a high-powered engine would be a major undertaking. I find myself skeptical. The Stanley brothers worked out a fair feed system, using the Stone Age tools and techniques of 70 years ago, and the Stanleys, compared with even the second-team talent available in battalion strength in Detroit today, were little more than whittlers and blacksmiths. A technology that can throw an unmanned rocket to the moon, make it take photographs and transmit them to earth, on a time schedule of plus or minus nothing, could, I feel, work out a way of squirting water into the boiler of a steam automobile at a rate compatible with a given speed. In comparison with the billions lavished on i.c.e. research, mills, not pennies, have been spent on steam down the years. Karl Ludvigsen, who has a significant reputation in automotive reportage, wrote, "The achievements of today's steam researchers on practically zero financial backing merely hint at what steam might be able to do with a full-scale industrial push behind it."

A switch to steam automotive power would, of course, cause a horrendous economic dislocation. It would wipe out uncounted numbers of component suppliers and it would turn into scrap metal millions of dollars' worth of i.c.e. tooling. It would affect the sensitive oil industry, to a degree, by destroying the gasoline market in favor of other crude-oil derivatives. This effect might not be wholly adverse, since a barrel of crude oil will give more kerosene than it will gasoline. Detroit argues that the only reason for considering the steam engine is its favorable emission characteristics and that comparable levels can be achieved by i.c. engines within a short time. Some authorities dispute this vigorously, on the grounds that currently favored emission-control systems are expensive, inefficient and short-lived. Spot checks in California have shown them breaking down at surprisingly low mileages, as little as 2000; and, like so many other environmental problems, smog will not wait: We are running 100,000,000 i.c.e. vehicles now, we will have 180,000,000 by 1980 and 360,000,000 by 2000. The heart of the matter, Senator Warren Magnuson has said, lies in the fact that "The increasing number of combustion vehicles will outdistance the effectiveness of pollution controls and air pollution will take a dramatic *rise.*" Because of the number of old cars in use, ten years will pass before all automobiles have emission-control devices. One New York City research group predicts that automobiles as presently used will make Manhattan uninhabitable by 1977. If pollution continues at the present rate, by 1980 we may have *irreversibly* contaminated the atmosphere.

Nothing less than a Federal mandate could effect a crash steamcar production program. Only a pollutant crisis very close to the point of producing death on an epidemic or plague level could call out such a mandate. To the extent that the Federal Government has taken a position, it has been one of hands off. Alan S. Boyd, Secretary of Transportation in the Johnson Administration, said that the Government should not actively help in developing new automotive-propulsion systems; and, in general, Washington's attitude has been that the problem is Detroit's. Nevertheless, Federal financing has supported a number of projects, but many have seemed nominal, and Ralph Nader°called the Federal moves "trivial and misdirected." The token-fund device is often used: $5,000,000 would have allowed the promising Republic Aviation–New York State safe-car project to build 15 prototype automobiles, but only $70,000 was granted. The idea that the automotive industry itself should produce new systems is probably wrong at the root: Radical breakthroughs are more likely outside the industries affected. Nylon, for example, originated in the chemical, not the textile, industry. On balance, it seems likely that air pollution by automobile will be a serious problem for years to come, but palliatives will prevent its reaching emergency level. Steam automobiles will be built during this decade but not in significant numbers.

And the electric?

The electric is no new thing; the first ran in Scotland in 1837, the creation of one Robert Davidson. In 1902, Charles Baker, who manufactured pleasant little two-seater electrics, built a racer with a design speed of 100 mph. It carried a two-man crew riding in hammocklike tandem seats reminiscent of those in today's Grand Prix cars: the driver in front, a mechanic behind him to work the switches. Baker was getting about 85 mph on a Staten Island circuit when spectators ran across the course. A rear wheel rim (made of steamed hickory, for lightness) broke under braking and wrecked him. Two years passed before a gasoline car, a Gobron-Brillié, did 100.

Many ordinarily farsighted people, in automobilism's beginning, found the electric a better prospect than the steamer and much better than the gasoline car. The electric was taken for granted, it was an important part of the scene: The first speeding ticket in New York City went to Jacob German (he was doing 12 mph on Lexington Avenue) and the city's first traffic fatality was a real-estate operator named Henry H. Bliss, done to death by an electric taxicab in 1899. Before the electrics gave up, in the Thirties, 70-odd firms had built them, and the square, glassy-looking town runabout was a fixture in American cities. Endearing was the word for those Detroit or Baker or Waverley coupes, nearly always black, slipping almost silently along the boulevards (they made a well-bred kind of hum). They were usually upholstered in rich gray cloth, the driver, most often a lady of means, holding across her lap the tiller, which in its main movement steered the vehicle, and regulated its speed with a twist-grip throttle thing at the end of it. There would be a brake pedal on the floor, a voltmeter and a speedometer, a bell to warn away the peasants and, nearly always, a cut-glass vase for flowers.

The standard electric was usually run at around 15–20 mph and had a full-power range of about 25 miles. It used lead-acid batteries and, as a rule, spent the night plugged into the house current. Battery cost dictated a price for an electric automobile almost twice that of a comparable gasoline car; this and its rigidly limited utility made it as much a class symbol as a contemporary country-club membership. It was marvelously suited to the pedestalized fragile-flower image of the well-to-do woman of the day; it needed no cranking, no firing, no tiresome warming up and, in relation to the two other types, it was about as complicated as a bent pin, reliable to the point of boredom. Its lady pilot needed to know nothing of its workings, because, except for running out of juice or blowing a tire, little could happen to it. There was no excuse for flatting the batteries, since the gauge on the dashboard registered the life they had left; and even if they did run down, a 15-minute standstill for recuperation would usually raise enough current to get home. And the electrics ran so slowly that tires lasted a long time.

Limited range and speed forbade them the highways and then, as now, some formidably qualified minds were intrigued by these problems: Henry Ford and Thomas Edison, for two. Spurred by the success of the great Model T, they projected a $600 electric, chassis and body by Ford, power by Edison's radical nickel-iron batteries. A couple of prototypes were built in 1914, but that was the end of it; the announcement that the work was in hand was the only tangible that came to the public, a story that was to tell itself again after the Congressional hearings of 1966 set off an electric-car boomlet.

"An electric car, priced at $840, [was] introduced . . . by Carter Engineering, Tamford, England. Top speed is said to be 40 mph, with a 50-mile driving range between rechargings."

Bulletins like that flooded automobile publications in 1967 and 1968. There were stirrings all around, in the United States, England, France, Germany, Italy and Japan, but busiest in the U.S., where at one time, 15 different Federal agencies were funding 86 research projects by universities and corporations. Most of the research was directed toward new batteries, because everything else the electric needed could be taken off 1920 shelves, dusted and put on the road. But the batteries were a real drag.

The emission crisis resurrected the electric, as it had the steamer. Air pollution hits hard, because we *must* breathe. Lake Erie may be covered with iron-hard scum from shore to shore, but we needn't walk on it, as we needn't swim in the Cuyahoga River where it's so oily it's a fire hazard; but air is something else.

An electric delivery truck trundling along the street—there are still a few in the U.S. and 100,000 in the United Kingdom—looks like the instant solution to auto pollution. It's 100 percent emission-free, isn't it? No. It does produce a small amount of ozone, a form of oxygen and a strong oxidizing agent. Ozone appears whenever a spark jumps in air, and it's a primary smog ingredient. Further, 85 percent of U.S. line electricity, needed for charging batteries, is generated by burning fossil fuels, smoke-making coal and oils. Some authorities think that substituting electrics for our present 100,000,000 i.c.e. vehicles wouldn't alter the level of pollution at all, the cars would be pushing out so much ozone and the power plants so much fossil-fuel smoke. On the other side of the fence, ozone production may be curbed, a properly managed fossil-fuel furnace burns its smoke, and that's academic, anyway, because all new electricity plants will be nuclear-fueled. The argument probably favors the electric car on balance; at least the vehicle itself doesn't turn out the horrifying brew of carcinogens and lethal gases (200 chemicals have been identified) that the i.c. engine emits.

Dr. George A. Hoffman of the UCLA Institute of Government and

Public Affairs thinks an urban electric should weigh 3000 pounds (49 percent batteries, 4 percent motor) and be capable of a sprint speed of 100 mph, with a range of 150 miles at 30 mph. A car meeting those standards would have a lot going for it. Its expensive batteries would probably be leased, as fork-lift batteries are now. Its 30-mph base speed would be more than adequate: The rate on feeder roads into New York City during rush hours is 13 mph and in the city proper, 8.5. As for range, the national average per car per day is circa 50 miles. The car's silence would have a profound effect on urban noise, 85 percent of which originates in i.c.e. vehicles. It might also alter certain of our psychological patterns. It would be difficult for an electric car to meet the status-symbol and virility-indicator requirements of the most sought-after i.c.e. automobiles.

Yes, but those batteries.

A battery is not hard to make, because whenever two materials of different electrical potentials are connected, a flow of electrons will occur. It's just that some materials are better than others. Lead plates and diluted sulphuric acid enclosed in a suitable box make a splendid battery from most points of view, but it doesn't register very high on the power-capacity standard, measured in watt-hours: 8–20 per pound. You can drain the lead-acid battery's energy slowly—take it out through a small hole, so to speak, as the old electric coupes used to do in a day's puttering around town at 10–15 miles an hour—or all at once, as the Autolite company has done with the fastest electric automobile of all time, the Lead Wedge, a single-seater that has done 138.863 mph at Bonneville. The Lead Wedge, so called because its configuration is like that of the wedge-shaped STP turbine cars, carried 20 standard lead-acid 12-volt automobile batteries wired in series to a rear-mounted General Electric torpedo motor designed to put out 40 horsepower at 10,000 revolutions per minute. It will accept a momentary overload to 150 horsepower.

The lead-acid battery is a fairly primitive rig; researchers have long looked for something better. There are new wonder batteries on the market and more in the laboratory pipelines: nickel-cadmium, silver-zinc, sodium-sulphur, zinc-air, lithium-chlorine, lithium-nickel-halide, lithium-tellurium. They tend to be powerful but expensive or tricky to use or short-lived or all three.

Ford researchers surfaced with a sodium-sulphur battery rated at 150 watt-hours, with a much greater potential, but it has drawbacks for automotive use: The sodium and sulphur, separated by permeable ceramic walls, must be maintained in a molten state, at

572 degrees Fahrenheit. This might make for awkwardness in an accident, and there's a second factor: The two chemicals react violently when mixed together or with water. General Motors has a lithium-chlorine battery that is stronger—250 watt-hours, with a final-development potential four times that—but it has to be maintained at around 1200 degrees Fahrenheit, with chlorine gas being continuously pumped into the cells. Lithium-tellurium batteries may have the highest potential of all, but tellurium, an element that usually occurs in nature in combination with gold or silver, is rare, costly and poisonous.

The silver-zinc battery is expensive at first pricing—about $2000, of which $1200 is the cost of the silver—but it works and it's four to five times as powerful as a comparable lead-acid battery. The silver in a silver-zinc battery is not consumed, it's fully recoverable, reusable over and over.

Silver-zinc batteries were used in what was probably the most advanced electric automobile so far produced, General Motors' Electrovair II. Erected on a 1966 Corvair chassis, this vehicle used 286 silver-zinc cells connected in series to an oil-cooled Delco motor, weight 130 pounds, horsepower 150, speed 13,000 rpm. Engine compartment and trunk space in the Chevrolet chassis were fully taken up by the batteries, motor, gearbox, oil pump, radiator, fan and the various controls. The Electrovair was meant to put out performance comparable with the production Corvairs and did so: 80 mph top speed, as against 86; and 0-to-60-mph acceleration in 16.7 seconds, as against 15.8. But maximum range on charge was only 40–80 miles, as against 250–300 miles on a tank of gas. The Electrovair did not have a regenerative braking system, in which the motor is used as a generator to recharge the batteries when the car is coasting with power off. The designers felt that ordinary city driving didn't provide enough power-off coasting to be worth while.

General Motors' reaction to the Electrovair was negative. The car's short range, slow recharge and short battery life (100 charging cycle) were cited as basic flaws. Then there was cost, cooling requirements (batteries get very hot under stress) and such difficulties as control-system noises, lack of power for heating and options and possible high-voltage dangers.

G. M.'s experimental technicians produced another electric vehicle, the Electrovan, using not batteries but fuel cells, which produce electricity in a different fashion. The battery can produce electricity only to the limit of the capacity of the materials sealed into it. The fuel cell is continuously fed and will make electricity indefinitely. Various combinations can be used; G. M. settled on liquid hydrogen and liquid oxygen. An electrolyte fluid is also needed; potassium hydroxide was chosen. Although simply stated in outline, delivery of electric power to the wheels was complex and components needed for fuel and electrolyte storage and transfer (550 feet of plastic plumbing, for example) for cooling and control, together with 32 fuel-cell units, brought the weight of the van to 7100 pounds, as against the standard 3250. It was seven seconds slower to 60 mph, one mile an hour slower in top speed, at 70, and its range was 100–150 miles, as against 200–250. There was, of course, no room in the van for useful pay load; the works were everywhere. The General Motors technical paper on the Electrovan, delivered to the Society of Automotive Engineers in January 1967, emphatically stated the vehicle's impractical aspects: weight, cost, complication, safety problems including collision hazards.

The paper's conclusion noted, significantly, that its authors had been working with the fuel-cell system as they had found it: "The build-up of an operating fuel-cell power plant gave us a realistic state-of-the-art evaluation. The many problems indicate that much research-and-development work remains ahead." It would, indeed, seem reasonable to suppose that the fuel-cell system, good enough at the moment to be used in space vehicles, in which reliability and weight are absolutely critical, could, within an acceptable expenditure of time and money, be brought to a state of utility in automobiles. Ralph Nader, in his *Playboy Interview* (October 1968), stated a conviction, not a supposition, that General Electric could, in two to three years, produce a fully efficient fuel-cell automobile with an 80-mph top speed and a 200-mile range.

Ford's prototype electric, the Comuta, was turned out by the British Ford research-and-engineering people and was a down-to-earth machine, carefully thought out, practical in limited application and pretty well ready for the market, should there be a market. The Comuta is small and boxy, only 80 inches over-all length, but will stow two adults and two children in modest comfort and move them for 40 miles at 25 mph with two five-horsepower motors and four 12-volt 85-amp/hour lead-acid batteries. It includes a good heater, fan driven and using waste heat from the motors and controls. A Ford of Germany version, the Berlina, is designed to accept alternative i.c.e. power.

The Comuta is probably the best of the urban electrics and

would be useful today in any major city, San Francisco possibly excepted because of its hills; but it represents no great technical advance over the Henney Kilowatt of 1961. This was a Renault Dauphine conversion using a 36-volt battery system to drive a seven-horsepower motor. It had a 35-mph top speed and 40 miles of range. I had one for a time. It was quiet, pleasant, surprisingly quick on acceleration, shortwinded on hills and expensive: $3600. True, the Comuta was not an adaptation but a new design from the wheels up. There have been many such in the past two or three years, most of them one-offs. The British, characteristically, ran out a whole covey, an amperage of electrics, some of them conversions of things such as the Mini-Minor, and some, such as Scottish Aviation's Scamp, wholly fresh designs, but all running on lead-acid. Enfield Automotive of England some time ago announced firm production plans for a four-seater electric pointed toward the U.S. market and selling at around $1000; so far this vehicle has not appeared on the market. The Enfield has a top speed of 40 mph, a 35-mile range, an eight-hour recharge period and is meant for city use, local suburban tasks (station car, child ferry) and as a personnel carrier for airports, multi-acre industrial complexes and the like.

Westinghouse announced, in 1966, a small two-passenger lead-acid to be called the Markette. It would be rated, the company said, at 25 mph and 50 miles and would sell for $2000. Production of 50 a week was planned; but after market testing in Phoenix, Westinghouse abandoned ship in 1968, saying that the vehicle didn't meet safety standards, an exit line most people thought uninspired. One thousand of the Mars II, a lead-acid Renault conversion, were contemplated for 1968, at $4800. General Electric had a four-seater prototype built by its Santa Barbara Division with the collaboration of the Illinois Institute of Technology, but it remained under cover. The numbers were impressive: 81-mph top, 300-mile range, eight-minute recharge! The Amitron, an American Motors–Gulton project, ran on lithium batteries.

The Rowan electric was a big thing at the 1967 London automobile show. British Motors Holdings, the U. K. giant, is said to be working on a zinc-air car. The zinc-air battery has unique advantages: Zinc is cheap—15 cents a pound—and a mechanical recharge is possible by dropping in new zinc plates. Tokyo Shibaura of Japan announced a 62-mph, 50-mile lead-acid car, which perhaps should be taken more seriously than others, since only the Japanese have put an electric into series production since World War Two. Toyota made 3300 electrics immediately after the armistice, when gasoline was almost unobtainable in Japan.

As with the steam auto, a practical electric urban car won't soon be turned out without Federal insistence backed by, say, the cost of two weeks' fighting in Vietnam. Utility companies would push hard for it, seeing a potential electricity-sales increase of fully 50 percent, and at the right times, too: late night and early morning. But it's hard to imagine how the Government could force an electric car into being at catastrophic cost to Detroit and Dallas, although, as auto writer Brock Yates has pointed out, the oil industry has so vast a future in petrochemicals and synthetic food that it might drop the gasoline business and never miss it.

There's been talk of the Wankel engine as a good power source for the urban car, but although it's now proved and practical, running on the road, and has the advantages of light weight and small size, it's still an internal-combustion engine, rotary instead of reciprocating, and it throws an exhaust that is notably dirty, although Mercedes-Benz and Mazda have developed separately successful correctives. The gas turbine is practical—Chrysler consumer-tested 50 turbines some years ago and is now running sixth-generation models—and offensive turbine emission is less than the i.c. engine's. George Huebner of Chrysler believes it wouldn't economically depress the industry, even though it has only 20 percent as many moving parts as present i.c. engines. The turbine uses cheap fuel, is quiet, light, smooth-running but expensive, because it's made of costly materials to critically tight tolerances.

Combinations of i.c. and electric power have interesting aspects, and the Department of Housing and Urban Development financed a $300,000 research project by the University of Pennsylvania and General Motors pointing toward a $1600 car with VW acceleration and a 100-mile range on the batteries alone. This is an old idea. Ferdinand Porsche built combination passenger cars before World War One, and during the War, the Austrian army used his giant gasoline-electric artillery prime movers. The urban combination, or hybrid, would ideally run on electricity on city streets and use its small, emission-controlled i.c. engine on open roads. It would combine clean exhaust in town with acceptable range and speed on the highway. The University of Pennsylvania–General Motors project, now called Minicars Incorporated and based in Goleta, California, envisions an ultrasmall automobile, probably running on both electricity and gasoline and used in a Minicar

Transit System on a rental basis. Customers would pick up a car at a terminal, register use of it through an on-board credit-card reader, drop it at another terminal, at one of many designated parking lots or perhaps on the street, to be picked up by a roving retrieval crew.

General Motors has carried the hybrid idea to a higher point than anyone else by using the Stirling engine for primary power. The Stirling is a creaking ancient in engine chronology: Its patents went to a Scots minister, Robert Stirling, in 1816. The Stirling engine is something like the steam engine, in that it's an external-combustion machine; but instead of burning fuel under a boiler and sending the resulting steam to do work in a piston cylinder, the Stirling burns fuel (kerosene) and passes the heat to a jacket around a sealed cylinder and piston containing hydrogen gas. The hydrogen expands, driving the piston down for a power stroke; expanded, the gas is cooled and fed back to the cylinder, ready to be heated again. Since there is no near-explosive fuel burning, as in an internal-combustion engine, the Stirling is silent, it's vibration-free and, since the fuel can be burned under precise control, the pollution level is radically reduced.

The Stirling-electric installation was made in a 1968 Opel Kadett and the engine used was rated at eight horsepower. Alone, it could propel the car at about 30 mph at a fuel consumption of 30–40 miles per gallon. With power from the 500 pounds of lead-acid batteries cut in, speed would rise to 55 mph, maintained for a maximum of 40 miles, when current consumption would overcome charging rate. With the vehicle stationary, the engine could be fully directed to battery charging.

Engine-compartment and trunk space in the Opel are stuffed with machinery, a situation to be expected, since practically all the components are off-the-shelf items designed for other use. Research and development presumably would speedily change the picture: Miniaturization is not an occult art. There are problems in the Stirling electric—batteries, heat rejection, the cost of a double drive system—but they are not so grave as to dull its intellectual appeal. It has the extra value of being presumably inoffensive to the oil and automotive industries and perhaps attractive to a third power, the utilities.

Until the great city-suburb complexes sag and crack under the maddening load of 4000-pound-car/160-pound-passenger traffic, and sag and crack they surely will, the urban automobile will be what it is today. After that, something small and squarish will appear, three of it parkable in an Eldorado's shadow and running a steam engine, maybe, an electric motor, perhaps, an emission-free i.c. engine, probably not, or a hybrid. Whatever the power source, it's most likely to be in the rear or under the floor, not in front. It will be small, since a 50-mph top speed will be adequate. The "three-box" basis on which automobiles have been designed from the beginning—one box each for engine, people and luggage—will have no relevance to tomorrow's urban design: It will be strictly "one-box." Indeed, a British designer has on the road at the moment a wheeled platform carrying a glass cube as its body. The general effort will be far less radical, the end result a cube rounded off on the edges and narrowing in all dimensions toward the top. Capacity will be two people, with less comfortable accommodation behind them for two children or one adult. There will be no luggage area except for minimal parcel stowage.

Seating will be straight up and down, since lateral space will be at a premium. There will be no doors as such: Part of the body, probably in front, will be hinged. One projected design allows the whole right front three quarters of the body to open, the windshield being in two parts, sealed on the center vertical line. The steering wheel (or yoke, or tiller) will fold out of the way.

To minimize maintenance, body metal will probably be anodized or otherwise colored at the source. All-round bumpers, perhaps hydraulic, will be standard ware, and minor traffic collisions will have no significance. Radio and tape rigs about the size of a present package of cigarettes will take care of the sound, and a cheap but adequate two-way radio-telephone will be standard. Like everything else on the road, the urban car will be air conditioned.

This transition vehicle will be succeeded by slot-track cars such as the Cornell Aeronautical Laboratory's Urbomobile, capable of hands-off automated travel on city-access trunk lines and driver-control street use. Beyond the Urbomobile, the crystal ball clouds into striated visions of 25-mph moving sidewalks, 250-mph gravity-vacuum subways, individual electron-rocket pods and the ultimate solution: material transference, or, I think—ZAP!—I'll go to Paris now.

in my opinion...

Ken Purdy has covered the problem of urban transportation fairly thoroughly as far as the movement of people is concerned. The problems of moving freight were not given any discussion in this article and were not relevant to it. It is my opinion, however, that any replacement that is developed for the internal combustion engine will wind up in trucks and public transportation vehicles in order to test further day-to-day reliability.

I agree with Mr. Purdy that steam engines are getting "the short end of the stick" in Detroit at present. The auto-makers apparently believe that the necessary re-tooling to produce steam rather than internal combustion engines would be more than the company could bear. Possibly the manufacturers of high performance internal combustion engine components have a hand in Detroit's rejection of steam power because steam engines don't require anything like all the expensive performance options that the internal combustion engine requires (in order to perform on a par with the steam engine).

Undoubtedly, re-tooling costs would be great but eventually the money lost would be regained. At present the Defense Department pays the re-tooling costs outright for many defense contractors in order to keep them in business; I see no good reason why a loan could not be set up through the federal government in order to facilitate re-tooling for steam by the auto-makers and their sub-contractors.

The special parts industry might also be included in such a deal because of the fact that it is such a big business and also because a great many people will probably always be wanting to improve the performance of their personal vehicles. Another reason for including the special parts industry is that this business employs a fairly large number of people who would lose their jobs in a shift from the internal combustion engine to the steam engine were it not for government help.

The manufacturers of transmissions also stand to lose a large source of income in any such change, but they would not lose out entirely since there is no company involved strictly in the manufacture of transmissions. This problem must be taken into account and dealt with when considering any change in power plant types. But even this can be worked out, I believe, by people who know a great deal more about the situation than I do. I must agree with Mr. Purdy that any nation which can send men and unmanned ships to the moon can surely find the brains and knowledge to effect a change-over in automobile power plants without destroying the nation's economy.

Electrical transportation does not offer, in my opinion, anywhere near the flexibility of steam or some other type of power source. I believe the major use for electric cars will be for neighborhood transportation and for such things as large warehouses and office building complexes where a good many electric "golf-cart" type vehicles are already in use. Electricity may also come back into use in fixed-route public transportation. Japan at present is criss-crossed with electric trains, some with underground power sources, but most, unfortunately (from an appearance standpoint), still above ground. However, this in itself is no problem at all.

In my opinion, Mr. Purdy has given a good account in his article on personal transportation. He has presented a few of the alternatives open to us, some or all of which will have to be implemented somehow if we are not all to choke to death on our own transportation.

kyle a. jones

questions

1. What are some of the factors which have made the personal automobile such an important symbol in today's society?

2. What are some of the effects of the lack of comfortable, dependable public transportation on society today?

3. Do you think that by the year 2000, our emphasis on the importance of individual transportation will have changed? If so, in what respects? If not, why not?

4. Should automobile makers be made to bear total responsibility for solving problems caused by their products? Explain.

5. What part do you think automation and the computer will play in the production of individual conveyances during the next thirty years?

7.

what did you really say? communication

communi-
cation

COMMUNICATION

john r. pierce

introduction and comment by robert scott thomas

The dictionary tells us that to communicate is to transmit or exchange knowledge and ideas. The process of communicating is, in its highest sense, essentially a human act, and at this point in time, our main medium for this transmission or exchange is the printed or spoken word. Some of the difficulties inherent in communication via words are considered in the article that follows.

Semanticists, moreover, have pointed out that the use of words alone frequently is not enough, primarily because the same word may mean different things to different people speaking the same language, and it certainly conveys a variety of meanings to individuals who must deal with the original idea in translation. If words like "democracy" and "freedom" have different connotations to statesmen attempting to draw up a treaty between two governments, it is obvious that the resulting document can be the subject of vigorous disagreement from the moment it is signed.

Communication, in another sense, can be an instrument for change. The expansion of communication media has been a major contributor to the uneasiness that marks this period of instability. It is not difficult to keep a people subjugated, despite the poverty of their existence, if they know of no better way of life; but if a communicating device such as a television set is provided for such an impoverished group, surprise is followed by resentment, resentment by demands for change.

A number of fascinating possibilities for improving our ability to communicate has come into focus during the past few years. One, for instance, is the suggestion that learning is essentially the result of chemical changes in the brain's protein molecules. If such actually proves to be the case, say the neuro-biochemists who are researching this hypothesis, why not knowledge by injection? Why not words and ideas transmitted by extrasensory perception?

At present, however, those devices which are having the greatest impact on the transmission of ideas are electronic in nature.

Inventions such as television, the telephone and the computer have unified people from continent to continent, but only to a certain extent. For example, we still do not *understand* our languages enough to program a computer capable of translating from one language to another. With accomplishments in understanding we should eventually be able to communicate much more effectively. Though television and the telephone, essential parts of mass communications, still do not guarantee unslanted facts about a certain issue, they are a step in the right direction, and this step is being enlarged through the use of communication satellites. These satellites enable live television to be transmitted over great distances. Thus the viewer can receive first-hand information concerning the world around him. The only problem here will be the expense of building and operating more satellites.

The home newspaper will be much more practical when it is produced on microfilm instead of paper, with an expensive viewing device the only possible limitation. Microelectronics (Integrated Circuits) have already contributed much to the production of computers and satellites, yet in the future their importance will be even greater since they are becoming more complex and reliable every day.

Another aspect of communications here on earth is one which has been used very little as yet—laser communications. The real problem here is lack of experience, but by the twenty-first century we should see the laser being used extensively. Eventually, science and technology should advance enough to be able to unify the various types of communication to create a common form for dealing with all the human senses simultaneously. Such a communication system would promote faster, more complete communications around the earth (and beyond), and also better understanding between human beings.

The reading that follows is a paper delivered at the California Institute of Technology Conference on Scientific Progress and Human Values by Dr. John R. Pierce.

r.s.t.

COMMUNICATION

Dr. John R. Pierce is a name well-known in electronics and electrical engineering. He received his Ph.D. from California Institute of Technology and is at present executive director of the Research and Communications Sciences Division of the Bell Telephone Laboratories, Inc. Winner of numerous honors and awards (including the Ballantine medal from the Franklin Institute, 1960; H.H. Arnold trophy, Air Force Association, 1962; and the Edison medal, 1963), Dr. Pierce is a member of the American Academy of Arts and Sciences and the Institute of Electrical and Electronic Engineers. He has done work with satellites and travelling-wave amplifiers, as well as the writing of Quantum Electronics, *1966;* Symbols, Signals and Noise, *1961;* Electronics and Waves, *1964; and numerous articles for science journals.*

Electrical communication has profoundly altered the world we live in and the way we live in it. Today's child accepts the telephone and television with the same sense of familiarity and lack of understanding that earlier generations accorded natural phenomena. We do not need to know the physical basis of telephony in order to use a telephone any more than we need to understand the biological intricacies of a horse in order to ride one. Familiarity and use are the same in each case. But the telephone is a product of man, and the telephone system, a huge and intricate assembly of complicated parts, is the outgrowth of research and understanding as we know them in science.

This sort of understanding is powerful but rare in our world.

Reprinted from Toward the Year Two Thousand: Work in Progress *by permission of* DAEDALUS, *Journal of the American Academy of Arts and Sciences, Boston, Massachusetts, Vol. 96, Summer, 1968.*

For example, although we talk and read and write everyday, we understand very little about language. In the past decade, attempts to use the computer to translate from one language to another have forcibly emphasized how little we do understand this universal intellectual tool. It soon became apparent in efforts at machine translation that an accurate grammar would be necessary, a grammar by means of which a computer could parse a sentence unambiguously (as we almost always can) and a grammar by means of which all grammatical and no ungrammatical utterances could be constructed. It became equally apparent that linguists could not supply even a reasonably satisfactory grammar for any language. The grammars we have are like tips for playing good golf. With their aid, and with the aid of our hidden and unformulated skills of speech, we can construct grammatical (and meaningful) sentences and interpret and parse such sentences. But because we do not consciously understand how we do this, we cannot tell a computer how to do it.

Language is central to our life and thought. Yet in the sense that we use *understanding* in science, we do not understand language. We know how to speak, but we do not know how we speak. We learn to use language through apprenticeship. We may be provided with some rules that can help us in a practical way to speak or write uniformly and intelligibly. But the foreigner who is full of rules does not speak or write our tongue as "correctly" as a well-apprenticed native without a rule in his head.

This has always been the pattern for most human life. Somehow, through the examples and precepts of others, we learn to live—to act, to interact, to choose, and to decide. As members of a society, we formulate and accept rules and precepts that help to guide us through life. But we are successful in acting as we are successful in digesting our food—not because we understand the process, but because we are able to carry it out.

There is an increasing side to our life that is quite different. Everyone uses language, but no one understands how we use it. In contrast, everyone uses television sets and telephones, and a few people do understand them completely. This is partly because a radio or telephone is very much simpler than a language or a human being. Chiefly, however, we understand a radio or a telephone because it has been created according to our understanding. Through our understanding of science, we see how we can make a useful device. We do this in a way that is understandable to us. It is no wonder, then, that the operation of the final product is understandable.

Science and technology inject into our environment an increasing part that is inherently understandable and controllable because man put it there through his understanding. We do not need to be told that this understandable, controllable element of our environment has a profound effect on all of our life; we see this whenever we drive a car, or fly in a plane, or make a telephone call, or watch television.

To all of these things we adapt, behaviorally and linguistically, in the old mysterious way in which man has always managed to live. We acquire new needs and new standards. A society that functioned well in the absence of telephones, automobiles, and electric power is replaced by a society that would collapse without these present necessities.

Communication is a particularly apt field in which to discuss and illustrate the impact, actual and potential, of the understanding of science and the power of technology on society. Electrical communication has changed our lives profoundly within the span of our memories.

Further, electrical communication clearly exemplifies the applicability and power of science. Few industries have a deeper or broader technological base. Within my lifetime communication has been profoundly changed by advances in electron tubes, by a rapidly changing solid-state art that has displaced these, by the invention and control of polymers that have replaced wood, paper, rubber, and even metals, and by a mathematical and logical insight into ways of organizing digital systems—such as computers and telephone switching systems.

Finally, electrical communication illustrates as no other field can the range from the comparatively simple, exemplified by the local broadcasting station and the home receiver, to the incredibly complicated and interdependent, exemplified in common-carrier communication systems.

This division between the technologically simple and the technologically complex reflects a difference in the purpose and function of mass communication, such as television, and personal communication, such as telephony. Mass communication is necessarily aimed at majorities or large minorities. It is one-way; it is aimed from the few to the many. It is a unifying and conservative element in our society. As such, its effects have been tremendous.

We are rapidly approaching a society without "sticks" or "boondocks," except those that are growing in the central slums of metropolitan areas. Television brings launchings from Cape Kennedy, sports from all parts of the continent, even (via satellite) live events from across the ocean, and a nationally uniform brand of music, comedy, and soap opera into the most remote house. The center of our society is no longer a physical region; it is a medium of communication that pours forth in every house.

In the face of television, it is difficult for differences of dialect, of interest, or of attitude to persist.

This makes television the greatest unifying force ever to act upon man. A voice and a picture on television may not yet be able to tell us what to think about a matter, but they very effectively decide what we will be thinking about, and that may be as remote physically as the war in Viet-Nam. Here on the other side of the globe we are made conscious of political implications that escape most of the Vietnamese themselves, who know government only through death and taxes.

Television is a direct and powerful tool in the hands of the central government. The President and members of his Administration can appeal directly to the people, without distortion or deletion of what they want to say. And what they say directly to the people, the newspapers must handle somehow.

This is powerful in a society that is already unified, but its impact and power could be far greater in an emerging nation that must achieve some sort of national unity and effective government for its well-being and indeed its survival.

The impact of the telephone and other common-carrier communication is quite different from that of mass communication. The telephone is inherently the tool of the individual, not of the majority or the society. It is the means by which we conduct the business of life—ordering groceries, calling the doctor, making appointments and reservations. It is our social tool for keeping in touch with friends and relatives, arranging dates, dinners, parties, and trips. And it is our intellectual tool for calling informed acquaintances to find out what is really behind public statements, and even for arranging protest marches and demonstrations.

Unlike mass communication, which could have a profound impact on even a primitive society, the telephone is an inherent part of a way of life that has been shaped by automobiles, airplanes, electric power, standardized, uniform merchandise, and a pattern of credit. We use the telephone because we have interests that lie beyond the home, the family, and the neighborhood; because we are willing in many cases to buy, without shopping, on the basis of past experience and information provided by advertisements that reach us by mail or through newspapers.

It seems to me that except for some government and business

usage, a telephone system would have little value in a primitive society. Its widespread use is a reflection of our way of life, a way of life that it has helped to bring into being.

So far, I have cited communication as an example of the impact of science and technology—of intellectual understanding, if you will—on society, and I have indicated how important this can be in the utterly different fields of mass communication and individual communication. I have not, however, indicated how the revolutionary powers of communication came into being; their source is discovery and invention. While this is a plausible and simple statement, it is an important one. Today we hear much about meeting the needs of society, and about planning and systems analysis and systems engineering as means for meeting those needs.

Planning and systems analysis and systems engineering are vital parts of technology, and are essential in making good and effective use of what we have at hand. They may even be effective in pointing out lacks that stand in the way of accomplishing what we want to do. Discovery and invention may—or may not—then remedy such recognized difficiencies. But discovery and invention often take us off on some entirely different tack.

I am sure that when Alexander Graham Bell invented the telephone, what common-carrier communication felt it *really* needed was better multiplex telegraphy, and perhaps practical automatic telegraphy. What the world got through this invention was a revolutionary system of communication that has swamped the telegram and, indeed, the letter as the means of interpersonal communication. We do what we can, not what we think we should or what we want to do, and needs are as often created as satisfied by discovery and invention. De Forest was seeking a detector for wireless telegraphy when he invented the vacuum tube. The invention led to worldwide telephony and to radio broadcasting. Television languished as an interesting idea for years until science and technology gave us an advanced electronic art, and Zworykin invented the iconoscope.

Babbage tried to make a sophisticated computer in the nineteenth century and failed. The computer was reinvented and easily realized, using the art supplied by telephone switching, by Aiken and Stibitz around 1940. The vacuum tube made it possible for Eckert and Mauchly to make a fast electronic calculator. Von Neumann provided the stored program. And the transistor made the computer economical, reliable, and profitable.

Discovery and invention have been the crucial elements in inaugurating and changing the course of communication. Systems engineering and systems development have been necessary in effectively exploiting discovery and invention, in realizing their full impact. But in most cases the discoverers and inventors have convincingly demonstrated the power and potentialities of what they have done before it seriously engaged the attention of systems engineers.

If discovery and invention have been so vital in the revolutionary effect that communication has already had on our lives, what may they do to and for us in the future? Here I shall consider only discoveries and inventions that have been made but not yet applied, or applied fully.

We may expect the effective extension of mass communication into countries with less advanced communication technology. The transistor radio has already provided a direct link between otherwise isolated peoples and their central governments. Even the Bedouin on his camel can hear that he is part of a nation and learn of its problems and aspirations.

We have all experienced the much stronger impact of television. In the United States network programs are transmitted between cities by common-carrier facilities provided by the telephone companies, and broadcast from a large number of high-power television transmitters. Many important and populous countries have neither the common-carrier networks to span the country nor the television transmitter to reach the viewer. Moreover, a television receiver is expensive and complicated compared with a transistor radio. But communication satellites may eventually make television available even in underdeveloped countries. At present it is impractical to broadcast directly from a satellite to a standard television receiver—the power required is too large. Such broadcasting will probably remain impractical for a considerable period.

It is practical, however, to launch a satellite that will send out a signal with a few hundred watts' power; in fact, the Soviet Union has done this. A ground station costing only a few thousand dollars could receive television signals from such a satellite. The received signals could be carried for short distances by cable or distributed in local areas by means of cheap, low-power transmitters.

Thus, by means of an entirely feasible communication satellite, television could be transmitted from the capital of a nation to many towns and villages where it could be viewed in schools or other public buildings. The cost of such a satellite television-distribution system would be considerable, but the impact could be tremendous.

Consider Nigeria, a nation of over fifty million people, which has established English as the language of its schools. Nationwide television could be of tremendous value there as a motivation for learning English, as a way of establishing and maintaining a standard English, and as a means for making nationhood meaningful and desirable to the population. Television of this sort would be almost as valuable in far more advanced nations, such as India and China.

Space technology has advanced to a point where satellites may be very economical for domestic communication. As we already have adequate domestic network facilities, satellites could not make television different for us, only cheaper to distribute. Indeed, the popular revolution in television distribution now under way is in quite the opposite direction—that is, in favor of wired distribution provided by CATV (community antenna television) services, rather than distribution by radio. CATV was initially established to supply television to remote or shadowed areas where the direct signal is inadequate. Signals from a hilltop antenna were amplified and distributed by cables, which themselves have amplifiers at regular intervals. It was found that subscribers were anxious to pay a few dollars a month for an adequate TV signal. And this has proved true even in cities where a fair (but inferior) signal can be obtained from a rooftop antenna.

But CATV has another potentiality as well. Through importation of signals from a distance, it can provide a community, large or small, with as many channels as are available to the residents of Los Angeles or New York. Here, indeed, is the ultimate in the abolition of the "sticks" and "boondocks."

CATV is a great advance, the wave of the future in comparison with anything else on the television horizon. It will be interesting to see whether CATV will continue to thrive. If it does, it may help to bring about another long-time dream—the delivery of newspapers to homes by wire. At least two problems must be overcome if this is to succeed. The smaller of these problems is economical broadband transmission; an extra channel on a CATV network could provide this. The other problem is that of the bulk of a newspaper. People *want* big papers, papers with lots of advertisements. But they do not want these to spew out onto the living-room floor, unfolded. They do not want to have rolls of newsprint delivered and stored away in their houses.

Although the production of a paper newspaper in the home seems to be clearly impractical, a microfilm newspaper might be acceptable. Its success would depend on an economical, convenient, high-resolution viewing device, and on some practical way of recording images with microfilm resolution. Conventional photography and even the Land Camera process seem inadequate. Perhaps science will provide an answer. If it does, the impact could be tremendous. Experience shows that people want local news and local advertisements in newspapers, as well as national news and national advertisements. In a newspaper distributed by wire, some news and advertisements could be tailored to specific neighborhoods if that proved profitable. Indeed, to some degree, mass communications might be nearly individualized in this process. Television could remain the truly national unifying force that it is.

In individual communication I foresee a revolution based on various specific advances that will make both transmission and the station equipment at the ends of transmission circuits less expensive. The cost of transmission goes down as we send more signals over a given path, which we accomplish by providing transmission paths of greater bandwidth. We have now advanced far beyond the era in which one pair of wires carried one voice signal. A digital transmission system called T1 can send twenty-four two-way telephone channels or 1.5 million data bits per second over two pairs of wires in cables. The L4 system sends thirty-six hundred telephone conversations one way over a single "pipe" in a coaxial cable, and there are twenty such pipes in the cable. A microwave transmission route can accommodate as many as twelve thousand telephone channels.

Using the telephone channels as a measure of transmission capability, we can say that a commercial TV signal uses about one thousand times as much bandwidth as a telephone signal, and a *picturephone* (service mark of A.T. & T. Co.) signal about one hundred times as much as a telephone signal. Facsimile signals and data signals fall somewhere between the telephone and the television bandwidth, though some data signals (teletypewriter) require only about a tenth of the telephone bandwidth.

What have science and technology provided that will enable us to send large bundles of channels economically? First, the extension of the operation of solid-state devices into the microwave range has made it possible to build microwave repeaters of extremely high reliability and extremely low power consumption. Thus, it is possible to build small, cheap, trouble-free repeaters and to power them economically. Perhaps this will lead to a new use of microwave repeaters, spaced at frequent intervals along roads rather than on remote hilltops. This would make possible the profitable exploitation of microwave bands (at 17 and 30 Gigahertz) at which transmission over conventional distances is seriously impaired by rain.

The same advances in electronics, together with boosters for the power of the Titan III, have made it immediately practical to launch communication satellites that could supply as many as one hundred thousand telephone circuits between, say, five or ten principal cities in the United States. Such a satellite system could be established in a few years, substantially increasing the number of long-distance circuits available in the country. Further, in concert with terrestrial facilities, the satellite could incorporate switching equipment that would transfer blocks of circuits from one pair of cities to another in meeting fluctuations of demand.

Work on transmission of millimeter waves through waveguides has made it technically possible to send two hundred thousand one-way television signals or one hundred thousand two-way telephone channels through a single tube two inches in diameter. The signal must be amplified and regenerated at intervals of about fifteen miles. Advances in the solid-state art have made it possible to do this entirely by means of solid-state devices of low power consumption. Such a waveguide system would be economical if there were sufficient traffic to justify it.

In the future, it will also become technologically possible to provide circuits of almost unlimited bandwidth by means of the coherent light generated by lasers. We already have suitable lasers; in lenses consisting of gas flowing through alternately hot and cold regions, a means for guiding light through buried pipes; modulators for impressing signals on the light; and detectors for translating the received light signals into electrical current. We are not, however, presently in a position to build a useful laser communication system. The performance of some of the components is not so good as we might desire; the modulators have inadequate bandwidth; and adequate detectors are not available for the longer of the wavelengths at which lasers operate. There is also a problem of accuracy of alignment of the system of guiding lenses, and of automatic correction of misalignment. But, too, there is lack of experience.

We could have new types of microwave systems, satellite systems with a capacity of over one hundred thousand telephone circuits, and millimeter waveguide systems at any time merely by deciding to go ahead and spend the money. In the case of optical transmission, we need more research and more experience.

Integrated circuits, or microelectronics, will make it possible to produce a complicated circuit almost as cheaply as a transistor. Circuit configurations are impressed, hundreds at a time, on the surface of a wafer of silicon; aside from this process, the steps in production are essentially those required in making single devices. Thus, it will be possible to put at a low cost very complicated yet highly reliable electronic equipment almost anywhere—a telephone set, a car, or even a pocket.

I have described briefly the technological advances that I see as shaping the future—cheaper broadband transmission, and a potentiality to provide complicated, cheap, and reliable terminal equipment through microelectronics—but I have not said what we will do with these tools, because I do not fully know how they will be used. I do feel, however, that their impact can be described as a general broadening of and an increase in our use of electrical communications.

Initially, in primitive electrical communication, we dealt with two apparently distinct inventions: the telegraph and the telephone. As we look back at the early telephone and the early telegraph, we see that they were as specialized as they were simply because of the limitations of the electrical art of that day. But the telephone and the telegraph were not entirely separate even then. Alexander Graham Bell discovered the telephone while working toward a harmonic telegraph, in which different distinct signals would be conveyed over the same pair of wires by electrical tones of different frequencies or pitches. Still, for a long time there seemed to be some sort of intellectual or electrical distinction between the sorts of signals that one used for telegraphy and telephony.

If we look at the nervous system of man, we find no such distinction. The nerve impulses involved in the senses of touch, sight, hearing, smell, and taste are all the same distinct spikelike electrical signals. They do not differ in quality. There is a uniform medium through which all our senses serve us.

The difference among the senses lies in the pickup organs, which are responsive to light or sound or touch, and in the interpretation we make of the signals we receive in our central nervous system. The human body uses this common communication system not only for its senses but in all its muscular activity as well. We simply are not built with separate and different communication networks for separate kinds of communication.

As the technologies of the telephone and the telegraph advanced, the distinction between them became vague. Telegraph signals were multiplexed, or transmitted many at a time, over telephone lines in much the way that Alexander Graham Bell had envisioned in his work on the harmonic telegraph. Finally, it became clear that telephone signals could be transmitted by off-on impulses, by a method which we call PCM or pulse code modulation. PCM is now coming into increasing use in the telephone system. Only since 1948, however, when Claude Shannon derived his mathematical theory of communication—has there been a broad, coherent, and useful theory of the process of communication that includes the telephone, the telegraph, and all other means of communication.

Through Shannon's work, our intellectual conception of communication has finally caught up to what has always existed in the nervous system—a common sort of communication for all modalities of sense. Our conception of communication has also come to fit what has increasingly existed in electrical communication systems—circuits that can be used interchangeably for telegraph, voice, or picture signals. We are now achieving, both conceptually and practically, something approaching the universality in electrical communication that was built into the communicating senses of man even before he had learned to talk and to write. As we know from our experience, man uses all forms of communication simultaneously, and in a supplementary rather than a divided manner. This is reflected in his nervous system and in the results of experiments that psychologists have made concerning the interaction of the various modalities of human communication.

The modern communication network transmits indifferently the signals we associate with the primitive telegraph, those we associate with the primitive telephone, and a great many other more complicated signals that have come into being through automatic switching, through facsimile and telephotograph transmission, through television transmission, through writing at a distance by means of telewriters, through high-fidelity and stereophonic speech and music.

In the future we can expect many new signals and many new uses of communication. Whatever these may be, we can be sure of two things. Modern electrical communication networks will be adaptable to the transmission of all of these forms of communication. Shannon's general theory of communication will be a common measure and tool for studying and relating all these forms of communication.

What will these new forms of communication be? I have already mentioned the possibility of greatly improved mobile telephony—car telephones and even pocket telephones. Microelectronics promises to provide complicated but economical equipment for such purposes. Of course, such service could only be realized if adequate frequencies were assigned for such use.

But future communications will embrace much more than voice. The Bell System is engaged in a determined effort to introduce person-to-person television or *picturephone* service on a large scale, to see if there is a real public demand for it. Facsimile may have an increasing use for business and library purposes. Even telewriting may find its place in connection with conferences and lectures convened through electrical communication rather than physical travel. Certainly, in conferences as in a two-party communication, we will want to make data available and to send letters and reports by means of data transmission. Indeed, I believe that within a few years virtually all business records and correspondence will be put into machine-readable form when first typed. If this is done, it will be possible to send text from office to office with the speed and ease of making a telephone call.

Furthermore, computers can index and search machine-readable material; they can be used in editing and correcting texts without complete retyping; they can even be used to a degree in proofreading. From a corrected machine-readable copy, computers can automatically produce printed material, correctly paginated and with justified lines. They can also construct charts, graphs, and line drawings, and insert them at specified points in the text. Thus, computers will take care of a great deal of office drudgery. And, by means of electrical communication, offices will be linked to other offices, to files, to reproduction facilities, and to other resources.

This linkage will extend through other business activities as well. The *touch-tone®* telephone set generates signals that, unlike dial pulses, can travel over any voice circuit, to any distant place. The *touch-tone* keyboard can, therefore, be used to query computers or to control machinery wherever the telephone can reach. This is already in limited use in banking and merchandising.

The computer can reply to queries in spoken words. At present, these words are recorded words, and voice recording is an inefficient means of information storage, alien to the digital computer. But there are good prospects that computers will be able to read aloud intelligibly from phonetically spelled data stored in their memories.

In the future, we may be able to query, from a distance, any number of information sources about weather, hotels, stores, sports, theaters, or other matters, and receive specific voice replies. We may even make such queries in simple English via a keyboard. As the computer will be able to respond to only simple, unambiguous questions, it will sometimes misunderstand or fail to understand. If it replies amiss or says that it did not understand the query, we will be able to try again, perhaps in words suggested by the computer.

Thus, the messages we receive from computers may be printed data, spoken words, diagrams, or drawings. While we may receive these by television or facsimile, we will in some cases have small local computers that can make drawings from concise and easily transmitted instructions received from afar. This will greatly reduce the cost of "transmitting" complicated pictorial material.

I have tried to sketch a few sorts of communication of the future; I am sure that I have missed many more. They are, however, all a part of one general trend—the *generalization* of communication, in the sense that human nerves have a generalized transmission function that is utilized in all our senses and powers.

Science and technology will increase the capacity of our common-carrier communication networks to provide all sorts of communication over the same channels. Microelectronics and other advances will provide terminal equipment or transducers that will link this network to all our senses and to a growing variety of uses.

What this will do to our life I can only guess. It will certainly provide an environment as different from the present as the pre-telephone world. Hopefully in the future we will be able to live where we like, travel chiefly for pleasure, and communicate to work; perhaps this is too optimistic. The certainty is that science provides an understanding that is alien to everyday life. We understand little in this way, but what little understanding we have is extremely powerful. Through research and development, this understanding has so altered our environment that we live lives that are essentially different from those of earlier generations. Science and technology are now creating, through advances in communications as well as many other fields, an entirely new environment in which life will again be different. As always, man will adapt to this world by apprenticeship, by the same sort of learning without understanding that enables him to speak and to walk. The man who successfully lives in the world of the future need not understand that world in the sense of scientific understanding, but it is the understanding of science that is bringing that world into being.

in my opinion...

Communication, or rather the lack of it, has been one of the most difficult problems of mankind's history. Imagine how many wars and loss of lives have resulted from poor communication! To simplify matters, consider the communication problems between two individuals. It is so easy for individual "A" to provoke individual "B" whether "A" uses his voice, eyes, or physical movements. If one individual misunderstands the meaning of a single word uttered by another, their relationship can be instantly thrown into chaos. Now, to understand the magnitude of this problem, multiply it by the 3.3 billion people living on earth today using hundreds of completely different languages! Essentially, almost all other problems facing man today (large or small) originate or result from the problem of lack of communication. It is logical that if we can solve our communication problem we will be on our way to eliminating many of our other problems. For this reason we must attempt to learn how to improve communications.

Scientists and technicians are deeply involved in the search for efficient solutions to our problem. The most promising of these solutions would be the development of a language-translating computer which would work as a central brain for the world, converting everything into a universal language. The problem here is not the computer (we already have computers capable of doing just this if we program them correctly), but rather the fact that we still do not *understand* our own languages. Communications expert John R. Pierce says that an accurate grammar is necessary for the computer to translate truthfully, but linguists cannot supply satisfactory grammar for any language. Because we do not understand how we construct grammatical sentences we cannot program a computer to do it! Another solution would be the use of extrasensory perception which the Rand Corporation has predicted by the year 2020.

Regretfully, this area cannot be covered in more detail because of lack of available information.

Maybe we will not *understand* well enough to communicate efficiently by the twenty-first century, but let's not get discouraged. Many preliminary means of communication must be tested and used in order to progress. Such things as satellite and laser communications, computers and microelectronics might be as common in fifty years as the telephone is today. They will act as stepping stones to more complete communications. Science may develop different types of communication networks capable of dealing with all our senses, thus providing the individual with a better means of communicating with other individuals. This would, of course, extend to better understanding among communities, cities, states, nations and complete continents. In my opinion, better communications is a major key to worldwide peace and understanding. It may not come in the twenty-first century, but someday (through more efforts on the part of present-day man and probably further evolution on his part), complete communications will come—it's only a matter of time.

robert scott thomas

questions

1. "Language is central to our life and thought. Yet in the sense that we use *understanding* in science, we do not understand language." What effect does this paradox mentioned by Pierce have on international politics?

2. Dr. Pierce states that "television is the greatest unifying force ever to act upon man." What are the negative and positive aspects of this force?

3. Arthur C. Clarke announced recently that the government of India expects to cover that country with education programs carried by communications satellites and television receivers in each town and village. The system is expected to become operative within the next three years. What are some of the results that might occur?

4. The enormous impact of television news broadcasts has created considerable discussion. How can the power of the TV screen be regulated without destroying our constitutional guaranty of freedom of the press?

5. This article concentrates on electronic communications. What other methods of communication may become a part of living in the 21st century?

8.
cornucopia of tomorrow? ocean- ography

OCEANOGRAPHY

roger revelle

introduction and comment by geraldine a. haynie

Seventy-one percent of the earth is covered by ocean! If we learn to understand and control this vast, strange expanse, the earth's populace could enjoy a better standard of living. While the ocean will not satisfy the total of man's needs, it can supplement the land.

Even if population control is successful, it is estimated that in the year 2000, there will be over five billion inhabitants on the earth—mouths to feed, homes to provide. There is no balance of creature comforts in the world. While many do live in comfort, hordes of human beings suffer from lack of reasonably decent living standards. By using the ocean to the utmost, there will be sufficient room for everyone. Future generations will enjoy better lives because the present generation is making a commitment to reverse some of the old destructive ecological mistakes. We must work with enthusiasm to reach a true balance of nature. We have been taking what we want with little thought that perhaps our grandchildren will have no fuel or clean water.

It is nearly impossible to fathom the space required to house five billion people. It is a problem situation, requiring immediate solutions. Buckminster Fuller, for example, foresees a tremendous potential for living on floating cities. Pilot projects are being built in such overpopulated countries as Japan. Such a city offers most of the conveniences of a land city. Power is provided by atomic energy. The generous water supply is desalinated by the atomic generators which also provide heat. Since the city is anchored in the ocean, boating will become a major form of transportation as well as an amusement. Boats will be used for travel to the degree that cars are used today. If man works at all, he might run his own boat the short distance to land, or ride the municipal shuttle boat. This aquatic city will be built in a tetrahedron shape with sufficient room for many families; we will have to overcome the customary idea of a home to be content on the ocean. There would not be green lawns or spacious yards, yet for those now living in poor conditions, this ocean home will appear spacious indeed. These are the people who will benefit most.

In the past we have used newly-mined mineral resources without regard for the future. We now realize that we must economize for the sake of generations to come, and that while the ocean is a vast treasure house of all kinds of natural wealth it will become depleted unless we show regard for the finite nature of these resources.

Efforts are being made to recycle discarded metal products. This procedure eliminates the need for disposing of this kind of debris as well as for preserving the metal for another generation's use.

Our technological knowledge is increasing rapidly. We can apply it to the problem of the advanced utilization of the sea's resources. None of the knowledge will be of value, however, unless every man in every country understands what is required of him and is willing to accept his role as a world citizen.

Roger Revelle, Assistant Director of Research at the Scripps Institute of Oceanography, describes the enormous potential of the oceans in the selection that follows.

g.a.h.

OCEANOGRAPHY

Roger Revelle has spent his adult life in research and teaching
in oceanography and geology. He received his Ph.D. from the
University of California, and honorary degrees from Pomona
College, 1957, Harvard, 1964, and Carleton College, 1966.
He has been Director of the Harvard Center for Population
Studies since 1964. Trustee of Scripps Clinic and Research
Foundation (1960–1966), he has also headed the Geophysics
Department for the Naval Reserve and was a member of panels
on pollution and on world population and food supplies of the
President's Science Advisory Committee. In addition, he is a
member of the National Academy of Sciences, American Academy
of Arts and Sciences and a Fellow of the San Diego Society
of Natural History. Recipient of United States and foreign
awards, Professor Revelle is doing research in physical
oceanography, geology of the sea floor and population studies.

What will we be doing in the ocean fifty years from now? One
answer is simple: Everything we are doing today. We will fish,
swim, and dive in it, sail on it, pollute it, study and measure it,
use it for defense and military operations, drill and mine it for
petroleum, natural gas, and minerals, obtain fresh water and other
chemicals from solution, farm it, and use it as a pasture for
protein production.

The major difference in these activities will be that some of
them will be conducted on a far larger scale than today. Much
of the entire ocean will be used by man, and not simply, as at
present, chiefly the inshore and coastal waters. But even in the
21st century the ocean areas near land will still be the principal
scene of man's marine activities. This will be so because these are

Reprinted from Toward the Year 2018 *by permission of the Cowles*
Book Company, Inc. Copyright © 1968 by Foreign Policy Association.

the regions where most of the fishes live, where most of the valuable fuel and mineral resources are concentrated, and where it is easiest for people to enjoy themselves in ocean recreation. We will also do some things that are not possible or necessary now. We may be able to change the weather over and in the ocean. We may want to live on it or in it. We may have to install an international system for detecting, identifying, and tracking missile-launching submarines, those most fearsome of all nuclear weapons-delivery systems. We may establish underwater national or international parks and marine wilderness areas. Possibly we will construct and use transoceanic pipelines to carry fossil fuels and other bulk cargoes.

boundaries will be pushed seaward

The likely expansion of existing activities and the creation of new ones will require far-reaching changes in the law of the sea and the public order of the oceans. Perhaps they will lead to a powerful and multifaceted international organization designed to ensure that all mankind can benefit from the sea's resources. The ancient doctrine of *res nullius*—that the resources of the sea are no man's property, and belong to him who captures them—is already being replaced by the concept of *res communis*—that marine resources are the common property of mankind, and should be managed and used in the interests of all.

Around every continent there is a submerged, shallow plain, formed by waves during the Ice Age, when a part of the ocean waters was locked up in the continental glaciers and the sea level was several hundred feet lower than at present. This "continental shelf" varies greatly in width, from a mile or so off Chile and Peru to several hundred miles off East and Southeast Asia. On it lie reefs of phosphatic rock, and fossil beaches with placer deposits of tin, diamonds, thorium, and magnetic iron. Beneath it are ancient marine sediments that contain enormous quantities of petroleum, natural gas, sulfur, and salt.

Beyond the shelf the continental platforms extend outward toward the deep sea, gradually deepening down to a mile or more. Like the shelf itself, this "continental slope" is underlain by sedimentary rock, and in many places it may also contain pools of oil, natural gas, and sulfur. Indeed, it has been estimated that as much as half of all the petroleum still remaining in the earth exists in the parts of the continents that lie beneath the ocean, even though these areas are less than a third the size of the dry land areas. The underwater reserves are probably at least 10 billion tons and may be more than 150 billion tons. At present prices, these amounts of oil, when recovered, would be worth from $250 billion to more than $3500 billion. Sixteen percent of world production of oil and gas already comes out of submarine wells, and drilling rigs are operating from the North Sea to the shores of Australia, and from West Africa to Alaska's Cook Inlet. About seventy-five nations are searching for off-shore oil, and production is underway or about to begin in twenty-four others. All this production comes from depths of less than 300 feet, but the technology is rapidly advancing, and drilling in depths from 600 feet to a mile of water will soon become possible.

These technological developments have raised an international political problem of the first magnitude. By accepted international convention, each coastal state has jurisdiction over exploration and recovery of the resources of the "seabed and subsoil" out to the edge of the continental shelf off its shores. But where is the edge? The question is relatively easy to answer when, as in the case of the North Sea, shallow water extends all the way from one coastal nation to another. The median line between two nations marks the limit of jurisdiction of each. In most places, however, the nations and their bordering shelves are separated by wide and deep ocean basins. The convention provides that the shelf extends out and down to the depths where exploitation is possible. Because it is likely that technology will soon be available for economic recovery of minerals at the greatest ocean depths, it is not hard to imagine the nations extending their claims out to the midline of the ocean basins that separate them, and thus attempting to establish sovereignty over areas vastly larger than their own land areas. The position is somewhat similar to that which existed before the Northwest Ordinance of 1787, when some of the former Thirteen Colonies declared that their boundaries extended between two parallel lines across the continent from the Atlantic to the Pacific.

Beside the obvious threat to the principle of *res communis,* there are two other uncomfortable aspects of this situation. Some former colonial powers, notably France and Britain, have kept possession of small islands throughout the world ocean; under the present convention, the "shelves" off these islands could be taken to extend for thousands of miles in several directions, to the median lines separating them from the continents. Elsewhere, small, sparsely populated coastal states can claim jurisdiction over very large areas. By leasing exploration and exploitation rights to corporations from the advanced nations, they may obtain huge royalties that will be used, if past experience with Saudi Arabia and such "ministates" as Kuwait, Bahrein, and the sultanates of Trucial Oman is a guide, largely for military hardware and conspicuous consumption by a small elite.

In the near future, the problem is likely to be most serious for the continental slope at depths from 600 to more than 6,000 feet. Off Africa, the slope covers a greater area than the continental shelf, though, on a worldwide basis, it is somewhat narrower than the shelf. An apparently rich and extensive deposit of metallic sulfide ores has been discovered recently in a mile-deep depression in the Red Sea about half way between Saudi Arabia and Ethiopia. Under what legal arrangements should it be exploited? Over a longer time horizon, deep salt-domes of the Gulf of Mexico (which probably contain sulfur and petroleum deposits) and the cobalt-, copper-, and nickel-rich manganese nodules of the deep-sea floor may be of real concern.

use of resources poses problems

The problem of the "shelves" of oceanic islands can probably be solved by accommodation among the great powers, but the question of the optimum use of the resources of the continental slopes and the deep-sea floor is a far more difficult one that may take several decades to resolve. If the less-developed nations are to gain much real benefit from these resources, it may be necessary to place them under the jurisdiction of an international agency that could grant exclusive licenses for exploration and exploitation in return for a share of the proceeds. Such an agency would need to be able to take decisive action in accordance with principles of economics and equity, and with due regard to the major interests involved, but without the international logrolling that stultifies many existing United Nations organizations. It should probably be newly created within the United Nations family. Perhaps it could best be governed by a board of directors representing major continental areas, rather than individual nations.

A new "International Ocean Agency" might gradually assume five other functions: conservation of high-seas fisheries; establishment of regulations to prevent pollution by tankers and other ships at sea; surveillance of nuclear submarines; promotion of international cooperation in oceanography; and equitable control of large-scale modifications of ocean weather.

By the beginning of the 21st century, it may be possible to

increase the harvest of ocean fish and other animals fourfold, from about 50 million tons gathered at present to 200 million tons, if present annual rates of growth can be maintained. This may require major advances in fisheries technology aimed at harvesting and processing many varieties of small fish that are not now taken, plus the "krill," or large planktonic crustacea of the Antarctic Ocean, that were the principal food of whales before these giant animals were virtually exterminated by a ruthless and short-sighted fishery. To sustain such a large catch will certainly require more effective international regulation of fishing industries than has been possible under present arrangements. To ensure economic returns and technological advances, these regulations may need to include control of entry into different fisheries, as well as catch limitations. The history of the whaling industry since World War II is a sorry example of the ineffectiveness of present international arrangements. Because the International Whaling Commission had no real authority, and could operate only by securing unanimous agreement among its member nations, it was impossible to limit the catch of any one species, but only, instead, the total weight taken from all species hunted by the fishery. The result was that the largest, and therefore most desirable, species was almost eliminated before the whalers turned their attention to the next largest, and so on through each of the species involved. Now, the numbers of all species have been driven down to such a low level that the prospects of recovery of the populations within the next fifty years is tragically slight.

mariculture—the farming of the future

Part of the anticipated increase in the marine harvest will come from ocean farming, primarily in estuaries and other near-shore areas. The Japanese have already had considerable success in growing oysters, and have made a beginning with shrimps and other crustaceans. In oyster farming, they have managed to increase the productivity of an acre of marine land from twenty-five- to fifty-fold, from around 500 pounds of animal tissue per acre to between 15,000 and 30,000 pounds. One of the keys to this success has been their practice of attaching the oysters to long ropes hanging from buoys, both to avoid predators and to use the entire volume of the ocean and not just the bottom. Using somewhat similar techniques, Italian mussel farmers have obtained yields of hundreds of tons per acre.

These results suggest that we need to think of mariculture in quite a different way than agriculture. In modern farming on land, large quantities of chemical fertilizers are added to the soil, and plant crops use these nutrients. In the case of marine farming, the ocean can provide not chemical fertilizer for plants but food for animals, that is, the plankton—tiny floating plants and animals —the animals we want to harvest feed upon. This means that the areas most useful for mariculture are not those that can be enclosed or fenced in and fertilized with chemicals, but rather those in which there is a continual through-put of plankton carried by tidal and other inshore currents past the locality where the animal crop is being grown.

Although mariculture will undoubtedly grow in importance in the future, particularly if it can be mechanized, the large-scale development of the living resources of the sea will probably depend to a much greater extent on range or pasture management, of somewhat the same kind as now practiced over many land areas in raising cattle and sheep. In the pastures of the sea, we should harvest a balanced catch of different fish species at the same ecological level and control the populations of unusable species, just as the manager of a livestock range tries to make sure that the cattle graze on both wanted and unwanted plants and controls the population of other animals that compete with the cattle for food. Control of predators is desirable in both land and sea pastures, as is improvement of the breeds of cattle and of such self-corralling fishes as salmon and other anadromous species. Both kinds of pastures may be made more productive by spraying them with relatively small quantities of minor nutrients, such as cobalt-containing compounds. In the ocean pastures, we may be able eventually to increase plankton production and, hence, the fishes' food supply, by changing circulation patterns or speeding up the vertical interchange of surface water and deep nutrient-containing water.

pollution increases foreseen

As recent accidents have shown, the likelihood of widespread pollution of the sea surface and beaches by the wrecking of the new large tankers is rapidly increasing with the growth of ocean oil transport. These new sources add to the old problem of pollution from the fuel tanks of ordinary cargo vessels.

To prevent tanker pollution, it may be necessary to prescribe the routes and destinations of these monster vessels, and to insist that they load and unload by means of underwater pipelines at a considerable distance from land. Special navigational facilities and means for monitoring their passage at all points, similar to those used for airplanes over the United States, may be required, and these could well be administered by the proposed International Ocean Agency. An alternative would be to abandon tankers altogether, and to transport oil through pipelines installed on the sea floor across the ocean basins. Some rough cost calculations indicate that such pipelines could be economically competitive with the largest present tankers.

undersea 'radar network'

Nuclear-powered missile-launching submarines are today a major component of the deterrent forces that maintain the balance of terror between the Soviet Union and the United States. Because of their mobility and invisibility, they have the great advantage that "first-strike" or "counter-force" weapons cannot be used effectively against them, and hence their response in a nuclear confrontation can be both delayed and measured. Thus, in a sense, they have much positive value in peacekeeping between the two superpowers.

But the seemingly inevitable proliferation of atomic weapons will almost certainly be accompanied by a similar proliferation of nuclear submarines. When many nations possess both these objects, submarine mobility and invisibility will change from a dubious blessing into an undoubted nightmare. The possibilities of international mischief-making by a smaller power deploying its submarines in distant waters are unpleasant to think about. One possible solution may be the establishment of an international surveillance system consisting of a network of underwater sound devices, possibly augmented by lasers, which would detect, identify, and track all large submerged vehicles at all times, much as objects in outer space are tracked today. This process of making the ocean "transparent" could well be one of the prime functions of the International Ocean Agency.

an unlimited horizon in technology

Oceanography can be defined in various ways: as the scientific study of the part of the earth that is covered by seawater, or, more broadly, as those activities within the ocean that have significant scientific or technological content.

A host of new instruments and new methods are on the horizon that could lead to an explosive growth in oceanography during the next several decades. Among these are: computers to investigate complex hydrodynamic models and to handle large quantities of data; worldwide navigational systems using satellites and ground-based radio stations that allow a ship almost anywhere to locate itself within a few hundred feet; new submersible vehicles of various kinds; the so-called man-in-the-sea programs, started by the French and now being vigorously pursued in the United States, which look forward to men living in the ocean for extended periods—going down even to great depths in the sea and staying there for weeks or months on end; the possibility of anchoring a network of instrumented buoys in mid-ocean that will make continuous observations over extended periods; the use of satellites to study the near-surface waters and the overlying atmospheric cloud patterns; free-floating and bottom-mounted instruments; the many scientific uses of underwater sound and the possible use of lasers to multiply the distance at which underwater objects can be seen, and, most exciting of all to geologists, the possibility of drilling and sampling the entire column of seafloor sediments and the underlying rocks.

cooperation among nations needed

Just as all men breathe the same air, and a storm over New England may have begun off Japan, so the ocean waters are indivisible, and events in one part of the sea eventually have effects at great distances. Oceanography is thus not only a natural field of international scientific cooperation, but also such cooperation is necessary if human understanding of the oceans is to keep pace with human needs. Only in this way can the knowledge required for improvements in long-range weather forecasting, development of ocean fisheries on a worldwide basis, better routing of merchant vessels, greater national security, and rational solutions of international controversies about ocean resources be obtained at a minimum cost to all interested nations.

Many marine problems demand international cooperation for their effective investigation, particularly in cases where:

¶ The scale of research is greater than can be mobilized by any one of the nations concerned.
¶ The research involves a greater diversity of scientific competence or facilities than possessed by any one of the interested nations.

¶ Solution of a problem requires access to data and experience possessed by several nations (for example, the assessment of the condition of a fish stock exploited by many nations requires the pooling of information).

¶ The cost-effectiveness of the research for each nation can be substantially increased by joining forces in an international operation (this is the case in nearly all multiship international investigations).

¶ The subject of research is affected by activities or laws of another nation (for example, many interesting geological features of the sea floor extend offshore from the coasts of different countries across the continental shelf).

¶ There is special need to reach agreement on the employment of comparable methods of research (an ocean-wide study of primary organic production by standard methods could probably be accomplished only through international cooperation).

¶ There is a need to establish mutual confidence in observations or analyses bearing on particular problems of international action (for example, when stock assessments have revealed a need for regulation of exploitation, as in the case of Antarctic whales, appraisal of the effects of alternative regulations requires joint analysis of biological statistics by scientists serving in an international capacity).

Among the most obvious reasons for international oceanographic cooperation is the need for taking censuses of fish populations in the world ocean. No one really knows how many fish there are in the sea, nor how rapidly they can reproduce themselves.

Some species of fishes and invertebrates of the high seas wander over great distances, and their distribution and abundance change with changes in the oceanic environment. To find the sizes, distribution, and interrelationships of these populations is important to the rapid development and indispensable for the conservation of world fisheries.

A second area where international cooperation is essential is in the making of systematic surveys of the shape of the deep-sea floor. At present, our maps of the deep ocean are about equal in accuracy and detail to the maps of the land published 200 years ago. The task of making ocean maps will require the continuous operation over several decades of a dozen or more specially equipped vessels, and an international navigation network. If this great task can be shared among all interested nations, the expenses to any one nation will not be burdensome.

weather forecasting can be improved

Recent meteorological studies show that changes in world weather patterns over periods of weeks to many years are closely related to changes in the temperature of the ocean waters. Because the sea behaves more sluggishly than the air, studies of these changes may make it possible to improve the accuracy of long-range weather forecasts. The present accuracy is low, but if it could be increased, great economic benefits would follow—for example, in planting and harvesting crops, in planning seasonal fuel transportation and storage, in the timing of building and road construction, and in flood and drought protection. In the United States alone, a real improvement in the accuracy of long-range weather forecasting could produce savings of billions of dollars every year.

Measurements at numerous points over vast areas are required to study the changes in the sea and the air. At the present time, no nation by itself has enough research ships or oceanographers to make all the needed measurements. Cooperation among oceanographers and meteorologists of different nations is essential.

the sea will become a playground

One of the most important uses of the ocean in the future will be for recreation. Much of this will be in the near-shore zone. In many parts of the world the shoreline needs to be stretched, or "wrinkled," in order to make it much longer than at present. This could be done by building peninsulas and offshore bars and islands, and by dredging estuaries and bays. But our knowledge of the oceanic processes that stabilize shorelines is still far from adequate to allow us to build and maintain such structures inexpensively and effectively.

The development of small submarines for recreational, scientific, and engineering purposes, and the man-in-the-sea programs are liable to change our very attitude toward the ocean. We human beings are land animals, even though the salt in our blood tells us that our remote ancestors were sea creatures. The sea surface has always been a nearly impenetrable curtain for us, whether we were on a ship at sea or looking at the wavy surface of the ocean from the beach. The new capacity to move and live under water will give us new insights and new interests—a feeling of being at home in the great volume of the ocean, and a capacity for thinking about the interior of the sea as a place for man.

Unlike space exploration, which can be indulged in only by a few men with enormous resources at their disposal, the voyage to inner space may turn out to be comparatively inexpensive. Before the turn of the century, it may be possible for anyone with about $5,000 to have his own submarine, which will go down to depths of several miles. There may be hordes of moderately well-to-do amateurs in small submersibles—perhaps getting in the way of scientific submarines; perhaps making new discoveries on their own; certainly getting into trouble at various times; in any case requiring many new developments of undersea technology to take care of them.

advances in marine sciences

Because the oceans are so vast and so little known, almost any nation that borders on the sea can make important contributions to oceanography, even with a modest effort. Oceanography deals with a familiar and visible, yet mysterious, part of the real world, consequently it is an easily understood kind of science, well suited to creating public understanding of the purposes and methods of scientific research. At the same time, the less developed nations need to learn a great deal about their bordering seas, as a basis for conservation and full development of their fisheries, and for many other purposes. But many of these nations are too small or too poor to be able to afford a sufficiently broad and strong oceanographic institution. Through the mechanisms of international collaboration, the oceanographic institutions of the rich nations can provide facilities and intellectual back-up to the scientists in the poor nations and work with them on their national problems.

International scientific cooperation in the marine sciences would be greatly strengthened by the creation of an effective and adequately budgeted international oceanographic organization on a worldwide scale. Because ocean science and technology, like agricultural research, must be mainly supported by governments, the basic international oceanographic organization should be intergovernmental, and, consequently, the proposed new International Ocean Agency might assume responsibility for planning and coordinating oceanographic cooperation as one of its functions.

In its scientific activities it would need a counterpart controlled by scientists and speaking with the voice of science rather than of governments. This might take the form of an international union of marine sciences, which could be one of the constituent Unions of the International Council of Scientific Unions. Two of its purposes would be to help marine scientists talk to each other through scientific meetings and publications and to develop the scientific infrastructure of standards, nomenclature, bibliographies, information exchange, and intercalibration of methods. But it would have another, more important objective, and that would be to exert an influence for scientific integrity and imaginative change on the International Ocean Agency. Like the players in "Hamlet," the principal task of a private world organization of oceanographers would be "to catch the conscience of the King."

We need to think about more than observation and measurement, or theory and understanding, or even forecasting and prediction. What can be done to control or change the ocean? There are many possibilities for both small- and large-scale changes.

Off the coast of California, most of the water is too cold to swim in. It may be possible to warm it up, particularly in the near-shore zone, by using waste heat from the large nuclear power plants of the future—plants that will generate many thousand megawatts of power. If a way could be found to keep a 200-meter-wide ribbon of water near the beach warm enough for comfort, the new recreational areas that could be developed might be worth a good many millions of dollars.

A first-order change might be brought about by spreading thin particles of reflecting materials near the sea surface in the areas of generation of tropical storms or hurricanes, in such a way as to prevent overheating, during the summer time, of the waters near the surface in these areas. There might be two consequences, one favorable and one unfavorable: (1) hurricanes might be prevented from forming, and (2) there might be a sharp decrease in rainfall over large land areas. Another possibility of the same kind, in reverse, would be to decrease the reflectivity of the earth and thereby increase solar heating by spreading a thin powder of nonreflecting materials over ice- or snow-covered areas. The potentialities for spreading small amounts of light-reflecting or absorbing materials over large regions will probably be considerably greater in the future.

These potentialities should be exploited with great caution, and only after we have gained much more understanding than we now possess of oceanic and atmospheric processes, so that we can predict all the probable consequences of our actions. Even under the best of circumstances, however, there are liable to be both favorable and unfavorable effects. Some people will be benefited and others will be worse off than they would have been if the natural processes had not been modified. The possibility of stopping hurricane formation, described above, is an example. Many lives might be saved and much property damage prevented, but the reduction in rainfall might bring serious losses to farmers. Here the International Ocean Agency might find its most important task—to make sure that the real benefits from ocean weather modification significantly exceed the real costs, and to arrange means for compensating those individuals and groups who suffer losses.

in my opinion...

There is a promise of better days to come for mankind. Perhaps a great hope for survival can be found in the oceans. We are willing to spend billions of dollars to explore outer space; it would seem more reasonable to spend whatever may be needed to develop areas in our own atmosphere, admittedly polluted, but still more familiar to us than moon dust and space suits. There is limitless wealth in and on the ocean, waiting to be used to man's advantage.

Education in things oceanic is primary. We need to understand this new world before we can seek out its possibilities. We must not waste the oceans as we have done the land. Discretion must be used to tap this wealth in a most frugal and practical manner. Logically, governments will set up international agencies which will work with science to determine lawful and fair boundaries. We would hope this action will avoid jealousy or infringement on other countries' rights. It would be to everyone's benefit if scientists from all nations pool their knowledge and efforts, thereby expanding and accelerating man's ultimate use of the ocean. Since events in one part of the seas affect all parts, such groups are necessary to explore in an economical way and to control the ocean and all it contains. It is possible that countries previously impoverished will find new pride in wealth found along their shores. Great stores of metals and minerals are found in natural deposits and much is washed down from the land by rivers and streams to collect on the ocean floor. Science will need to develop specific methods to retrieve these assets efficiently.

Science will expand its knowledge regarding currents and sea conditions, and how they indicate natural resources. It will be possible to determine successfully where and how man can live in and on the ocean. Weather forecasting is feasible as an aid to accurate farming seasons and industrial efforts. Nations from various parts of the earth will have to be involved to make any efforts in this area worthwhile. Defense will be simplified through checks by international governmental organizations, and more sophisticated technological equipment will assure mankind some measure of protection from any would-be aggressor by worldwide surveillance. Subsurface craft already have the potential of reaching great distances without frequent contact with conventional bases. When sea-bases are established, such craft will have unlimited range and capability.

Water is of such great value that wars have been fought for its possession. Imagine the impact of abundant desalinated water on a country which previously could not feed its people. Imagine the self-respect people will develop for themselves as nations and as individuals, growing crops on their own land instead of accepting humiliating arrangements made by wealthier countries on their behalf. This will be possible with sufficient water and fertilizer produced from unplatable fish and seaweed. With education, man can learn to enjoy products of the sea; he must and will adapt. He will learn to enjoy foods which are not presently part of his diet. He must take seriously the need to overcome these inhibitions if he is to enjoy future generations on this earth. There are many strange types of fish and sea creatures which are not only nutritious, but also quite palatable. For example, some countries enjoy national dishes made from algae and seaweed. The more affluent nations will have to participate in experimental foods also, or they may find themselves nutritionally poor.

The sea is the answer. Name any of man's most pressing problems, and the sea offers a solution. It is waiting for future-oriented minds to seek the answers it holds.

geraldine a. haynie

questions

1. Professor Revelle suggests the utilization of a new "International Ocean Agency" under the aegis of the United Nations as an overseeing agency for the world's oceans. What factors would determine the effectiveness of the new agency?

2. Are those nations which are landlocked entitled to a share in ocean wealth? Why?

3. Since oceans are bordered by many nations, what steps should be taken to protect against pollution?

4. What conditions would be necessary in order to develop our ocean wealth for the greatest possible benefit of mankind?

5. If you were a government planner, what justification could you give for spending more money on ocean research than on space travel?

9.

how far to where? space travel

TO THE STARS

arthur c. clarke

introduction and comment by john r. balfour

In looking at where we have been, it is rather difficult to guess where we are going. Man has had a great history of dreams, and as time passes, more and more of these dreams have become reality, as everyday as opening his eyes in the morning. It seems that we have quite an accelerated rate of fulfillment which leads to the question: what are man's limitations? We see a creature with unlimited wants and limited resources, but how limited are these resources? Fifty years ago who would have thought of having television, or an automatic dishwasher? Man seems to have the knack for taking on ideas and making them into solid objects. Thus, we seem to have had at some time, someone who, just "because they were there," wanted to reach for the stars.

The idea of space travel isn't really new, however; few years have passed since man first left earth and its atmosphere. It was a well-known "fact" that man would never fly, but we have received television pictures from the moon taken by men whom our technology has put there. Mars will be one of our next targets, and it's just a matter of time before we have a president phoning person-to-person to Pluto, his call relayed by Bell Telephone of Jupiter. We know we can do it, which is almost saying it is done. But what next? Will man be satisfied with nine planets travelling around a mediocre-sized star? What are the possibilities in terms of distance? Our closest neighbor is 4.3 light-years away, which is quite a contrast to the few light-hours distance to Pluto; with the speeds of our present-day space craft, we would hardly say it is worth leaving earth. Such a journey, according to Clarke, would take an estimated million years.

It is new ideas that we will make for our future journeys. Many of those laws, inventions, techniques and designs have never even been considered. Power is one problem, speed, another; but the most important problem is time. Can we risk sending a man to a star only to find that—as Clarke mentions—it has been colonized by much faster ships launched years after his departure? Our knowledge is increasing at such a swift rate that computers, highways, cars, books and varied electronic equipment are obsolete before completion and distribution. The idea does rather leave us open to the future with no visible end in sight. How far will man go in his reach for the stars?

Arthur C. Clarke, author of several dozen fiction and non-fiction volumes on space and the future, possesses the astounding ability to predict scientific progress. In *The Exploration of Space,* published in 1951, a description under an illustration reads:

The little rocket (the last step of a far larger machine) left the Earth 250 days ago and during that time has been coasting freely, like a comet, along the path that leads to Mars with the least expenditure of fuel . . . Under the guidance of a tiny yet extremely complex electronic brain, the missile is now surveying the planet at close quarters. A camera is photographing the landscape below, and the resulting pictures are being transmitted to the distant Earth along a narrow radio beam . . .

This is the Arthur Clarke who, in the chapter that follows, discusses man's future in space.

j.r.b.

TO THE STARS

Arthur C. Clarke, who took first class honors at King's College, University of London, is one of the best-known science fiction writers of this century. During his Royal Air Force service in World War II, he served as technical officer in charge of the first experimental "ground-controlled approach" unit. He proposed the use of synchronous satellites for communication as early as 1945 in an article in Wireless World. *He is a member of the Royal Astrological Society in Britain and the International Academy of Astronautics, and wrote the script for the film* 2001: A Space Odyssey *with Stanley Kubrick. Some 5 million of his books have sold in 20 languages; more than 300 articles and short stories have appeared in* Horizon, Holiday, Harper's, Playboy, New York Times Magazine, Vogue, Life *and others. His books of fiction include* The Sands of Mars, *1951; and* A Fall of Moondust, *1961. Non-fiction work includes* Interplanetary Flight, *1950;* The Exploration of Space, *1951 (a Book-of-the-Month Club selection);* The Challenge of the Spaceship, *1959;* The Coming of the Space Age, *1967, and many others.*

Travel to the stars is not difficult, if one is in no particular hurry. . . . Today's vehicles could send substantial payloads to Proxima Centauri, especially if they went by way of Jupiter. Unfortunately, the voyage would take the better part of a million years.

However, no one doubts that there will be enormous increases in spacecraft velocities, especially when we have discovered really efficient ways of harnessing nuclear energy for propulsion. Theoretically, a rocket operating on the *total* annihilation of matter should be able to approach the speed of light—670 million mph. At the moment, we can reach about 1/20,000 of this figure; clearly, there is plenty of room for improvement.

Let us be very pessimistic and assume that rocket speeds increase tenfold every century. By the year 2000 we will certainly have vehicles which could reach the nearer stars in 100,000 years, carrying really useful payloads of automatic surveying equipment.

But there would be no point in building them, for we could be sure that they would be quickly overtaken by the ten-times-faster vehicles we would be building a hundred years later. And so on.

The situation, in round figures, might look something like this:

Launch Date	Time To Proxima Centauri (Years)
2000	100,000
2100	10,000
2200	1,000
2300	100
2400	10

Clearly, there is no point in making anything but paper studies until about the year 2300; but after *that,* it is time to start thinking about action. A wealthy, stable, scientifically advanced society would be accustomed to making hundred-year plans, and it might well consider building space probes to survey the nearer stars, as our Mariners have surveyed Mars and Venus. They would report back along tight laser beams to gigantic reflecting telescopes orbiting the Earth; or they might even come back themselves, loaded with quantities of information too enormous to be transmitted across the light-years in a period less than their own transit time.

This proxy exploration of the universe is certainly one way in which it would be possible to gain knowledge of star systems which lacked garrulous, radio-equipped inhabitants; it might be the only way. For if men, and not merely their machines, are ever to reach the planets of other stars, much more difficult problems will have to be overcome. Yet, they do not appear to be insoluble, even in terms of the primitive technology we possess today.

We will first of all assume—and the evidence is overwhelmingly in favor of this—that it is impossible for any material object to attain the velocity of light. This is not something that can be explained; it is the way that the universe is built. The velocity of light represents a limit which can be more and more closely approached but never reached. Even if all the matter in the cosmos were turned into energy and that energy were all given to a single electron, it would not reach the speed of light, but only 99.999999-9999—and so on, for about 160 digits—per cent of it.

We may eventually be able to build rockets driven by the *total* annihilation of matter, not the mere fraction of a per cent that is all we can convert into energy at present. No one has the faintest idea how this may be done, but it does not involve any fundamental impossibilities. Another idea that had been put forward is that, at very high speeds, it may be possible to use the thin hydrogen gas of interstellar space as fuel for a kind of cosmic, fusion-powered ramjet. This is a particularly interesting scheme, as it would give virtually unlimited range, and remove the restrictions imposed by an on-board propellant supply. If we are optimistic, we may guess (and guessing is all that we can do at this stage) that ultimately speeds of one-tenth of that of light may be attained. Remember that to make even a one-way voyage, this would have to be done *twice*—once to build up velocity, the second time to discard it, which is just as difficult and expensive. (Atmospheric braking is not going to work very well at 70 million mph. Even at 1 g it would take many times the width of the Solar System to slow down from such a speed.)

On this assumption, we will be able to reach the nearer stars in a few decades, but any worthwhile explorations would still have to last thousands of years. This has led some scientists to make the striking pronouncement: Interstellar flight is not an engineering problem, but a medical one.

Suspended animation may be one answer. It requires no great stretch of the imagination to suppose that, with the aid of drugs or low temperatures, men may be able to hibernate for virtually unlimited periods. We can picture an automatic ship with its oblivious crew making the long journey across the interstellar night until, when a new sun was looming up, the signal was sent out to trigger the mechanism that would revive the sleepers. When their survey was completed, they would head back to Earth and slumber again until the time came to awaken once more and greet a world which would regard them as survivors from a distant past.

Another solution was first suggested, to the best of my knowledge, in the 1920's by Professor J. D. Bernal in a long-out-of-print essay, *The World, the Flesh, and the Devil,* which must rank as one of the most outstanding feats of scientific imagination in literature. Even today many of the ideas propounded in this little book have never been fully developed, either in or out of science fiction.

Bernal imagined entire societies launched across space, in gigantic arks which would be closed, ecologically balanced systems. They would, in fact, be miniature planets upon which generations of men would live and die so that one day their remote descendants would return to Earth with the record of their celestial Odyssey.

The engineering, biological, and sociological problems involved in such an enterprise would be of fascinating complexity. The artificial planets (at least several miles in diameter) would have to be completely self-contained and self-supporting, and no material of any kind could be wasted. Commenting on the implications of such closed systems, *Time* magazine's science editor, Jonathan Leonard, once hinted that cannibalism would be compulsory among interstellar travelers. This would be a matter of definition; we crew members of the three-billion-man spaceship Earth do not consider ourselves cannibals, despite the fact that every one of us must have absorbed atoms which once formed part of Caesar and Socrates, Shakespeare, and Solomon.

One cannot help feeling that the interstellar ark on its 1,000-year voyages would be a cumbersome way of solving the problem, even if all the social and psychological difficulties could be overcome. (Would the fiftieth generation still share the aspirations of their Pilgrim Fathers, who set out from Earth so long ago?) There are, however, more sophisticated ways of getting men to the stars than the crude, brute-force methods outlined above.

The ark, with its generations of travelers doomed to spend their entire lives in space, was merely a device to carry germ cells, knowledge, and culture from one sun to another. How much more efficient to send only the cells, to fertilize them automatically some twenty years before the voyage was due to end, to carry the embryos through to birth by techniques already foreshadowed in today's biology labs—and to bring up the babies under the tutelage of cybernetic nurses who would teach them their inheritance and their destiny when they were capable of understanding it.

These children, knowing no parents, or indeed anyone of a different age from themselves, would grow up in the strange artificial world of their speeding ship, reaching maturity in time to explore the planets ahead of them—perhaps to be the ambassadors of humanity among alien races, or perhaps to find, too late, that there was no home for them there. If their mission succeeded, it would be their duty (or that of their descendants, if the first generation could not complete the task) to see that the knowledge they had gained was someday carried back to Earth.

Would any society be morally justified, we may well ask, in

planning so onerous and uncertain a future for its unborn—indeed, unconceived—children? That is a question which different ages may answer in different ways. What to one era would seem a cold-blooded sacrifice might to another appear a great and glorious adventure. There are complex problems here which cannot be settled by instinctive, emotional answers.

At the moment, our whole attitude to the problem of interstellar travel is conditioned by the span of human life. There is no reason whatsoever to suppose that this will always be less than a century, and no one has ever discovered just what it is that makes men die. It is certainly not a question of the body "wearing out" in the sense that an inanimate piece of machinery does, for in the course of a single year almost the entire fabric of the body is replaced by new material. When we have discovered the details of this process, it may be possible to extend the life span indefinitely if so desired—and this would drastically reduce the size of the universe from the psychological point of view.

Whether a crew of immortals, however well balanced and carefully chosen they might be, could tolerate each other's company for several centuries is an interesting subject for speculation. But the mobile worldlet in which they would travel might be larger—and would have incomparably greater facilities in every respect—than the city of Athens, in which small area, it may be recalled, a surprising number of men once led remarkably fruitful lives.

If medical science does not provide the key to the universe, there still remains a possibility that the answer may lie with the engineers. We have suggested that one-tenth of the speed of light may be the best we can ever hope to attain, even when our spacecraft have reached the limit of their development. A number of studies [1] suggest that this is wildly optimistic, but these are based on the assumption that the vehicles have to carry their own energy sources, like all existing rockets. It is at least conceivable that the interstellar ramjet may work, or that it is possible to supply power from an external device, such as a planet-based laser, or that the universe contains still unknown sources of energy which spacecraft may be able to tap. In this case, we may be able to approach much more closely to the speed of light, and the whole situation then undergoes a radical change. We become involved in the so-called time-dilation effect predicted by the Theory of Relativity.

It is impossible to explain *why* this effect occurs without delving into very elementary yet subtle mathematics. (There is nothing at all hard about basic relativity mathematics; most of it is simple

[1] See the papers by Sebastian von Hoerner and Edmund Purcell in the volume *Interstellar Communication,* ed., A. G. W. Cameron (1963).

algebra. The difficulty is all in the underlying concepts.) Nevertheless, even if the explanation must be bypassed, the results of the time-dilation effect can be stated easily enough in nontechnical language.

Time itself is a variable quantity; the rate at which it flows depends upon the speed of the observer. The difference is infinitesimal at the velocities of everyday life, and even at the velocities of normal astronomical bodies. It is all-important as we approach to within a few per cent of the speed of light. To put it crudely, the faster one travels, the more slowly time will pass. At the speed of light, time would cease to exist; the moment "now" would last forever. Let us take an extreme example to show what this implies. If a spaceship left Earth for Proxima Centauri at the speed of light and came back at once at the same velocity, it would have been gone for some eight and a half years according to all the clocks and calendars of Earth. *But the people in the ship, and all their clocks or other time-measuring devices, would have detected no interval at all.* The voyage would have been instantaneous.

This case is not possible, even in theory. But the one that follows does not involve any physical impossibility, though its achievement is so far beyond the bounds of today's—or tomorrow's—technology that it may never be realized in practice. Nevertheless, since it illustrates the working of the universe, it is worth careful study.

Imagine a spaceship that leaves the Earth at a comfortable 1-g acceleration, so that the occupants have normal weight. Today's rockets could maintain this rate for about twenty minutes, but we will assume that our X-powered supership can keep it up indefinately. Its velocity and its distance from Earth would increase as follows:

TABLE 12
1-G VOYAGES

Duration	Velocity, MPH	Distance, Miles
1 hour	80,000	40,000
1 day	192,000	2,300,000
1 week	1,344,000	101,000,000
1 month	5,760,000	2,080,000,000
1 year	70,000,000	305,000,000,000
5 years	350,000,000	7,600,000,000,000
(10 years)	(700,000,000)	(30,500,000,000,000)

The last line of the table is in parentheses, as after ten years at 1-g acceleration the ship would have exceeded the velocity of light (670 million mph) according to this straightforward, nonrelativistic calculation, and this is impossible. It is surprising to see how long it does take, at an acceleration that men can tolerate, to build up interstellar speeds. Even after five years at 1-g, we have reached only half the speed of light—and have traveled less than one-third of the way to the nearest star. But if we want to stop at Proxima Centauri, in a year or two we must start to decelerate, because we need exactly as much time, and space, to slow down as to build up speed.

So even if we had unlimited power, it would take us about fifteen years to reach Proxima Centauri, for reasons that have nothing to do with Einstein and the velocity of light. We could not stand the acceleration required for faster trips unless we spent the whole journey floating in liquid or frozen in blocks of ice.

Of course, we are at liberty to assume that a technology which could attempt such feats might also have a "space drive," which acted upon every atom of matter in its domain, so that it could produce acceleration without any apparent force. As gravity does precisely this, the idea does not violate any known laws. So if we had artificial gravity plus an infinite power source, we could cut our transit time to Proxima Centauri—4.3 light-years away— down to perhaps five years.

But asking for two miracles is a little greedy; let us stick to one, and see what happens when we continue our 1-g acceleration beyond five years, reaching speeds which are now more than 50 per cent of the velocity of light.

What *does* happen now depends on the point of view of the observer. To the people in the ship, the thrust is constant and their instruments tell them that they are gaining 80,000 mph every hour. Everything is perfectly normal.

But an observer back on Earth, if he could look into the ship,[2] would see that something very strange was happening. It would be like watching a film that was slowing down.

When the ship had reached 87 per cent of the speed of light (580 million mph), everything inside it would seem to be taking twice as long as it should from the point of view of the outside observer; two hours of ship time would be only one hour of Earth time. At 98

[2] I am fudging some philosophical points here and hope that relativistic purists will forgive me for describing observations which, even in principle, cannot be performed.

per cent of the speed of light the time rate would be slowed five-fold, at 99.5 per cent tenfold, at 99.99 per cent a hundredfold. Thus the effect increases very rapidly as one nears the velocity of light; but once again it must be emphasized that to the crew of the ship, not only does everything appear normal—everything *is* normal. They are not responsible for the peculiar behavior of the rest of the universe; their clocks and tape measures are just as good as anybody else's.

Only when they had slowed down, turned around, and come home again would they discover any discrepancy, and then they would be confronted with the most famous paradox of the Theory of Relativity. For centuries might have passed on Earth, while they had aged only a few years aboard their speeding ship.

It is not really a paradox, of course; it is the way the universe is built, and we had better accept it. (A tiny minority of mathematicians—Professor Herbert Dingle is their most vehement spokesman—still refuses to accept a universe in which this sort of thing can happen. But the weight of the evidence is against them.)

In 1522 the Western world was suddenly confronted by a paradox which must have seemed equally baffling to many people at the time. Eighteen sailors landed at Seville on a Thursday, whereas by their own careful reckoning it was only Wednesday aboard their ship. Thus they were, in their view, a day younger than the friends they had left behind.

They were the survivors of Magellan's crew—the first men to circumnavigate the world—and they presented the Church with the frightful problem of deciding just when they should have kept the various Saints' days on the latter half of their voyage. Four and a half centuries later, we have learned to get along with the International Date Line, though it is going to cause us more and more trouble with the advent of global television. Perhaps four and a half centuries from now, time dilation will present no greater intellectual difficulties—though it may certainly cause grave social ones, when young astronauts return home to greet their senile great-grandchildren.

The effects that time dilation will produce have been calculated by Dr. von Hoerner for various 1-g round trips, with the fascinating results shown in the table below. It will be seen how spectacularly the time-stretching increases with speed; the power consumption and engineering difficulties, unfortunately, increase even more rapidly. In the opinion of most scientists, Table 13 begins at a level of mere absurdity and swiftly mounts to the utterly preposterous; yet it is (*pace* Professor Dingle) mathematically sound.

TABLE 13
INTERSTELLAR ROUND TRIPS AT CONSTANT 1 G

Duration (Out and Back), Years		Distance Reached, Light-Years
On Board Ship	On Earth	
1	1.0	0.06
2	2.1	0.25
5	6.5	1.7
10	24	10
15	80	37
20	270	137
25	910	455
30	3,100	1,560
40	36,000	17,500
50	420,000	208,000
60	5,000,000	2,470,000

(Adapted from Sebastian von Hoerner, "The General Limits of Space Travel," in Interstellar Communication, *ed. A. G. W. Cameron, N.Y., 1963.)*

Similar results have been calculated by Dr. Carl Sagan in a paper with the forthright and uncompromising title, "Direct Contact Among Galactic Civilizations by Relativistic Interstellar Spaceflight," the gist of which will be found in his book (with I. S. Shklovskii) *Intelligent Life in the Universe*. Dr. Sagan takes these ideas quite seriously and concludes that as far as energy requirements are concerned, there are no fundamental objections to high-speed (near-light-velocity) travel to the stars.

As a final example of the time-dilation effect, which also gives some idea of the energy requirements, it would be rather difficult to surpass a calculation made some years ago by the late Dr. Eugen Sänger. He considered a spaceship *circumnavigating the cosmos*—assuming that this represents a distance of ten billion light-years. If the ship could achieve 99.999,999,999,999,-999,996 per cent of the velocity of light, the crew would imagine that the journey had lasted thirty-three years—yet ten billion years would have elapsed before they returned to Earth (if it still existed, and they could find it). Since this feat would require the complete conversion into energy of a mass approaching that of the Moon, Sänger decided that this far surpassed the limits of the technically feasible.

Of course, he may be right. But because now we know that there are energy sources in the universe which appear to be turning Moon-sized masses into radiation every ten seconds, it might be best to reserve judgment even on this point.

Everything that has been said in this chapter is based on one assumption, that the Theory of Relativity is correct. However, we have seen how Newton's theory of gravitation, after being unchallenged for three hundred years, was itself modified by Einstein. How can we be sure that this process will not be repeated and that the "light barrier" may not be shattered, as the once formidable "sound barrier" was a generation ago?

This analogy is often drawn, but it is quite invalid. There was never any doubt that one could travel faster than sound, given sufficient energy; rifle bullets and artillery shells had been doing it for years. (In fact, manmade objects first broke the sound barrier at least 10,000 years ago, though very few people would guess how. Think it over before you look at the footnote.) [3]

During the last half century, however, the equations of relativity have stood up to every test that can be applied, and billions of dollars' worth of engineering have been based upon them. The giant accelerators that speed atomic particles up to almost the velocity of light simply would not work unless Einstein's formulas were obeyed to as many decimal places as can be measured.

Nevertheless, there is a faint possibility that even this apparently insuperable barrier may be breached and that we may be able to signal—conceivably, even travel—faster than light, with all that this implies. And we might do it *without* violating the Theory of Relativity.

I am indebted to Professor Gerald Feinberg of Columbia University for these ideas, which are taken (I hope accurately) from his stimulating paper "On the Possibility of Faster Than Light Particles." Professor Feinberg makes a point which is usually overlooked: the Theory of Relativity does *not* say that nothing can travel faster than light. It says that nothing can travel *at the speed of light;* there is a big difference, and it may be an important one. As Professor Feinberg puts it, the speed of light is a limiting velocity, but a limit has two sides. One can imagine particles or other entities which can travel *only* faster than light; there might even be a whole universe on the other side of the light barrier, though please do not ask me to explain precisely what is meant by this phrase.

[3] The crack of a whip is a sonic bang.

It may be argued that even if this were true, it could never be proved and would be of no practical importance. Since we cannot travel *at* the speed of light, it seems obvious that we can never travel any faster.

But this is taking an old-fashioned, pre-twentieth-century view of the universe. Modern physics is full of jumps from one condition of energy or velocity (quantum state) to another *without* passing through the intermediate values. There are electronic devices on the market now which depend on this effect—the tunnel diode, for example, in which electrons "tunnel" from one side of an electrical barrier to the other without going through it. Maybe we can do the same sort of thing at the velocity of light.

I am well aware that this is metaphysics rather than physics; so are even more *outré* ideas like shortcuts through higher dimensions—the "spacewarps" so useful to science-fiction writers. But we have been wrong so many times in the past when attempting to set limits to technology that it would be well to keep an open mind, even about surpassing the speed of light.

J. B. S. Haldane once remarked: "The universe is not only queerer than we imagine—it is queerer than we *can* imagine." Certainly no one could have imagined the time-dilation effect; who can guess what strange roads there may yet be on which we may travel to the stars?

in my opinion...

As far back as I can remember, I have wanted to travel. I loved movies of ships travelling round the world, or of flights to Africa for safari travel, and I read every bit of science fiction I could. I watched all the American space flights on television, memorizing so-called worthless statistics; by the time man had landed on the moon I was completely bored with the idea of moon travel. From what I had read, the pictures from space were nothing special, in fact, they were rather "old hat."

I was born in the space age and watched the first American go into space. I plan on hearing about the first man going to the stars.

In my opinion we will travel to the stars. I feel that even with all his stupidity and laziness, man will make it; after all, the 21st century is not just a twelve month period. It consists of one hundred years and we still have a few years before it starts.

Mr. Clarke has done an excellent job of presenting not only the problem of star travel, but figures of voyages, distances, and time involved. I do feel, however, that he could have put more thought into the possibility of travelling faster than light. In recent years, research had been done on the possibility of particles that travel faster than light; if these particles prove to exist, the speed of light may, like the speed of sound, be just another so-called barrier to cross.

Through my research I honestly believe that, although at present we are not capable of travelling at such great speeds, the next fifty years will not only prove us capable of doing it, but will also provide us with the equipment to do it. The problem lies with people, not with machinery.

For colonization attempts and long distance flights, the "time dilation" effect could be a great asset for the large groups of people who are travelling. The craft would be a city in itself, and the trip's duration, which would be the lifetime of the city, would really be a short time. Ordinary city functions would take the boredom out of flight. A craft of this type would be enormous in size, dwarfing even the Titan series used in Apollo missions.

Power and the type of space drive will be very important. It seems very clear that we cannot carry the vast quantity of fuel needed by our present-day chemical rockets. The amount of energy needed for such an excursion is almost incomprehensible, yet we need and will have such power sources in order to make these journeys.

As we have eliminated chemical drives as a power source, we naturally turn to atomic fission and fusion type power sources on an ion drive engine. This is as far as our technology has brought us.* It only seems that if these are not powerful enough, technology will invent something else.

The spacemen of tomorrow will also be much different than today's astronauts. They will probably be specialists in individual fields. It is possible that they will unionize and flights in the solar system will probably be scheduled. There will

---

* That is to say we do have the ideas, but none in use. There are ion engines on the drawing boards and some are in the working model stage.

continue to be exploratory groups, but for interstellar flights the spacemen will probably consist of families. A ship will cover more distance in miles in one trip than all of man's trips in his history to date, but man will still not be satisfied unless he reaches for further stars.

john r. balfour

questions

1.   Based on our present attitudes and human values, discuss the moral aspects of some of Clarke's suggestions about long distance space travel. Cannibalism? Computer-trained generations? Multi-generation trips?

2.   Inevitably, a star journey will last quite a while. Discuss a "colony" long journey and what it might be like.

3.   Assuming that we make such a long journey, how will the time–dilation affect the travelers of a return trip, finding their grandchildren and great-grandchildren old and grey?

4.   In view of the fact that we have made our first tentative space flights and that there exists the potential for far more ambitious exploration, what speculations can be made that more advanced civilizations than ours have already examined our planet?

5.   Man does have limitations. Discuss these in terms of how far he can go despite these limitations.

10.
everyman
a genius:
genetics

ON LIVING IN A BIOLOGICAL REVOLUTION

donald fleming

introduction and comment by stephen w. shaner

Man has almost completely eliminated the process of natural selection in his species. No longer do only the strongest, most intelligent, or better-adapted individuals survive to pass on beneficial genes. So also do the genetically inferior and defective.

Because of man's recent technological improvements in his immediate environment, and through his humanitarian or sympathetic feelings for others of his kind, he has eliminated the need for all people to fend for themselves in the seemingly harsh and brutal world of nature wherein natural selection works best. Except where a lethal genetic trait is present, the reproductive capacity destroyed, or a severe social problem exists because of a genetic defect, inferior genes in any individual will be passed on into the next generation's gene pool by people who — had man not interfered—would probably have died or been unable to reproduce.

The desirability, perpetuation, and existence of any human gene is now no longer determined by ecological pressures, as is the case in most living organisms. The desirability of a genetic characteristic or trait is now determined by goals set by the conscious human mind. Those who would argue that we should not interfere with man's genetic makeup and basic physiology, but rather leave nature to its course (it having done such a perfect job until now), must not forget that mankind has already influenced or tampered with nature to such an extent that intervention and remedial action are currently necessary to avert disaster both to ourselves and to all other forms of life on earth.

Biological engineering concerning human physiology is of course only part of what needs to be done to make man's technology compatible with other life forms that share the earth. But it is an important part as far as our species is concerned. The existence of the universe, the basis of life and of nature as it is now, is solely dependent on the physical properties of matter, the atom and various sub-atomic particles and their ability to combine into and interact with other molecules. Life, or more specifically, the cell, exists only because it was possible for it to do so; and the odds were that at some time such a highly complex chemical system would evolve.

I can see no reason for declining to "tamper" with nature, other than for the reason that it may be disastrous to ourselves if we do not understand all aspects of our actions, and all possible consequences of them. There is no "purpose" to life or nature; the purposes we may consider it to have, if we feel it has any at all, are our own personal goals and ambitions, and the purpose we give to it.

What, then, about the people who believe, on religious grounds or for any other reason, that it is either unethical or unwise to alter or reorganize human physiology? They should certainly then have the right to leave their own bodies alone or unaltered. However, they should also not interfere with those who might wish to attempt an alteration of their physiology or genetic make–up. When we come to the matter of determining the composition of future generations, we feel we have an obligation to the unborn.

Future generations do not exist at present, and the people composing the human population of the future do not "desire" anything at the present time either. However, they will have to live with our set of values, whether they want to or not. If our genetic make–up is changed, it will, of course, become the genetic make–up of our children, assuming that reproduction is based on chromosomal inheritance from parent organisms. If we feel obliged to do anything at all for the people of the future, perhaps it should be to provide them with a physiological composition most adaptable and receptive to further change, so that they can determine for themselves what they shall be.

It would be possible then to use this same reasoning to argue that we should not alter our genetic make–up at all, since anything we can do for (or to) ourselves at the present can certainly still be done in the future. This argument could be used to postpone any kind of action indefinitely. However, the present generation is just as important (even more so to me) as the next generation, or the one following. Therefore, if the technology is available now, we should use it.

By now I have probably brought to mind a picture of our future planet inhabited by all sorts of strange and frightening monsters that once were or are the children of men. I don't discount the possibility, but if we proceed carefully, biological engineering has the potential for providing a fantastic number of benefits for mankind. Our fears are largely the result of the negative attitude of some science fiction writers toward the subject, as well as the nightmares they have presented to us since we were first old enough to know the meaning of the word "monster".

Most can probably agree that it would be desirable to eliminate physical and mental defects which create invalids and their suffering, who impose a burden on the society that must care for them. A solution to this problem acceptable to nearly everyone is, or should be, our major goal.

But beyond this, what should man do with the soon-to-be-available technology which will enable him to control and manipulate his own body, mind, and even consciousness in whatever way he chooses?

Dr. Donald Fleming presents some of the philosophical implications of the world of genetics in the excerpt that follows.

S.W.S.

ON LIVING IN A
BIOLOGICAL REVOLUTION

*Donald Fleming, educator and historian, was born in Maryland
in 1923. After receiving degrees at Johns Hopkins University
and at Harvard, he began teaching at Brown University in 1947.
In 1959 he was associate professor in the history of science
at Yale as well as visiting professor at Harvard. Fleming is a
Fellow of the American Academy of Arts and Sciences and a
member of the American Historical Association. He is the
author of several biographies and* The Rise of Modern Medicine.

Here are a dozen things that we have discovered in the last fifteen
years.

1) We have discovered the structure of the genetic substance
DNA—the double helix of Watson and Crick—The general nature
of the process by which the chromosomal strands are replicated.

2) We have discovered in viruses how to achieve the perfect
replication of DNA molecules that are biologically effective.

3) We have discovered the code by which DNA specifies the
insertion of amino acids in proteins.

4) We have discovered how to produce hybrid cells between the
most diverse vertebrate species, including hybrids between man
and mouse; and some of these hybrids have gone on multiplying
for several (cellular) generations.

5) We have discovered the power of viruses to invade bacterial
and other cells and to insert the genes of the virus into the genome
of the host; and we have good reason to conjecture, though not
yet to affirm, that this phenomenon is involved in cancer.

6) We have discovered hormonal contraceptives and grasped in

principle the strategy for devising a contraceptive pill for both sexes, by knocking out certain hormones of the hypothalamus, the master sexual gland of the body.

7) We have discovered on a large scale in the livestock industry that deep-frozen mammalian sperm, suitably mixed with glycerol, can be banked indefinitely and drawn upon as desired to produce viable offspring.

8) We have discovered in human females how to produce super-ovulation, the release of several eggs into the oviduct at the same time instead of the customary one, with the possibility on the horizon of withdrawing substantial numbers of human eggs for storage, culture in test tubes, or surgical manipulation, without destroying their viability.

9) We have discovered in rabbits how to regulate the sex of offspring by removing fertilized ova from the female before they become implanted in the wall of the uterus, "sexing" the embryos by a technique entailing the deletion of some 200 to 300 cells, flushing embryos of the "wrong" sex down the drain, and then in a substantial minority of cases, successfully reinserting in the uterus embryos of the desired sex that proceed to develop normally.

10) We have discovered drugs, above all the hallucinogens, that simulate psychotic states of mind; and have thereby rendered it plausible that the latter are the product of "inborn errors of metabolism" and as such remediable by the administration of drugs.

11) We have discovered in principle, and to a certain extent in practice, how to repress the immunological "defenses" of the body.

12) We have discovered a combination of immunological and surgical techniques by which the kidney, liver, or heart can be transplanted with fair prospects of the recipient's survival for months or even years—the first constructive proposal for turning our death wish on the highways to some advantage.

Each of these is a major discovery or complex of discoveries in itself, but they add up to far more than the sum of their parts. They constitute a veritable Biological Revolution likely to be as decisive for the history of the next 150 years as the Industrial Revolution has been for the period since 1750.

Definitions of what constitutes a revolution are legion. An undoctrinaire formulation would be that every full-scale revolution has three main components: a distinctive attitude toward the world; a program of utterly transforming it; and an unshakable, not to say fanatical, confidence that this program can be enacted —a world view, a program, and a faith.

In this sense, Darwinism did not usher in a full-scale biological revolution. Darwinism was a profoundly innovating world view, but one that prescribed no steps to be taken, no victories over nature to be celebrated, no program of triumphs to be successively gained. Indeed, one of the most plausible constructions to be put upon it was that nothing much *could* be done except to submit patiently to the winnowing processes of nature.

This defect was not lost upon Darwin's own cousin Sir Francis Galton, who tried to construct an applied science of eugenics for deliberately selecting out the best human stocks. But Galtonian eugenics was sadly lacking in any authentic biological foundation.

Once the science of Mendelian genetics came to general notice about 1900, a more promising form of eugenics began to commend itself, the effort to induce artificial mutation of genes in desirable directions.

This was long the animating faith of one of the most extraordinary Americans of the twentieth century, the geneticist Herman J. Muller. He was the actual discoverer, in 1927, of artificial mutation through X-rays. But this great achievement, for which he got the Nobel Prize, was a tremendous disappointment to Muller the revolutionary. There was no telling which genes would mutate in which direction, and he came to suspect that the vast majority of mutations were actually harmful in the present situation of the human race.

Muller at the end of his life—he died in 1967—was thrown back upon essentially Galtonian eugenics. He did bring this up to date by his proposal for sperm banks in which the sperm of exceptionally intelligent and socially useful men could be stored for decades and used for artificial insemination. He also envisioned, in the not too distant future, ova banks for storing superior human eggs. But none of these modern touches, these innovations in technique, could conceal the fact that this was still the old eugenics newly garbed, but equally subjective and imprecise.

The Biological Revolution that Muller failed to bring off was already in progress when he died, but on very different terms from his own. There is a new eugenics in prospect, not the marriage agency kind, but a form of "biological engineering." When this actually comes to pass, chromosomes, segments of chromosomes, and even individual genes will be inserted at will into the genome. Alternatively, germ cells cultured in laboratories will be enucleated and entire tailor-made DNA molecules substituted. Alternatively still, superior genes will be brought into play by hybridization of cells.

The detailed variants upon these general strategies are almost innumerable. They all have in common the fact that they cannot be accomplished at present except in viruses and bacteria or in cell cultures. But it would be a bold man who would dogmatically affirm that none of these possibilities could be brought to bear upon human genetics by the year 2000.

That is a long way off for the firebrands of the Biological Revolution. The Nobel Prize winner Joshua Lederberg in particular has been pushing the claims of a speedier remedy, christened by him "euphenics," and defined as "the engineering of human development." The part of human development that fascinates Lederberg the most is embryology, seen by him as the process of initially translating the instructions coded in the DNA into "the living, breathing organism." Embryology, he says, is "very much in the situation of atomic physics in 1900; having had an honorable and successful tradition it is about to begin!" He thinks it will not take long to mature—"from 5 to no more than 20 years." He adds that most predictions of research progress in recent times have proved to be "far too conservative."

The progress that Lederberg has in mind is the application of new embryological techniques to human affairs. He is at once maddened and obsessed by the nine-months phase in which the human organism has been exempted from experimental and therapeutic intervention—such a waste of time before the scientists can get at us. But the embryo's turn is coming. It would be incredible, he says, "if we did not soon have the basis of developmental engineering technique to regulate, for example, the size of the human brain by prenatal or early postnatal intervention."

Nothing as sensational as this has yet been attempted, but the new phase in embryology that Lederberg heralded is undoubtedly getting under way. The most conspicuous figure at present is Robert Edwards of the physiology laboratory at Cambridge University. In 1966 Edwards reported the culture of immature egg cells from the human ovary up to the point of ripeness for fertilization. He made tentative claims to have actually achieved fertilization in test tubes. The incipient hullabaloo in the newspapers about the specter of "test tube babies" led Edwards to clamp a tight lid of security over his researches in progress.

In the spring of this year, however, he and Richard Gardner announced their success in "sexing" fertilized rabbit eggs before implantation in the wall of the uterus and then inducing 20 percent of the reinserted eggs to produce normal full-term infants. The aspect of these findings that attracted general attention, the prospect of regulating the sex of mammalian offspring, is not likely to be of permanent interest. For this purpose, Edwards' and Gardner's technique is obviously a clumsy expedient by comparison with predetermining the "sex" of spermatozoa—presently impossible but certainly not inconceivable within the next generation.

The real importance of Edwards' and Gardner's work lies elsewhere. They have opened up the possibility of subjecting the early embryo to micro-surgery, with the deletion and "inoculation" of cells at the will of the investigator, *and* the production of viable offspring from the results. The manufacture of "chimeras" in the modern biological sense—that is, with genetically distinct cells in the same organism—is clearly in prospect.

Work in this vein has just begun. The only branch of euphenics that has already become something more than a promising growth stock in science is the suppression of immunological reactions against foreign tissues and the accompanying, highly limited, successes in the transplantation of organs.

The technical details and immediate prospects in eugenics and euphenics, however fascinating, are less important than the underlying revolutionary temper in biology. The most conspicuous representatives of this temper are Lederberg himself, the biochemical geneticist Edward L. Tatum, and Francis Crick of the model— all of them Nobel Prize winners, with the corresponding leverage upon public opinion. Robert Edwards, though slightly singed by the blast of publicity about test tube babies, is clearly in training for the revolutionary cadre.

One of the stigmata of revolutionaries in any field is their resolute determination to break with traditional culture. For a scientist, the most relevant definition of culture is his own field of research. All of these men would angrily resent being bracketed with biologists in general. Biology has always been a rather loose confederation of naturalists and experimentalists, overlapping in both categories with medical researchers. Today even the pretense that these men somehow constitute a community has been frayed to the breaking point.

At Harvard, for example, the revolutionaries have virtually seceded from the old Biology Department and formed a new department of their own, Biochemistry and Molecular Biology. The younger molecular biologists hardly bother to conceal their contempt for the naturalists, whom they see as old fogies obsequiously attentive to the world as it is rather than bent upon turning it upside down.

In one respect, the molecular biologists do overlap with the contemporary naturalists and indeed with most creative scientists in general—in their total detachment from religion. In a way, this is a point that could have been made at any time in the last seventy-five years, but with one significant difference. Herman Muller, for example, born in 1890, had no truck with religion. But he was self-consciously antireligious.

The biological revolutionaries of today are not antireligious but simply unreligious. They give the impression not of defending themselves against religion but of subsisting in a world where that has never been a felt pressure upon them. They would agree with many devout theologians that we are living in a post-Christian world, to such an extent that some of the most doctrinaire biological revolutionaries are able to recognize without embarrassment, and even with a certain gracious condescension, that Christianity did play a useful role in defining the values of the Western world.

The operative word here is in the past tense. Francis Crick says that the facts of science are producing and must produce values that owe nothing to Christianity. "Take," he says, "the suggestion of making a child whose head is twice as big as normal. There is going to be no agreement between Christians and any humanists who lack their particular prejudice about the sanctity of the individual, and who simply want to try it scientifically."

This sense of consciously taking up where religion left off is illuminating in another sense for the revolutionary character of contemporary biology. The parallel is very marked between the original Christian Revolution against the values of the classical world and the Biological Revolution against religious values.

All the great revolutionaries, whether early Christians or molecular biologists, are men of good hope. The future may or may not belong to those who believe in it, but cannot belong to those who don't. Yet at certain points in history, most conspicuously perhaps at intervals between the close of the Thirty Years' War in 1648 and the coming of the Great Depression in 1929, the horizons seem to be wide open, and the varieties of good hope contending for allegiance are numerous. But the tidings of good hope don't become revolutionary except when the horizons begin to close in and the plausible versions of good hope have dwindled almost to the vanishing point.

For the kind of good hope that has the maximum historical impact is the one that capitalizes upon a prevalent despair at the corruption of the existing world, and then carries conviction in pointing to itself as the only possible exit from despair. Above everything else, revolutionaries are the men who keep their spirits up when everybody else's are sagging. In this sense, the greatest revolutionaries of the Western world to date have been precisely the early Christians who dared to affirm in the darkest days of the classical world that something far better was in process and could be salvaged from the ruins.

Both of these points are exemplified in the Biological Revolution that has now begun—despair at our present condition, but infinite hope for the future if the biologists' prescription is taken. Anybody looking for jeremiads on our present state could not do better than to consult the new biologists. "The facts of human reproduction," says Joshua Lederberg, "are all gloomy—the stratification of fecundity by economic status, the new environmental insults to our genes, the sheltering by humanitarian medicine of once-lethal genes."

More generally, the biologists deplore the aggressive instincts of the human animal, now armed with nuclear weapons, his lamentably low average intelligence for coping with increasingly complicated problems, and his terrible prolificity, no longer mitigated by a high enough death rate. It is precisely an aspect of the closing down of horizons and depletion of comfortable hopes in the second half of the 20th century that conventional medicine is now seen by the biological revolutionaries as one of the greatest threats to the human race.

Yet mere prophets of gloom can never make a revolution. In fact, the new biologists are almost the only group among our contemporaries with a reasoned hopefulness about the long future—if the right path is taken. There are of course many individuals of a naturally cheerful or feckless temperament, today as always, but groups of men with an articulated hope for the future of the entire race are much rarer. The theologians no longer qualify, many Communists have lost their hold upon the future even by their own lights, and the only other serious contenders are the space scientists and astronauts. But just to get off the earth is a rather vague prescription for our ills. Few people even in the space program would make ambitious claims on this score. In a long historical retrospect, they may turn out to have been too modest.

This is not a charge that is likely ever to be leveled against the new biologists. It is well known by now that J. D. Watson begins his account of his double-helix double by saying that he had never seen Francis Crick in a modest mood. But after all, modesty is not the salient quality to be looked for in the new breed of biologists. If the world will only listen, they *know* how to put us on the high road to salvation.

What exactly does their brand of salvation entail? Perhaps the most illuminating way to put the matter is that their ideal is the manufacture of man. In a manufacturing process, the number of units to be produced is a matter of rational calculation beforehand and of tight control thereafter. Within certain tolerances, specifications are laid down for a satisfactory product. Quality-control is maintained by checking the output and replacing defective parts. After the product has been put to use, spare parts can normally be supplied to replace those that have worn out.

This is the program of the new biologists—control of numbers by foolproof contraception; gene manipulation and substitution; surgical and biochemical intervention in the embryonic and neonatal phases; organ transplants or replacements at will.

Of these, only contraception is technically feasible at present. Routine organ transplants will probably be achieved for a wide range of suitable organs in less than five years. The grafting of mechanical organs, prosthetic devices inserted in the body, will probably take longer. Joshua Lederberg thinks that embryonic and neonatal intervention may be in flood tide by, say, 1984. As for gene manipulation and substitution in human beings, that is the remotest prospect of all—maybe by the year 2000. But we must not forget Lederberg's well-founded conviction that most predictions in these matters are likely to be too conservative. We are already five to ten years ahead of what most informed people expected to be the schedule for organ transplants in human beings.

a coming value revolution too?

The great question becomes, what is it going to be like to be living in a world where such things are coming true? How will the Biological Revolution affect our scheme of values? Nobody could possibly take in all the implications in advance, but some reasonable conjectures are in order.

It is virtually certain that the moral sanctions of birth control are going to be transformed. Down to the present time, the battle for birth control has been fought largely in terms of the individual couple's right to have the number of babies that they want at the desired intervals. But it is built into the quantity-controls envisioned by the Biological Revolution, the control of the biological inventory, that this is or ought to be a question of social policy rather than individual indulgence.

Many factors are converging upon many people to foster this general attitude, but the issue is particularly urgent from the point of view of the biological revolutionaries. In the measure that they succeed in making the human race healthier, first by transplants and later on by genetic tailoring, they will be inexorably swamped by their own successes unless world population is promptly brought under control. The irrepressible Malthus is springing from his lightly covered grave to threaten them with catastrophic victories.

The only hope is birth control. The biologists can contribute the techniques, but the will to employ them on the requisite scale is another matter. The most startling proposal to date for actually enforcing birth control does not come from a biologist but from the Nobel-Prize-winning physicist W. B. Shockley, one of the inventors of the transistor. Shockley's plan is to render all women of childbearing age reversibly sterile by implanting a contraceptive capsule beneath the skin, to be removed by a physician only on the presentation of a government license to have a child. The mind boggles at the prospect of bootleg babies. This particular proposal is not likely to be enacted in the near future, even in India.

What we may reasonably expect is a continually rising chorus by the biologists, moralists, and social philosophers of the next generation to the effect that nobody has a right to have children, and still less the right to determine on personal grounds how many. There are many reasons why a couple may not want to be prolific anyhow, so that there might be a happy coincidence between contraception seen by them as a right and by statesmen and biologists as a duty. But the suspicion is that even when people moderate their appetite in the matter of babies, they may still want to have larger families than the earth can comfortably support. The possibility of predetermining sex would undoubtedly be helpful in this respect, but might not be enough to make people forego a third child. That is where the conflict would arise between traditional values, however moderately indulged, and the values appropriate to the Biological Revolution.

This issue is bound to be fiercely debated. But some of the most profound implications of the Biological Revolution may never present themselves for direct ratification. In all probability, the issues will go by default as we gratefully accept specific boons from the new biology.

Take, for example, the role of the patient in medicine. One of the principal strands in Western medicine from the time of the Greeks has been the endeavor to enlist the cooperation of the patient in his own cure. In certain respects, this venerable tradition has grown much stronger in the last century. Thus the rising incidence of degenerative diseases, like ulcers, heart trouble, and high blood pressure, has underscored the absolute necessity of inducing the patient to observe a healthful regimen, literally a way of life.

This has been the whole point of Freudian psychiatry as a mode of therapy, that cures can be wrought only by a painful exertion of the patient himself. We often forget, for good reasons, how traditional Freudianism is after the one big shock has been assimilated. In the present context, it actually epitomizes the Western tradition of bringing the patient's own personality to bear upon his medical problems.

Where do we go from here? The degenerative diseases are going to be dealt with increasingly by surgical repair of organs, by organ transplants, and later on by the installation of mechanical organs and eventually by the genetic deletion of weak organs before they occur. The incentive to curb your temper or watch your diet to keep your heart going will steadily decline.

As for mental illness, the near future almost certainly lies with psychopharmacology and the far future with genetic tailoring. Though the final pieces stubbornly decline to fall into place, the wise money is on the proposition that schizophrenia and other forms of psychosis are biochemical disorders susceptible of a pharmacological cure. If we are not presently curing any psychoses by drugs, we are tranquilizing and antidepressing many psychotics and emptying mental hospitals.

Neuroses, the theme of Freudian psychoanalysis, are another matter. It is not easy to envision a biochemical remedy for them. But even for neuroses, we already have forms of behavioral therapy that dispense with the Freudian tenet of implicating the patient in his own cure. For the *very* long future, it is certainly not inconceivable that genetic tailoring could delete neurotic propensities.

Everywhere we turn, the story is essentially the same. Cures are increasingly going to be wrought upon, done to, the patient as a passive object. The strength of his own personality, the force of his character, his capacity for reintegrating himself, are going to be increasingly irrelevant in medicine.

This leads to what many people would regard as the biggest question of all. In what sense would we have a self to integrate under the new dispensation? The Princeton theologian Paul Ramsey has now been appointed professor of "genetic ethics" at the Georgetown University Medical School, presumably the first appointment of its kind. He thinks that genetic tailoring would be a "violation of man." To this it must be said that under the present scheme of things, many babies get born with catastrophic genes that are not exactly an enhancement of man. Our present genetic self is a brute datum, sometimes very brutal, and anyhow it is hard to see how we can lose our identity before we have any.

As for installing new organs in the body, there is no evident reason why the personality should be infringed upon by heart or kidney transplants per se. Brain transplants would be different, but surely they would be among the last to come. States of mind regulated by drugs we already possess, and obviously they do alter our identity in greater or lesser degree. But even here we must not forget that some identities are intolerable to their distracted possessors.

We must not conclude, however, that the importance of these developments has been exaggerated. The point is that the immediate practical consequences will probably not present themselves as threatening to the individuals involved—quite the contrary. Abstract theological speculations about genetic tailoring would be totally lost upon a woman who could be sure in advance that her baby would not be born mentally retarded or physically handicapped. The private anxieties of individuals are likely to diminish rather than increase any effective resistance to the broader consequences of the Biological Revolution.

One of these is already implicit in predicting a sense of growing passivity on the part of patients, of not participating as a subject in their own recovery. This might well be matched by a more general sense of the inevitability of letting oneself be manipulated by technicians—of becoming an article of manufacture.

The difficulty becomes to estimate what psychological difference this would make. In any Hegelian overview of history, we can only become articles of manufacture because "we" have set up as the manufacturers. But the first person plural is a slippery customer. We the manufactured would be everybody and we the manufacturers a minority of scientists and technicians. Most people's capacity to identify with the satisfactions of the creative minority is certainly no greater in science than in other fields, and may well be less.

The beneficiaries of the Biological Revolution are not likely to feel that they are in control of the historical process from which they are benefiting. But they will not be able to indulge any feelings of alienation from science without endangering the specific benefits that they are unwilling to give up.

The best forecast would be for general acquiescence, though occasionally sullen, in whatever the Biological Revolution has to offer and gradually adjusting our values to signify that we approve of what we will actually be getting. The will to cooperate in being made biologically perfect is likely to take the place in the hierarchy of values that used to be occupied by being humbly submissive to spiritual counselors chastising the sinner for his own salvation. The new form of spiritual sloth will be not to want to be bodily perfect and genetically improved. The new avarice will be to cherish our miserable hoard of genes and favor the children that resemble us.

in my opinion...

It is doubtful that we shall pass tranquilly into this new era without problems, perhaps even crises unimaginable at present. By what values and standards will society determine the composition of future generations? Will people become mere articles of manufacture by a relatively small number of scientists and technologists? How will feelings toward the worth or value of human life be affected, with the availability of as many people in any form as society needs? Who will comprise "society"? Will society become a rigidly-controlled caste system determined by intelligence levels, a 21st century Brave New World?

It is unlikely that all of these problems will confront us by 2000 A.D., but by the end of the 21st century, most of them will have to be solved. Perhaps we don't even have enough sense of reality of things to come, and our solutions or answers to the problems will be rendered invalid or irrelevant by future circumstances. Some scientists are now saying that there ought to be a moratorium on further research for a while, to give the rest of society time to catch up on facts and to realize the significance of what scientists are doing—and then decide on future action.

Before we attain the ability to alter our entire population, new discoveries in genetics will help solve problems that have plagued man since he first began to live in primitive communal societies.

Irrational and antisocial behavior has always existed in some people, perhaps latently in us all. The seemingly high incidence of an extra Y-chromosome in extremely aggressive, antisocial, and criminally-oriented individuals is now being studied by scientists who believe there may be a connection between this genetic variation and its undesirable type of behavior. Research is still being done on this, but it or a similar defect may someday lead to the elimination of the more incompatible members of our society.

It is also possible, if not inevitable, that mental and physical invalids will be eliminated, relieving mankind of the burden of providing for their existence. This would, of course, eliminate the need for penal institutions and reformatories, not to mention a variety of medical clinics and centers for physically and mentally handicapped people. New techniques in immunology and genetic manipulation may render the human body resistant to most serious diseases and crippling genetic defects. Near immortality or an extreme lengthening of lives will inevitably be possible, through natural and artificial organ transplants, possibly of any part of the body except the brain (and perhaps even that). The benefits of a longer life are obvious, regardless of the motivation. Something similar to a generation gap may then either reach catastrophic proportions or disappear altogether. Extensive interplanetary exploration will soon be upon us, and man may be able through genetic and thus physical transformation of the body to adapt himself to the temperature extremes of the moon, the chemically different atmospheres and gravitational fields of other planets, and a host of other environmental conditions. A physiological change could also be brought about, some people becoming chemolithotrophs—requiring only inorganic material to sustain life or a variety of other mechanisms to obtain energy.

Although the benefits we stand to receive during the latter

part of this and the next century are numerous, great also is the potential for disastrous errors in our handling of our new knowledge. How we shall apply this knowledge to the betterment of all mankind is a problem that we must thoroughly understand; we must not be too long in making our decision on our future courses of action.

stephen w. shaner

questions

1.   What types of controls should be established by society over genetic research, both immediate and future, on the federal, local, and possibly international level?

2.   Should a moratorium on further scientific research be initiated to give society a chance to evaluate and re-direct our course in biological engineering? Why?

3.   What programs, if any, should be put into effect to educate and prepare the general populace for the coming biological revolution?

4.   In a non-biological sense, what should become society's definition of life, of a human being, of individual rights and equality—if such definitions are possible?

5.   What improvements on the human body or its genes do you think would be of immediate or near-future benefit to us?

II.

to be or not to be: conservation and ecology

OUR SHRINKING LIVING SPACE
EPILOGUE: NOT QUITE UTOPIA

stuart chase

introduction and comment by patricia a. bonn

Spaceship Earth: The year 2000. Only thirty years away. Isn't *now* the time to think about the damage man is doing to his world? There is mounting evidence that man and his works are disrupting the numerous complex and interrelated processes upon which this planet's web of life depends.

Professor L. C. Cole of Cornell University has pointed out that the Aswan Dam may yet be the "ultimate disaster for Egypt" because of its likely effect on the salinization of that country's soil. His description of the possible dangerous consequences of a sea-level canal across Central America—one that would permit large masses of cold Pacific Ocean water to enter the warm Caribbean—raises issues that have been almost totally ignored in discussions of this project. And if the tanker Torrey Canyon had been carrying a concentrated herbicide instead of petroleum, what would have happened to the North Sea?

Our attitude toward nature has scarcely altered from that of our ancestors. We still believe in the myth of nature's inexhaustible wealth. It is undeniable that the earth is being pillaged despite the efforts of conservationists and considerable technical progress. The major problem is to safeguard natural resources throughout the world and provide mankind with the means of survival.*

A complete reappraisal should thus be made of the whole problem of man's relationship to nature. All forms of life, including man, have slowly developed over the passage of millions of years. This slow development has actually been a continuous adjustment to all the other elements of the environment, both living and non-living, an adjustment that has created a situation where each form of life has grown to

* Jean Dorst, "A Biologist Looks at the Animal World (Beasts and Men)", UNESCO Courier, January 1969, 22:17.

depend on the existence—the presence—of all the other
elements. This interdependence or relationship must be
maintained . . . or something dies.

Our failure to develop an environmental awareness and
understanding is a failure of our society. Now we are faced with
some of the results of this failure. Never before has the
environment been changed so much, so rapidly. Never before
have so many life forms disappeared in so short a time;
never before has the world been in such a state of unrest.
Never before have the air, water and soil been so foul. And
never before has the environment been challenged by any
form of life as powerful or as destructive as man.

Noted author Stuart Chase graphically describes the dangers
that confront man in the technological age; he also delineates
what we might attain if we make the effort.

p.a.b.

OUR SHRINKING LIVING SPACE

Stuart Chase, economist and author, was educated at Massachusetts Institute of Technology and at Harvard. A prolific writer, his works include more than twenty books, many of which are regarded as classics in various fields, as well as frequent contributions to journals and magazines. Among his books are: The Tragedy of Waste, *1925;* Men and Machines, *1929;* Rich Land, Poor Land, *1936;* The Tyranny of Words, *1938;* Idle Money, Idle Men, *1941;* The Road We Are Travelling, *1942;* Democracy Under Pressure, *1945;* The Proper Study of Mankind, *1948;* Guides to Straight Thinking, *1956;* Live and Let Live, *1959;* American Credos, *1962; and* Money to Grow On, *1964.*

Mr. and Mrs. Chase live in Redding, Connecticut, where he is active in community affairs, conservation, and outdoor sports.

* * *

It is sobering to remember that only about 12 percent of the surface of the earth is fit for human habitation. That surface has been called a "thin lamination." We live between an ocean of air above and a rocky crust beneath. The air must be reasonably pure if we are to breathe, the soil must be arable if we are to eat, the water must be clean if we are to drink. Two-thirds of the globe's surface is salt water, while polar ice, tundra, high mountains, deserts, swamps, and rain forests reduce the land on which we can live with any comfort to not more than one-eighth of the earth's surface.

How many of us in affluent societies have any conception of

the meaning of these limitations? If we do not like where we are, we get in the car and go somewhere else. Yet living space is only a small part of the planet's surface, and now a series of technologies on the loose are squeezing it smaller. The man-land density is increasing, not only because land is limited and population is going up, but because more and more of the land is becoming unfit for human living. We have sturdily refused to accept our place in nature. "If any biological system," observed Dr. Dickerman Richards of Columbia, "were to have the kind of chaos our social system has, it would not survive five minutes."

Every once in a while, amid the stupendous chaos of ramming a new superhighway across the continent, the motorist sees a lonely frame house surrounded by great mounds of up-rooted earth and blasted rock. It has been abandoned by its owner, but the bulldozers have not got around to pulling it down. This may be a fair analogy for what is happening to all our homes: the bulldozers have not got around to pulling them down. Day by day the roar grows louder. When they do get around, where shall we live?

eight assaults on living space

That modern dinosaur, the bulldozer, went into mass production during World War II, which it helped to win. Today it is a familiar sight, driven by an impetuous young man in a state of high exhilaration, leveling hills, obliterating brooks, toppling large trees. No forest, meadow, or shore is safe, as it roots out the habitat of plants and animals, including, in the last analysis, man. The bulldozer, indeed, can be taken as a symbol of a shrinking environment. It represents a technological trend only less menacing than the growth of population and the arms race.

We could begin the analysis far up in space, even at the moon. The military have splendid plans for burning up a continent with missiles fired from the moon. Then we could descend to the stratosphere and find more trouble, especially radioactive fallout. Descend again to normal atmosphere and note what is perhaps the most acute threat of all at present, air pollution. Then down to earth for disturbances in the balance of nature, governing land and water. But it may be better to arrange the assaults by their current urgency. There are at least eight of them, as follows:

pollutants of the air

Water can be channeled in aqueducts and mains, but not so air. New York City is now discovering that any real control of smog is hopeless if it can roll across the bay from New Jersey on prevailing west winds. It bloweth where it listeth, to be sure, but it must carry whatever cargo presents itself. A raw mixture of carbon, sulphur, nitrogen compounds, water vapor, and stockyard odors hangs constantly over the Jersey meadows, awaiting transport.

The word "smog," coined as a combination of "smoke" and "fog," has lost its original meaning. Los Angeles, the most publicized producer, has little smoke today and almost no fog. The term, however, is apparently here to stay and the definition must be expanded. It now refers to any condition of the air we breathe that offers a danger to health—from a slight headache to a fatal coma.

Smog seldom becomes serious without the condition known as "temperature inversion," where hot air does *not* rise and blow away as it normally should. The inversion sits like a lid over the landscape. In certain geographic areas the warm air, by causes not yet well understood, is prevented at times from rising, and any impurities stay in it, keeping foul air at nose level.[1]

The inversion is not caused by a city as such. The Los Angeles area undoubtedly suffered from it long before people settled there. Some cities have spells of inversion, others do not. Dublin does not, thanks to much wind and rain. Inversion has been noted in Tokyo, Paris, Leningrad, New York, Buenos Aires, Mexico City, Sydney, San Francisco, among others. It can even be found in the middle of the Kansas prairie. Inversion plus pollution killed 12,000 Londoners in 1952—the estimate of excess deaths due to a smog in which visibility was reduced to three feet. Inversion killed 20 and made 6,000 very sick in Donora, Pennsylvania, in 1948. London had another attack in 1956, and again in 1962. New York had excess deaths from inversion in 1953, 1963, and, with enormous publicity, and no little irony, on Thanksgiving Day, 1966. In the Japanese town of Yokkaichi, children play in

[1] Donald E. Carr, *The Breath of Life: The Problem of Poisoned Air*, New York: W.W. Norton, 1965.

the school yards equipped with gas masks.[2] Scientists suspect, says *Time,* that thousands of deaths in cities around the world can be linked to air pollution. It is particularly hard on lung patients. It is hard, too, on plants and trees. Certain nursery crops can no longer be grown where air pollution is heavy.

When inversion clamps down its lid, trouble comes for everyone who breathes. It comes in two forms, and from two major sources. One form is the visible particles of carbon dirt, coating the windowsill, which are known to all city-dwellers. The other form, and far more serious, is invisible gas; it accounts for some 90 percent of all air pollution. The major source for a hundred years has been smoke and gas from factory chimneys, where coal and oil are burned. Now, an even greater producer is the rear end of an automobile. Los Angeles, the prize example of inversion because of the city's encircling mountains, has long since compelled industry to use fuels with low sulphur content, but "smog" is worse than ever. Why? Because there are more cars than ever.

Stop-start driving in congested areas releases, along with carbon monoxide (a favorite compound for suicides), various hydrocarbons and nitrogen oxides, and the higher the engine compression, the more perverse they become. No gadget so far designed is able to do more than somewhat reduce the exhaust danger, and Dr. Carr doubts if an effective gadget can be designed.

Meanwhile Dr. Philip A. Leighton, professor emeritus of chemistry at Stanford, concentrating on the nitrogen oxides (which seem to be the most insidious of the lot), has made the following calculation: A full-sized American car cruising at 60 miles an hour emits about three liters of nitrogen oxides per minute. To dilute this blast to safe breathing limits requires more than 60 million liters of fresh air per minute, "a rate which is enough to supply the average breathing requirements, over the same period, of five to 10 million people." This causes Dr. Leighton to wonder if the resource which will really force the control of population, will be not land, food or water, but *air* . . . sixty million liters of fresh air per car per minute.[3]

Here is a dilemma indeed. We have been quite unable to prevent bigger and better traffic jams, which produce bigger

[2] *Time* has a picture of them in its issue of January 27, 1967, together with full-page color photographs of many cities wreathed in sulphur dioxide.

[3] *Geographic Review,* April, 1966.

doses of nitrogen oxides. We managed to ban the testing of nuclear bombs in the atmosphere because of fallout, but to ban the burning of gasoline promises to be a much more serious business. It would not only bring Detroit and the petroleum industry in on the double-quick, but create a great outcry from the public, in defense of its most cherished artifact. John W. Gardner, Secretary of Health, Education, and Welfare, showed real courage when he declared at a 1966 conference that the gasoline automobile and the welfare of the American people are on a collision course: "None of us would wish to sacrifice the convenience of private passenger automobiles, but the day may come when we may have to trade convenience for survival."

The following figures furnish eloquent proof of the dilemma:

ANNUAL AIR POLLUTANTS IN THE UNITED STATES [4]

	Millions of Tons
From transportation engines, cars, trucks, etc.	85
manufacturing plants	22
electric power plants	15
space heating	8
refuse burning	3
Total	133

That means more than half a ton descending on every man, woman, and child in the country, every year.

fallout

High above the exhaust fumes, fallout from nuclear explosions circles the globe in the stratosphere, gradually sifting down. It does not confine its donations to Los Angeles, New York, or London, but distributes them impartially to all mankind. True, the atmosphere of the planet, extending about 30 miles up, has been assailed with substances harmful to human beings ever since volcanoes erupted, or large forest fires were set by lightning, or certain rock formations gave off radiation. Such emissions were "Acts of God," assaults on living things by nature. In the last few years, however, man himself has led the radioactive assault.

Following the Test Ban Treaty of 1963, nuclear explosions have been conducted underground by the United States, Russia, and Britain, but the other members of the "Nuclear Club," France

[4] United States Department of the Interior *Year Book,* 1966.

and China, have continued to throw poisons into the air we breathe, and to coat with poison some of the plants we eat. The danger is certainly not building up at the rate that prevailed before the test ban, but there is plenty of toxic matter still aloft. Dr. Linus Pauling, Nobel laureate in chemistry, has predicted that millions of defective babies will be born over the years as a result of fallout which descended before 1963.

controlling the weather

Contrails from the proposed supersonic airliners may upset weather by accident, but both the military and the rainmakers have larger designs. The former want to make weather very unpleasant for an enemy, while the latter want, for example, to alleviate such droughts as afflicted the New York area in the 1960's, and hopefully to dissolve hurricanes with silver iodide.

The National Science Foundation at Washington, however, considers tampering with the climate about on a par with a nuclear explosion. The Foundation calls for a good deal more research before swinging into action. This should include a study of the biological, social, economic, political, and legal effects of changing the established climate in a given area. The last promises to occupy platoons of lawyers and judges, both national and international. What if Canada wants rain for its wheat crop, while the state of Washington, on the other side of the boundary, is inundated by floods? Who wins when skiers and resort owners want snow and motorists want clear roads?

noise

Sound waves traverse the air, and when they have unpleasant effects on eardrums, can be called a kind of air pollution. A whisper is rated by the sound engineers at 20 decibels, ordinary conversation is rated at 60, factory operations and cocktail parties compete at 85 to 90.[5] If you are subjected to 120 decibels for any length of time, you are likely to suffer permanent damage to your hearing.

It is estimated that average sound levels in the U.S. have increased by some 30 decibels in recent years. Indeed, why not?

[5] Harland Manchester in the *National Civic Review,* September, 1964. Traffic noise on New York sidewalks is rated at 103 decibels; subway coaches at 100.

It seems a modest estimate. A few decades ago one might lie in his hammock in once-rural Connecticut, where I now live, and hear the croaking of frogs, the singing of birds, the lowing of cattle, the barking of dogs over the hill, perhaps a neighbor pounding nails, the occasional clatter of hooves on the dirt road, the complaint of a heavily loaded wagon, punctuated by the crack of a whip and a cry of "Giddap, you Dobbin!" That is about all he would hear.

Now, sitting on an aluminum garden chair where the hammock used to be, what does one hear? Some of the old sounds to be sure—birds and dogs—but no horses, no creaking wagons, no lowing cattle. You hear the woosh of car after car on the blacktop, the laboring gears of a 20-ton truck hauling sand and gravel to the new superhighway, the roar of motorcycles, a loudspeaker dispensing *Pagliacci* from a neighbor's house, a power lawn mower chattering, the rhythmic thump of a well driller, the screech of power saws clearing the telephone line, the grunt of bulldozers as they tear out a new subdivision, the wailing of an ambulance siren en route to the Danbury Hospital. These are not simultaneous decibels, to be sure, but they are all sounds I have entered in my notebook as occurring within a few hours.

In the troubled air, meanwhile, mingled with the alarms of crows, you can hear trainer planes from the Danbury Airport, helicopters from Sikorsky's, big four-engine props heading for La Guardia, and mammoth jets from across the Atlantic coming down in thunder to Kennedy Airport 50 miles away. This is what you hear in my rustic retreat today—with the bright promise of a "sonic carpet" descending tomorrow.

The sonic carpet is a truly uproarious item in the curve of technology. The term has been used by a Swedish engineer, after a study of sonic boom was made in Oklahoma in 1965.[6] The "carpet" delimits the broad swath of living space made momentarily uninhabitable by sonic boom. When a plane goes faster than the speed of sound (640 miles an hour), it may enter a less turbulent area in the sky, but the turbulence below becomes fantastic. It generates a minor earthquake, breaking windows, dishes, and nervous systems from coast to coast.

Dr. Lundberg reports that the Oklahoma effects were worse than expected. The boom carpet, he says, is between 50 and 80 miles wide, so that cities, suburbs, and countryside alike

[6] Dr. B. K. O. Lundberg in *Bulletin of the Atomic Scientists*, February, 1965.

are blasted. Furthermore, he says, the boom is intensified by certain atmospheric conditions and can be more than doubled by reflection from walls; it seems that the decibels bounce. There will be intolerable insomnia for all in the boom carpet, much physical damage, and many serious accidents. "The comfort and safety of millions of people will be sacrificed to the convenience of a few travelers."

the pollution of waters

There is no major river in the United States which is not grossly polluted. People still drink the water after heavy chlorination, though many buy expensive bottled water, even for tea and coffee. The alarm some of us raised a generation ago has had very little effect.

The despoliation of American rivers is an old and dishonorable story, but lately the fate of Lake Erie has held the headlines. President Johnson made a special journey in 1966 to inspect the desolation. In the same week came a story from Russia that Lake Baikal in Siberia was threatened with the chemical wastes of a vast new pulp mill complex. Russian conservationists promptly moved to head off the disaster.

Lake Erie is a large inland sea, covering 2,600 square miles, large enough, one would expect, to be proof against any trash men might throw into it. Not so. From Detroit on the west to Buffalo on the east, city sewage and the offscourings of industry flush filth into waters which millions of American have long depended upon for drinking, swimming, fishing, and boating. The bathing beaches are now closed, and the boat liveries bankrupt. *Newsweek* in April, 1965, tells the sad story:

Lake Erie is dying. Called *eutrophication,* this death comes ironically from too much nutrition, as when as obese man eats until his heart quits. Nitrogen, phosphorus and filth in the lake feed immense blooms of green algae that burn up oxygen at the lake's bottom needed by higher forms of life . . . useful water life has already been smothered. . . . Revitalization will require more than elaborate pollution-control schemes, for *eutrophication,* once started, feeds on itself.

At the other end of New York State, to the east, lies the Hudson River, in almost as sad a plight. Sixteen cities, from Troy southward to New York Harbor, contribute raw sewage, while other towns give it only a sketchy treatment. The U.S.

Public Health Service estimates that the Hudson gets the waste of 10 million people. "That is what one would expect if, for these 158 miles, both banks of the river were lined solidly with outhouses." [7]

Additional wastes pour into the Hudson from scores of factories: fibers from paper mills, grease and flesh from slaughterhouses, dyes from chemical plants, chemicals from drug makers, acids from metal-processing, oils from automobile paint shops . . . a long way from the year 1609 when Henry Hudson found the river "clear, blue and wonderful to taste."

The Mississippi River, down which Huck Finn and Jim floated on their immortal raft in the old steamboat days, has been equally despoiled. Huck and Jim would not relish going overboard for a swim today. Meanwhile pesticides have been killing the few types of fish which can survive the standard load of pollution. A serious difficulty is that sewer mains and storm drains are combined in most American cities. A big rain is often too much for the sewage treatment plant, if there is one, and the excess overflows into the river along with the storm water.

When the rivers with their heavy burdens come down to the coast, bathing beaches, oyster beds, and lobster pots are abandoned as the bacteria count goes up. Nor are the rivers alone the source of coastal grief. Oil dumped from oceangoing tankers comes washing ashore, ruining the beaches for bathers, preventing shellfish from breeding, and killing gulls and terns. When a bird's feathers are coated with oil, the poor creature can neither swim nor fly, and must die of starvation.

water supply

As in the case of air, the world's water supply is strictly limited. Only 3 percent of the total is fresh water, and most of this is locked in polar ice caps and mountain glaciers. Modern cities want more water for air-conditioning units; farmers want more for irrigation. Arizona, for instance, now depends on underground waters for cities and farms and the water table is steadily falling —some 300,000 acres of cropland have been abandoned. Unless nuclear desalting of sea water becomes practical within a decade, a lot of people may have to move out of Arizona. Meanwhile California, Arizona, and Mexico are in a chronic legal battle as to which gets how much water from the Colorado River. A more sanguinary battle goes on between Jordan and Israel as to who controls the waters of the Jordan River.

[7] Peter T. White in the *New York Times Magazine,* July 17, 1966.

There is, of course, a hopeful note in the coming desalting of sea water by nuclear energy. Intensive R & D [Research and Development] is bringing costs per gallon down so rapidly that some coastal areas will surely receive a new and permanent supply of fresh water within a decade. How far inland desalted water can economically be pumped is another question. A further optimistic note from R & D is the recycling of used and dirty water. It is not particularly pleasant to contemplate, but the engineers say that it will taste all right. Foul water is recycled by nature too, but in a larger and slower operation.

pollution of the land

Beside the road day-lilies grow
Amid the beer cans, row on row.

There are worse pollutants than empty beer cans, but in America, at least, few things are more visible as one drives along the roads, except, of course, billboards. I pick up the cans, flung gaily from cars which pass in the night, every morning around my front gate. They are a symbol of the stupendous piles of junk and refuse which our affluent society throws off.

In *God's Own Junkyard,* Peter Blake superbly documents the trend—with the most dreadful photographs. One reason why junk grows faster than people is the up-and-coming merchandising of the container—the idea being to sell the package rather than what is in it. A comfortable 60 percent of Americans are now in the affluent class, with access to all the good things of life. This does not impress Marya Mannes: "Americans had better be told," she says, "that the more people attain the good things of life, the less good resides in these things." The American Academy of Sciences adds a statistical note. In 1920 the average American threw away 2.75 pounds of refuse a day. In 1965 he threw away eight pounds. "As the earth becomes more crowded, there is no longer any 'away.' One person's trash basket is another's living space."

The junk yards, the roadsides, and the beaches can someday hopefully be cleaned up—perhaps by using manpower made obsolete by automation—*if* enough people are sufficiently revolted by the "effluent age." Soil erosion, however, will take longer to heal. It is not so much the up-and-down plowing which causes it now as the runoff from blacktop highways. Soil, as well as air and water, can be so poisoned as to render it unfit for growing food. This condition results, says the U.S. Department of Agriculture, from adding waste products to the soil faster than they decompose. Pesticides also contribute to soil pollution, and so does fallout. A kind of somber cooperation exists where, says the Department, "air pollutants—such as automobile exhausts, industrial smoke and radioactive fallout—ultimately become soil pollutants as well."

The most spectacular destruction of the good earth is, of course, open-pit mining for coal and other minerals. Without careful and expensive replacement of the soil when the operation is over, nothing may ever grow there again. By contrast, in Germany a mine cannot be opened unless plans are first filed to heal the wound, with severe penalties for their neglect.

The United States lags far behind Europe in protecting its land, but the President's Advisory Committee on Environmental Pollution makes the sound point that *there should be no right to pollute.* Antipollution measures should take their place along with public schools as a mandatory public service. In due course industry must include the costs of pollution control together with materials and labor.

outer space

Above the land, the waters, and the air lies outer space, safe from all human interference until a certain day in 1945 when the first nuclear bomb was exploded in a New Mexico desert. Its ancient peace is now violated so frequently that someone has proposed, not entirely humorously, that the United Nations send up a platoon of space policemen to control the traffic.

If space is ever used in thermonuclear war, it will be quite possible, scientists say, to incinerate a substantial fraction of a continent by firestorm. We remember Mr. Khrushchev's threat when he was head of the Russian state: "Germany will burn like a candle." Germany can be burned even more efficiently now, with the latest nuclear hardware.

Real damage, rather than speculative, occurred when the U.S. exploded a device in outer space a few years ago. It broke up the so-called Van Allen belt, which guards the earth from too much radiation. Scientists, including Dr. Van Allen himself, were shocked by this reckless act.

the spirit of st. francis

From the beer can tossers to the open-pit miners to the disrupters of the Van Allen belt, the trend continues almost unabated. Not only in North America but all over the world, living space is under concentrated attack.

No creature purposely destroys its home, and the only excuse for Homo sapiens is that most of us are still unaware of what we are doing. In our ignorance we suppose that air, water, and land are unlimited. We have in fact become, as the great ecologist Paul Sears once said, a kind of geologic force, more destructive in the long run than hurricanes or earthquakes.

This behavior is deep-rooted, and some students, such as Professor Lynn T. White, trace it back down the centuries to the very foundations of our Judeo-Christian culture. Though Copernicus demonstrated the fallacy of the Ptolemaic system, which had made man the center of the universe, with sun, planets, and the stars revolving deferentially around him, the theologians of the time were far from being defeated. They continued to regard man as the sole possessor of the planet, with dominion over the fish of the sea, the fowl of the air, and over every living thing that moveth upon the earth, and, to make it final, dominion over all the earth. Only St. Francis of Assisi seriously challenged this doctrine; he was bold enough to believe that other living creatures had some rights.

One might add, in all deference, that our children's children have some rights too.

The pollutants now at large—in space, in the air and water, and on land—are not confined to any one city or state or nation. The Van Allen belt fiasco affected the whole world. The "air shed" of New York City includes at least four states and may drift into Canada. Remedial measures and laws which apply to a single political division will be mostly unavailing. The protection of living space is a matter for the federal government in Washington, on one level; for all the countries of North America, or of Europe, on another level; for the United Nations on a planetary level. It is evident that we must make our peace with nature herself, as well as with the fact of thermonuclear bombs.

* * *

To go a step further, we need a supranational Bureau of Standards to screen technological inventions before putting them into mass production, by either industry or government. "All mankind," says the *New York Times*, "can be threatened by unexpected consequences. The need is for worldwide appreciation of the serious warnings now given, and worldwide efforts—perhaps through the United Nations—to meet a worldwide problem."

The *Times* asks whether the race to beat the Russians to the moon is a worthwhile example of government support of science. The spin-off in the form of new knowledge is alleged to be great, but what does it really amount to? Who has taken an impartial inventory? Perhaps the whole NASA operation should be removed from the Rose-Bowl-championship-football class and organized as a sober, careful, probably manless, exploration of space by the United States, Russia, and all high-energy societies, in a joint scientific enterprise under the auspices of the United Nations.

There are plenty of other innovations ripe for screening. High on the list might come the antimissile missile. What will it do in the way of exacerbating the arms race, increasing the danger of war by accident, and what will it cost—$50 billion or $100 billion?

Again, how about biological and chemical warfare, now in active R & D? What can this elaborate mischief-making do to the total human environment and the complex balance of nature? Nobody knows.

Can the supersonic airliner (S.S.T.) really serve a human need on this small planet, while it smashes a 50-mile-wide corridor of sonic boom?

And what promises to be the ultimate effect on the planet's climate of releasing carbon dioxide from industry and motor vehicles at the present rate? One estimate, as noted earlier, is a 4-degree Centigrade increase in world temperature by the year 2000. How soon thereafter will polar ice caps begin to melt, and the oceans to rise?

The United Nations might well be the home of such a Bureau of Standards, and the depository for all relevant scientific information on large technological innovations which can seriously affect society.

One could sleep better at night if some such screening bureau were at work in its laboratories and in the field, manned by scientists who were also philosophers. It would give political leaders, furthermore, firm ground on which to stand, and make decisions. The path to knowledge might really begin to open, and the jungle to be pushed back.

* * *

epilogue: not quite utopia

A faculty member of the Westchester State College, let us say, walks out to his mailbox for the Sunday *New York Times* on a spring morning in the year 2001. The shad-blow is almost over and the orioles are back. The *Times* weighs just half a pound, rather than the present eight. It is charged to his personal account in the computerized credit system to which every American citizen belongs. His salary is of course credited. Competitive advertising has largely disappeared, leaving chiefly news, reviews and comment.

As he looks up, the sky is a deep, unpolluted blue.

A squirrel is chattering, but he hears no thundering jets, no sonic booms, no grinding trucks, roaring motorcycles, screeching station wagons, or grunting bulldozers.

Along the clear, almost transparent road, faintly luminous at night, comes a fuel-cell car, small, quiet, easy to park, shockproof, fumeless. . . . An electric truck follows. Yellow daffodils are blooming by a roadside innocent of beer cans.

Water from the nuclear desalting plant at Greenwich is cold and free of chlorine, with plenty for lawn, garden, and community swimming pool. Private, unguarded pools are banned—too many children were drowned in this struggle for prestige. The fear of drought has disappeared forever—at least in coastal areas.

There are no commercials on television, a service now charged to citizens in the national credit system along with other public utilities.

The beaches of Long Island Sound are white and clean, and shore birds are thick in the wide salt marshes. Power boats with fuel cells are as silent as the sailboats, and water skiing is assigned a separate area, with stiff penalties for leaving it. The waters of the Sound are clear and clean. Great schools of shad are running up the Hudson and Connecticut rivers, shellfish are healthy and abundant. Even Lake Erie is slowly beginning to breathe again.

Through a gap in his tall pine grove, the professor can see on the horizon the towers of the New Town near White Plains. It is one of a dozen local centers in the New York urban field, helping to take the pressure off Manhattan. Its symphony orchestra, he recalls, won the recent All-American competition.

No private automobiles are now permitted in Manhattan, not even for the grandest politicos. Electric buses, electric trucks for night deliveries, plenty of fuel-cell taxis, bicycles on the special paths constitute the vehicles aboveground. The professor can go from a station near his home to Manhattan in 20 noiseless minutes underground. It takes him no longer to the international airport, where Stol-planes rise and descend vertically with almost no noise. The supersonic liners have been abandoned, pending a solution of the sonic boom problem. The professor can get anywhere in the world comfortably in a few hours, as it is.

A good half of New York City's area is now open space, following the Great Demolition of the 1980's, and population is down to an unhurried five million. No crowds yell at a would-be suicide, "Go ahead and jump!" The parks are safe at night; the malls with their fountains, flowers, and sidewalk cafés are pleasant for shopping or for meditation by day.

The United Nations has left New York for an island of its own in the Indian Ocean. It has a powerful legislative body responsible to no nation but to mankind, and the whole organization is intensively devoted to settling disputes between nations, enforcing disarmament, and balancing the world economy. Its lordly budget of over $100 billion a year comes from royalties on various supranational resources, drawn from the sea, from Antarctica, and from the earth's mantle. A cut in the tolls of the new sea-level canal across Nicaragua also helps.

The last substantial war, beyond UN control, ended in Southeast Asia in the early 1970's, when the governments of both belligerents were overwhelmingly displaced by their exasperated, bereaved, and impoverished citizens, and the UN was called in to mandate the whole devastated area. The explosion of several nuclear weapons on each side was the dreadful price for bringing permanent peace on earth.

The cold war between the U.S. and the U.S.S.R. was finally abandoned in the late 1960's. One reason was that Russian scientists discovered and gave to the world a cure for cancer. The impact even dissolved the John Birch Society.

China and a reunited Germany are now strong supporters of the United Nations. As a result of the steady growth of the mixed economy, the opposing ideologies of Communism and the Radical Right have all but withered away. Mr. William F. Buckley, Jr. devotes his still energetic mind to raising delphiniums.

No human landings on Mars or Venus are now planned. The terrible disaster on the return from the moon by the first astronauts determined that. Outer space is obviously inhospitable for long trips by earthlings; there are too many unknown variables. Exploration is still vigorously carried on, but by unmanned vehicles and instruments, under the direction of scientists in UNESCO.

Competition between nations is largely confined to advances in the arts, research, and the Olympic Games. Deprived of its military function, a nation is now a nostalgic homeland, and a much more decent and friendly institution. Capital punishment has been abolished in most countries, the crime rate is down, and there is no point to stealing money in a society devoted to computerized credit.

Every child on earth now learns the world language—with its phonetic spelling and simple structure—through television lessons and plays. A little fiction and poetry have recently been written in this synthetic tongue, but its literary value remains to be proved, however excellent it may be for international conferences.

Nearly every child on earth receives all the education his genes permit. He grows up an independent thinker, informed by the scientific attitude. This has gone far to heal race relations, but no final solution can yet be announced. There is however, no *Apartheid* in South Africa and no "Black Power" in the United States.

The American population is growing at half of one percent a year, down from 1.6 percent in 1965. The world rate stands at 0.7 percent. Though birth control is universally available, with some extraordinary new techniques in both sterilization and tranquilizing the sex drive, these growth rates are known to be too high. Planetary policy aims at a rate of *zero* by 2025, with world population thereafter never to exceed seven billion children, women, and men. That seems to be the maximum our living space can comfortably support. It is no longer a question of the food supply setting the total, but elbow room.

The food supply in calories is now growing at 1.3 percent, almost twice the rate of population. Some African children are still undernourished, but the dreadful famines of the 1970's and 1980's will never come again, and the insidious and deadly new variety of plague which then originated to balance births with deaths has at last been conquered by the World Health Organization.

Nuclear power plants, using the fusion process with hydrogen from all the oceans as raw material, are now beginning to raise living standards everywhere, and the area once known as the Hungry World—two-thirds of mankind—has lost its title. The battle now is with the temptations of material abundance rather than with the deprivations of scarcity. Economic textbooks are at last being rewritten on this principle.

Our professor walks back from his pleasant roadside, waving to a neighbor on horseback, hacking along the parallel trail. He breathes deep of the fresh spring air, notes the dogwood buds almost ready to create their annual snowdrift, and enters his pleasant home, warmed and serviced by wireless pulsations of energy. He opens the Sunday *Times* to read the latest instrument analysis from Mars. Yes, once there were probably living creatures on Mars, and then . . . ?

in my opinion...

Mr. Chase has assembled in a relatively small package the "eight assaults on living space" which conservationists have worked on individually for the past decade with increasing intensity. It is indeed helpful to have each of these problems examined at close view, since any one or a combination (with the exception of noise pollution) could make our world a wilderness.

Although the points discussed were supported by American statistics, the trends are worldwide, affecting all cultures. Whether the oil covering a beach is Asian, European or American makes no difference: the damage has been done.

A supranational bureau is essential to protect man from himself. But Mr. Chase neglected to mention the feasibility of this. The problem is two-fold: there must be universal awareness of the pending catastrophe and universal agreement among the peoples of the world. As herculean as this job sounds, it must be done before the turn of the century—before our present destructive trends are irreversible.

The projections of the future in the Epilogue can be considered as science fiction. This "brave new world" will exist when man faces the reality of his using godlike powers with more godlike wisdom.

Mr. Chase did present several ideas which can and should be initiated now. As practical and economical desalinization of sea water is within our grasp, the water shortage problem may be forestalled.

City planning is becoming widely-accepted. The question of what to do with the present megalopolis was handled well: restrict the population and relocate the excess. Although it sounds terribly inhumane, would it not be more inhumane to maintain the slums of Rio de Janiero or Hong Kong?

The fuel-cell car and Stol-plane are necessities of the future. Today's automobiles and jet aircraft are luxuries that our small planet cannot afford. Our science and technology have the ability to develop noiseless, pollution-free means of transportation. But man must first realize the need for these things.

The projections about world politics in the twenty-first century sound like wishful thinking. A supranational agency, possibly an expanded United Nations, is indeed probable and desirable. Its sphere of influence will be universal but I doubt that the basic nature of man will have changed sufficiently within the next thirty years to erase national prejudices.

Perhaps the haunting tone of the projection on space travel should be heeded by scientists and governments alike. And what about a zero birth rate? It is extremely doubtful that this could occur unless a catastrophe, either man-made or natural, takes place between now and the millennium.

The fate of mankind is no longer an abstraction. Mr. Chase acknowledges the danger but in words which may soon be forgotten. No outcry can be too loud. Man no longer has the margin for error which space, time, and his relative lack of power once provided for his ecological mistakes.

"Yes, once there were probably living creatures on Earth, and then . . . ?"

patricia a. bonn

questions

1. The U.S. Army used the Atlantic Ocean as a tomb for deadly nerve gas while the world looked on seemingly helpless. Conservationists fought and lost in U.S. courts against this action, yet little was heard from the countries along the Gulf Stream which would be directly affected in the event of an accident. Do you think worldwide outcry could have altered the Army's plan? Would this strategy be effective in future ecological crises?

2. It is the opinion of some experts that an automobile smog control device will never be perfected. The automobile and

petroleum industries have acknowledged this fact and are in the process of developing a pollution-free form of transportation. Until this new vehicle is available, should Detroit continue to manufacture thousands of automobiles daily? Why?

3. Information released by the aircraft companies about the super jet transport (SST) did not include the fact that it would create a huge sonic carpet. Law suits have been filed against airlines, aircraft manufacturers and airports by private citizens. Has private industry the legal right to disrupt and possibly destroy for its own profit? Explain.

4. It has been estimated that if the multi-million dollar job of restoring Lake Erie were started now, it would take 50 years to return it to "reasonable" purity. As federal, state, and local governments are politically and financially involved, would a special commission of private citizens be desirable to head this project in order to speed up its implementation? Why?

5. If a supranational screening board were established as an extension of the United Nations, do you think private industry would cooperate? Do you think the private citizen would consider such an agency to be interfering with his personal freedom? Explain.

12.
too many,
too soon?
population

THE POPULATION BOMB

paul r. ehrlich

introduction and comment by patricia hubbard

The population of the world is increasing at an alarming rate. The human race is reproducing so fast that we are threatening our own existence. Overpopulation produces such problems as pollution of the environment, food shortages, disease caused by poor sanitation, psychological problems due to over-crowded conditions, and even war. Although many are aware of the immediacy of the situation, great numbers of people continue in their ignorance of the dangers or are perhaps ignoring them with the hope that they will all go away by themselves. This problem is too urgent to be ignored for even a year or two. Something must be done *now* to educate the world about the impending catastrophe of too many people.

Much has been written in recent years about the population problem. Dr. Paul R. Ehrlich, professor of Biology and Director of Graduate study for the Department of Biological Sciences at Stanford University, has written *The Population Bomb,* which has been lauded by the Sierra Club as well as other similar groups because of its vivid, accurate account of the population problem. In the prologue of his book, Dr. Ehrlich dramatically describes the urgency of the situation:

The battle to feed all of humanity is over. In the 1970's the world will undergo famines—hundreds of millions of people are going to starve to death in spite of any crash programs embarked upon now. At this late date nothing can prevent a substantial increase in the world death rate, although many lives could be saved through dramatic programs to "stretch" the carrying capacity of the earth by increasing food production. But these programs will only provide a stay of execution unless they are accompanied by determined and successful efforts at population control. Population control is the conscious regulation of the numbers of human beings to meet the needs, not just of individual families, but of society as a whole.

In *The Population Bomb,* Dr. Ehrlich discusses the dangers of war, pestilence, and famine at great length.

Famine is the most obvious danger of overpopulation. It follows logically that if the world can produce only "X" amount of food for "2X" amount of people, some people are going to starve to death. It doesn't take too much thought to figure out the mathematics involved in this part of the problem.

Pestilence, however, is somewhat more abstract. In a sense, this type of pestilence is man-made. Pollution and imbalances in nature are the by-products of our population explosion. The irresponsible spraying of chemicals to control insect pests has already resulted in conditions that are worse than the conditions they were supposed to control. Pollution is also the direct result of man's irresponsibility toward his natural environment. Every day thousands of tons of wastes, some of them extremely toxic, are dumped into our already diseased environment. Overpopulation multiplies this problem. The result, eventually, may be widespread disease.

War is the most dangerous problem of all and is also the most difficult to understand. It is common knowledge that man has the power to destroy himself completely at any time. But the threat of war because of overpopulation has not yet been fully understood. As the most critically overpopulated areas of the world (Red China, for example) face massive famines, the threat of atomic war may intensify, according to Dr. Ehrlich. The United States cannot produce enough food to supply these people—therefore they may become increasingly hostile toward us. If we sit on our hands, this situation could eventually materialize into World War III and the end of Homo sapiens on earth.

p.h.

THE POPULATION BOMB

Dr. Paul R. Ehrlich is professor of Biology and Director of Graduate Study for the Department of Biological Sciences at Stanford University. His specialty is Population Biology; he is the founder and president of Zero Population Growth, Inc., and vice president of the Society for the Study of Evolution. Trained as an entymologist, he received his B.A. in Zoology from the University of Pennsylvania and Ph.D. from the University of Kansas. He is an associate at the Center for the Study of Democratic Institutions, and has credits as a committeeman for the International Association for Ecology. He is a member of the California Academy of Sciences, and is on the executive council of the Lepidopterist Society. Dr. Ehrlich has written How to Know Butterflies, *1960;* Process of Evolution, *1963; his best-selling* The Population Bomb, *1968; and* Population, Resources, Environments: Issues in Human Ecology, *1970.*

Americans are beginning to realize that the undeveloped countries of the world face an inevitable population-food crisis. Each year food production in undeveloped countries falls a bit further behind burgeoning population growth, and people go to bed a little bit hungrier. While there are temporary or local reversals of this trend, it now seems inevitable that it will continue to its logical conclusion: mass starvation. The rich are going to get richer, but the more numerous poor are going to get poorer. Of these poor, a minimum of three and one-half million will starve to death this year, mostly children. But this is a mere handful compared to the numbers that will be starving in a decade or so. And it is now too late to take action to save many of those people.

In a book about population there is a temptation to stun the reader with an avalanche of statistics. I'll spare you most, but not all, of that. After all, no matter how you slice it, population is a numbers game. Perhaps the best way to impress you with numbers is to tell you about the "doubling time"—the time necessary for the population to double in size.

It has been estimated that the human population of 6000 B.C. was about five million people, taking perhaps one million years to get there from two and a half million. The population did not reach 500 million until almost 8,000 years later—about 1650 A.D. This means it doubled roughly once every thousand years or so. It reached a billion people around 1850, doubling in some 200 years. It took only 80 years or so for the next doubling, as the population reached two billion around 1930. We have not completed the next doubling to four billion yet, but we now have well over three billion people. The doubling time at present seems to be about 37 years.[1] Quite a reduction in doubling times: 1,000,000 years, 1,000 years, 200 years, 80 years, 37 years. Perhaps the meaning of a doubling time of around 37 years is best brought home by a theoretical exercise. Let's examine what might happen on the absurd assumption that the population continued to double every 37 years into the indefinite future.

If growth continued at that rate for about 900 years, there would be some 60,000,000,000,000,000 people on the face of the earth. Sixty million billion people. This is about 100 persons for each square yard of the Earth's surface, land and sea. A British physicist, J. H. Fremlin,[2] guessed that such a multitude might be housed in a continuous 2,000-story building covering our entire planet. The upper 1,000 stories would contain only the apparatus for running this gigantic warren. Ducts, pipes, wires, elevator shafts, etc., would occupy about half of the space in the bottom 1,000 stories. This would leave three or four yards of floor space for each person. I will leave to your imagination the physical details of existence in this ant heap, except to point out that all would not be black. Probably each person would be limited in his travel. Perhaps he could take elevators through all 1,000

[1] Since this was written, 1968 figures have appeared, showing that the doubling time is now 35 years.

[2] J. H. Fremlin, "How Many People Can the World Support?" *New Scientist,* October 29, 1964.

residential stories but could travel only within a circle of a few hundred yards' radius on any floor. This would permit, however, each person to choose his friends from among some ten million people! And, as Fremlin points out, entertainment on the world-wide TV should be excellent, for at any time "one could expect some ten million Shakespeares and rather more Beatles to be alive."

Could growth of the human population of the Earth continue beyond that point? Not according to Fremlin. We would have reached a "heat limit." People themselves, as well as their activities, convert other forms of energy into heat which must be dissipated. In order to permit this excess heat to radiate directly from the top of the "world building" directly into space, the atmosphere would have been pumped into flasks under the sea well before the limiting population size was reached. The precise limit would depend on the technology of the day. At a population size of one billion billion people, the temperature of the "world roof" would be kept around the melting point of iron to radiate away the human heat generated.

But, you say, surely Science (with a capital "S") will find a way for us to occupy the other planets of our solar system and eventually of other stars before we get all that crowded. Skip for a moment the virtual certainty that those planets are uninhabitable. Forget also the insurmountable logistic problems of moving billions of people off the Earth. Fremlin has made some interesting calculations on how much time we could buy by occupying the planets of the solar system. For instance, at any given time it would take only about 50 years to populate Venus, Mercury, Mars, the moon, and the moons of Jupiter and Saturn to the same population density as Earth.[3]

What if the fantastic problems of reaching and colonizing the other planets of the solar system, such as Jupiter and Uranus, can be solved? It would take only about 200 years to fill them "Earthfull." So we could perhaps gain 250 years of time for population

[3] To understand this, simply consider what would happen if we held the population constant at three billion people by exporting all the surplus people. If this were done for 37 years (the time it now takes for one doubling) we would have exported three billion people—enough to populate a twin planet of the Earth to the same density. In two doubling times (74 years) we would reach a total human population for the solar system of 12 billion people, enough to populate the Earth and three similar planets to the density found on Earth today. Since the areas of the planets and moons mentioned above are not three times that of the Earth, they can be populated to equal density in much less than two doubling times.

growth in the solar system after we had reached an absolute limit on Earth. What then? We can't ship our surplus to the stars. Professor Garrett Hardin [4] of the University of California at Santa Barbara has dealt effectively with this fantasy. Using extremely optimistic assumptions, he has calculated that Americans, by cutting their standard of living down to 18% of its present level, could in *one year* set aside enough capital to finance the exportation to the stars of *one day's* increase in the population of the world.

Interstellar transport for surplus people presents an amusing prospect. Since the ships would take generations to reach most stars, the only people who could be transported would be those willing to exercise strict birth control. Population explosions on space ships would be disastrous. Thus we would have to export our responsible people, leaving the irresponsible at home on Earth to breed.

Enough of fantasy. Hopefully, you are convinced that the population will have to stop growing sooner or later and that the extremely remote possibility of expanding into outer space offers no escape from the laws of population growth. If you still want to hope for the stars, just remember that, at the current growth rate, in a few thousand years everything in the visible universe would be converted into people, and the ball of people would be expanding with the speed of light! [5] Unfortunately, even 900 years is much too far in the future for those of us concerned with the population explosion. As you shall see, the next *nine* years will probably tell the story.

Of course, population growth is not occurring uniformly over the face of the Earth. Indeed, countries are divided rather neatly into two groups: those with rapid growth rates, and those with relatively slow growth rates. The first group, making up about two-thirds of the world population, coincides closely with what are known as the "undeveloped countries" (UDCs). The UDCs are not industrialized, tend to have inefficient agriculture, very small gross national products, high illiteracy rates and related problems. That's what UDCs are technically, but a short definition of undeveloped is "starving." Most Latin American, African, and Asian countries fall into this category. The second group consists, in essence, of the "developed countries" (DCs). DCs are modern, industrial

[4] "Interstellar Migration and the Population Problem," *Heredity* 50: 68–70, 1959.
[5] I. J. Cook, *New Scientist,* September 8, 1966.

nations, such as the United States, Canada, most European countries, Israel, Russia, Japan, and Australia. Most people in these countries are adequately nourished.

Doubling times in the UDCs range around 20 to 35 years. Examples of these times (from the 1968 figures just released by the Population Reference Bureau) are Kenya, 24 years; Nigeria, 28; Turkey, 24; Indonesia, 31; Philippines, 20; Brazil, 22; Costa Rica, 20; and El Salvador, 19. Think of what it means for the population of a country to double in 25 years. In order just to keep living standards at the present inadequate level, the food available for the people must be doubled. Every structure and road must be duplicated. The amount of power must be doubled. The capacity of the transport system must be doubled. The number of trained doctors, nurses, teachers, and administrators must be doubled. This would be a fantastically difficult job in the United States—a rich country with a fine agricultural system, immense industries, and rich natural resources. Think of what it means to a country with none of these.

Remember also that in virtually all UDCs, people have gotten the word about the better life it is possible to have. They have seen colored pictures in magazines of the miracles of Western technology. They have seen automobiles and airplanes. They have seen American and European movies. Many have seen refrigerators, tractors, and even TV sets. Almost all have heard transistor radios. They *know* that a better life is possible. They have what we like to call "rising expectations." If twice as many people are to be happy, the miracle of doubling what they now have will not be enough. It will only maintain today's standard of living. There will have to be a tripling or better. Needless to say, they are not going to be happy.

Doubling times for the populations of the DCs tend to be in the 50-to-200-year range. Examples of 1968 doubling times are the United States, 63 years; Austria, 175; Denmark, 88; Norway, 88; United Kingdom, 140; Poland, 88; Russia, 63; Italy, 117; Spain, 88; and Japan, 63. These are industrialized countries that have undergone the so-called demographic transition—a transition from high to low growth rate. As industrialization progressed, children became less important to parents as extra hands to work on the farm and as support in old age. At the same time they became a financial drag—expensive to raise and educate. Presumably these are the reasons for a slowing of population growth after industrialization. They boil down to a simple fact—people just want to have fewer children.

This is not to say, however, that population is not a problem for the DCs. First of all, most of them are overpopulated. They are overpopulated by the simple criterion that they are not able to produce enough food to feed their populations. It is true that they have the money to buy food, but when food is no longer available for sale they will find the money rather indigestible. Then, too, they share with the UDCs a serious problem of population distribution. Their urban centers are getting more and more crowded relative to the countryside. This problem is not as severe as it is in the UDCs (if current trends should continue, which they cannot, Calcutta could have 66 million inhabitants in the year 2000). As you are well aware, however, urban concentrations are creating serious problems even in America. In the United States, one of the more rapidly growing DCs, we hear constantly of the headaches caused by growing population: not just garbage in our environment, but overcrowded highways, burgeoning slums, deteriorating school systems, rising crime rates, riots, and other related problems.

From the point of view of a demographer, the whole problem is quite simple. A population will continue to grow as long as the birth rate exceeds the death rate—if immigration and emigration are not occurring. It is, of course, the balance between birth rate and death rate that is critical. The birth rate is the number of births per thousand people per year in the population. The death rate is the number of deaths per thousand people per year.[6] Subtracting

---

[6] The birth rate is more precisely the total number of births in a country during a year, divided by the total population at the midpoint of the year, multiplied by 1,000. Suppose that there were 80 births in Lower Slobbovia during 1967, and that the population of Lower Slobbovia was 2,000 on July 1, 1967. Then the birth rate would be:

$$\text{Birth rate} = \frac{80 \ (\text{total births in L. Slobbovia in 1967})}{2,000 \ (\text{total population, July 1, 1967})} \times 1,000$$

$$= .04 \times 1,000 = 40$$

Similarly if there were 40 deaths in Lower Slobbovia during 1967, the death rate would be:

$$\text{Death rate} = \frac{40 \ (\text{total deaths in L. Slobbovia in 1967})}{2,000 \ (\text{total population, July 1, 1967})} \times 1,000$$

$$= .02 \times 1,000 = 20$$

Then the Lower Slobbovian birth rate would be 40 per thousand, and the death rate would be 20 per thousand. For every 1,000 Lower Slobbovians alive on July 1, 1967, 40 babies were born and 20 people died. Subtracting the death rate from the birth rate, and ignoring migration, gives the rate of increase. If the birth rate is 30 per thousand per year, and the death rate is 10 per thousand per year, then the rate of increase is 20 per thousand per year (30 — 10 = 20). Expressed as a percent (rate per hundred people), the rate of 20 per thousand becomes 2%. If the rate of increase is 2%, then the doubling time will be 35 years. Note that if you simply added 20 people per thousand per year to the population, it would take 50 years to add a second thousand people (20 × 50 = 1,000). But the doubling time is actually much less because populations grow at compound interest rates. Just as interest dollars themselves earn interest, so people added to populations produce more people. It's growing at compound interest that makes populations double so much more rapidly than seems possible. Look at the relationship between the annual percent increase (interest rate) and the doubling time of the population (time for your money to double):

Annual percent increase	Doubling time
1.0	70
2.0	35
3.0	24
4.0	17

Those are all the calculations—I promise. If you are interested in more details on how demographic figuring is done, you may enjoy reading Thompson and Lewis's excellent book, *Population Problems*.[7]

There are some professional optimists around who like to greet every sign of dropping birth rates with wild pronouncements about the end of the population explosion. They are a little like a person who, after a low temperature of five below zero on December 21, interprets a low of only three below zero on December 22 as a cheery sign of approaching spring. First of all, birth rates, along with all demographic statistics, show short-term fluctuations caused by many factors. For instance, the birth rate depends rather heavily on the number of women at reproductive age. In

---

the death rate from the birth rate gives us the rate of natural increase of Lower Slobbovia for the year 1967. That is, 40 — 20 = 20; during 1967 the population grew at a rate of 20 people per thousand per year. Dividing that rate by ten expresses the increase as a percent (the increase per hundred per year). The increase in 1967 in Lower Slobbovia was two percent. Remember that this rate of increase ignores any movement of people into and out of Lower Slobbovia.

[7] McGraw-Hill Book Company, Inc., New York, 1965.

the United States the current low birth rates soon will be replaced by higher rates as more post World War II "baby boom" children move into their reproductive years. In Japan, 1966, the Year of the Fire Horse, was a year of very low birth rates. There is widespread belief that girls born in the Year of the Fire Horse make poor wives, and Japanese couples try to avoid giving birth in that year because they are afraid of having daughters.

But, I repeat, it is the relationship between birth rate and death rate that is most critical. Indonesia, Laos, and Haiti all had birth rates around 46 per thousand in 1966. Costa Rica's birth rate was 41 per thousand. Good for Costa Rica? Unfortunately, not very. Costa Rica's death rate was less than nine per thousand, while the other countries all had death rates above 20 per thousand. The population of Costa Rica in 1966 was doubling every 17 years, while the doubling times of Indonesia, Laos, and Haiti were all above 30 years. Ah, but, you say, it was good for Costa Rica— fewer people per thousand were dying each year. Fine for a few years perhaps, but what then? Some 50% of the people in Costa Rica are under 15 years old. As they get older, they will need more and more food in a world with less and less. In 1983 they will have twice as many mouths to feed as they had in 1966, if the 1966 trend continues. Where will the food come from? Today the death rate in Costa Rica is low in part because they have a large number of physicians in proportion to their population. How do you suppose those physicians will keep the death rate down when there's not enough food to keep people alive?

One of the most ominous facts of the current situation is that roughly 40% of the population of the undeveloped world is made up of people *under 15 years old*. As that mass of young people moves into its reproductive years during the next decade, we're going to see the greatest baby boom of all time. Those youngsters are the reason for all the ominous predictions for the year 2000. They are the gunpowder for the population explosion.

How did we get into this bind? It all happened a long time ago, and the story involves the process of natural selection, the development of culture, and man's swollen head. The essence of success in evolution is reproduction. Indeed, natural selection is simply defined as differential reproduction of genetic types. That is, if people with blue eyes have more children on the average than those with brown eyes, natural selection is occurring. More genes for blue eyes will be passed on to the next generation than will genes for brown eyes. Should this continue, the population will have progressively larger and larger proportions of blue-eyed people. This differential reproduction of genetic types is the driving force of evolution; it has been driving evolution for billions of years. Whatever types produced more offspring became the common types. Virtually all populations contain very many different genetic types (for reasons that need not concern us), and some are always outreproducing others. As I said, reproduction is the key to winning the evolutionary game. Any structure, physiological process, or pattern of behavior that leads to greater reproductive success will tend to be perpetuated. The entire process by which man developed involves thousands of millenia of our ancestors being more successful breeders than their relatives. Facet number one of our bind—the urge to reproduce has been fixed in us by billions of years of evolution.

Of course through all those years of evolution, our ancestors were fighting a continual battle to keep the birth rate ahead of the death rate. That they were successful is attested to by our very existence, for, if the death rate had overtaken the birth rate for any substantial period of time, the evolutionary line leading to man would have gone extinct. Among our apelike ancestors, a few million years ago, it was still very difficult for a mother to rear her children successfully. Most of the offspring died before they reached reproductive age. The death rate was near the birth rate. Then another factor entered the picture—cultural evolution was added to biological evolution.

Culture can be loosely defined as the body of nongenetic information which people pass from generation to generation. It is the accumulated knowledge that, in the old days, was passed on entirely by word of mouth, painting, and demonstration. Several thousand years ago the written word was added to the means of cultural transmission. Today culture is passed on in these ways, and also through television, computer tapes, motion pictures, records, blueprints, and other media. Culture is all the information man possesses except for that which is stored in the chemical language of his genes.

The large size of the human brain evolved in response to the development of cultural information. A big brain is an advantage when dealing with such information. Big-brained individuals were able to deal more successfully with the culture of their group. They were thus more successful reproductively than their smaller-brained relatives. They passed on their genes for big brains to their numerous offspring. They also added to the accumulating store of cultural information, increasing slightly the premium placed on brain size in the next generation. A self-reinforcing selective trend developed—a trend toward increased brain size.[8] But there was, quite literally, a rub. Babies had bigger and bigger heads. There were limits to how large a woman's pelvis could conveniently become. To make a long story short, the strategy of evolution was not to make a woman bell-shaped and relatively immobile, but to accept the problem of having babies who were helpless for a long period while their brains grew after birth.[9] How could the mother defend and care for her infant during its unusually long period of helplessness? She couldn't, unless Papa hung around. The girls are still working on that problem, but an essential step was to get rid of the short, well-defined breeding season characteristic of most mammals. The year-round sexuality of the human female, the long period of infant dependence on the female, the evolution of the family group, all are at the roots of our present problem. They are essential ingredients in the vast social phenomenon that we call sex. Sex is not simply an act leading to the production of offspring. It is a varied and complex cultural phenomenon penetrating into all aspects of our lives —one involving our self-esteem, our choice of friends, cars, and leaders. It is tightly interwoven with our mythologies and history. Sex in man is necessary for the production of young, but it also evolved to ensure their successful rearing. Facet number two of our bind—our urge to reproduce is hopelessly entwined with most of our other urges.

Of course, in the early days the whole system did not prevent a very high mortality among the young, as well as among the older members of the group. Hunting and food-gathering is a risky business. Cavemen had to throw very impressive cave bears out of their caves before men could move in. Witch doctors and shamans had a less than perfect record at treating wounds and curing disease. Life was short, if not sweet. Man's total population size doubtless increased slowly but steadily as human populations expanded out of the African cradle of our species.

Then about 8,000 years ago a major change occurred—the

---

[8] Human brain size increased from an apelike capacity of about 500 cubic centimeters (cc) in *Australopithecus* to about 1,500 cc in modern *Homo sapiens*. Among modern men small variations in brain size do not seem to be related to significant differences in the ability to use cultural information, and there is no particular reason to believe that our brain size will continue to increase. Further evolution may occur more readily in a direction of increased efficiency rather than increased size.

[9] This is, of course, an oversimplified explanation. For more detail see Ehrlich and Holm, *The Process of Evolution*, McGraw-Hill Book Company, Inc., New York, 1963.

agricultural revolution. People began to give up hunting food and settled down to grow it. Suddenly some of the risk was removed from life. The chances of dying of starvation diminished greatly in some human groups. Other threats associated with the nomadic life were also reduced, perhaps balanced by new threats of disease and large-scale warfare associated with the development of cities. But the overall result was a more secure existence than before, and the human population grew more rapidly. Around 1800, when the standard of living in what are today the DCs was dramatically increasing due to industrialization, population growth really began to accelerate. The development of medical science was the straw that broke the camel's back. While lowering death rates in the DCs was due in part to other factors, there is no question that "instant death control," exported by the DCs, has been responsible for the drastic lowering of death rates in the UDCs. Medical science, with its efficient public health programs, has been able to depress the death rate with astonishing rapidity and at the same time drastically increase the birth rate; healthier people have more babies.

The power of exported death control can best be seen by an examination of the classic case of Ceylon's assault on malaria after World War II. Between 1933 and 1942 the death rate due directly to malaria was *reported* as almost two per thousand. This rate, however, represented only a portion of the malaria deaths, as many were reported as being due to "pyrexia." [10] Indeed, in 1934–1935 a malaria epidemic may have been directly responsible for fully half of the deaths on the island. In addition, malaria, which infected a large portion of the population, made people susceptible to many other diseases. It thus contributed to the death rate indirectly as well as directly.

The introduction of DDT in 1946 brought rapid control over the mosquitoes which carry malaria. As a result, the death rate on the island was halved in less than a decade. The death rate in Ceylon in 1945 was 22. It dropped 34% between 1946 and 1947 and moved down to ten in 1954. Since the sharp postwar drop it has continued to decline and now stands at eight. Although part of the drop is doubtless due to the killing of other insects which carry disease and to other public health measures, most of it can be accounted for by the control of malaria.

[10] These data and those that follow on the decline of death rates are from Kingsley Davis's "The Amazing Decline of Mortality in Underdeveloped Areas," *The American Economic Review,* Vol. 46, pp. 305–318.

Victory over malaria, yellow fever, smallpox, cholera, and other infectious diseases has been responsible for similar plunges in death rate throughout most of the UDCs. In the decade 1940–1950 the death rate declined 46% in Puerto Rico, 43% in Formosa, and 23% in Jamaica. In a sample of 18 undeveloped areas the average decline in death rate between 1945 and 1950 was 24%.

It is, of course, socially very acceptable to reduce the death rate. Billions of years of evolution have given us all a powerful will to live. Intervening in the birth rate goes against our evolutionary values. During all those centuries of our evolutionary past, the individuals who had the most children passed on their genetic endowment in greater quantities than those who reproduced less. Their genes dominate our heredity today. All our biological urges are for more reproduction, and they are all too often reinforced by our culture. In brief, death control goes with the grain, birth control against it.

In summary, the world's population will continue to grow as long as the birth rate exceeds the death rate; it's as simple as that. When it stops growing or starts to shrink, it will mean that either the birth rate has gone down or the death rate has gone up or a combination of the two. Basically, then, there are only two kinds of solutions to the population problem. One is a "birth rate solution," in which we find ways to lower the birth rate. The other is a "death rate solution," in which ways to raise the death rate— war, famine, pestilence—*find us.* The problem could have been avoided by *population control,* in which mankind consciously adjusted the birth rate so that a "death rate solution" did not have to occur.

in my opinion...

In my opinion, Dr. Ehrlich dare not be ignored any longer.
The entire world must listen to him and try to stop this race toward doom. There is just barely enough time left to save us from extinction by overpopulation. In other words, not a month, day or week can be wasted in the fight to control the population of the world. Extreme steps must be taken because

time is so short. In another section of *The Population Bomb,*
Dr. Ehrlich states this situation as plainly as is possible:

*I wish I could offer you some sugarcoated solutions, but I'm
afraid the time for them is long gone. A cancer is an uncontrolled
multiplication of cells; the population explosion is an
uncontrolled multiplication of people. Treating only the symptoms
of cancer may make the victim more comfortable at first, but
eventually he dies—often horribly. A similar fate awaits a
world with a population explosion if only the symptoms are
treated. We must shift our efforts from treatment of the symptoms
to the cutting out of the cancer. The operation will demand
many apparently brutal and heartless decisions. The pain may
be intense. But the disease is so far advanced that only
with radical surgery does the patient have a chance of survival.*

The biggest problem, as I see it, is how to overcome opposition
to programs of population control. Many religious groups
oppose population control and so do many people just on general
principles. How can these people be prevented from spreading
their threatening dogma? They must be convinced in some
way that such control is absolutely necessary.

On the question of population control it is very easy to
become pessimistic. I would allow myself to feel this way except
for the fact that I believe that we can be saved if something
is done now. If nothing is done within the next five years at most,
there will be no year 2000 for the people on the earth. We
will have populated ourselves into oblivion.

Each person must do all he can to help bring into existence
a worldwide program of control. If everyone does not do his
part, there may be no one to worry about it. It is as simple as
that—alarmingly simple.

patricia hubbard

questions

1. Why has so little been done to save the world from the doom of overpopulation in the United States?

2. What type of agency could be set up to administer a program of population control?

3. Awareness of threats to our ecology have become, fortunately, a part of the American social and political ethos. It has been far more difficult to arouse the nations of the world to take more positive action with regard to population control. Why? How can this resistance be overcome?

4. How many children do you plan to have? Why?

5. What is being done to control overpopulation in the underdeveloped nations today?

13.

we won't make it: the threat of nuclear war

WOULD CIVILIZATION SURVIVE A NUCLEAR WAR?

linus pauling

introduction and comment by jay r. bourne

The two brothers strolled casually into the field. The first was at home; the second was a visitor. And the visitor did not know that as he gazed elsewhere, his brother raised a weapon. The weapon was lowered quickly and forcefully. ". . . and Cain slew Abel." With this action, Homo sapiens were marked with a trait which has stayed with the species and made it different from any other animal. Man became the first animal ever to plot and kill one of his own kind.

Since that day, mankind has retained this capacity to take the life of another of his own species—or any other species. Man also acquired an enemy which is the most feared by all other animals—that enemy is man himself. It has been man's strange and wondrous ability to kill anything, anywhere and at anytime which has truly established man's presence on earth.

There are many environmental problems which are contributing factors to mankind's self-destruction, as was noted by Stuart Chase. These problems are not new. The population of the world has been increasing. The number of pollutants being added to the air is on the rise. These two threats have been rapidly increasing in magnitude.

Man, with all his scientific knowledge, may improve the standard of living, increase the longevity of human life, and expand his ability to cope with environmental problems. The question is: Can man survive long enough to have his dreams of "progress" come true?

Science and technology have been the tools and the toys of man. Is it now possible that these two pious partners in progress can also be the means of man's doom? One fact remains quite clear: never before has man possessed the power totally to destroy himself and almost every other form of life on this planet.

No matter how advanced or "civilized" man becomes, somewhere on this earth at least one man will be plotting to

kill another man. This is the major problem; man has killed
man and will continue to do so. The extent and magnitude to
which this killing takes place will depend largely upon
the weaponry and the availability of that weaponry.

As the number of inhabitants of the earth has increased, so
has the number of weapons. As the number of weapons has
increased, so has the possibility for mass murder. And in addition
to this frightening parallel, man has invented the super-weapons.

World War II not only saw the introduction of the most
majestic mass murder weapon yet devised—the H-bomb—but
also saw the German hierarchy deliberately kill approximately
6 million people by means of the "gas-method". It is the
first of these two methods of mass murder which deserves
particular attention. The two nuclear weapons used against
Japan in the war were relatively small, but they ushered in the
first use of nuclear energy as a weapon. The bomb also
demonstrated our capability for the total destruction of human life.

We would only be hiding the truth from ourselves if we did
not admit that nuclear weapons are numerous. It would
likewise be deceiving to say that these weapons are not readily
available.

It is difficult to assume that the super-weapons of man's
arsenal will never be used. It is more realistic to assume that
when these weapons are used, they will be used in force.
Even more possible is the chance that a "mistake" could
set off the chain of events leading to World War III. Will man
exist three decades from now?

Double Nobel Laureate Linus Pauling details our omnipresent
dangers.

j.r.b.

WOULD CIVILIZATION SURVIVE
A NUCLEAR WAR?

*Controversial Dr. Linus Pauling earned his Ph.D. at the California
Institute of Technology where he has been the Chairman of its
Chemistry division since 1931. He has studied at the Universities
of Munich, Copenhagen and Zurich. Recipient of honorary
doctorates from twenty-five United States and foreign universities,
he was a Guggenheim and National Research Council fellow.
Since 1963 he has been Research Professor of Physics and
Biological Sciences at the Center for the Study of Democratic
Institutions.*

*In 1952 the Society of France presented the Pasteur medal in
Biochemistry to Dr. Pauling and the awards and honors have
not stopped their flow. Two Nobel prizes are among the
most noted: in Chemistry in 1954 and the Nobel Peace Prize in
1963. Innumerable medals, awards, fellowships and scholarships,
visiting professorships and orders of merit have also been
granted to him. He is noted for the application of quantum
mechanics to chemistry, and has written books too numerous
to mention.*

In his book *Has Man a Future?*, Bertrand Russell said, 'What exact
degree of damage would be done by a nuclear war with present
weapons is uncertain, and we must all hope that it will remain so.
It is just possible that, after a nuclear war between NATO and the
powers of the Warsaw Pact, some neutral nations might retain a
degree of social cohesion which would enable them to keep civilization alive.'

The intensity of our efforts to prevent the catastrophe of a great

Reprinted from Ralph Schoenman, ed., Bertrand Russell: Philosopher of
the Century *by permission of the author and publisher. Copyright © 1967
by George Allen and Unwin Ltd.*

nuclear war may be to some extent determined by our estimates of the probability of destruction of a major part of the world, perhaps of civilization itself, in such a war, were it to take place. In this essay I shall attempt to estimate the size of the world's stockpile of nuclear weapons and the effects of a possible nuclear war in which these weapons were used.

a small nuclear war

In 1958, in my book *No More War!,* I discussed the probable effects of a hypothetical nuclear attack on the United States with 2,500 megatons of bombs (50 percent fission and 50 percent fusion), and an attack on the Soviet Union with 5,000 megatons of bombs. It is estimated that, because of the larger size of the Soviet Union than of the United States, about twice as much nuclear explosive would be needed to cause the same damage in the USSR as in the US.

An estimate of the damage that would be done to the United States by a nuclear attack of 2,500 megatons is to be found in the volumes *The Nature of Radioactive Fallout and its Effects on Man.* Hearings before the Special Subcommittee on Radiation of the Joint Committee on Atomic Energy of the Congress of the United States, May 27, 28, 29, and June 3, 1957. The 250 nuclear weapons were of three sizes: 5-megaton, 10-megaton, and 20-megaton. There were 144 areas of attack: fifty-three of the areas were basically population and industrial centres, fifty-nine were basically military installations, and fifty-two were intermediate in character. The attack was assumed to take place during two hours of one day.

The analysis of the effects of this hypothetical attack was made by Dr. W. W. Kellogg of the Rand Corporation and Mr. Charles Shafer of the United States Weather Bureau (on assignment to the Federal Civil Defense Administration). Their estimate, corrected for the increase in population since 1957, is that sixty days after the day on which the attack with 2,500 megatons took place 98,000,000 of the 190,000,000 American people would be dead and 28,000,000 would be seriously injured but still alive, and there would be about 70,000,000 relatively uninjured survivors, who, however, would be suffering some radiation effects. It was estimated that about half of the deaths and injuries would be the result of blast and fire and the other half the result of high-energy radiation, including that from local fallout.

Similar estimates have been made by other scientists. Especially valuable is the extensive study of the distribution and effects of fallout in large nuclear-weapon campaigns that was carried out by Hugh Everett, III, and George E. Pugh, of the Weapons Systems Evaluation Division, Institute for Defense Analyses, Washington, D.C. Their report is published in the volume *Biological and Environmental Effects of Nuclear War,* Hearings before the Special Subcommittee on Radiation of the Joint Committee on Atomic Energy of the Congress of the United States, June 22–26, 1959. Their estimate is that sixty days after a 2,500-megaton attack, with the intensity of the attack in various regions proportional to the population density, 103,000,000 of the 190,000,000 American people would be dead, 23,000,000 injured, and 64,000,000 relatively uninjured.

There is, I think, a considerable possibility that the United States could survive such an attack and that the Soviet Union could survive a corresponding attack with 5,000 megatons. I have, however, reached the conclusion that it is not justified to hope that a nuclear war would be such a small one, if it were to be initiated. On the basis of the information available to us about the size of the stockpiles of nuclear weapons possessed by the United States and the Soviet Union, I conclude instead that the nuclear war, if it were to occur in the near future, would be about ten times as great as this small hypothetical one.

the size of the stockpiles of nuclear weapons

Neither the United States nor the Soviet Union has announced the size of its stockpile of nuclear weapons. On the basis of the bits of information that have been released, I have reached the conclusion that at the middle of the year 1963, the stockpile of nuclear weapons in the possession of the United States totalled 240,000 megatons. Taking into consideration the fact that the Soviet Union was about three years later in starting and may be assumed to have worked about as intensively in its military activity, I guess that the Soviet stockpile amounted to about 80,000 megatons.

In recent years the United States has been purchasing uranium at the rate of about 30,000 tons per year. Some of this uranium is used to make the fissionable substances uranium-235 and plutonium-239. In April 1957 James Van Zandt, who was at that time a Congressman and a member of the US Joint Congressional Committee on Atomic Energy, stated that the United States then had enough fissionable material for 35,000 atomic bombs and that the Soviet Union had an estimated stockpile of 10,000 bombs. In

January 1959 I received a letter from Lester Pearson, of Canada, in which he wrote that he had information that he considered to be reliable that for the preceding two years the United States had been manufacturing plutonium at the rate of 200,000 pounds per year. Although no official statement has been made about this matter, it seems likely that ten pounds of plutonium is enough to constitute the explosive material of a small atomic bomb or the first-stage material of an H-bomb or superbomb (fission-fusion-fission bomb). The manufacture of plutonium at the rate of 200,000 pounds per year would accordingly permit the addition of 20,000 atomic bombs to the US stockpile each year.

Dr. Ralph E. Lapp, an able American physicist who has played an outstanding part in educating the American people about the nature of the nuclear age, has estimated on the basis of the amount of uranium feed material flowing into the plutonium plants and uranium-235 plants, the amount of electric power the plants use, the capital investments in the plants, and the annual sums spent for operation of the plants that in 1960 the American stockpile of fissionable material amounted to 700,000 pounds, enough for 70,000 atomic bombs.

A 20-megaton bomb has as its explosive materials ten pounds of plutonium for the first stage, about 200 pounds of lithium deuteride for the second-stage nuclear fusion reaction, and 1,000 pounds of ordinary uranium metal for the third stage (fission). The supply of lithium deuteride is great enough so that each of the 20,000 atomic bombs that may be added to the stockpile each year could be converted into an H-bomb. Moreover, the third stage of 1,000 pounds of ordinary uranium metal could be added to each of the 20,000 bombs with use of only one third of the uranium stockpiled each year. The supply of fissionable and fusionable materials is accordingly such that 20,000 superbombs with explosive energy 20 megatons apiece could be added to the US stockpile each year, a total increase of 400,000 megatons per year.

We know, however, from the statements of military and governmental authorities in the United States that many of the nuclear weapons in the American stockpile are smaller ones. Some missiles, such as Polaris and Minuteman, carry at the present time a nuclear warhead of only one or two megatons explosive energy (the new warheads will be larger). Moreover, it has been the announced policy of the US Department of Defense and Atomic Energy Commission to develop small nuclear weapons, possibly to be used in a limited war, as well as the great nuclear weapons, and many of the nuclear tests carried out by the United States have been in the range from 0·001 to 0·1 megaton. The bombs exploded over Hiroshima and Nagasaki in 1945 were small nuclear weapons; each had explosive energy 0·02 megaton, 1000 times smaller than the 20-megaton bomb exploded by the United States on March 1, 1954.

In January 1960 President John F. Kennedy mentioned 30,000 megatons as the size of the world's stockpile of nuclear weapons. Nearly one year later, in December 1960, the scientists of the Pugwash Conference in their discussions made use of the estimate 60,000 megatons, without discussing the basis of the estimate. I used the estimate 120,000 megatons in January 1962 and 240,000 megatons in January 1963, and my present estimate is somewhat over 320,000 megatons.[1]

These estimates do not contradict one another; instead, they are mutually consistent.

The explosive power of the stockpiled weapons in the world has been increasing exponentially over the last eighteen years. The rate of exponential increase corresponds to doubling every year.

During the Second World War conventional bombs, with chemical explosives such as TNT, were used at the rate of about one megaton per year. It is reasonable for us to take one megaton as the amount of military explosive in the world's stockpile in 1945. By 1946, with plutonium and uranium-235 being produced in the United States at the rate of a few pounds per day, about fifty old-fashioned atomic bombs of the Hiroshima-Nagasaki type (0·02 megaton apiece) had been made, increasing the world's stockpile of explosives to two megatons. The rate of production of fissionable material doubled during the next year, and the stockpile became four megatons. The development of H-bombs and three-stage superbombs later led to a great increase in the explosive power of the individual bombs, permitting the exponential increase in the size of the world's stockpile to continue.

After eighteen years of annual doubling of the stockpile, it would have reached 2^{18} megatons, that is, 262,144 megatons.

Increase by the factor two each year accordingly explains the change from President Kennedy's 30,000 megatons in January 1960 to 60,000 megatons a year later, 120,000 megatons two years later, and 240,000 megatons three years later.

It seems unlikely that the exponential increase will continue, even though it is possible. The stockpiles of nuclear weapons have long ago become irrationally great.

[1] Late 1963.

My present estimate that the United States has 240,000 megatons of nuclear weapons can be made credible by consideration of the following facts. On the 12th of November US Secretary of Defense Robert S. McNamara stated that the United States Strategic Air Command includes 630 B-52s, 55 B-58s, and 1,000 B-47s, a total of 1,685 great bombers. It is known that these bombers carry about fifty megatons of bombs apiece—two 25-megaton bombs on each bomber. Accordingly these 1,685 intercontinental bombers carry a load of bombs totalling 84,000 megatons. I do not believe that any person would contend that the bombs for these bombers do not exist. Secretary McNamara has also stated that we have over 10,000 other vehicles (bombers, fighter-bombers, Polaris missiles and other missiles) capable of carrying nuclear weapons in the megaton range.

In the days following October 22, 1962, during the Cuba crisis, 750 great SAC bombers were deployed at airfields about the United States on 15-minute alert. Events might have developed in such a way that these 750 bombers would have set off for the Soviet Union, with the probability that most of them would have reached their goal. Even if 20 per cent of them were prevented from delivering their weapons, the attack on the Soviet Union by this fraction of the SAC bombers alone would have amounted to 30,000 megatons.

If the Cuba crisis had not been resolved, but had led to nuclear war, the initial attack on the Soviet Union by the 750 SAC bombers that were on 15-minute alert would have been supplemented within a few hours by an even greater attack carried out by the remaining SAC bombers and the other vehicles able to deliver nuclear weapons. Our knowledge about the number of SAC bombers and about their payload indicates clearly that in a nuclear war between the United States and the Soviet Union the bombs exploded over the Soviet Union might well amount to far over 50,000 megatons.

It would, I think, be optimism of an entirely unjustified sort to assume that the attack on the United States by the Soviet Union would be less than 25,000 megatons, which would achieve the same amount of damage.

the nature of a great nuclear war

Everett and Pugh made studies of hypothetical nuclear attacks on the United States and the Soviet Union with weapons totalling between 100 megatons and 50,000 megatons. From their careful studies we may conclude that an attack carried out in the near future on the United States with 10,000 megatons or more of nuclear weapons would kill nearly everybody and would destroy the nation essentially completely. A similar result would be achieved with an attack on the Soviet Union with 20,000 megatons or more of nuclear weapons. It is interesting that, according to their estimates, the same fraction of the people of the United States, 88 per cent, would be dead sixty days after a nuclear attack with 10,000 megatons whether the weapons were exploded in various areas in amounts proportional to the population density or were exploded with uniform distribution over the entire country. For attacks smaller than 10,000 megatons a greater yield of deaths is achieved by distributing the weapons proportionately to the population density, and for attacks greater than 10,000 megatons a greater yield is achieved by distributing the bombs uniformly over the country. The explanation of the paradox in the last statement is that for large nuclear attacks some of the weapons would be wasted over completely destroyed areas if they were distributed proportionately to population density.

A 10,000 megaton attack on the United States, of either type, would, according to Everett and Pugh, achieve the result that sixty days after the day on which the war was fought about 170,000,000 of the 190,000,000 American people would be dead, 15,000,000 seriously injured, and 5,000,000 alive and uninjured, except for the effect of some exposure to high-energy radiation.

As to the final result, we may quote from Everett and Pugh: 'Finally, it must be pointed out that the total casualties at sixty days may not be indicative of the ultimate casualties. Such delayed effects as the disorganization of society, disruption of communications, extinction of livestock, genetic damage, and the slow development of radiation poisoning from the ingestion of radioactive materials may significantly increase the ultimate toll.'

An attack on the United States with 10,000 megatons would lead to the death of essentially all of the American people and to the destruction of the nation. An attack on the Soviet Union with 20,000 megatons would achieve the same result there. The present stockpiles and the present means of delivery are such that it is not unlikely that the attacks on these countries, in case that there were to be a great nuclear war, would be much larger than 10,000 and 20,000 megatons, respectively. I think that a great nuclear war would destroy these two nations. Moreover, it is probable that some fraction of the nuclear weapons would be used in attacks on

European nations and other nations in which there are weapons bases, and that most of the people in these countries would also be killed.

the degree of overkill

Using 20,000 megatons as the amount necessary to destroy the Soviet Union completely and my estimate 240,000 megatons for the present US stockpile, I may say that we have a 12-fold degree of overkill capability; similarly, with 10,000 megatons needed to destroy the United States completely and a stockpile of 80,000 megatons, the Soviet Union has an eight-fold overkill capability.

There is another way of discussing the factor by which the powers of destruction have been needlessly amplified. In the course of the First World War about 20,000,000 people were killed, and in the course of the Second World War about 40,000,000. We might follow a logarithmic curve in extrapolating in a 'rational' way to the Third World War, and conclude that the war might be expected to come to an end (with one side victorious) when 80,000,-000 people had been killed.

In their analysis, Everett and Pugh assumed that the nuclear weapons would not necessarily be delivered very accurately—they assumed that one half of them would explode within 100 miles of their targets, and one half would explode at a greater distance from the targets. Missiles have now been developed that permit nuclear weapons to be delivered with probable errors of only a few miles, and we may turn our attention to a small war waged with missiles with high accuracy.

*   *   *

Correcting the populations to 1963, the reported estimate is that such a hypothetical attack, involving a total of only 567 megatons, would find 52,000,000 Americans dead at the end of sixty days and 21,000,000 seriously injured. An attack with twice as much megatonnage on the cities of the Soviet Union would kill and injure about the same fraction of the Soviet people: that is, about 66,000,000 of the Soviet people would be killed and 26,000,-000 seriously injured. Accordingly a nuclear war in which the United States used about 1,100 megatons and the Soviet Union about 550 megatons of bombs would be a greater war than the 'rational' Third World War corresponding to geometric extrapolation from the First and Second, as a war that, if nuclear weapons had not been developed, would have caused enough destruction and enough death to force the nations to bring it to an end.

On this basis the United States has an overkill capability greater than 200, and the Soviet Union has an overkill capability greater than 140.

During the Second World War about 3,000,000 tons of high explosive were used in strategic bombing of Germany and Japan. The total amount of explosives used was about twice as great—the war could be called a six-megaton war. The significance of the presently stockpiled total of about 320,000 megatons of nuclear explosives may be brought out by the following statement: if there were a six-megaton war (equivalent to the Second World War in the power of the explosives used) tomorrow, and another such war the following day, and so on, day after day, for 146 years, the present stockpile would then be exhausted—but, in fact, this stockpile might be used in a single day, the day of the Third World War.

the need for disarmament by international agreement

As we consider the facts about the capabilities of destruction that are possessed by the Soviet Union and the United States (with, of course, some contribution by Great Britain and a small one by France), we are forced to the conclusion that we are doomed to die if the world continues along the path of insanity. Unless some steps are taken immediately in the direction of disarmament, beginning with the international agreement to stop the testing of all nuclear bombs, the United States and the Soviet Union and probably many other countries in the Northern Hemisphere will be destroyed. It is possible that the civilization developed by man during the past few thousands of years will come to its irrational end.

I believe that we can prevent this great catastrophe, that we can meet the challenge of the crisis. The time has come when it is essential that an international agreement be made to stop the testing of nuclear weapons, to be followed by other agreements leading to general and complete disarmament. We must abandon the mistaken policy of transferring nuclear weapons to NATO, where they may come under the control of the West Germans. Immediate steps should be taken to set up demilitarized zones in the areas of greatest tension, beginning with Central Europe. We are now forced to eliminate from the world the immoral institution of war, and to replace war by international law, based upon the principles of justice and morality. I believe that we are going to grasp this opportunity, which will eliminate the suffering caused by war but will also permit the world community to be freed from hunger, disease, illiteracy, and fear, and will permit us to achieve economic, political, and social justice and to develop a culture worthy of man.

in my opinion...

The views of Professor Pauling deserve attention. Particularly important are the facts and the statistics which definitely show that man is very capable of destroying himself. Some of the statistics he presents are outdated, but for practical purposes, his figures can be used as a base.

It is my belief, however, that the major threat to the world in regard to nuclear weaponry is not the U.S.A. or the U.S.S.R. but Red China. A very interesting event occurred on April 18, 1970: on that day, the Red Chinese launched a satellite-bearing missile. The importance of this event lies in the fact that China now has a delivery system for its nuclear weapons.

With an area roughly the size of the U.S.A., China contains 23% of the world's population. In the U.S.A. the population per farmable acre is approximately 250/1. In China, the population per farmable acre is 1410/1. Obviously, this creates a tremendous problem of over-crowding.

This is why it is my belief that any upcoming World War III will be initiated by Red China, not the U.S.S.R. The cause of its actions is the problem it faces in attempting to feed 800 million to 1 billion people. (It might be noted that the exact population of China is not known. Sources which were checked varied between 750 million to 1.1 billion. One source stated that not even the Chinese Government knew its total population; it could only make an educated guess.)

It is not a secret that the world will shortly be faced with a population problem. The population problem and the food problem go hand-in-hand. And this is why China will make the move that starts the war. When a man—or a country—is dying of hunger, there is nothing to lose—nothing but life. I believe that a starving man will risk his life for food. And in China there is a greater number of starving people, which means there are more people with nothing to lose. Also, with the governmental control in China as it is, I doubt if a Chinese will turn against another Chinese for food.

Here, it should be noted, is where that important date— April 18, 1970—enters into the picture. With a nuclear weapon, with the newly-gained delivery system, with the food problem, I believe China will waste no time in threatening every country bordering it. In my opinion, the Chinese will begin their move for food in the immediate future.

The next seven years will prove whether or not man will make it into the 21st century. The political decisions which will be made in this period will define and decide the course of action which each of the various countries will take in confronting the world's problems.

Prophesying, I would say these will be the reasons for the destruction of the world: (1) There are so many theories as to which is right for which group. (2) There are so many past hatreds and dislikes which have been built up over the centuries that seven years will not be long enough for man to "pull down his fences" and admit that he needs his fellow man in order to survive. (3) There are so many people who really don't give a damn about anything. The conflict of ideas will be the final blow.

Is there hope that mankind will somehow forget his past and work for a future, together? Personally, I doubt it. And I can base this speculation on nothing other than the fact that man and his personal groups, and the ethnocentrism that he feels toward these institutions, are enough to make him damn all others and take his chances on outliving the next short, brief and mightiest of all wars. And in addition, man can, man has, and man will, do away with man.

jay r. bourne

questions

1. Assuming that Professor Pauling is correct in his hypothesis about the outcome of a 10,000-megaton war, is there any chance of any organism living through a 500,000–megaton war?

2. With many countries working to develop a nuclear weapon, or maintaining their present nuclear armaments, is there any real way to have a nuclear ban treaty that works? Explain.

3. Should the United Nations have the power to control nuclear weapons, or must this be done on a nation-to-nation basis? Why?

4. If the Red Chinese did start World War III and if the U.S.A. antimissile system was 100% efficient (keeping in mind that China, the U.S.A and Soviet Union, and the rest of the countries in the Northern Hemisphere all share the same hemispherical wind currents), is it possible that there would already be a sufficient amount of radiation in the atmosphere to kill off human beings in both the Eastern and Western hemispheres?

5. In the last section of Dr. Pauling's article, he presents a definite need for disarmament. Do you think the steps of action he mentions would solve the nuclear war threat that we are faced with? How?

14.

what next for eve? the role of women

MY OWN UTOPIA

elisabeth mann borgese

introduction and comment by kathryn baker

Throughout history women have been matter-of-factly regarded as an inferior class. It all started with Eve—created by God as an afterthought to his universal plan. She was formed from one of Adam's spare parts. Her function: to help him. Her goal: to tempt him with the power of the devil. Thus, the biblical prototype of woman.

Today the inheritors of the Bible have elevated its biases into religious truths. The daily ritual prayers of Orthodox Jewish men include thanks "that Thou hast not made me a woman." Catholic theology likewise emphasizes the inferiority of the female. The eminent Catholic philosopher, Saint Thomas Aquinas, stated that "a female is something deficient." Marriage ceremonies in Protestant faiths included, until quite recently, the bride's promise to obey her husband.

Organized religion, however, cannot be credited with sole responsibility for the present state of women. Freudian psychology has been the single most significant factor in woman's repression in the twentieth century. Before Freud's theories exploded on the American scene, a few advances had been made. However, these were confined to changes in the law— not changes in attitude. Proponents of Freudian theories were able, by first admitting the intelligence of women and then producing the sacred cow of psychology—a subject in which few women were qualified to argue—to convince women that subservience was their natural role. They succeeded. After World War II, women participated in a massive retreat to their homes.

Inextricably linked with Freudian psychology's effects on women are the effects of education. Women, in schools throughout America, are taught that it is a woman's "destiny" to be a wife and mother, that she should spend her time in school preparing for this inevitability. Success in school inhibits social life. Girls are pressured into early dating, popularity struggles, and early marriage. (More than half of American women are married before the age of twenty-one.) Intellectual striving is an "aggressive" activity, making it, according to Freudian thought, inherently masculine. If a girl is so stubborn as to demand an education to prepare her for professional life, she is warned that she will have to choose between marriage and a career. When faced with the prediction of lifelong loneliness as a direct result of a meaningful career, is it surprising that many capable women choose to drop their career plans? It is estimated that 75% of all qualified high school students who do not attend college are female. One study revealed that 70% of the women who did decide to attend a certain Midwestern university were there to get their "MRS" degree. Women B.A.'s are less than half as likely to try for a graduate degree as equally qualified men.

Women's magazines perpetuate the myths of femininity. Their goal, which is to sell the products advertised within, is accomplished by linking each product with "femininity." Women who are trying to reconcile themselves with the "real nature" of femininity quite naturally snap up anything which promises them femininity.

The magazines emphasize woman's role as wife and mother. Teen-age magazines are almost exclusively manuals for success in dating. When a woman has succeeded in "trapping" a husband, she is treated to such magazines as *McCall's, Redbook,* and *Ladies' Home Journal.* These devote their pages, for the most part, to cooking, sewing, child-rearing, and other homey themes which reflect the only interests of a "feminine" woman. If, for some reason, the first marriage fails, *Cosmopolitan* is prepared with advice on how to catch another man.

Today, however, there appears to be reason for hope. Our whole society is undergoing ruthless examination. Young people, especially, are no longer satisfied with accepting what society decrees. The question "Why?" is being asked more and more frequently. "Why must I marry?" "Why must I not become a career woman?" "Why is it not feminine to be intelligent?" We are on the verge of a new era. Attitudes regarding society will change drastically in the next thirty years. Now is the time for women to ensure that new attitudes concerning their proper role in society form an integral part of the social changes to come. Women, Unite!

k.b.

MY OWN UTOPIA

Elisabeth Mann Borgese is a Fellow of the Center for the Study of Democratic Institutions. She is author of To Whom It May Concern, The Language Barrier, *and* Ascent of Woman, *1963. Ms. Borgese presently resides in Florence, Italy.*

Children will be born, I hesitate to say, pretty much along the lines suggested satirically by Huxley in *Brave New World,* and more seriously by . . . Herman Muller, by Haldane [1] and others. There will be great establishments, where banks of deep-frozen reproductive cells, both male and female, will be maintained, along with multiplying cultures of them. This procedure will make the most precious genetic heritage of all humanity available for nurturing into childhood and adulthood.

Let us most fervently hope that the transition to this type of procreation will not be hastened by the genetic unfitness of a large part of the population due to an atomic holocaust. The deformation of pregnancy and the hazards of viviparous birth, at any rate, will be remembered as simply beastly.

But I do not think we will breed alphas, epsilons, and semi-moronic gamma-minuses, as Huxley fancies. We do not need immutable castes, ant-like, in our society to come; that society, far from stunting individual development, will create a new, specifically human, synthesis of individualism and collectivism.

We will breed only the best: all alpha-pluses.

At the age of two, or thereabouts, these children will leave

[1] John B. S. Haldane, *Daedalus, or Science and the Future* (London, 1924).

the Establishment and be adopted by family groups. For the raising of children will be a favorite hobby of the leisure mass— the beauty of children, the contact with the magic world of children, a main source of their inspiration.

There will be no difference between boys and girls. They will be children, that is all. They will all have the same education, the same way of dressing, the same games, the same purpose in life. Imagine them romping, on a holiday, in the playground, where centrifugal accelerators and pressure-shoots, modeled on those that prepared the cosmonauts and astronauts for their adventures, will have taken the place of the old merry-go-rounds and Ferris wheels. For all the children will be getting ready to be spacemen, one day.

Between the ages of eighteen and twenty, when their primary education is completed, they will *all* grow to be *women*. For to be a woman no longer means to bear children. Femininity will rise out of social context and reflect a psychological, a psychosomatic condition.[2] These women will be tall and strong and beautiful, like Michelangelo's angels. They will bear the brunt of the work in this new world. During the four years of the labor draft they will learn how the economy of this world state ticks, from the lowest echelons to the highest. Drafted women will be burdened with whatever drudgery is left in agriculture and industry and services.

When they come back from the labor draft, the women will be scientists, doctors, professional women, business executives, administrators, educators, and social workers. The bulk of the international income will go through their hands; which means, they will be an enormous political power. Their power, and their experience, will carry them into public office: practically all positions of the executive branch of government will be filled by women, including that of President of the World Republic. The collectivist character of this new society brings that with it; there's no way of getting around it. But let no one fear: these women will be fully suited to their high position—by birth, by character, and upbringing.

When they get out of the labor draft, the women will also be ready to found families. (Where the men come from we shall see shortly.) These families, obviously, will have little in common with the closed, patriarchal family of our own time. The post-

---

[2] For cultural determination of sex, see Ashley Montague, *Man in Process* (New York, 1962).

individual family, like the pre-individual family, will be a group; an open group, including six to fifteen adults and four to six children each.

The family will be a working community, dedicated to all those types of work that are not owned or run by the State: all work that embellishes the life of the community, from fancy cooking to all the arts and crafts, fashion, dance, drama, music, plastic arts, poetry, philosophy. Much of the family work will be done for and with the children: the creation of myth and lore, of new forms of art, of new forms of play and happiness.

Although the products of this work may and will enter into commerce, enriching the family and raising its standard of living, the family is not founded primarily on economic interests but on a community of taste and on the common pursuit of the true and the beautiful. This, the women—who are young, fair, receptive, willing to sacrifice, loyal, eager to serve—will learn from the men, who are older, more mature: "capable of communicating wisdom and virtue," while the young women are "seeking to acquire them with a view to education and wisdom." And when physical love and spiritual love thus coincide, "and meet in one, then, and only then, may the beloved," in our case, the woman, "yield with honor to the lover," in our case, the man.

The words between quotation marks are taken—the reader may guess—from Plato's *Symposium*. And the love between men and women, in our post-individual community, will indeed be Platonic, in that it will unite physical and spiritual love and will be aimed at creating beauty immortal, rather than mortal children. Love will be harmony, the reconciliation of elements that are not opposite, but harmonized. For men and women, in our society, cannot be considered as opposite elements.

The men, as we said, will be older—between forty-five and seventy-five years old—and more experienced than the women. They will be the masters, the teachers, the inspirers of women. They will be the great inventors and explorers. They will be the great artists and architects. In public life they will fill all the positions in the legislative branch of government as well as in the lower judiciary. But Supreme Court justices, the great historians and prophets, the high priests of the new society, will be human beings past seventy-five, up to, say, one hundred years of age, who will be neither male nor female—individuals rich in three or four life experiences, and approaching a perfection and greatness unknown at present.

When the children in a family have all grown into young women, gone away from home, joined the labor force; when the men have either died—which, owing to the advanced state of medicine, will occur only quite exceptionally—or, what may happen more commonly, are missing in the cosmos; or when the men have become sexless superindividuals: then, of course, comes the moment for a woman to grow and mature into manhood. The transition will be smooth and spontaneous. The woman, who is now about forty-five years old, has had a full life, has raised her children, has learned from the man she loves, whose disciple she was, what she was able to learn. If now she is herself "capable of communicating wisdom and virtue," she will naturally feel attracted toward a young person "seeking to acquire them." She will grow into the position of a man; she will become a man.[3]

We have seen . . . how sex reversal is common on the lowest levels of life, and how, in forms in which sex reversal is usual, the physiological state established by the hereditary constitution is readily overridden through the environment: how, before becoming *caste,* sex was *phase.* Remember our remote ancestor, the "boatshell" snails of the genus *Crepidula:* after a juvenile period that is essentially asexual, Professor Allee tells us, the growing *Crepidula* first becomes a male, and later, sometimes only at long last, transforms into a female—femaleness, at that stage of evolution, being the crown of success of life.

* * *

We have seen beasts changing sex, under the biochemical action of "social hormones." We have seen gods changing sex, under the subconscious action of social context. Why should we

---

[3] Nietzsche anticipated something of this type of changing relationship when, in *Human, All too Human,* he suggests that every man marry twice: an older, experienced woman, when he is in his twenties, and a young girl, when he is in his thirties, after which marriage is a dangerous nuisance anyway. "Thus one might wonder whether Nature and Reason would not suggest to man several successive marriages, in such a way that at first, at the age of twenty-one or thereabout, he should marry an older woman, his superior intellectually and morally, who would become his guide through the dangers besetting his 'twenties (ambition, hate, self-contempt, passions of all sorts). The love of this woman would transform itself later into a purely motherly love; and not only would she tolerate, she would most wholesomely want her man, now in his thirties, to enter into relationship with a younger woman whose education he could take into his hands. Marriage is an institution that is necessary between twenty and thirty, useful between thirty and forty; but in later years it often becomes harmful and causes a process of spiritual involution in man."

be amazed at seeing human beings do the same? Magic, plus social context, has wrought sex reversal on prophets and shamans. Biochemistry, plus social context, may achieve as much.[4]

But evolution, on our graph, ever open, runs no risk of turning into involution, and none of the gains made in the process are sacrificed.[5]

Not all women, of course, will arrive at the turning point, at least at the beginning. Only the better, the more gifted ones will get there—which, in a collectivist society, will be the majority. A minority, however, will not make the grade; at least for some time to come. They will remain women, will age as women. Individual failure, seen from an individual angle. The action of the group-*Gestalt* on the sex balance, seen from the statistical point of view —the physiology of numbers.

The group-force in a collectivist society, as we have seen, engenders a numerical superiority of females. Thus, women will comprise the entire age group from eighteen to forty-five, plus, let us say, thirty per cent of the age group, forty-five–seventy-five; that is, sixty-five per cent of the sexually mature population. Men will comprise seventy per cent of the age group, forty-five– seventy-five; that is, thirty-five per cent of the sexually mature population. This proportion should fairly reflect the degree of basic collectivism and marginal individualism of society, during the initial phase.

It may be easily imagined that the women above forty-five will not command the highest respect of the community. They will be considered as failures in life, as "arrested men," to use a term coined by Herbert Spencer for women in general. We may even fancy that in moments of tension, of mass hysteria, which can develop whenever the collectivist component of our social psychology overpowers the individualist—that in such moments these

[4] "From the words 'Till we all come to a perfect man, to the measure of the age and the fullness of Christ,' and from the words 'conformed to the image of the Son of God,' some conclude that women shall not resurrect as women, but that all shall be men, because God made man only of earth and woman of the man."—St. Augustine, *City of God.*

[5] It occurs to me that this evolutionary curve, tracing *forth* what has been traced *back* since the origin of life, with the never-ending and the never-beginning meeting at an imaginary point, expresses something very analogous to what Hermann Broch expressed poetically in the archemythical dream of death agony in *The Death of Vergil.* The soul of the dying poet, *rising* through various stages of its ontogenetic liberation to eternity, is at the same time *descending,* backward, through the phylogenetic stages of evolution: from being human, it becomes mammal, bird, fish, mollusk, primordial-ultimate nonbeing.

poor aging women may be persecuted as witches. . . . As this society moves toward a perfect equilibrium between individualism and collectivism, between male and female components, this group of unfortunate women will disappear, and all women will mature to manhood. The proportion between men and women will then be one to one.

in my opinion...

Elisabeth Mann Borgese, in her visualization of Utopia, presents an original view, to say the least. However, I find the underlying concepts to be both illogical and reflective of her apparent uneasiness regarding human sexuality.

The prediction of laboratory-produced babies seems reasonable—indeed, in the light of recent discoveries, seems but a few decades, at most, away. Whether this method will become the only accepted mode of reproduction is quite another question. The desire to perpetuate a part of one's self appears to be a deeply-rooted human quality, not easily cast aside, even for the seeming perfection of a generation of geniuses.

The idea of communal child-raising is a viable one. Such rearing occurs, albeit infrequently, today and the dramatic increase in demands for day-care centers, the increase in employment opportunities for young mothers, and the general questioning of society in regard to the merits of the nuclear family indicate that the trend will continue.

That children be brought up without the chains of sexual stereotypes is my fervent hope for the future. Today's increasing awareness of such sex-typing seems to me a hopeful sign. Society cannot for long tolerate such a repressive system when its full ramifications are brought to light. The movement for women's liberation can, incidentally, be credited with single-handedly making the American people conscious of their own sexual attitudes.

Except for the above-mentioned points, Ms Borgese's logic escapes me. She, after carefully rearing children without sexual stereotypes, would now have them all female, with their "femininity" to "rise out of social context." This seems to me to be a crash indoctrination course in subservience. First, as women, all are "burdened with whatever drudgery is left". After four years of this labor, they are permitted to become professional workers in the society—doctors, scientists, educators, etc. After reaching the age of forty-five, woman will "grow and mature into manhood". Of course not all will be worthy of the supreme gift of a penis, "only the better, the more gifted ones". Those unfortunates who are not eligible for this "will be considered as failures in life".

Men will be "the masters, the teachers, the inspirers of women". Only men will be artists, inventors, explorers, legislators. Thus, while on superficial examination it appears women will have finally achieved a rightful role in society, they will still be subservient to the creativity endowed only to males. Women will be the technicians of this "Utopia", men the thinkers and innovators.

Ms Borgese seems to be subscribing to that old "anatomy is destiny" tripe. Being a woman apparently is synonymous with having an undeveloped personality. Woman is not capable of abstract thinking; her purpose in life is to serve society (comparable to one huge family?), while man's role is to develop as an individual.

The strangest twist of Ms Borgese's plan is the sexlessness of the most esteemed members of society, those "approaching a perfection and greatness unknown at present". This suggests that Ms Borgese regards sex in itself as degrading. Those of us burdened with being male or female can never hope to attain the lofty heights achieved by the sexless. By denying sex, Ms Borgese is denying an essential part of the experience of humanness. The human body is not mentioned in her Utopia, except as some alien thing to be adorned with sex organs. Even physical love described in the piece is strangely bodiless. Passion is totally ignored; sex becomes a cerebral union "aimed at creating beauty immortal"—whatever that is. "Love is harmony", says Ms Borgese. But where is the vitality, the excitement, of two people coming to terms with each other on both the physical and spiritual levels? Love would seem to be a spiritless affair (no pun intended) in Utopia. Harmony may be pleasant, but isn't it a bit dull after a while? Isn't the joy attained by two vital people more than compensatory for the periods of turmoil experienced?

I would not be satisfied with life in Ms Borgese's Utopia. Although I may be tempted by the challenging intellectual life she envisions, I am not ready to sacrifice my body to my mind. Being human is living on both a physical and intellectual plane—development of greater humanity does not involve the sacrifice of one to the other.

kathryn baker

questions

1.   What is the woman's role in society today, and how is it changing?

2.   Should the concepts of male and female include a division of emotional and/or intellectual characteristics?

3.   What are the advantages and disadvantages of communal child-rearing?

4.   Is sexlessness a requisite for human attainment of the "perfection" represented by the superindividuals?

5.   What effects on present concepts of love would unlimited sex reversal have?

15.

can we make man human? psychology

WALDEN TWO

b. f. skinner

introduction and comment by randall swanson

Prediction and control of human behavior is based on the knowledge that members of a given species will originally react similarly to a given stimulus. These regularities are instrumental in learning.

Since we minimize pain and maximize pleasure, the penalties and rewards of society condition us into the "certain, certain way we live our own private lives."

Although primary needs are constant, desired standards and acceptable modes of gratification are flexible. The kind of control advocated by B. F. Skinner allows the individual to do what he wants to do, but first ensures that what he wants to do is in the best interest of the group.

Selfishness is unavoidable. Everything one does, one believes to be in his self-interest. Selfishness leads to competition which fosters suspicion and distrust, which evolves into fear, hatred and hostility. Aggression can be minimized if the culture does not provide the means with which to be selfish.

We dwell in groups, therefore the individual's impulses must be contained. When freedom is stifled, frustration occurs. We are adjusted if we relieve this frustration directly or vicariously in an acceptable manner. If we do not or cannot rid ourselves of this resentment in a way which is socially blessed, we will seek relief either by denying reality or by creating our own.

Adjustment carried too far can be defined as complacency. The more one must restrain one's self, the more frustration is incurred, and the more escapes are needed. The stress barrage is clearly evident in congregations, where the normal reaction is to grow progressively more defensive and insensitive.

Therapy is used to harmonize the individual with his culture. Traditional therapy demands that the patient be displeased with his present conduct enough to want to reform it. The patient bears the responsibility; the therapist just reconciles. In behaviorist therapy, the patient can be helped in spite of himself, providing the practitioner is able to deprive and satiate.

Contemporary Americans are preoccupied with treating symptoms and manifestations of personal disorders and social defects. Our misplaced emphasis is upon correction—or, worse yet, repression—rather than on prevention. Our unwillingness to recognize problems and their sources precludes solutions.

Our self-image is formed by accepting preconceptions and comparing performances. These spurious indicators of worth promote deprecation and aggrandizement. Everyone should step to the music which he hears, and strive to be, as John Kennedy described himself, "an idealist without illusions".

One achieves self-control through self-understanding. Self-understanding proceeds from correct exposure and reflection. A disciplined individual is marked by his ability to 1) balance his emotions with his logic, 2) take setbacks in stride, and 3) tolerate immediate frustration for greater long-range satisfaction.

The greedy ogre within us cannot be tempered with appeasement. "We have met the enemy, and he is us" is an epigram which at least turns us in the right direction.

One's apparent powerlessness could easily result in despair, but instead should encourage a deliberate, selective altruism. At any rate, our behavior coincides with our beliefs. If on the species level, we eventually do harness avarice, it will undoubtedly be more because of what we fear than because of what we desire.

Those who are afraid of themselves and infatuated with avoidance façades will shun the chance to be free from the aimlessness of drifting. Those who are constructively discontented and can visualize the opportunity for improvement unleashed by the knowledge which enables us to control our own destiny will welcome and partake of its grace.

In psychology's exciting future, the empirical will support the rational and the sciences will complement the humanities. Theories, even in psychology, must be verifiable and according to observation. Adequately controlled experimentation has been lacking in the social sciences because of the human variable. Conditions are frequently too provincial to insure safe induction; the relative strengths of contributing factors are nearly unknown. Hopefully, the importance of a scientific attitude—especially toward our own behavior—will be realized and appreciated by the year 2000.

In *Walden Two,* Harvard's famed Professor B. F. Skinner explains how the characteristics of tomorrow's man are developed.

r.s.

WALDEN TWO

Dr. Burrhus Frederic ("B.F.") Skinner resides at Harvard
University as Edgar Pierce Professor of Psychology. He is the
inventor of the teaching machine and programmed learning, and
is the fount of behaviorist psychology. A Harvard and Guggenheim
Fellow, Dr. Skinner received his Ph.D. from Harvard and is
a member of the National Academy of Science, the American
Academy of Arts and Sciences, and received in 1958 the
award of the Psychological Association. In 1968 he received the
National Medal for Science. Dr. Skinner has written Behavior
of Organisms, *1938;* Science and Human Behavior, *1953;*
Verbal Behavior, *1957;* The Technology of Teaching, *1968; the*
world-famous Walden Two, *and his most current work*
Beyond Freedom and Dignity, *1971.*

"Each of us," Frazier began, "is engaged in a pitched battle with
the rest of mankind."

"A curious premise for a Utopia," said Castle. "Even a pessimist
like myself takes a more hopeful view than that."

"You do, you do," said Frazier. "But let's be realistic. Each of
us has interests which conflict with the interests of everybody else.
That's our original sin, and it can't be helped. Now, 'everybody
else' we call 'society.' It's a powerful opponent, and it always wins.
Oh, here and there an individual prevails for a while and gets what
he wants. Sometimes he storms the culture of a society and
changes it slightly to his own advantage. But society wins in the
long run, for it has the advantage of numbers and of age. Many
prevail against one, and men against a baby. Society attacks
early, when the individual is helpless. It enslaves him almost

before he has tasted freedom. The 'ologies' will tell you how it's done. Theology calls it building a conscience or developing a spirit of selflessness. Psychology calls it the growth of the super-ego.

"Considering how long society has been at it, you'd expect a better job. But the campaigns have been badly planned and the victory has never been secure. The behavior of the individual has been shaped according to revelations of 'good conduct,' never as the result of experimental study. But why not experiment? The questions are simple enough. What's the best behavior for the individual so far as the group is concerned? And how can the individual be induced to behave in that way? Why not explore these questions in a scientific spirit?

"We could do just that in Walden Two. We had already worked out a code of conduct—subject, of course, to experimental modification. The code would keep things running smoothly if everybody lived up to it. Our job was to see that everybody did. Now, you can't get people to follow a useful code by making them into so many jacks-in-the-box. You can't foresee all future circumstances, and you can't specify adequate future conduct. You don't know what will be required. Instead you have to set up certain behavioral processes which will lead the individual to design his own 'good' conduct when the time comes. We call that sort of thing 'self-control.' But don't be misled, the control always rests in the last analysis in the hands of society.

"One of our Planners, a young man named Simmons, worked with me. It was the first time in history that the matter was approached in an experimental way. Do you question that statement, Mr. Castle?"

"I'm not sure I know what you are talking about," said Castle.

"Then let me go on. Simmons and I began by studying the great works on morals and ethics—Plato, Aristotle, Confucius, the New Testament, the Puritan divines, Machiavelli, Chesterfield, Freud—there were scores of them. We were looking for any and every method of shaping human behavior by imparting techniques of self-control. Some techniques were obvious enough, for they had marked turning points in human history. 'Love your enemies' is an example—a psychological invention for easing the lot of an oppressed people. The severest trial of oppression is the constant rage which one suffers at the thought of the oppressor. What Jesus discovered was how to avoid these inner devastations. His technique was to *practice the opposite emotion.* If a man can succeed in 'loving his enemies' and 'taking no thought for the morrow,' he will no longer be assailed by hatred of the oppressor or rage at the loss of his freedom or possessions. He may not get his freedom or possessions back, but he's less miserable. It's a difficult lesson. It comes late in our program."

"I thought you were opposed to modifying emotions and instincts until the world was ready for it," said Castle. "According to you, the principle of 'love your enemies' should have been suicidal."

"It would have been suicidal, except for an entirely unforeseen consequence. Jesus must have been quite astonished at the effect of his discovery. We are only just beginning to understand the power of love because we are just beginning to understand the weakness of force and aggression. But the science of behavior is clear about all that now. Recent discoveries in the analysis of punishment—but I am falling into one digression after another. Let me save my explanation of why the Christian virtues—and I mean merely the Christian techniques of self-control—have not disappeared from the face of the earth, with due recognition of the fact that they suffered a narrow squeak within recent memory.

"When Simmons and I had collected our techniques of control, we had to discover how to teach them. That was more difficult. Current educational practices were of little value, and religious practices scarcely any better. Promising paradise or threatening hell-fire is, we assumed, generally admitted to be unproductive. It is based upon a fundamental fraud which, when discovered, turns the individual against society and nourishes the very thing it tries to stamp out. What Jesus offered in return for loving one's enemies was heaven *on earth,* better known as peace of mind.

"We found a few suggestions worth following in the practices of the clinical psychologist. We undertook to build a tolerance for annoying experiences. The sunshine of midday is extremely painful if you come from a dark room, but take it in easy stages and you can avoid pain altogether. The analogy can be misleading, but in much the same way it's possible to build a tolerance to painful or distasteful stimuli, or to frustration, or to situations which arouse fear, anger or rage. Society and nature throw these annoyances at the individual with no regard for the development of tolerances. Some achieve tolerances, most fail. Where would the science of immunization be if it followed a schedule of accidental dosages?

"Take the principle of 'Get thee behind me, Satan,' for example," Frazier continued. "It's a special case of self-control by altering the environment. Subclass A 3, I believe. We give each child a lollipop which has been dipped in powdered sugar so that a single touch of the tongue can be detected. We tell him he may eat the lollipop later in the day, provided it hasn't already been licked. Since the child is only three or four, it is a fairly diff—"

"Three or four!" Castle exclaimed.

"All our ethical training is completed by the age of six," said Frazier quietly. "A simple principle like putting temptation out of sight would be acquired before four. But at such an early age the problem of not licking the lollipop isn't easy. Now, what would you do, Mr. Castle, in a similar situation?"

"Put the lollipop out of sight as quickly as possible."

"Exactly. I can see you've been well trained. Or perhaps you discovered the principle for yourself. We're in favor of original inquiry wherever possible, but in this case we have a more important goal and we don't hesitate to give verbal help. First of all, the children are urged to examine their own behavior while looking at the lollipops. This helps them to recognize the need for self-control. Then the lollipops are concealed, and the children are asked to notice any gain in happiness or any reduction in tension. Then a strong distraction is arranged—say, an interesting game. Later the children are reminded of the candy and encouraged to examine their reaction. The value of the distraction is generally obvious. Well, need I go on? When the experiment is repeated a day or so later, the children all run with the lollipops to their lockers and do exactly what Mr. Castle would do—a sufficient indication of the success of our training."

"I wish to report an objective observation of my reaction to your story," said Castle, controlling his voice with great precision. "I find myself revolted by this display of sadistic tyranny."

"I don't wish to deny you the exercise of an emotion which you seem to find enjoyable," said Frazier. "So let me go on. Concealing a tempting but forbidden object is a crude solution. For one thing, it's not always feasible. We want a sort of psychological concealment—covering up the candy by paying no attention. In a later experiment the children wear their lollipops like crucifixes for a few hours."

> " 'Instead of the cross, the lollipop,
>   About my neck was hung,' "

said Castle.

"I wish somebody had taught me that, though," said Rodge, with a glance at Barbara.

"Don't we all?" said Frazier. "Some of us learn control, more or less by accident. The rest of us go all our lives not even understanding how it is possible, and blaming our failure on being born the wrong way."

"How do you build up a tolerance to an annoying situation?" I said.

"Oh, for example, by having the children 'take' a more and more painful shock, or drink cocoa with less and less sugar in it until a bitter concoction can be savored without a bitter face."

"But jealousy or envy—you can't administer them in graded doses," I said.

"And why not? Remember, we control the social environment, too, at this age. That's why we get our ethical training in early. Take this case. A group of children arrive home after a long walk tired and hungry. They're expecting supper; they find, instead, that it's time for a lesson in self-control: they must stand for five minutes in front of steaming bowls of soup.

"The assignment is accepted like a problem in arithmetic. Any groaning or complaining is a wrong answer. Instead, the children begin at once to work upon themselves to avoid any unhappiness during the delay. One of them may make a joke of it. We encourage a sense of humor as a good way of not taking an annoyance seriously. The joke won't be much, according to adult standards— perhaps the child will simply pretend to empty the bowl of soup into his upturned mouth. Another may start a song with many verses. The rest join in at once, for they've learned that it's a good way to make time pass."

Frazier glanced uneasily at Castle, who was not to be appeased.

"That also strikes you as a form of torture, Mr. Castle?" he asked.

"I'd rather be put on the rack," said Castle.

"Then you have by no means had the thorough training I supposed. You can't imagine how lightly the children take such an experience. It's a rather severe biological frustration, for the children are tired and hungry and they must stand and look at food; but it's passed off as lightly as a five-minute delay at curtain time. We regard it as a fairly elementary test. Much more difficult problems follow."

"I suspected as much," muttered Castle.

"In a later stage we forbid all social devices. No songs, no jokes—merely silence. Each child is forced back upon his own resources—a very important step."

"I should think so," I said. "And how do you know it's successful? You might produce a lot of silently resentful children. It's certainly a dangerous stage."

"It is, and we follow each child carefully. If he hasn't picked up the necessary techniques, we start back a little. A still more advanced stage"—Frazier glanced again at Castle, who stirred uneasily—"brings me to my point. When it's time to sit down to the soup, the children count off—heads and tails. Then a coin is tossed and if it comes up heads, the 'heads' sit down and eat. The 'tails' remain standing for another five minutes."

Castle groaned.

"And you call that envy?" I asked.

"Perhaps not exactly," said Frazier. "At least there's seldom any aggression against the lucky ones. The emotion, if any, is directed against Lady Luck herself, against the toss of the coin. That, in itself, is a lesson worth learning, for it's the only direction in which emotion has a surviving chance to be useful. And resentment toward things in general, while perhaps just as silly as personal aggression, is more easily controlled. Its expression is not socially objectionable."

Frazier looked nervously from one of us to the other. He seemed to be trying to discover whether we shared Castle's prejudice. I began to realize, also, that he had not really wanted to tell this story. He was vulnerable. He was treading on sanctified ground, and I was pretty sure he had not established the value of most of these practices in an experimental fashion. He could scarcely have done so in the short space of ten years. He was working on faith, and it bothered him.

I tried to bolster his confidence by reminding him that he had a professional colleague among his listeners. "May you not inadvertently teach your children some of the very emotions you're trying to eliminate?" I said. "What's the effect, for example, of finding the anticipation of a warm supper suddenly thwarted? Doesn't that eventually lead to feelings of uncertainty, or even anxiety?"

"It might. We had to discover how often our lessons could be safely administered. But all our schedules are worked out experimentally. We watch for undesired consequences just as any scientist watches for disrupting factors in his experiments.

"After all, it's a simple and sensible program," he went on in a tone of appeasement. "We set up a system of gradually increasing annoyances and frustrations against a background of complete serenity. An easy environment is made more and more difficult as the children acquire the capacity to adjust."

"But *why*?" said Castle. "Why these deliberate unpleasantnesses—to put it mildly? I must say I think you and your friend Simmons are really very subtle sadists."

"You've reversed your position, Mr. Castle," said Frazier in a sudden flash of anger with which I rather sympathized. Castle was calling names, and he was also being unaccountably and perhaps intentionally obtuse. "A while ago you accused me of breeding a race of softies," Frazier continued. "Now you object to toughening them up. But what you don't understand is that these potentially unhappy situations are never very annoying. Our schedules make sure of that. You wouldn't understand, however, because you're not so far advanced as our children."

Castle grew black.

"But what do your children get out of it?" he insisted, apparently trying to press some vague advantage in Frazier's anger.

"What do they get out of it!" exclaimed Frazier, his eyes flashing with a sort of helpless contempt. His lips curled and he dropped his head to look at his fingers, which were crushing a few blades of grass.

"They must get happiness and freedom and strength," I said, putting myself in a ridiculous position in attempting to make peace.

"They don't sound happy or free to me, standing in front of bowls of Forbidden Soup," said Castle, answering me parenthetically while continuing to stare at Frazier.

"If I must spell it out," Frazier began with a deep sigh, "what they get is escape from the petty emotions which eat the heart out of the unprepared. They get the satisfaction of pleasant and profitable social relations on a scale almost undreamed of in the world at large. They get immeasurably increased efficiency, because they can stick to a job without suffering the aches and pains which soon beset most of us. They get new horizons, for they are spared the emotions characteristic of frustration and failure. They get—" His eyes searched the branches of the trees. "Is that enough?" he said at last.

"And the community must gain their loyalty," I said, "when they discover the fears and jealousies and diffidences in the world at large."

"I'm glad you put it that way," said Frazier. "You might have said that they must feel superior to the miserable products of our public schools. But we're at pains to keep any feeling of superiority or contempt under control, too. Having suffered most acutely from it myself, I put the subject first on our agenda. We carefully avoid any joy in a personal triumph which means the personal failure of somebody else. We take no pleasure in the sophistical, the disputative, the dialectical." He threw a vicious glance at

Castle. "We don't use the motive of domination, because we are always thinking of the whole group. We could motivate a few geniuses that way—it was certainly my own motivation—but we'd sacrifice some of the happiness of everyone else. Triumph over nature and over oneself, yes. But over others never."

"You've taken the mainspring out of the watch," said Castle flatly.

"That's an experimental question, Mr. Castle, and you have the wrong answer."

Frazier was making no effort to conceal his feeling. If he had been riding Castle, he was now using his spurs. Perhaps he sensed that the rest of us had come round and that he could change his tactics with a single holdout. But it was more than strategy, it was genuine feeling. Castle's undeviating skepticism was a growing frustration.

"Are your techniques really so very new?" I said hurriedly. "What about the primitive practice of submitting a boy to various tortures before granting him a place among adults? What about the disciplinary techniques of Puritanism? Or of the modern school, for that matter?"

"In one sense you're right," said Frazier. "And I think you've nicely answered Mr. Castle's tender concern for our little ones. The unhappinesses we deliberately impose are far milder than the normal unhappinesses from which we offer protection. Even at the height of our ethical training, the unhappiness is ridiculously trivial—to the well-trained child.

"But there's a world of difference in the way we use these annoyances," he continued. "For one thing, we don't punish. We never administer an unpleasantness in the hope of repressing or eliminating undesirable behavior. But there's another difference. In most cultures the child meets up with annoyances and reverses of uncontrolled magnitude. Some are imposed in the name of discipline by persons in authority. Some, like hazings, are condoned though not authorized. Others are merely accidental. No one cares to, or is able to, prevent them.

"We all know what happens. A few hardy children emerge, particularly those who have got their unhappiness in doses that could be swallowed. They become brave men. Others become sadists or masochists of varying degrees of pathology. Not having conquered a painful environment, they become preoccupied with pain and make a devious art of it. Others submit—and hope to inherit the earth. The rest—the cravens, the cowards—live in fear for the rest of their lives. And that's only a single field—the reaction to pain. I could cite a dozen parallel cases. The optimist and the pessimist, the contented and the disgruntled, the loved and the unloved, the ambitious and the discouraged—these are only the extreme products of a miserable system.

"Traditional practices are admittedly better than nothing," Frazier went on. "Spartan or Puritan—no one can question the occasional happy result. But the whole system rests upon the wasteful principle of selection. The English public school of the nineteenth century produced brave men—by setting up almost insurmountable barriers and making the most of the few who came over. But selection isn't education. Its crops of brave men will always be small, and the waste enormous. Like all primitive principles, selection serves in place of education only through a profligate use of material. Multiply extravagantly and select with rigor. It's the philosophy of the 'big litter' as an alternative to good child hygiene.

"In Walden Two we have a different objective. We make every man a brave man. They all come over the barriers. Some require more preparation than others, but they all come over. The traditional use of adversity is to select the strong. We control adversity to build strength. And we do it deliberately, no matter how sadistic Mr. Castle may think us, in order to prepare for adversities which are beyond control. Our children eventually experience the 'heartache and the thousand natural shocks that flesh is heir to.' It would be the cruelest possible practice to protect them as long as possible, especially when we *could* protect them so well."

Frazier held out his hands in an exaggerated gesture of appeal. "What alternative *had* we?" he said, as if he were in pain. "What else could we do? For four or five years we could provide a life in which no important need would go unsatisfied, a life practically free of anxiety or frustration or annoyance. What would *you* do? Would you let the child enjoy this paradise with no thought for the future—like an idolatrous and pampering mother? Or would you relax control of the environment and let the child meet accidental frustrations? *But what is the virtue of accident?* No, there was only one course open to us. We had to *design* a series of adversities, so that the child would develop the greatest possible self-control. Call it deliberate, if you like, and accuse us of sadism; there was no other course." Frazier turned to Castle, but he was scarcely challenging him. He seemed to be waiting, anxiously, for his capitulation. But Castle merely shifted his ground.

"I find it difficult to classify these practices," he said. Frazier emitted a disgruntled "Ha!" and sat back. "Your system seems to have usurped the place as well as the techniques of religion."

"Of religion and family culture," said Frazier wearily. "But I don't call it usurpation. Ethical training belongs to the community. As for techniques, we took every suggestion we could find without prejudice as to the source. But not on faith. We disregarded all claims of revealed truth and put every principle to an experimental test. And by the way, I've very much misrepresented the whole system if you suppose that any of the practices I've described are fixed. We try out many different techniques. Gradually we work toward the best possible set. And we don't pay much attention to the apparent success of a principle in the course of history. History is honored in Walden Two only as entertainment. It isn't taken seriously as food for thought. Which reminds me, very rudely, of our original plan for the morning. Have you had enough of emotion? Shall we turn to intellect?"

Frazier addressed these questions to Castle in a very friendly way and I was glad to see that Castle responded in kind. It was perfectly clear, however, that neither of them had ever worn a lollipop about the neck or faced a bowl of Forbidden Soup.

in my opinion...

The quality of life can be improved if we understand ourselves. For this reason, psychology is the quintessential adventure.

Proliferating knowledge is fraught with confrontation. How should it be applied? How will it be applied? Who should decide? Who will decide? The fate of mankind is rather precariously hinged on the answers to these four questions. By the twenty-first century, our motivations are likely to be under definite design, and our behavior under efficient coordination. Personality formation and character training will probably be planned and controlled.

Please imagine that you are in the early part of the twenty-first century. What do you see? Are you shuddering from the terrifying image of organizational robots, or smiling from your

encounters with humans? Is the atmosphere characterized
by deceit and lack of challenge, or by awareness, empathy and
accomplishment? All right now, please return. Before we
ponder the experience, we should try to understand, through
observation, how we behave, and why we behave the way we do.
Our actions and expectations are largely reflections of our
self-image. To a great extent, we are what we think we are and
will be what we anticipate ourselves to be.

Our behavior is based on reflex and nature. We are animals,
and share common peculiarities with our primate cousins.
Superimposed on this framework is behavior originating from
learning and cultural conditioning. If we try distilling our
hereditary compulsions from our environmental education, we
can determine the exciting range of human potential.

We are, like other organisms, innately endowed with a
passion for self-preservation which creates a craving for comfort
and security. Sex likewise drives us into a search for love
and approval.

Behavior is regulated in the mind by the subconscious and
conscious, by feelings and reasoning; but it is comprised of
nerve cells which do no more than receive, process and
transform stimuli into responses.

An individual's freedom is relative within and among societies,
but it is always limited in a cultural context. By social experiences,
everyone is coerced one way or another into his particular
pattern of thought and action. Despite inherent variety in
individual abilities, we prefer creating artificial (and exploiting
superficial) *differences* to exploring *similarities.*

In spite of the havoc created by society's pogroms and
vengeance, we are still united in our needs. For sheer survival,
we require: 1) a favorable climate, 2) sustenance (to breathe,
eat, drink, sleep and defecate), 3) protection, implying restrictions
and their enforcement, 4) an identity with a belief in something,
and 5) assimilation into a life style. In addition, children
must be procreated and cared for.

An individual's potential and the collective capacity are
genetically governed, however, within the inherited extremes;
development of our resources depends upon our surroundings.

The goals of applied psychology are to adjust the individual
to his culture, and to adapt his culture to humanitarianism.
But the most effective means of pointing behavior into more
prudent designs inflames controversy.

Disturbances are produced by the conflicts between how one

sees one's self and one's impression of how one should behave. The intensity of the clashes between one's conceptions of his reality and his ideal determine one's mental health. Discord arises from distorted perspectives. Today we are by and large adjusted, but to ridiculous hypocrisies (such as feeling superior while feigning equality).

Although poets and playwrights have been delineating our behavior for centuries, the dynamics of psychology did not truly begin to unfold until Wilhelm Wundt founded his laboratory at Leipzig in 1879. Dr. Skinner's behaviorism seems to be a most valid solution.

randall swanson

questions

1. For "protection", we must surrender authority to a central government. Corresponding to this is a loss of personal freedom. How much less is inevitable? When does it become intolerable?

2. What were your first reactions to Frazier's description of *Walden Two's* child-training methods? Did they change as you read further? Why?

3. Behaviorists believe that the kind of training that Dr. Skinner describes in this chapter from his novel will prepare all children for the problems which they will face. Examine the effect of the methods described on the very bright child.

4. If we again assume a society which is leisure-oriented, will it be necessary to reorganize our methods of teaching? Why?

5. Can you imagine something which you have never experienced? Does seeing imply something seen? Always?

16.
the unwanted: can we change the criminal mind?

LET'S BRAINWASH OUR CRIMINALS

steve allen

introduction and comment by thomas krupinski

Historically, man's freedom was often measured by his acceptance of society's norms, mores, taboos and customs. To the extent that these were violated, his freedom was restricted. By the act of placing limitations on the liberty of the individual, society managed to remove the social deviate from its midst.

Concern for those imprisoned was minimal if it existed at all. Prisoners were left to rot in their own filth, or, on occasion, forced to labor for the benefit of their jailors. The removal of the individual's freedom was a form of punishment as well as a means of eliminating the participation of the prisoner in the culture.

From time to time, there were attempts to provide a form of correction along with punishment. These were crude, at best. In the United States, while correction and reform are widely heralded as the main thrust of our penal system, in many cases it is punishment which is supposed to provide the main deterrent to crime and deviation from socially acceptable behavior.

In an era of change, in an affluent society, we should give serious consideration to our own motives with regard to the radical non-conformist, regardless of whether his "crime" is against the mores and laws of society, or, as may more frequently be the case in the decades ahead, simply his determined opposition to "the way things are". Is our penal policy to be dictated by fear—of violence, of subversion, of the whole spectrum of criminal acts? Or should it be predicated on a positive effort to improve the quality and capacity of those who have gone beyond the limits of acceptable human behavior?

Social scientists, psychologists and penologists have labored long to find solutions to problems that are becoming more acute from year to year. Biochemists have suggested the possibility that a gene abnormality may be a basic cause of anti-social behavior. Newspaper headlines flay police officials, political conservatives berate our courts, and vast numbers of our Middle Americans triple-lock their doors at night and dream of the good old days when the sole occupant of the town jail was the town drunk. Washington appoints committees—and quickly and quietly locks up their reports, adding them to a collection of similar treatises which contain similar disturbing suggestions as to why crime happened and how it could be eliminated. Politicians bemoan "crime in the streets", garner millions of votes on the basis of stronger "law and order" programs, but carefully avoid the dollar-consuming programs that might minimize, if not eliminate the major source of criminal activity— the recidivist.

Over-simplified, the question becomes simply this: is it within the power of our technology-oriented culture to truly reform at least the majority of those individuals who have violated the laws of the society in which they live? Can we formulate a program which can convert the deviate into a contributing member of society?

And if such a program were constructed, would the public accept it, even if only on a trial basis? Can we afford it? Can our culture, at long last, reject the "eye for an eye" principle and take positive steps toward reclaiming the wrong-doer?

Steve Allen, pianist, composer, writer, television comedian —and thoughtful, sensitive human being—has proposed such a program in the selection that follows.

t.k.

LET'S BRAINWASH OUR CRIMINALS

Actor, composer, musician, comedian, writer, TV and radio performer, thinker and social commentator—this is a partial portrait of Steve Allen, student for one year each at Drake University and Arizona State University (then Arizona State Teachers College). Deeply concerned with social problems, he has made scholarly studies of such subjects as criminology and psychology and has written on subjects as varied as humor and politics, as well as an autobiography and a book of poetry. Among the prolific Mr. Allen's works are: 14 for Tonight, *1955;* The Funnymen, *and* Wry on the Rocks *(verse), 1956;* Mark It and Strike It, *1961;* Not All Your Laughter, Not All Your Tears, *1962;* Letter to a Conservative, *1965;* The Ground is Our Table, *1966; and* Bigger than a Breadbox, *1967.*

Many people who deplore criminal violence seem to have an insatiable appetite for it, to judge by the popularity of television and radio programs, motion pictures, books and periodicals that depict murders, kidnapings, assaults, rapes and burglaries.

Society, I suspect, would feel cheated if someone were to invent a pill that could convert a murderer into a decent, law-abiding citizen.

Well, society had better get interested in a change soon. The present crime wave is going to assume tidal proportions in the years ahead. Hiring more policemen and making penalties more severe will not solve the problem. The typical American prison is anachronistic and harmful.

For thousands of years society has punished neurotics and psychotics. The sicker they were the more severe the punishment. It

Reprinted from the Science Digest, *Hearst Corporation, 1968, by permission of the author.*

hasn't worked. But society has rarely given up practices simply because they haven't worked. The truth is, we tend to overlook the fact that a crime is essentially an irrational act.

Does punishment deter irrational acts—crime? The rate of repeatism in the federal prison system increased from 61 to 67 percent between 1949 and 1958. It has been argued that a young man who has never been punished by society might somehow feel immune from retribution. But the same cannot be said for a man who has already spent several years in prison. He knows the nature of the punishment that faces him. He has had ample evidence of the misery, the degradation, the monotony and general horror of prison exlstence. Nevertheless, he is irrational enough to go back to a life of crime as soon as he is released.

Man, in general, reasons more poorly than he supposes. We are creatures of strong physical and animal needs from the moment of birth. Only gradually and painfully do we learn to reason. Most of us, unfortunately, do not learn very well. Even at our fullest intellectual development, we still carry within us a tremendous burden of factual ignorance, erroneous information, superstition, prejudice, fear, hostility and other detrimental baggage.

These powerful emotional undercurrents enable us to stifle concern over possible detection, conviction and punishment. If detection and punishment were certain and immediate, formal deterrence might work. Tell a thirsty man that if he drinks a cold glass of water placed before him he will be shot on the spot, and he will not drink it—unless he becomes maddened by thirst. He may then suspect that you do not really mean what you said about shooting him. Or he may gamble that your courage will fail. Or he will decide that the momentary satisfaction of assuaging his thirst is worth dying for.

But, in reality, deterrence always has been pretty much a failure. Millions of people believe in a real, material hell, with actual flames that burn actual bodies. Yet their conduct does not appear to be statistically different from those who do not share such a belief.

Some will argue that if threat of imprisonment is no deterrent, then prisons ought to be abolished. I see no reason why the assumption must lead to the conclusion. It could still be argued that prisons protect society simply by keeping dangerous people off the street.

No society has ever justified its prison system purely on this thesis, however. Prisons have sprung up as the result of a tendency to do something "civilized" with offenders. In early times evil-doers were torn limb-from-limb, drawn and quartered, eaten alive by animals, burned at the stake, skinned alive, boiled in oil, stoned, crushed, impaled on spears, crucified, strangled, shot and so forth.

For lesser offenses, eye-for-an-eye "ingenuity" was employed. A man who lied might have his tongue torn out, a spy might have his eyes gouged out, a thief might have one or both hands chopped off. This last punishment persists to this day in parts of the Arab world.

Parenthetically these barbaric atrocities have not been inflicted by demented criminals, but by the authority of the state, frequently with the blessings of the church.

death or banishment

We in the West like to believe that human rights are more precious to us than property rights. But when we turn from pious theory to practice, something gets lost. As the European masses broke from feudalism, attacks upon private property increased. More than 200 offenses were punishable by death. Not every criminal could be killed, under the new enlightenment, so more were locked up. Some were put on sailing ships and banished—not always to Australia, either. Many were sent to America.

The first English prisons were the workhouses. It would be impossible to exaggerate the horror of them. They housed not only criminals, but the insane, the impoverished, lepers, women and children.

In the United States, Dr. Benjamin Rush, a signer of the Declaration of Independence, proposed that criminals be classified and segregated. Gradually two philosophies of imprisonment emerged. One, the Pennsylvania System, was based on solitary confinement and hard labor. The other—the New York, or Auburn, system—held that absolute silence would improve the prisoner. Both were nonsensical and cruel. Eventually they employed beating, flogging, strait-jackets, chains, thumbscrews and other forms of torture.

Every penal system in turn has come to be recognized as generally a failure. Certain side-approaches had value: probation, parole, democracy within the convict population, the industrial prison. Finally the idea of offering the prisoner a few educational opportunities emerged. After that the ideal of psychological counseling was introduced. I use the word *ideal* to suggest that little has been done to develop the kind of sweeping program that is really required.

My own prescription is a revolutionary and radical one.

The field of psychology has yielded up a considerable body of knowledge and theory concerning the impressionability of the human mind. Chinese Communists apparently were able to take perfectly average GIs, brainwash them for a few months, and produce important changes in their basic outlook. Think of it! In a few months of daily indoctrination—without resort to torture or drugs or any James Bondian devices—men who had lived 20 or 25 years in one culture were induced to accept ideas of another in which they had spent only a short time.

These same techniques, among others, ought to be used in a new kind of model institution to promote reasonable and socially useful ideals and attitudes.

The success of the Chinese admittedly was less than is popularly supposed. But this does not mean that nothing can be learned from the experience. Communism is an unattractive philosophy to Americans. Communist purges, slave labor camps, subversion, firing squad executions, Berlin Walls, etc., have produced in most American minds an unsympathetic image of communism. Let's assume we are trying to sell worthwhile products—reason, honesty, decency and other civilized virtues. The results might well be different and better.

The Synanon experience in rehabilitation of narcotics addicts, and the effectiveness of Alcoholics Anonymous, have given a number of interesting results. One reason is that the addicted individual is approached by someone who has successfully overcome the identical predicament, rather than someone who simply lectures from a position of virtuous, inexperienced authority. Our model institution, therefore, should include some staff members who are former convicts. Synanon has succeeded not only in curing addicts but in imbuing them with a desire to help other troubled people. This suggests that it might be possible to select and train individuals from the prison population.

Experiments could be conducted in sensory deprivation, or sensory restriction. Studies undertaken in 1957 at Princeton University showed that immediately following periods of isolation the capacity of subjects for learning certain kinds of material was improved. Here is something that deserves further study. Experiments in sleep deprivation may also hold clues that would be valuable.

It has been determined that one of the most important factors connected with indoctrination procedures is isolation—not only physical isolation, but separation from one's culture group. There is an opportunity in prisons to initiate experimental procedures which, regardless of the degree of their effectiveness, are clearly preferable to the treatment presently accorded a majority of those incarcerated.

Since monopoly of influence is desirable, a *small* institution is better than a giant one. At present, a state prison inmate spends most of his time in the culture of other prisoners, whose values may contradict those that the authorities are trying to inculcate. He is faced with a conflict between his new desire for civilized conduct and his previously established sense of loyalty to the rest of the prison group, to which he feels he belongs. Even in the absence of any such sense of group loyalty, there is sometimes the fear of retaliation or contempt from the peer group, for being a "stool pigeon." These considerations support the idea, not only of a small total inmate group, but its subdivision into even smaller and more manageable teams.

group influences actions

Actually, advantage can be taken of a susceptibility to "go along with the group." A good example is the experiment in which an individual is told he is one of a group of five being tested. In reality, the other four apparent subjects are cooperating with those administering the tests. A simple question is asked, to which the four "shills" deliberately give an incorrect answer. In a high percentage of cases an individual will deny what he knows to be the correct answer simply because the majority response makes him doubt the validity of his own initial response. Why shouldn't the same principle be applied to the rehabilitation of anti-social minds?

The learning process is already going on in our prisons. After spending a year or two in a prison in the company of more experienced criminals, a youngster comes out knowing exactly how to jimmy a door, where to go to buy or sell narcotics, how to hold up a bank. Therefore we are not concerned to debate the question: Should a man learn anything in prison or not? He *is* learning something. Much of it is bad. It is, I admit, possible for a man to acquire some formal education in arts and crafts in prison today, but present programs represent a drop in the bucket.

One of the tragic lessons being learned by the Head Start Program is that, while dramatic improvement can be made in the learning ability of small children who live in poverty areas, these same children tend to fall back into their former condition. Powerful influences in home and neighborhood tend to defeat the influences available in the schools. The hard truth seems to be that we can't properly educate young people who continue to live in a ghetto. In a totalitarian society you solve this by ordering the children out of the ghetto and into boarding schools. But we are not a totalitarian society.

There is one situation, however, when at least a small percentage of socially deprived young people are forcibly taken out of their slum homes and neighborhoods. That is prison. What an opportunity to educate and indoctrinate a captive audience! What are we waiting for?

But what kind of teaching am *I* talking about? Two kinds: Standard academic teaching, and intensive, out-and-out brainwashing designed to produce important personality changes. I am not competent to map out a complete program. As for grade school, high school and college curricula, I should think them essential.

For mind-changing indoctrination, I would rule out practically nothing. Closed-circuit television would be a must, as would tape-recording and playback equipment, with earphones available for individual concentration. High-quality public address equipment for simultaneous communication to all hands is possible. Lectures and informal talks by prominent authorities should be part of the program. The presence of public figures would suggest to patients that society is interested in them and cares.

The institution should be provided with teaching machines and programmed instruction books and devices. Instructions in remedial reading and speed reading would be essential. Video-tapes and motion picture films that were not only instructive but interesting—even entertaining—would be important.

Fundamentals of psychology and a course in general semantics might do wonders. General semantics programs already have proved strikingly effective in a few prisons. The patient would be photographed, and shown the pictures, tape-recorded and made to listen to the sound of his voice, patterns of his speech, the techniques of his thinking. He should be given standard psychological tests. The results should be discussed with him in whatever way medically qualified supervisors deemed best to bring the man into realistic focus in his own eyes. For probably the first time in his life the patient would be given an enormous amount of personal attention, made to feel a sense of dignity and importance. There have been startling conversions of hardened criminals through religion. It should be tried.

restore self-respect

The kind of institution I envision would set out deliberately to "coddle" inmates—but not in the literal sense. Inmates would *not* be served breakfast in bed, offered a choice of dinner entrees, given manicures or massages or driven to nearby golf courses. The institution would, however, make up to the inmate for the deprivations, raw deals and shortchanges that society has generally meted out to him since his birth. This might include good food, instructions about proper diet, the prescribing of decent medicines used in a normal home environment, a complete athletic program, an educational system, a library, a music room, the privilege of wearing something other than a prison uniform on special occasions. By such means, "authority" would be saying, "You have committed a crime and been deprived of the freedom to live in your accustomed environment. But you have not been sent here to be beaten, intimidated, starved, ignored, rejected or brutalized. We have one objective: to help you to help yourself."

We have ample evidence that the best efforts to control or alter human conduct rely on developing self-control and self-direction in the patient, not on authoritarian, external control.

it's a family affair

It is commonly assumed that the home is the place where sound attitudes toward social responsibility, sex, marriage and parenthood are learned. There is increasing evidence, unfortunately, that it is within the American home itself that much serious social trouble originates. The rehabilitative program I recommend, therefore, should have as one of its parts a method for involving the inmate's home environment through consultation and participation.

Primitive man commonly asked the question "what?" (What is that light in the sky? What is the stranger—friend or enemy?) Later, he asked "how?" (How can I tie these sticks together? How can we make fire?) Finally comes "why?"

Today we consider ourselves civilized and intelligent. We should be asking "why?" about a lot of things. *Why* does a prison look like a prison? The architecture carries an 18th century influence, when prisons were designed to keep dangerous people in. They were copied, at that time, from structures that were designed to keep dangerous people out—castles and fortresses.

It is no longer necessary that a prison resemble a medieval

fortress. We have better means in this age of electronics for maintaining effective security. The prison of the future should look as little like a prison as possible. Nor need it be isolated from the community. Is it because we don't want to face the reality of our mental hospitals and prisons that we hide them from our sight behind the nearest mountain range, or on a bleak island? The chief result of this stupidity—whatever the reason for it—is that patients or inmates are deprived of the important benefits of easy contact with families and friends.

What I propose is visionary and utopian. Such rehabilitation for criminals will not be constructed tomorrow. But what I propose is easier than creating nuclear weapons or putting a man on the moon.

What would a pilot institution cost? I don't know or care. More than two and a half million offenders move through our prison system each year, many of them recidivists. State and local governments spend roughly one billion dollars a year keeping convicts locked up, but less than a fifth of that trying to rehabilitate them. Fewer than four percent of prison staff people are concerned with treatment; more than 90 percent are zoo keepers.

My idea is better than that.

in my opinion...

Quite frankly, in my research in the area of penal reform, I hardly expected to find the most exciting article on the subject written by a famous entertainer. Most fortunately, I think, Allen's position as a public figure made it possible for his proposal to be heard.

When Allen said that society would somehow feel cheated if crime were abolished, I feel that he is close to the truth—at least, in terms of today. Although generally a threat to the public, the criminal frequently displays characteristics which many envy. Have we not deified Bonnie and Clyde? Jessie James? And how about the Nielsen rating of "To Catch a Thief?"

Perhaps there is a hidden streak of "The Sundance Kid" in all
of us . . .

I also imagine the society would severely miss the criminal
deviate as a scapegoat. Today, at least, when all else fails,
we can condemn, distrust and fear those who have not followed
the rules. (Perhaps we condemn to an even greater extent
those who have not been caught. "He couldn't possibly have
made that much money if he was on the level!")

But if we are moving, as we hope, toward a better world, then
our planning must transcend our own weaknesses, and a
positive program to conserve human resources must be a part
of our thinking. Perhaps Allen's Coercive Persuasion has
enough promise to merit a trial.

I think, however, that successful reform of the average criminal
will take more than a few months of daily indoctrination. A
deep-felt motivation must be built into the program, a motivation
which is of value upon the criminal's return to the outside
world. How can you sell someone on the ideals of decency,
honesty and reason if the society he sees "outside" disregards
those same principles? If we cannot upgrade our own values,
a few hours of exposure to a world of selfishness and deceit will
quickly destroy any newly-established traits. What a travesty
it would be if our most idealistic citizens were ex-cons!

I agree with Allen that the institution should provide two types
of education for deviates, although I am not sure which should
have priority. Much depends on the state of our culture at
the time. I have the feeling the author gives preference to
attitudinal changes; if this is so, I would concur, simply because
I do not think that academic training could be successful
before at least partial philosophic changes had taken place.

I cannot agree with Allen when he states that his purpose is
visionary. We must find a high priority for prison reform. We
cannot wait for the cybernetic revolution to do away with many
of the causes for criminal acts. And we cannot afford—now—to
keep correctional reforms on a scale with zoo construction.
From generation to generation, this problem has been shunted
aside; with each generation it has become more acute. We can
no longer justify barbaric, inhuman, wasteful treatment of
those unfortunates who, as Allen points out, are fundamentally
emotionally disturbed.

One final question. Brain-washing can be for good or for evil
purposes. In all of our discussion of the twenty-first century, we

consistently come back to the question of controls: who is to decide what is good and what is not? Whole nations have been brain-washed, degraded and destroyed. We retained our hopes for man as a thinking creature. We must create hope for deviates.

thomas krupinski

questions

1.　Discuss the possible effects of a guaranteed annual income on the number of criminal deviates there will be in forthcoming generations.

2.　Criminal behavior is being attacked from two directions today other than the penal system. What possibilities are there in the chemical treatment of the criminal mind? Neuro-electronic therapy?

3.　What dangers can you see in the program suggested by Allen?

4.　What factors are contributing to the increase in criminal activity at the present time?

5.　Justify spending huge sums of money that would be needed to reform our present penal system.

17.

science or religion? a christian view

CONCERNING THE RELATION BETWEEN SCIENCE AND RELIGION

martin j. heinecken

introduction and comment by russell j. blanchette, jr.

Organized religion has been in existence for about as long as recorded history can determine. "God" has been the explanation for the rising sun, the falling rain, and all conceivable natural events. Modern Man, with his increasing knowledge of the causes of physical phenomena, is faced with a decreasing need to believe in "God" as an explanation for physical occurrences. Some conceive of Man's mind as the supreme knowledge, capable of absorbing within its spongy confines the answers to the sea of problems which surround him .

America is on the threshold of a new era. Our society has sufficient knowledge to produce practically all that is basic to Man's sustenance, plus the goods which make life increasingly comfortable. It is possible that Man's knowledge will enable him to produce these goods with a decreasing amount of human labor utilized in their production. It is conceivable that in an era of abundant material goods, we will have only a small minority engaged in their production, with the major segment of our society not engaged in productive employment. This cybernetic dream would not have been possible if it were not for a religious ethic which has been deeply ingrained within us from our very inception as a nation: The Christian Work Ethic. This ethic, present in all Christian religions in one form or another, has been responsible for our growth as a nation. From the settlement of the first colonies through the industrial revolution, "Idle hands do the devil's work" is a cliche which has been accepted, without equivocation, as true. This very ethic, which has been responsible for our unparalleled industrial growth, may require close scrutinization; for if a major portion of our population will have idle hands, are we to scorn them for something over which they have only minimal control, or will we re-examine our religious ethics?

One of the primary purposes of religion, from the time of Moses to our own, through iconoclastic revolution and insurrections, has been to meet the intrinsic needs of Man and provide him with a relevant guidebook to his path through life. When Man's religions have become dogmatic and irrelevant to his needs, one of two things has occurred: either the existing religions determined where their lack of relevance lay, and modified themselves to continue to meet the needs of Man; or Man developed new religions which filled his intrinsic needs and provided him with a legible guide to life. A declining church attendance in our society over the past ten years may indicate that people are not finding the answers to the problems of this century in their religious institutions. Many people today believe in a manner of living which closely resembles that of the Man from whom Christianity takes its name. He indicated the irrelevance of certain religious rules during his time, initiating what would now be called situational ethics. Today's college students are inquiring into the existing religious institutions. Many feel that these age-old relics have condoned war while advocating peace; tolerated the accumulation of wealth (as well as amassing wealth of their own), in the glaring presence of poverty; and advocated racism, in spite of the philosophy of the Man for whom their religion is named. People starve to death in India, their religion depriving them of a ready food supply, making virtually impossible any change of their position in life.

There was a time when infant mortality was high, and life expectancy low. It was essential to Man's very existence that he propagate his race at a prolific rate. The relevance of the religious institution which advocated this could hardly be questioned, for Man's survival depended upon adequate numbers. During our century, science and medicine have made progress, eradicating many of the causes of infant mortality, and increasing the duration of life. Now we are confronted with an over-crowded planet, and the world's population is expanding astronomically. In view of the population problem, the purpose of this institution's position should be re-examined. If we believe that human life is sacred, should we allow its indiscriminate creation—making us helpless to prevent its destruction by starvation or by any of the other means of death which result from unlimited people competing for limited resources?

Man can now travel to the moon and planets, possibly beyond. The chance is increasing that we will discover some form of life elsewhere, that life is not confined to our small, insignificant planet. What effect will this have upon our existing religious institutions? What of our concept of God? Will it be modified, or destroyed? What of our concept of the nature of Man? The problems to be confronted by our religious institutions are innumerable. Will these rocks of security continue their existence in an age of growing knowledge, changing concepts, and expanding communication among men of all religious convictions? Or will they erode and eventually crumble as the growing waves of science and technology continue a relentless onslaught at their aged foundations?

Martin J. Heinecken, Professor of Systematic Theology at the Lutheran Theological Seminary, addresses himself to these questions in the selection that follows.

r.j.b., jr.

CONCERNING THE RELATION
BETWEEN SCIENCE AND RELIGION

Martin J. Heinecken has been Professor of Systematic Theology at the Lutheran Theological Seminary at Mt. Airy, Philadelphia since 1945. He has also taught at Wayne College, Staten Island, New York, and in South Australia, and served parishes in the midwest. He is a representative of the United Lutheran Church, and has been instrumental in formulating theological documents for the Lutheran World Federation and the National Council of the Churches of Christ, U.S.A. He is the author of The Moment before God, *a study of Soren Kierkegaard (1950);* Christ Frees and Unites; Truths We Live By; *and* Basic Christian Teachings *(1949); in addition to* God In The Space Age, *1959.*

The advent of the space age, with all its implications for the future, is only the dramatic climax of the road which science has been traveling for many years, and so it brings into sharp focus the place that science is to be given in our life in general, and its relation to religion and the Christian church in particular. A man cannot live a schizophrenic existence, in the laboratory and in his everyday life, depending upon scientific method, and then on Sundays and whenever he says his prayers, somehow shifting gears. There must be not just a working truce but a reasonable unification into a meaningful whole, even if this includes many an irrational, given fact which we fail to understand, but which does, nevertheless, exist.

the warfare between science and theology

There is a long history of the warfare between science and theology. This presents us with a pugnacious problem. Prophet, priest, and scientist have not always seen eye to eye nor pulled together very well under a common yoke.

Whenever there was a new discovery which went counter to the traditional beliefs, the church and its leaders were quick to protest. Puny man was presuming to know more than God. He was getting too big for his britches. He was once more building the Tower of Babel to rival God and make a name for himself on the earth.

As the Middle Ages drew to a close, the Roman Catholic Church tried and convicted some of the proponents of the new world view of heresy. Giordano Bruno was burned at the stake in 1600 because he no longer believed in a finite, enclosed universe. Because he held space to be infinite, he could find in it no abode for God as a being separate from the world. He was condemned, therefore, not because he was an advocate of learning, but because he was a pantheist and held that God was immanent in, that is dwelling in the universe itself and in no way separable from the creation.

In 1632, Galileo was forced to recant his conviction that the earth revolved and not the sun, but he is said to have murmured under his breath after his recantation, "Nevertheless it moves." This shows how persistent is the drive toward truth and how impossible it is to force a man to change a conviction honestly arrived at. The only thing that can change a man's mind is persuasive counterevidence.

Churchmen have been suspicious of new views. Martin Luther did not think well of Copernicus for contradicting the cosmology of the Bible. So he said in the usual gruff fashion he used whenever addressing himself to one whom he considered the Lord's enemy, "People gave ear to an upstart astrologer who strove to show that the earth revolves, not the heavens or the firmament, the sun and the moon. Whoever wishes to appear clever must devise some new system, which of all systems is of course the very best. This fool wishes to reverse the entire system of astronomy; but sacred Scripture tells us that Joshua commanded the sun to stand still, and not the earth." [1]

Calvin also said, "Who will venture to place the authority of Copernicus above that of the Holy Spirit?" [2] and continued, "The world also is stablished that it cannot be moved." Ps. 93:1. It was also under Calvin's regime that Michael Servetus, who anticipated the discovery of the circulation of the blood, was convicted of

---

[1] Andrew D. White, *A History of the Warfare of Science with Theology in Christendom* (New York: George Braziller, 1953), p. 26.
[2] *Ibid.*

heresy and burned to death in Geneva in 1553. Again, it was not because of his scientific views, but because he denied the traditional doctrine of the Trinity. In the eighteenth century, John Wesley held that the new views of the universe tend toward infidelity.

It is also common knowledge that the church opposed other scientific innovations which it believed to be counter to God's word, such as inoculation, anesthesia, birth control, and above all, the theory of evolution. It is said that one divine finally found Biblical sanction for the use of anesthesia in childbirth by citing the fact that God himself caused a deep sleep to fall on Adam when he operated on his rib to produce Eve. There were repeated witch-hunts, and the last burning in Scotland was as late as 1731 and in France, 1718. In New England, there was a great rash of witch-hunts at the end of the seventeenth century.

So almost every advance of science had to win its way against the opposition of the church, but we must be fair to both sides of the issue. The church and the theologians were concerned with defending God's sovereignty and the truth of God's revelation. It was not always just fanatical opposition to all innovation; but there were genuine issues at stake, as in the case of Giordano Bruno and his pantheism, Servetus and his denial of the Trinity, and in the assertion of a chance evolution and only a quantitative instead of a qualitative difference between man and the animal. The trouble lay in the fact that neither the church nor the scientist always recognized their own limitations.

We should not forget, either, the fact that most, if not all, of the great scientists through the years have been devout members of the church, quite willing to bow to the authority of the church in matters of their soul's salvation, provided only they were left free to investigate in their own realm. The common notion that all scientists are godless is false. Many of them intended only to glorify God and to help mankind by their studies. To mention only a few: Copernicus was a canon of the Roman Church; Galileo was a devout Roman Catholic; Kepler was a Christian mystic. Robert Boyle aspired to the Christian ministry, but considered himself unworthy; Isaac Newton was an Aryan Christian; Joseph Priestley was a devout Unitarian; Michael Faraday was a devout member of a small evangelical sect; Arthur Eddington was a convinced Quaker; Louis Pasteur's Christian faith was the spur to his scientific activity.[3]

[3] See: Arthur F. Smethurst, *Modern Science and Beliefs* (New York: Abingdon, 1957).

When the British Royal Society was founded in 1645, it was stated by Sprat, its first historian: "I do here in the beginning most sincerely declare that if this design [of a Royal Society] should in the least diminish the reverence that is due to the doctrine of Jesus Christ, it were so far from deserving protection that it ought to be abhorred by all the politic and prudent, as well as by the devout part of Christendom." [4]

The debt which the development of the scientific method owes to Christianity in general should also be acknowledged. It was not until Christianity had made clear the distinction between Creator and creature and rid the world of demons which capriciously interfered with ordered events, that science became possible. A dependable, ordered nature is the precondition of all purposeful, spiritual life.[5]

Above all, if there is to be a proper scientific control, God himself must be excluded from the world that man gets under his control. The world of nature, man can control, but not the God who made it. Pantheism, and in fact all monistic views, have a fatal inconsistency. Purpose, plan, responsibility, both human and divine, are impossible except on the basis of a real dualism, not of matter and spirit, but of Creator and creature.

how to reconcile science and religion?

How then shall we go about reconciling science and religion? Socrates, the gadfly of Athens, the despair of his shrewish wife, Xantippe, was declared by the oracle at Delphi to be the wisest of men. To test the oracle, Socrates went back to his old haunts in the market place of Athens and continued his disconcerting game of questioning all whom he could buttonhole by the lapels of their togas. In the course of his questionings he discovered that almost everyone knew more than he did about something or other. The shipbuilder knew more about shipbuilding, the cobbler knew more about cobbling, the horsemen knew more about horses, the lute player knew more about "luting," the orator knew more about the art of persuasion and of making the worse appear the better cause, the statesman knew more about governing wisely, the warrior knew more about the "noble" art of slaughtering and putting to rout the enemy, the wrestler knew more fantastic holds than even

---

[4] C. A. Coulson, *Science and Christian Belief* (Chapel Hill: The University of North Carolina Press, 1954), p. 12.

[5] See: John Baillie, *Natural Science and the Spiritual Life* (New York: Oxford University Press, 1951).

Socrates' vivid imagination could conjure up, the housewife knew more about folding diapers and getting a hot meal on the table in between whatever was the equivalent of today's bridge game. In short, the infallible oracle seemed at last to have toppled from its throne: everyone was wiser than Socrates.

But then came the vindication. The ambiguous statements of the oracle could never prove false. When King Croesus asked the oracle whether he should make war on King Cyrus, he was told that a great empire would be destroyed if he did. And so it was; but not the empire that Croesus expected it would be. So also in Socrates' case there was a hitch in the oracle's ambiguous wisdom. As Socrates did his questioning, he discovered one fatal flaw in the wisdom of all those who knew more than he did in some special area of concern. Every expert in some speciality also made pretensions beyond the area of his competence. When the politician went to the races or the wrestling matches, he pretended also to be an expert judge of horseflesh, and to hear him extol his favorite grunter and groaner you would think that he was himself the champion wrestler of the Peloponnesus, with his skinny legs and stringy muscles. Whenever the artisans gathered in the market place, everyone knew all the answers as they discussed the latest tragedy or comedy, the latest fad in "schoolteaching," the state of the nation, the progress of the defensive war, the high price of perfumes, the state of morals and religion, and just who was responsible for corrupting the youth of Athens.

So each one in his own foolish way betrayed his ignorance, simply because he did not recognize the limitations of his competence. Because he was expert in one thing, he presumed to be expert in all. Because one method worked in one area, he supposed that it would do to solve all problems. Because the best way to get a donkey's attention was to beat him over the head, he applied this method universally. Because the oarsmen moved forward while facing to the rear, he supposed that this was also the way to ride down the *chaussée* in a chariot. Because absolutely certain knowledge came to him when he related his ideas to one another in perfect and indisputable clarity, he supposed that this was the only avenue to truth. Truth was attained only by clear thinking in abstraction from all the messed-up contradictions of life. When people worshiped the gods of the Olympus and the personified forces of nature because a surge of emotion overwhelmed them at the sight of the sunset or at the patter of the rain after the drought of summer, then this was all dismissed as superstition. The philosopher and not the priest was to be king. While, for his part, the priest had his pretensions, too. Nothing would succeed if the omens were not favorable. Everything depended on the shape of the kidney and the size of the bladder the sacrificing priest held in his bloody hands. Even the sun would not rise if the priest did not perform the right sacrifice. The priest held the keys to the kingdom not only of this world but also of the next. Pretension to knowledge meant pretension to power and this meant corruption, for the oft-quoted dictum was as true then as it is now: "All power corrupts and absolute power corrupts absolutely."

the proper recognition of limitations

So Socrates came to the conclusion that the oracle was correct after all. He alone of all men was wise in the knowledge of his ignorance and his lack of pretensions to power over men. He alone knew his limitations. He alone knew that he did not know and did not pretend to knowledge when all he possessed was opinion, hearsay, or the flimsiest kind of evidence. He knew both the values and the dangers of specialization. He knew the bane of the limited perspective. He knew that what worked in one area would probably get a person horribly fouled up in another. He himself had once been enamored of mathematics and astronomy and of all the so-called objective sciences, where a man looks away from himself at the world and the solid facts about him and lets them correct his own wayward desire of how he would like things to be. But then he discovered that this did not solve the riddle that man was to himself; it did not solve the inner contradictions of his being; it did not still the restless longing of his heart or take away life's loneliness, or silence the cries of an aroused conscience. So he turned, as he says, from the study of the numbers and the stars to the study of man himself, and he made his motto, "know thyself," because he was convinced that all truth was within every individual. This is why he derided the Sophists who pretended to teach men wisdom and charged tremendous fees for their fulminations. He himself would not charge a sou for his services. His mother was a midwife, and he himself proposed to follow her profession. He compared himself to a midwife assisting at the birth of ideas when the prodigiously pregnant youth of Athens came to him in their birth pangs. With his subtle questioning, he helped along the labor and then he examined the progeny to see whether it was just a wind egg or something more substantial. So he felt that every teacher should be humble before his pupils and only help them to develop their own inner capacities. These ideas he held to be sufficient to solve all man's problems. To know yourself properly was in the end to know God and all things. Within man himself lay the answer, and life's great adventure was the search for the truth within; and even if the answers were not always found, Socrates felt that there was still the glory of the quest.

". . . Some things I have said of which I am not altogether confident. But that we shall be better and braver and less helpless if we think that we ought to inquire, than we should have been if we indulged in the idle fancy that there was no knowing and no use in searching after what we know not;—that is a theme upon which I am ready to fight, in word and deed, to the utmost of my power." [6]

the truth is within the learner

So now we seem to have arrived at a contradiction. Socrates began by saying that everyone should recognize his limitations and that only he who knows that he does not know is wise. Then he concludes by saying that after all, everyone knows everything because all the truth is always within every learner himself. While this seems to be a contradiction, there is a resolution of it, and it is this resolution which should also help us toward the resolution of our problems concerning the relation between science and religion. It is still true that Socrates held that everyone should know his limitations and that true wisdom consists in the knowledge of ignorance. Nevertheless, this does not preclude the possibility that with the proper training, everyone should be able to arrive at the truth that matters. Socrates was not interested in just knowledge, for that, after all, is an abstraction. What he was interested in was the good life. The question concerning knowledge was for him always the question concerning the good. To know the good was the same as to do it, for Socrates held it impossible that anyone should really know the good and yet act in contradiction to it.

This is the Socratic presupposition with which we must come to terms, for it will have everything to do with how we solve the problem of the relation between science and religion and a proper division of labor. Does this square with the facts or does it reveal a far too optimistic view of human nature? Does it underestimate

[6] Jowell (trans.), Plato's *Meno* (New York: Tudor Publishing Company), pp. 35–36.

the radicalness of evil in the world? Is evil always just the result of ignorance, and does to know the good mean to do the good? Does all the truth lie within the learner, and is all that is necessary for this truth to be brought to birth the right maieutic process, that is the proper midwifery? Or is there something else necessary? Perhaps, after all, man's real problem in his existence is not solved when he goes within himself, and, so to speak, communes with himself. Perhaps the solution to life's problems is not in this kind of intellectual navel staring.

help from the gods

While the ancient Greek philosophers played at their intellectual game of chess, the people still crowded to the theaters where the part the capricious gods and the inscrutable fates played in the lives of men was so vividly portrayed, reflecting the comedy and tragedy of life itself. In addition, all of them took part in the so-called "mysteries." These were, in part at least, joyous nature festivals in which everyone rejoiced over the return of spring and the changing seasons of the year, each with its own peculiar charm. The word, mystery, comes from the Greek word *muo,* which means, to shut the mouth, as you do when you pronounce the letter M. In the mystery, therefore, a man was reduced to silence before an ineffable experience. As in the tragedies on the stage, he became aware of his basic dependence upon powers, both good and evil, which, try as he would, he could not control. So the solution to his real problem did not come from self-communing. It came only when help came from another, when the god himself appeared in the cleft of the rock or at the side of the fountain.

man's struggles for survival

Here lies the answer concerning the relation between science and religion. There are many problems that man can solve with the aid of a midwife as he gives birth to that which lies within him. It is true that the whole drama of man's struggle for survival against the forces of nature and his rise from barbarism and helplessness before storm and disease and death is due exactly to that kind of discovery of truth within. Only because man has the innate capacity to think, to frame universals by abstracting from the particular, to count, to draw geometrical figures, to make inductions and deductions, has he risen above the fox, his brother in cunning, and the tiger, his rival in ferocity. All animals are guided by their instincts and, apart from that, they are utter idiots. The lower in the scale of life an animal, the more specialized it is; for example, the bee, which builds its beautifully symmetrical honeycombs always in the same way, and goes through its routine of honey-making without long lessons from the teacher of honeymaking. But the more specialization an animal acquires, the more dependent it is upon the vagaries of environment. Man alone is not hampered by instincts. He is free to develop himself in almost any direction. The little monkey is independent of his mother almost as soon as he leaves the womb, and there is no long period of schooling for him.

But the human child must be taught everything he knows. Slowly through the years, that which is latent in him must be drawn out and developed. But it is precisely this which gives him his flexibility, as the powers that make him the crown of creation and only a little lower than the angels are developed. Man, created in the image of God, stands a qualitative leap above the animals. Part of what this means is his power of reasoning, and with it to conquer the earth and subdue it. (*See* Gen. 1:28.) It was a great day in the history of mankind when man made his first abstraction, and instead of dealing only with this particular tree and that particular animal and that particular woman, began to think in terms of trees and animals and women as a class. What he did was to abstract, that is, to take away from all the many particular trees that which they all had in common and to form the universal tree. From the many particular women of his acquaintance, he abstracted that grace of form and figure which distinguished them from the members of the opposite sex, and he called it "woman." He learned to count, and it was a great day when he ascertained the knowledge that one plus one is two, and that this is a truth quite independent of adding one apple to another apple and getting applesauce, instead of two apples. Here we can see most clearly what is involved in abstraction from actual existing things. Numbers and their relations, geometrical figures, perfect squares and circles and triangles exist in their perfection nowhere in the actual realm of things. A mathematical point occupies no space, and a line has no width whatsoever. These are all abstractions of the mind, and yet with them man is able to make himself master of the actual things in the world. The grocer can count out his apples and try to reconcile the actual number of apples in the bag with the unchanging, eternal numbers that he "knows" with his mind. He can be mistaken in his count and he can count over and over again, but he can never have the same absolute certainty that he has not miscounted, as he has of the number with which he is trying to make the apples agree.

This, at the same time, gives us the notion of absolute certainty, or apodictic certainty as it is also called, because it cannot be contradicted. No one can deny that two times two is four, unless he means something else by it. This is the notion of self-evidence. The evidence for the truth of the number relations lies in themselves alone. He who has the rational power to form the number concepts need only look at them to see that they are what they are and could not be otherwise. It is not possible that two plus two should be anything else but four. This fact exhausts the possibilities. Of course, if you add two things to two things, that is a different matter, and you can never be sure what you will get. Two quarts of liquid added to two other quarts may end up in a profusion of quarts, just as boiling rice can overflow into the whole kitchen, or other combinations may end up in a tremendous explosion and an expensive funeral. The possibilities of adding two things to two things are not exhausted by the number four, but the relation between the abstract number two plus the abstract number two is definitely exhausted in that one possibility of the abstract number four.

This is man's power of abstract thought, and it is a tremendous gain because it frees him from the particular and enables him to generalize and thus to soar in his imagination to the most distant realms. It makes him creative and marks the beginning of his conquest of nature. It is the beginning of what we today call science, although we ought to be much more exact and call it natural science, that is, the science which has to do with what we ordinarily call nature, all the things and animals and forces about us that man can manipulate and make to serve his purposes. How far this sphere extends—that is just the point in question, and we shall have to deal with it later.

Of course, this business of abstracting from the particular also involves a great loss. It is no longer this particular Mary Brown, with uniquely raised eyebrow and inimitable "unbaptized movements," and the whispered words that are meant for only one person in the world to hear, but it is just "woman in general," of which there are a million and more instances. No one wants a "woman in general," but each one wants his particular Eve, even though she falls far short of the perfection of beauty.

the power of induction and deduction

With the power to abstract and formulate universals went also the power of induction and deduction. By induction is meant the ability to go from the many particulars to the universal, or from many instances of a phenomenon to a generalization. The philosophers today are not agreed on just how this phenomenon is accomplished and what degree of certainty attaches to generalizations, but about the phenomenon and its benefit to mankind there is little doubt. Because the sun has for innumerable years risen in the east and set in the west and there have been no instances to the contrary, the generalization is made that the sun always rises in the east and sets in the west. Because water boils at a certain temperature under the same atmospheric conditions, it is concluded that it will always do so and that there are no exceptions to this so-called "law of nature." But we should be able to see that this is not a self-evident proposition. Saying that the sun will rise in the east does not exhaust the possibilities. There are three other points of the compass from which it could also rise, and then there is also the possibility that it should not rise at all, or that some day it should come up black as pitch and burned to a cinder, instead of shining all golden in its splendor. So the best you can get for any induction of this kind is a high degree of probability, high enough to make you wager a considerable amount but hardly high enough to make you stake your life on it.

There is a different kind of certainty connected with deduction. Every valid deduction is absolutely certain as a deduction from the given premises. If all men are mortal and Socrates is a man, then it is a valid deduction to conclude that Socrates is mortal. The generalization, however, that all men are mortal is not absolutely certain. It has only a high degree of probability, since it is not self-evident and does not exhaust either the possibilities or the instances. Even if all men in the past have died, this does not absolutely exclude the possibility that some day the fountain of youth and of immortality may be discovered. Some day some Siegfried may slay the fabulous dragon and bathe in his blood and make himself impervious to death without having any spot into which a treacherous Hagen may plunge the fatal spear. This always remains as a possibility, however unlikely. The generalization that all men are mortal is an induction from the particular instances to the universal and is highly probable, in view of the fact that there are no negative instances; while the deduction itself is absolutely certain from the universal to the particular. If there are two concentric circles, the one smaller than the other and contained within it, and there is a fly in the smaller circle, then it is absolutely certain that the fly will also be contained within the larger circle. This is only one instance of a valid deduction such as we are constantly making, and without which orderly thought would be impossible. All this is part of man's native equipment and it has enabled him to make all the progress he has made. Some truths are given to men by what we may call insight or intuition. He sees into them because he has the kind of mind he has. We may call these *truths of the reason* because they concern the ideas which man has and their relations to each other. Other truths come to man only slowly, on the basis of observation and experience, and it is through a combination of these two, the insights of the reason and the results of observation of experience, that man builds up his fund of knowledge. Whatever knowledge is gathered in this fashion we may call science, or *scientia,* from the Latin word *scio,* which means "I know." This is then a much broader term than we are accustomed to when we speak of science today and mean what the English schoolboy calls "stinks," that is, chemistry or any other of the natural sciences based as they are on the insights of mathematics plus careful observation and experiment.

the development of modern science

It has been only since about the year 1600 that man has been making the phenomenal progress in his knowledge of the world about him and in his control of the forces of nature that has culminated today in the splitting of the atom and the advance into outer space. It was then that the so-called method of induction, based on observation and experimentation, was more fully developed, and discovery followed upon discovery because men ceased relying upon authority and given premises, and accepted nothing that they could not verify for themselves and press into some useful service. Prior to that time there had, of course, been much learning, and the foundation of the scientific method already had been laid by Aristotle, who was as keen an observer of nature as ever lived. Nevertheless, tradition and the authority of the church stifled progress and fresh venture into the truth. Men usually proceeded by deduction from given premises rather than by induction from the observed facts to the generalizations. The authority of the church and of the Bible went for the most part unquestioned, and if observed facts contradicted the Bible, then the Bible won out.

There has been told what is probably an apocryphal story of the learned doctors deducing the number of teeth in a horse's mouth from some fantastic premise, and no one questioned their deduction until the stableboy came along, opened the hourse's mouth, and counted the teeth, and so got it "straight from the horse's mouth." Francis Bacon was the great spokesman for the new method of induction. He compared the method of deduction to that of the spider which spins its web all out of itself, while the method of induction he compared to that of the bee which flits from flower to flower and so gathers its store of honey. So it was stated that there must be seven planets because seven is the number of perfection, as there are seven golden candlesticks and seven letters to the churches in the Book of Revelation. The astronomer, however, learns the number of the planets from his actual observation of the heavens.

It was, then, from about 1600 and on that the method of the natural sciences was more and more carefully developed, until today it has been developed into an almost foolproof method, and there is in the hands of men an almost infallible method of prediction and control. For this is what the method of the natural sciences is, a method of prediction and control which increases man's power, enables him to overcome his insecurity, makes him less the victim of his environment and caprice. But, as we have already said, to call this method simply a matter of induction that begins without presuppositions, which nothing but the facts, would be a great mistake. The method of the natural sciences involves both deduction and induction and is never without accepted presuppositions which are themselves not capable of proof.

the presuppositions of the method of the natural sciences

For one thing, there is the acceptance of all mathematical relations and the belief that they apply to the given world of things. As we have already tried to state, these truths of mathematics are really based on insight. However true it may be that men first learned to count by actually manipulating their fingers and their toes or by proceeding from one object to another, the insights of mathematics, once gained, stayed with them as indubitable, and only by means of them were men able to continue their progress.

Furthermore, they presupposed the orderliness of nature and a strict cause and effect sequence. Nothing in the world of nature happened by chance, but only through the operation of a cause. Every event was a link in an interminable chain, linked to the event that preceded it as the effect to the cause and in turn linked to the event that followed it as the cause to the effect. Every happening thus played a dual role as both cause and effect. The acceptance of this kind of determined order was quite a shock to devout believers who thought of this as their Father's world in which no sparrow falls without his will, who believed in miracles, in divine interventions, in answers to prayer. And it was not only the devout believers who found it hard to believe in this kind of determinism, but also others who believed in human freedom and responsibility.

The philosopher Kant spent a lifetime in vindication of the fact of man's freedom of decision and his responsibility for that decision in the face of the inviolable order of nature. Two things, he said, filled him with unutterable awe, the starry skies above and the moral law within. By the starry sky above he did not mean just the torchlit heavens as they delighted lovers the world around, but he meant the inviolable order of nature according to which the stars return in their courses, after millions of years, with split-second precision. What room is there for freedom of decision and action in such a world? And yet every man feels in himself the pull of obligation, of duty, of responsibility, of that "ought" which lays a burden upon him that, try as he may, he cannot throw off. But this feeling of ought requires freedom or it would make no sense, and an unfree, determined being would scarcely feel in himself such an imperious pull. The idea implied in "I ought" is that "I can."

This is not the place to discuss the ingenious way in which Kant tried to reconcile the observed, inviolable order of nature with the observed fact of responsibility and freedom. It is recognized as one of the great achievements of human thought and still has its adherents today. The point is simply that men were presented with a real problem, not only for their faith in the Bible and in God, but for their belief in human dignity and responsibility, once they accepted the premise of an ordered world in which there is no room for freedom. Yet this presupposition of the orderliness of nature and of a cause and effect sequence remains the necessary presupposition of all the natural sciences, and without it no natural scientist can operate. He can perform no experiment, conduct no research, make no predictions, exercise no control if he does not assume this order. No chemist developing a new plastic, no bio-

chemist developing a new vaccine, no doctor performing an operation, no engineer building a bridge, no farmer sowing his seed and
crossbreeding his cattle, no housewife baking a cake, no barefoot
boy spinning his top can accomplish anything, except as they all
rely on this order.

Later on, we shall have something to say about Heisenberg's
so-called principle of indeterminacy and of the humility with which
the scientists view their generalizations as being nothing but
statistical averages and never indubitably certain. Now it is enough
to assert that every working scientist, and in fact every human
being, begins with and operates with the presupposition of an
inviolable and dependable order, and we are constantly making
deductions from our assumptions and hypotheses.

the method of the natural sciences

On the basis of these presuppositions, we can then state what is
peculiar about the method of the natural sciences. But we cannot
do this either, unless we recognize that what distinguishes the
scientist is, first of all, not so much a method as it is a spirit, an
attitude, a total orientation toward life. It is this idea that J. B.
Conant develops so well in *On Understanding Science,*[7] in which
he points out that the rise of the scientific attitude was due not
primarily to the actual practitioners of science, but to men who
disciplined their minds in the pursuit of knowledge, who insisted
on the most careful distinctions, and who, like Socrates before
them, made the distinction, above all, between what they knew
and what they did not know. They were not the actual experimenters and inventors who passed on to succeeding generations
much useful information, but they were the ones who had new
ideas that were fruitful in the search for truth. Such men were not
just interested in nature, in things, but in man himself, and in truth
for its own sake. They were the ones who went in pursuit of the
facts, without prejudice, in all areas of inquiry and were willing to
stick by these facts without fear.

Now the preliminary definition of science which Conant gives is
a much more inclusive one, and at the same time a narrower one
than the one generally given. It has to do with the disinterested
search for truth through the power of the human mind, and it
becomes fruitful wherever, on the basis of careful attention to and

---

[7] See: James B. Conant, *On Understanding Science* (New Haven: Yale
University Press, 1947).

observation of all the facts, the mind produces new concepts and ideas. Conant writes, "As a first approximation [that is, to a definition], we may say that science emerges from the other progressive activities of man to the extent that new concepts arise from experiments and observations. The case histories drawn from the last three hundred years show examples of fruitful and fruitless concepts. The texture of modern science is the result of the interweaving of the fruitful concepts. The test of a new idea is therefore not only its success in correlating the then-known facts, but much more its success or failure in stimulating further experimentation or observation which in turn is fruitful. This dynamic quality of science viewed not as a practical undertaking but as development of conceptual schemes seems to me to be close to the heart of the best definition." [8]

With this definition we can contrast that of Bertrand Russell: "Science is the attempt to discover, by means of observation, and reasoning based upon it, first, particular facts about the world, and then laws connecting facts with one another and (in fortunate cases) making it possible to predict future occurrences. Connected with this theoretical aspect of science there is scientific technique, which utilizes scientific knowledge to produce comforts and luxuries that were impossible, or at least much more expensive in a pre-scientific age." [9]

John Dewey is quite explicit in restricting the road to truth to the scientific method. "The mind of man is being habituated to a new method and ideal: There is but one sure road of access to truth—the road of patient, cooperative inquiry operating by means of observation, experiment, record and controlled reflection." [10]

It makes no difference at this point whether we accept Conant's definition, which puts the emphasis on fruitful concepts, or the other definitions which put the emphasis on the actual method employed in arriving at valid generalizations, in which fruitful concepts certainly play a vital part. In either case, the ultimate outcome is a greater control over his destiny on the part of man. According to Conant, this is not the conscious concern. The true scientist is interested only in knowing. The power of control which this gives him is secondary to this distinterested search.

According to Dewey, however, all thinking is problem solving,

[8] *Ibid.*

[9] Bertrand Russell, *Religion and Science* (New York: Oxford University Press, 1935), p. 8.

[10] John Dewey, *A Common Faith* (New Haven: Yale University Press, 1934), p. 32.

and man is always intent on overcoming some limitation. The only way to do this is to follow, step for step, the method that has proved successful in the natural sciences. This method must be extended to all the sciences if they are worth the name. If they cannot describe accurately, state causes, make predictions, and so exercise control, then they are not scientists, but philosophers or poets or prophets. This would apply to the sciences involving human beings as well as to those dealing with the subhuman.

Whatever still needs to be said about the limitations of this method of the natural sciences, there can be no question about what it is to lead to: the kind of prediction and control that is exercised in physics and chemistry. Meteorology is an exact science to the extent that it can predict and control the weather, warn against hurricanes, break these up or send them scurrying. Psychology is an exact science to the extent that it can predict behavior and so weed out the pilots who will crack up, predict incompatible marriages, or cure maladjustments. Sociology is an exact science only insofar as it gives insight into group behavior, social trends, and the like, so that evils can be guarded against and desirable ends achieved.

Granting then that science is more than a method, that it is a spirit of inquiry, that it is at best a disinterested passion for the truth, that it depends upon the fruitfulness of the concepts which it develops, there is, nevertheless, a scientific method which can be successfully employed in the giant laboratories of today where many thousands are working on the same problem. This method is, sooner or later, assured of success.

The method may briefly be described as follows: First of all, there must, of course, be a felt difficulty, which must be precisely located and defined. In other words, the problem under investigation must be clearly stated and limited. The next step is the gathering of relevant facts, and this implies some knowledge and some hypotheses; that is, guesses of what may and may not be relevant. So this is practically inseparable from the next step which is the setting up of possible solutions. It is here, especially, that deductive reasoning takes place and that the uniformity of nature is assumed. The reasoning is simple: if p then q. If the bite of the Anopheles mosquito is the cause of malaria, then the malaria occurs only where there are those mosquitoes. If the mosquito can be eliminated, then malaria can be eliminated. This assumes the causal connection and the uniformity of nature, and the trick is, of course, really to establish the causal connection by controlled experimentation and verification.

The most common fallacy at this point is that of *post hoc, ergo propter hoc,* "after this, therefore on account of this." The rustic who sees the girl kiss her soldier boy good-by at the train window just as the train starts moving supposes that it is this potent blast which sends the train catapulting. All primitive magic is based on the assumption that there is a causal connection between the mumbled incantation and that which follows. The hunter who relies on his tried and tested knowledge, the bow and the arrow fashioned perfectly after many a trial and error and a few fortunate flashes of insight, the lairs and habits of his prey carefully observed, nevertheless recognizes some factors over which he has no control. There are too many variables. The best arrow, most carefully aimed, from the tautest bow, at precisely the right moment, nevertheless fails to reach its mark, for in that split second the protective God whispers a warning into the ear of the deer, and it drops its head. These are the factors the hunter hopes to control with his magic, his charm, his mumbo jumbo. Once it worked, *post hoc, ergo propter hoc,* so he will take chances. Not so the scientist, who must carefully verify his hypotheses, and under controlled experimentation reassure himself that he really is in control. The Salk vaccine was not put into use until—as far as was humanly possible—it had been established that it worked and that there would be no deleterious effects.

It is at the point of the setting up of hypotheses that the flash of insight as to a possible solution is so important. In giant laboratories it is largely a matter of continued trial and error, and the company that can afford the biggest laboratories and perform the most experiments is likely to come up first with the best plastic. Nevertheless, this by no means eliminates the sudden flash of insight. Here the difference between the brilliant genius who, as the word indicates, has an inborn capacity beyond that of others, and the ordinary hack comes in. While it may be true that "inspiration is ninety-nine per cent perspiration," there nevertheless is the factor of the given capacity which man does not control. There is also that other intangible, the will, the desire, the drive to know or to serve, which is not under control.

the limitations of the scientific method

The flash of insight, the gift of genius, the push of the will, therefore, remain as uncontrolled and, we believe, uncontrollable factors, and this will have an important bearing on the conclusions at which we shall ultimately arrive. Granted that the aim of the scientist—in the narrow sense defined—is to make himself the master, either in just knowing for the sake of knowing, or in order that he may predict and control and so make his lot and that of his fellow men more bearable, the big question remains whether or not there are not definite limits to this method. A view that sees no limits to the applicability of the scientific method and that regards it as the only avenue to truth we may designate as "scientism." Like all "isms," it fails to see the rich complexity of life, that there are more things 'twixt heaven and hell than men dream of in their philosophy. It tries to reduce everything to one simple system and insists fanatically that its truth is the only truth. This is the height of unwisdom, as we tried to show earlier by the reference to Socrates, the master of those who know, because he distinguished between what he knew and what he did not know.

There are others, therefore—and these are scientists themselves—who recognize that there are different levels of existence, different ways of arriving at truth, different kinds of truth. There is no one scientific method, but there are many, and a method appropriate in one area may not be appropriate at all in another. Therefore, a legitimate science is one which operates consciously within given presuppositions, with its own categories, and has its own aims. The natural scientist, therefore, cannot ever give up the method and the aim that are peculiar to him. His task is to manipulate. He stands, as we shall develop later, in an I-It relation to the objects with which he deals, and pushes them around. When he is, however, confronted by another person, another Thou, another center of decision and responsibility, then there is erected a holy "no trespassing sign." An angel with a flaming sword guards this sanctuary. Another person may never be manipulated as is a chemical in a pot, unless, of course, he is being treated so as to restore to him precisely that freedom of decision and responsibility which constitutes him a person.

So there are different levels within which one operates legitimately. If the Christian church begins with a divinely given revelation of God and then operates strictly within the given, employing those categories that are demanded by such given revelation, then the charge may not be made against it that it is unscientific. It is dealing precisely with matters which, in the very nature of the case, cannot be brought under human control, which cannot be verified experimentally, where no control situation can be set up. The causal connection between the words, "Thy sins are forgiven thee," and the actual forgiveness cannot be established. Moreover, cause and effect is the wrong category to employ in this relation.

It is within the personal relation that the forgiveness takes place, setting up a new relation. Whether or not there is a life hereafter, in the sense of a final judgment, is in the very nature of the case not experimentally verifiable. There is, therefore, a realm—not set apart from the affairs of daily life, but most intimately tied up with them—the most distinguishing characteristic of which is that here man is not in control, but is himself under control. This is the realm of faith, of surrender to God, of obedience, of acceptance of what God has to offer.

When we are, therefore, speaking of the relation between science and religion, it is, from this viewpoint perverse to defend *all* religions. "Religion" may mean the grossest superstition, and be quite incompatible with the assured findings of scientific investigations. Christianity, with its gospel of the God who comes to men as the gracious God, in Jesus the Christ, means to put an end to all the religions in which men try to work themselves into the right God-relation. The story of the religions of the world is the story of man's aberrations, misunderstandings, and confusions with respect to the true God as he is revealed in the Bible. This is, of course, a most presumptuous affirmation of faith. But so be it! All religion which means to manipulate God, or whatever supernatural powers there are believed to be, instead of surrendering to the will and promise of a God of love, is idolatry. The Christian religion means to supplant, to correct radically and fulfill all other religions, and not just to supplement them with further insights. A religion which means to put man in control, in matters of ultimate concern, comes under the judgment of the Christian proclamation, and so does science itself, if it becomes a religion, and means to give man control of his ultimate destiny.

Again it is, therefore, a matter of a proper evaluation and a proper division of labor between scientist and priest, each sticking to his appointed task. As a matter of fact, there has been such a change in the whole scientific outlook that the way is opened to a harmonious cooperation.

in my opinion...

The title of Martin Heinecken's *God In the Space Age* is an exciting one, and indicative of the scope of the discussion of God which promises to be contained within its covers. Difficulty arises when one realizes after several chapters that more questions are being raised about God than are being answered. The scope of this work is limited by Heinecken's concept of what, exactly, composes the "Space Age". He appears preoccupied with the idea of space travel to the exclusion of other important areas of concern, such as changing morality; increasing automation of jobs; expanding communications; exploding population; and the other problems which organized religion, if it is to survive, must aid man in solving in our time. God is of paramount importance, and one must be constantly striving to develop an understanding of a higher power than himself. A working concept of God, as with any other concept, reaches its height in application: how do we apply a concept of God to achieve moral solutions to the problems which confront us? This should have been of primary concern to Heinecken, a theologian, and thus have been reflected in his book.

In the introduction of his work, Heinecken quotes Wernher von Braun, scientist extraordinaire:

It is the ultimate objective of our great Technological Revolution to free Man from the slavery of heavy physical labor, to elevate mankind from its historical bondage to a race of masters, in whose service toils an array of mechanical and electrical slaves. This liberation through technology will enable Man to devote more time to think and to dream; it will raise all our civilizations to levels never before attained in human history.[1]

[1] Wernher von Braun, "Space Travel and Our Technological Revolution," article presented at the American Rocket Society, New York City, Apr. 4, 1957, and the Evangelical Academy, Loccum, Germany, Feb. 28, 1958.

Heinecken calls this statement by one of the most outstanding scientists of our time an "extravagant claim". In the summary of the chapter selected from *God In The Space Age,* he speaks of a division of labor between scientist and priest, each concerned primarily with his appointed task. It would appear, if this is done, that science and religion could co-exist. It is difficult to understand the theologian's fear of science, for it would seem that an integrated mind would be able to assimilate scientific facts, and modify dogma in view of new facts. Von Braun, in contrast to Heinecken, appears to have a well-integrated comprehension of God and Man, as well as of technological skill:

Science and scientists should put this simple but widely unknown truth across to people everywhere. With all the modern means at our disposal, with schools, churches, educational institutions, press, radio and television, we should tell the world that religion and science are not incompatible; that, on the contrary, they belong together. For only with God reinstated in the heart of the world, will He furnish mankind and its leaders the ethical guidance through the dangers and pitfalls of the Technological Revolution.[2]

We live in a rapidly changing world, and the rate of change is accelerating. In the past ten years we have accumulated more technological knowledge than in all of our previously recorded history. It is the responsibility of organized religion to direct us in the moral application of this knowledge, for the advancement of humanity. If the existing religions do not meet this need within Man, they will perish. Man is becoming increasingly moral and concerned with problems relevant to the totality of humanity. He will either make his religions more relevant and moral, or he will create new ones which are.

russell j. blanchette, jr.

[2] *Ibid.*

questions

1. It would seem that Dr. Heinecken did not foresee all of the technological changes which are presently occurring. What future changes might possibly transpire which could threaten the existence of our present religious institutions? Consider changes in ecology as well as in technology.

2. What changes do you feel will probably have to take place within religious institutions if they are to survive into the 21st century?

3. It is interesting to note that throughout the article by Dr. Heinecken, the word "man" is written in lower case. In the quotations of Dr. von Braun, "Man" is capitalized. Might this be a reflection of a difference in concepts between Dr. Heinecken and Dr. von Braun, and if so, what might the nature of that difference be?

4. Why has there been an increasing interest on the part of many students in the religions of the East? In what ways has technology contributed to this increased interest?

5. In view of the expansion of communication between cultures, possibly religions should be seeking points of agreement instead of emphasizing differences in beliefs. What similarities, based upon the article, do you feel Christianity has with non-Christian religions?

18.

good, bad or indifferent: the dynamics of human values

VALUES AND VIEWPOINTS

donald michael

introduction and comment by michael v. opel

Human values have been the most important factors governing man's thoughts and actions since he became an animal capable of thinking and reasoning. Over the passage of time many of these values have been altered and others lost. And the future, always unpredictable, will offer us still more values, some of which will seem very strange to today's society.

But what exactly are "human values"? How and why do they affect us as individuals and as a society? Are today's youth treating the values of their parents differently from the way past generations of young treated theirs? Finally, how will this treatment of values by the young affect their judgment when they become the people in control, "The Establishment"?

The first question is at the same time perhaps the easiest and the most complex. Value implies worth—therefore, one element of human values is what an object or idea is *worth.* It also implies prestige—therefore, status enters the picture. The status of an object or idea is a human value: here status is used to determine position in society. *Respect* is another factor of human values. By pooling these factors and applying one word to what they have in common, human value can be defined quickly and precisely. The one word is *belief:* human values are those values that man *believes in.*

How and why do these values affect us as individuals and as a society? As a being alone, man is a nonentity. Given something upon which he can base life, he becomes an entity: an individual of enough significance to have an effect on other individuals. This belief manifests itself in two possible ways: it becomes a perfection, that is to say, an idol, something which the individual places above himself, knowing he can never be its equal. The alternative is that the belief becomes a goal, to be reached and even surpassed. As a goal, the belief is valued above all else. The individual will readily support any other belief or value which adds significance to his own. Yet, bring forth an opposing view, one that attempts to bring down the pedestaled goal, or in part change it, and the entity becomes rebellious or encloses himself in a world that will not be changed. He either fights or goes into hiding, living in his own little world, ignoring the changes around him until it is too late.

Society as a whole behaves in much the same way. If a specific societal group values an idea which is threatened with change or destruction, drastic retaliatory measures may be taken. Witness democracy as a value, threatened by the tyranny of Hitlerism. *Individuals grouped together as a functioning society will act as one in protecting their beliefs, i.e., their human values.*

This brings us to the next question: is today's youth challenging, changing, or discarding the values of their elders in any way different from the ways of past generations of young people? The answer is an emphatic *yes*. The difference is, however, that for the first time, on a large scale, much of the "now" generation is acting *together* to challenge the values of their elders. Many children have challenged their elders before, but almost always on an individual basis or in small groups. Now for the first time in history almost a whole generation is rebelling against the materialistic, moralistic and aesthetic values of their parents. The mass movements of the young for peaceful coexistence and an end to all wars were never as evident as they are today. The rejection of the "almighty dollar" and the widespread use of drugs (as mind-expanders) and contraceptives are powerful examples of the discarding and altering of values by the younger generation. Today's young are like no generation before them. Not only do they ask *why* are things the way they are; now they are asking *why not change them?*

The last question is the most difficult to answer. How will the treatment of values by today's youth affect them when they become The Establishment? The question is a philosophical one, of course. Who can, with reasonable accuracy, foretell the future? No one can, or has, or will. But, predictions are being made. The future of man has been continuously a source of literary release for fiction, fantasy and, finally, proven fact. The following excerpt from a chapter in Dr. Donald Michael's *The Next Generation* constitutes one such prediction. There are many such predictions, some optimistic, some not. Most are based on the philosophies of the past. Can the past be counted on to predict the future? Only time will tell.

m.v.o.

VALUES AND VIEWPOINTS

*Dr. Donald Michael is a social psychologist currently with
the Institute for Policy Studies in Washington, D.C. His background
in the social and physical sciences stems from his education
at both Harvard and at the University of Chicago, with a Ph.D.
from Harvard. After working in the weapons system evaluation
group of the Joint Chiefs of Staff (1953–1954) and on survival
methods for the national science policy studies of the National
Science Foundation (1954–1958), he served as director of
the Peace Research Institute from 1961 to 1963. In 1965 he began
work with the Commission to Study the Organization of Peace.*

*He has published many essays and reports on social and
psychological challenges produced by today's rapidly-changing
technology. Among his works are the* Proposed Studies of the
Implications of Peaceful Space Activities for Human Affairs,
1961; The Next Generation, *1965; and* The Unprepared Society,
1968.

This chapter is at once a partial review and synthesis of what has
gone before and an exploration of factors not conveniently falling
into previous chapters. It is concerned with states of mind growing
out of and influencing factors discussed earlier. As such, it is
concerned with the values and viewpoints surrounding youth in
various parts of the adult population. This adult population, which
has been alive for at least twenty years, will continue to exert a
profound influence over most if not all of the factors affecting
youth over the next twenty years. This chapter is concerned, too,
with the values of today's youth as they grow from the present into
the future, and with the values of the generation of youth which
will succeed them, who will not be as much products of the road

already traveled as are today's youth. It is also concerned, if only inferentially, with the attitudes, hopes, pettinesses, and greatnesses of those who now have the tasks of planning formal youth development programs. For after all, these people are partially of the past too, though some of those who are youth today should in the near future begin making contributions to such programs: indeed, a few in their teens already are.

Thus, this chapter is a look at the values and viewpoints that grow out of and will influence the factors we have looked at earlier. Values and viewpoints are certainly as important for youth's world as are work and leisure—indeed, more so, since they underlie the choices made in both.

The next twenty years will hold many challenges for prevailing American values and viewpoints. Many of the coming situations are not new ones but the degree and type of reaction to them may be significantly different. More people will be sensitive to issues and circumstances as a result of better education and because, even with no changes in percentages, their absolute numbers will be larger. More people will be personally involved in the outcomes because more issues and circumstances will involve social welfare. Equally important, there will probably be more people for whom these issues and circumstances will have little significance, being removed from personal preoccupations or too complex. The contrast between those who respond to society's challenges and those who do not will have greater political and social consequences for the conduct of democracy and national policy.

The growth in social complexity, which will require increasing rationalization of society, will result in more intense and widespread priority conflicts between traditional community interests. Indeed, part of the issue will be: whose traditional institutional positions are to be preserved and whose changed? Dilemmas will deepen between individual responsibility to conscience and social responsibility to national purpose and to organizational affiliations. International issues involving consequences for the maintenance of peace or the conduct of war will become more amorphous, and the chances will diminish for discovering firm moral positions regarding a given military or political event—especially if, as is likely, brushfire wars, guerrilla actions, and subversion are deliberately encouraged or supported by the United States more frequently. What is morally and ethically right and what is wrong will be perceived differently as the political and social context in which the judgment is made is narrowed or expanded through the information and event-defining sources available to the concerned individual.

The sheer growth in numbers of people—and hence in numbers of events and their consequences—will mean a steadily increasing opportunity to sense the world as full of disaster, crises, violence, danger. For the same reasons there will also be increasing numbers of examples of the safety and support provided in some parts of the world. But these are no more likely to be part of the public image of the world than they now are; the upsetting and disrupting will still provide most of the headlines and spot news interruptions. Putting these events in perspective will mean treating them as percentages. This will bring its own value dilemma (as currently exists in the prototype of future public-issue dilemmas: does one evaluate bomb-testing fallout in terms of the *per-cent* increase in tragedies or in terms of the increased *number* of tragedies?).

These deepening dilemmas of interpretation and action will lead to more polarization of personal solutions. Some will find themselves searching more deeply for a moral basis for action: some will find a moral basis for dogmatism, some for relativism. Some will opt out, turning to private preoccupations. Others, especially among those who rise to power, will obsessively pursue the same techniques which we like to think have produced our successes: the calculated manipulation of environment and man by the exploitation of technology and organization.

dispossession, potency, and participation among adults

As the next two decades proceed, a larger proportion of adults, especially older ones, will find themselves dispossessed in one way or another of lifelong jobs, of favored views or ideas, of a sense of being in close touch with what is happening to man and his world. Whereas more of the younger generation than in the past will, to a somewhat greater extent, be brought up to expect dispossession in one form or another, older adults will not as a group adjust easily to this. For them, anxiety, depression, annoyance, and hostility arising from felt incompetence and in reaction to being pulled out of deep ruts, will accompany forced changes in jobs and viewpoints. By and large, people in middle life and older don't like to change the way they have been doing and seeing things—especially if the change is required in the midst of economic and social insecurity.

This sense of dispossession will be especially frustrating because its sources will be exceedingly difficult to "get at" by conventional political methods. The scientists, technicians, and rationalizers will be deep in the interstices of the bureaucracies of government and industry, their products and programs based on esoteric equations and computer programs and on the subtle jargons of the natural and social sciences.

Unless these changes are made in ways that take into account the emotional needs of those being dispossessed, there will be resistance to them. Indeed, we can expect the older groups to exert political pressures intended to protect themselves from either the experience or the consequences of material, ideological, or emotional dispossession. The growing size and political potency of this older group will confront the nation with priority conflicts over how to meet the economic, social, and physical needs of both youth and older generations.

At the same time, much of the well-educated younger generation and the older, versatile, and well-trained professional group will be happy with or, at least, indifferent to the high rate of change. For many, the world will be as inspiring and as full of opportunity, by virtue of the rate of change, as it will for others be a source of despair.

For most of that population which concerns itself with attention to public issues, the trend will be toward feeling less and less competent to understand or influence larger national and international problems. In part, this will be due to a heightened realization of the overwhelming range of events as conveyed by expanded mass media. In part, it will be due to the inability of those who try to remain alert and involved in the issues to keep up with the rapid and interacting social and technological changes that will define these issues. In part, it will be caused by a growing sense of being locked into a system so complex and so large that the individual (including many so-called leaders) cannot understand it, much less affect its operation. Many will recognize that the intellectual prerequisites will be great indeed for effective participation in the idea-producing, decision-making, policy-planning activities at top levels of big institutions. Not very many who have more leisure time, then, are likely to spend it wrestling with these relatively abstract issues when so many opportunities for direct experience will be readily available.

Probably one victim of the period ahead will be a "sense of history." As Kenneth Keniston puts it, describing the plight of some of today's youth: ". . . the past grows more remote and irrelevant psychologically . . . the future grows more remote and unpredictable . . . the present assumes a new significance as the one time in which the environment is relevant, immediate and knowable."[1] The same will hold for many of tomorrow's adults, especially the better educated who, in earlier days, would have looked to history for insight. For many, even the present will seem so subject to alternative interpretations that it will tend to lack the definitiveness expected of events that "go down in history." Among the most sophisticated it will be understood that events often will lack definitiveness even for those making history: such will be the complexity and pace of events that whatever records there are will, in important ways, often be inadequate for future historical interpretation. How the teaching of history will be tied to this kind of present remains to be worked out.

For those not particularly aware of issues except when they become crises (of which there will be a continuing supply, some real and some locally contrived to meet the demand for novelty and sensation), the continuing international and national dangers, frustrations, and difficulties will probably heighten feelings of generalized, unfocused uneasiness, shorten time perspectives, and amplify needs for evidences of personal sure-footedness. The latter will be sought chiefly through the consumption of things and symbols, especially in connection with increasing opportunities for leisure-time activities.

Nevertheless, given the strong tendencies of most people to make sense of the world in ways compatible with what they already believe, the views and values of much of the adult population are unlikely to be subject to far-reaching changes, except possibly in emphasis, over the next several years. Most of their time, the majority of adults will, as now, be almost unaware of the complexities of this world. When events coalesce into headlines, they will interpret and evaluate the issues in terms of their conventional values and beliefs about self, nation, right and wrong, and "the other guy," transforming the complexities of policy and events into the equivalent of everyday household, interpersonal experiences.

Some of those who can cope with the complexity of values and events will continue to try to make sense out of and take action on national and international issues. They will also find themselves increasingly incapable of discovering adequate syntheses for what is happening, or values sufficient to meet the ambiguity

[1] Kenneth Keniston, "Social Change and Youth in America," in Stephen R. Graubard, ed., *Daedalus, Youth: Change and Challenge.* Vol. 91, No. 1, American Academy of Arts and Sciences, Winter 1962, pp. 152–153.

and amorphousness that will characterize this world. Those who need to pursue their values or relieve their frustrations and sense of disconnectedness through action will increasingly do so through involvement in very local civic and political issues and through participation in voluntary service organizations where the values involved will be familiar and malleable.

Others in this group will seek a sense of solidity and adequacy of viewpoint by avoiding involvement in the big issues, or crises, turning instead to intense interpersonal and private experiences such as love, sex, religion, hallucinatory drugs, art, teaching, and other individual and small-group activities that stress the immediate, personal experience of self.

Others, aware of changing circumstances, needing a rigid framework of values for coping with them, will commit themselves to extremist groups. In particular, many people, particularly older adults, will seek evidences of sure-footedness by supporting conservative and reactionary causes and philosophies. They will espouse traditional and pseudo-traditional viewpoints emphasizing ideas and actions, which they will see as means for producing a world in which they can again be potent. During this period some late adolescents and young adults who feel dispossessed will make common cause with the older disaffected.

viewpoints of youth

A growing group (at least, insofar as the numbers in this age group will be growing) of the most talented, sensitive, and searching of young adults and adolescents will be repelled by what they interpret as politicking, commercialism, high-pressure bureaucracy, and the "big" society, and by logic and the esoteric, "dehumanized" and "hemmed-in" experience of the devoted scientist.[2] They will seek expression and careers in the arts, the humanities; in teaching in primary and secondary schools; in social service in the emerging nations and at home; in organized and unorganized political action social protest, and so on. Uncynical commitment to an uncorrupted task will be their goal. They will also turn intensively to self-emphasizing experiences with love, family, sex, religion, hallucinatory drugs, and so on. These youth will often make very necessary and very important social contributions, but thereby some of our best talent will be

[2] Paul Goodman, *Growing Up Absurd.* New York: Random House, Inc., 1956.

exported or otherwise unavailable for other social tasks where precisely this sensitivity will be much needed. This "skill" shortage will become more serious, too, over the next twenty years.

Another group of the well educated will, as they always have, be undaunted by the ambiguities and contradictions of the times, will be aiming for and beginning to move into management and politics, manipulating men and events to serve pragmatic goals.

A third group will move into the professions, and more or less submerge their value conflicts and the events engendering them under the pressures, constraints, and attractions of professional competition and accomplishment.

The rest—that is, most adolescents becoming adults during the next ten years—will not be much better or worse as citizens than their recent predecessors; their cultural pedigrees will not be essentially different from those of today. The trends surveyed suggest that during the second decade a substantially larger proportion of young people will fall into the above three categories, but how the proportions will be allocated depends on the actual rate and distribution of other changes discussed—to say nothing of those overlooked.

Those adolescents and young adults exposed to conventional levels of education and occupations in the next decade, including those who develop as a new class of skilled technicians, will have less interest than the highly educated in the problems of the times and less ability to confront them at a significant level of understanding of self and society. They will not be devoid of values and beliefs any more than their equivalents are today, but their viewpoints will not be much more adequate than they are today for deeply understanding the world and their place in it.

The adolescents and young adults who are relatively poorly educated or who receive almost no education will increasingly develop their own values and beliefs, justifying withdrawal from or violence toward the rest of society. Here, unorganized crime will continue to flourish and, probably, will increase. Without enormous and carefully planned and programed efforts, it will become steadily more difficult to convince these people it is in their interest and within their ability to share the values and viewpoints of the society which has so grievously deprived them.[3]

[3] Oliver Moles, Ronald Lippitt, and Stephen Withey, *A Selective Review of Research and Theory on Delinquency*. Survey Research Center, Institute for Social Research, University of Michigan, Ann Arbor, Mich., 1959.

ethnic viewpoints

Ethnic identity, an important factor in American politics, will gradually lose its potency over the next two decades. Among the older workers now living in ethnic communities some dispersal will occur when, retrained, they move to other areas where jobs, but not necessarily ethnic-based neighborhoods, will be found. Pressures for joint urban attacks on regional problems will provide political excuses to set aside first consideration to ethnic interests and attitudes. The first generation of college students from ethnic communities will find these ties weakened as they take on occupational and social identities with less parochial perspectives. Implicit in this development will be the further attenuation of attachment to the past, to history—even ethnically oriented history. Also implicit probably will be greater freedom of choice for Federal foreign policy, unfettered by concern for ethnic bloc votes.

image of man

During the next two decades, belief in man as unique in himself and in his relation to the rest of the universe will, in many of the influential decision-making and policy-planning levels of society, become substantially secondary to viewing him as subject to the same manipulation and attention as other dynamic parts of social and physical systems. Certain developments in science and technology will contribute to this state of mind, as will other social factors discussed in this report.

Medical technology intimately linking man with machinery, some ability to replace organs with machinery or with those of another person, and specific and general-purpose drugs for maintaining health and curing sickness will continue to remove the mystery from at least the more prevalent maladies. The body will increasingly be accepted as maintainable and repairable, much as any fine piece of equipment which is cared for by "preventive maintenance" and through specific repair.

Emphasis on human engineering and on precise training so man and machine can work well and comfortably together will emphasize man as a biomechanical link. The growing use of chemicals in special situations to control moods and mental efficiency will add to this image. Finally, the synthesis of life in primitive forms and possibly the discovery of life forms on Mars will, for some, subtract from the mystery of life by making it less unique.

There will also be an increasingly vocal body of informed opinion asserting that man is infinitely more than a manipulable thing and that, indeed, our troubles stem from treating him as if that were all he is. But lip service to man's uniqueness may well ease reluctance to treat him otherwise. (This ritual acknowledgment is already part of many government and business policy-planning papers and program reports.) It is hard to see, however, how this "antimanipulation" viewpoint could be incorporated into the growingly popular statistical approach based on computer-oriented rationalization, or how it could significantly change the viewpoints of those exhilarated by the opportunity to apply economics, behavioral science, systems analysis, and computer methods to the social processes. Over the long run, as unhappy experience leads to understanding that rationalization involves more than logic and computer-encompassable efficiency, this humanistic viewpoint may begin to carry real weight. The long run may come about late in the period we are talking about. (We will return to the possibility that those who argue for the broader view of man will find a larger audience among the dispossessed, disaffected, and disemployed.)

manipulation of the social environment

The emphasis on manipulation of the environment, the growing treatment of man as a thing within the environment, and the quantification (both pseudo and real) of the behavioral sciences will encourage the application of social engineering wherever fad and practicability make it useful to do so. It will be practiced—and sometimes corrupted—by behavioral engineers, as well as by others who seek to influence various publics for various purposes, although not all the purposes will be evil by any means. After all, the needed programs we have spoken of will require the cultivation of public support. The behavioral sciences will also be over-sold, not so much by the scientists as by those who want them to do the job. In most cases, during the next decade at least, the results will be as conclusive as those who use them would hope. But this will not stop most people from believing they have been manipulated—or stop many from believing that such manipulation is desirable and socially necessary in many circumstances.

Nevertheless, growing acceptance of the manipulation of man will encourage the careful application of valid behavioral science methods and facts to social problems. As has been the case with the application of other expertise, interpretations from the behavioral sciences will often be employed to emphasize or to obscure issues so that, while used more, the behavioral sciences will only occasionally be the final arbiter of policy in the next decade.

During the 1970's, the behavioral sciences will probably be applied and effective to about the extent that economics is today (and will probably be no more internally schismatic than today's economic theory and practice). Their accumulating record of success in business and in the military will legitimize their application to many national problems. For by 1970 we will have to face truly critical problems in education, urban development, public-opinion manipulation and political-economic warfare, and only the behavioral sciences (often combined with economics) will have the expertise to deal with them.

It is not unlikely that the philosophy of law will be influenced by the factors we have discussed. In particular, the growth of knowledge about the wellsprings of behavior and the general trend toward rationalization will encourage, in the appropriate areas, the increasing application of law as a means to individual therapy in and to potency for deprived groups. Emphasis on abundance rather than scarcity, on consumption rather than possession, may be reflected in some changing views about the meaning of property.[4]

attitudes toward experts and issues

Natural science and technology will grow as a pervasive and powerful lobby for their own interests, emphasizing a manipulative and rational approach to society and its problems. Inevitably, this lobby and its supporters will make intensive use of public relations to sell itself to those publics, decision-makers, and opinion-makers who will listen. The already evident disquiet among some scientists and laymen will deepen as the struggle between disinterested and "political" science and technology factions becomes more intense.[5] Respect for facts and for the means for discovering them will remain high, though corruptible; indeed, the consumers of science and technology will themselves gradually become more respectful of the integrity of facts. But although

[4] Donald McDonald, Edward Bennett Williams, and Bethuel M. Webster, *The Law*. Santa Barbara, Calif.: Center for the Study of Democratic Institutions, 1962.

[5] Carl F. Stover, *The Government of Science*. Santa Barbara, Calif.: Center for the Study of Democratic Institutions, 1962.

the growing influence of scientists and engineers is a precursor of the mind-oriented world of work, some of these professionals have shared and more frequently will come to share some of the operating values and goals of their beneficiaries and sources of support—government, industry, and the military. As the tasks of scientists and engineers become more closely tied to the goals of their clients, interpretation of the facts and defense of the interpretation will become more subject to the values of their nonscientist clients.[6] Then, too, competing interpretations of the facts and "competing" facts (because their relationship to each other is not understood) and facts about the limits or meaning of other facts will frequently produce exceedingly complex communications problems and encourage oversimplification and self-justifying selection and emphasis. Scientists have never been unemotional, unbiased, and unfailingly ethical in defending their interpretations of facts. In the future, these human weaknesses will be more evident outside the science community, in part because the behavior will be more prevalent within it, and in part because other segments of the science community will be deeply and vocally concerned with the ethical problems engendered.

On major issues, the conflicting positions of experts and the arguments they use to defend themselves will be more exposed as an increasingly large educated audience makes it economically sensible for some of the media to air them. But it is very likely that the arguments, except in one's own specialty, will demonstrate the inability of the nonexpert to contribute to the resolution of the issues or to convince himself that he knows what the answers (or, often, the questions) really are. Today's debates about fallout, defense policy, insecticides, and manned-space efforts typify what is to come. When the questions involve national policy, the conscientious voter who knows he doesn't know for sure will find his democratic obligation a particularly frustrating one.

That issues will be subtle, complex, and interrelated will not discourage some from making them "causes." One way of dealing with a sense of being overwhelmed and dispossessed will undoubtedly be to join causes. From time to time a popular cause will force or channel government action, especially if the cause derives from economic deprivation. But, although the increased media outlets will make it easier for groups to get their message "out," it is not at all clear that such messages will be very influential. (It is not at all clear that such messages are often very influential now!)

[6] Albert Wohlstetter, "Scientists, Seers and Strategy," *Foreign Affairs*, Vol. 41, No. 3, Council on Foreign Relations, Inc., April 1963, pp. 466–478.

Most causes will probably tend to become chiefly a means for preserving the *forms* of popular democracy at the citizen level.

Those insufficiently educated to appreciate the nature of the controversies are no more likely to be aroused by them than they are now. But as the media report on an increasing number of important topics, many of which are subjects of controversy by experts, those with mediocre education will feel even more a sense of being left out and incompetent to deal with the issues which they recognize as somehow defining their lives and futures. A means for coping with these feelings will be cynicism about the utility of experts in general, and belief, often well founded, that "experts have their rackets just like everybody else." It may also be that if these people feel sufficiently left out and frustrated about the issues they feel they have a stake in, they will find their own spokesmen, who will speak in simpler terms uncomplicated by conflicting facts or the vested interests of the parties arguing at higher levels.

Among those already adult today there will be, of course, large numbers who will remain or grow indifferent to these controversies. Active cynicism or resentment or indifference toward the technical issues on the part of some people and real, if frustrated, concern with the issues in others will deepen the difficulties for policymakers of contriving meaningful and useful decisions calculated to strengthen and preserve democratic processes.

in my opinion...

As a member of "the next generation" of which Mr. Michael writes, I find myself in a slightly awkward situation. On the one hand lies the author's predictions which, for the most part, I find optimistic and sensible. I agree with him in many areas under discussion. On the other hand are my own feelings as a member of a generation which characteristically repudiates all such predictions and tries very hard to do the exact opposite, or at best, pursues a tangent to what is expected of it by its elders. I shall try to give an unhypocritical point of view of the subject.

The first substantial claim put forth by Mr. Michael is that history, long an invaluable instructor to the young, will lose much of its significance for the adults of tomorrow. This becomes evident when one realizes that in our technological world, man, for the most part, has absolute control over his fate. With the push of a few buttons on a computer, man can redirect the course of his life—or end it. Where in history is present-day man to look for advice on how to handle this situation? This example, alone, is enough to separate the next generation from any of the past.

To a large extent the coming generation will be similar in many ways to those before it. Many of its members will believe in the values of their elders without any hesitation. They will be aware of the world around them in much the same way. When an occurrence of some magnitude is brought to their attention they will only ask, "How will this affect me and my family and the way we live"? Few, if any, will ask, "*Why* does this affect me"?

There will be, however, a number of people who will react to the world about them. This is not new or unusual. The remarkable fact lies in the quantity of people and the affect they will have on the rest of humanity. I gather from Mr. Michael's writing that he feels this group will be a minority and their influence, though noticeable, will also be minor. On this point I must disagree: I foresee this group becoming a very influential minority and possibly, the majority. I say this because most of this group, students today, are becoming increasingly influential through mass belief and participation. When these students reach adulthood and pass on to their offspring the tenets they hold (assuming that these offspring are no more stubborn than the present crop), the possibility that today's minority will become a majority may well be realized.

We now approach the question of the "viewpoints of youth." That these viewpoints will be influenced enormously by the educational level attained by my generation is obvious. Through advanced, high-level education should come comprehension of current views and opinions. Once these are understood, the logical next step, that of changing and of exploring new outlooks, will become a commonplace occurrence. These new outlooks will blend smoothly with current beliefs, thus offering a pleasant change when compared to the chaotic intermingling of views of youth (as opposed to the views of their elders) which we witness today.

It is unfortunate that those with a high level of education will be fewer in number than those with conventional or no education. (You will recall that I said more people will react to world events and that this group may in time become a majority. However, they need not all be of a high educational level; conventional education can inspire an awareness of the world also.) To a great extent the conventionally-educated and the unschooled will continue to let the world move around them, interjecting their presence into the mainstream only when they are in some way immensely affected by it. It seems that this is an age-old problem which probably cannot be solved. The lower classes (intellectually and materially) have never involved themselves in world events unless they thought their existence was being threatened.

The ethnic question Michael discusses is one which until approximately one hundred thirty years ago was more or less an unasked one. Since then, however, it has often been repeated, with more emphasis each time until, within the last decade, the answers started erupting sporadically and then with more consistency. At present, to the serious questions raised by minority groups in activities ranging from reasoned to violent, the final answer has yet to be revealed. The end result, however, is obvious and inevitable. Eventually *all men will be equal in regard to race.* This equality will take much longer than the period in question but it will be advanced greatly during that time. That it may take longer in some areas as compared to others is obvious. However, equality, a product of education and time, will come.

The coming generations will have one large advantage over past generations: they will be able, without qualm, to question their own values as well as the older values of their predecessors. This is something which only a few individuals in other generations have had the courage to do. Human values of the next century promise to be exciting and shocking, but I am sure that mankind will survive that shock.

michael v. opel

questions

1. Dr. Michael describes the difficulties which will be experienced among older people in adjusting to change. What examples of these difficulties do you see today?

2. From your own experience with your peers, how flexible is your generation?

3. What are the negative and positive factors regarding the suggested increase in the use of the behavioral sciences in the next two or three decades?

4. What place do you think formal education should play in helping to develop value-judgments for all generations?

5. Do you think that by the year 2000 a human being will be more capable of understanding why his values must be flexible?

19.
learning without pain: education

VISITING DAY, 2001 A.D.

george b. leonard

introduction and comment by gayle shanks

Modern man must get away from the preconceived notion that education is merely one facet of our compartmentalized life and come to the realization that not only is education not a separate segment, but that it is total living and awareness. The shortcomings and failures of education in our modern cybernetic-oriented society can be better realized after a close analysis of the problems and a look at one man's idea of a utopian learning community.

In today's ethos, the term education implies schooling, usually beginning at age five and terminating in the youth's early twenties—as if one's learning capacity can be started and stopped in the same manner as one would turn a switch on and off. No allowances are made for those children who may be capable of learning at two or three years of age or those who may not be mentally or physically ready until age seven or eight. The idea of compulsory attendance at institutions enters into the problem at this stage. If the parents of a child do not feel that he is ready for formal schooling, they are forced to send him regardless of their objections. To carry this further, after enrolling in a school the child is required to continue, being excused only for illness or family tragedy. The history of this concept of mandatory school attendance dates back to the Industrial Revolution in America. Instead of sending them to school, parents sent small children to factories and mines to supplement family income. Laws requiring school attendance were instituted to keep children in school and away from hazardous, unhealthy work situations. Such outmoded laws should not rule the lives of school-age children today. As much if not more knowledge can be acquired at home, in parks, on farms—any place a child is living, absorbing, and evaluating the world he resides in.

The second major problem in the system is the heavily structured student-teacher relationships which exist. Children cannot learn by simply being told; they must confront the issue and then draw their own conclusions based on their own observations, confirmed and criticized by their peers. This empirical form of problem-solving should be the base from which a student-teacher relationship develops. The joy of discovery and evaluation of ideas should be aided—and in some instances directed—by an educator who intervenes only at the request of his students or at such a time as he feels the students will not benefit from their own methods of research and investigation. This is a total reversal from the standard method of imparting knowledge in which the child is told by the teacher (in most instances) those things which he will be expected to know—with an explanation given at the discretion of the teacher.

The core of today's educational system is still a teacher, a student, a lecture, a textbook, a test, a report card. The main objective of learning is to secure enough information to pass a test, and to pass enough tests with scores good enough to merit a high grade on the report card. In elementary school, children get their first exposure to the multiple choice, yes-no answer tests (used because they are easy to tabulate); then there is the complaint as the years progress that for some reason children are not able to articulate their thoughts clearly.

The previously-mentioned faults in our present-day educational system do not even begin to note the problems that progressive educators need to cope with. These are merely structural flaws. Perhaps even more important, emphasis should be placed on the crushing of the spirit of children at an early age. This is done in various ways, but regardless of the method used, the end result is the same. It is much easier for a teacher to have a room full of average, passive students than to have a room full of students all working at different levels and all having individual preferences about specific fields of learning. Rather than meet the needs of all students, it is easier to condition the child to do as he is told, to accept the fact that the teacher knows what is best for him. If he strays from the established path, he is punished and made to understand that being creative or different from his classmates does not make him a good student. For his deviation, he is threatened with unsatisfactory grades in such areas as "makes good use of time" and "follows instructions." After continual warnings the student usually succumbs and performs in the desired way. His spirit of adventure and his natural instincts of curiosity and resourcefulness are lost and in some instances never regained. Many unexplainable phobias and anxieties which occur in later life can be traced to events of early school days. An unthinking music or art teacher who is too critical can curb a child's total interest in fine arts. A librarian who feels she knows better than a child which books he should and is able to read can cause a hatred for all printed matter. Who knows better than a child himself what books he can or cannot read? In whose eyes should a work of art be viewed?

Many men directly and indirectly concerned with the field of education have spoken out against the system and in turn offered plausible solutions to the problems. One such man is George B. Leonard, who writes of a utopian scholarly community which could and should exist today.

g.s.

VISITING DAY, 2001 A.D.

George B. Leonard was born in 1923 in Macon, Georgia, and was educated at the Georgia Institute of Technology and at the University of North Carolina. He majored in journalism and in 1953 began working for Look *magazine, where he is now a Senior Editor. His other activities include the Vice Presidency of the famed Esalen Institute in Big Sur, California, a pioneer establishment in the "human potential movement" where "sensitivity" and "encounter" groups are conducted as part of the human growth effort.*

A spring morning, 2001 A.D. It is visiting day, but not in any special sense; every day is visiting day. We are among those parents who frequently drop by Kennedy School when our children are there or even on those rare days when they choose not to attend. We go not through any sense of duty (though I guess that old-fashioned word would apply to what we feel for our children), but out of sheer fascination. In fact, there's a certain amount of kidding among members of our adult learning group about how much time we spend in our children's early-school—"lifting ideas for our own projects."

We catch a glimpse of the school before driving our electric down the ramp and into the underground parking lot. The sight, as always, pleases us—gleaming geodesic domes and translucent tentlike structures scattered randomly among graceful trees; a large grassy playfield encircled with flowers; all of it a testament to the foresight of community planners who set aside the land decades ago. Educators in the great strip cities haven't had it so easy. Some of them have had to build vertically; others are still engaged in lengthy negotiations for enough land for a few trees and flowers.

We walk up a ramp to an entrance. Two postgrads, an eleven-year-old boy and girl, welcome us with hugs and kisses. The girl finds our electronic identification devices on a large board, and we clip them to our clothing. The boy gives each of us a flower—a large orchid-like bloom, orange speckled with deep red, for my wife; a lavender rose for me—the products, we know, of botanical experiments by a group of six- to ten-year-olds. We thank our hosts with another embrace and stroll through a grove of oaks toward the Basics Dome, where we may find our three-year-old, Sally. Even if we knew Sally was somewhere else, we'd probably go there first anyway.

On the way, we pass children of various ages in various states of consciousness. Some are walking aimlessly, alone or in small groups, perhaps toward some destination, perhaps not. Others are running. We notice a group of around seven of the older children with two of the educators in impassioned encounter near one of the biggest trees. Almost in our pathway sits a little girl with long black hair and dark skin—probably of Mexican-Indian extraction. Her enormous black eyes seem to hold a powerful dream, and we tiptoe around her, so as not to disturb her inner voyaging. But she looks up and, for a moment, shares with us something mysterious.

A total of some 800 children between three and ten are enrolled in Kennedy, but on a typical morning only about 600 (around seventy-five of each chronological age) are on the school grounds. Most of the educational environments are in operation from eight in the morning until six in the afternoon. Children can come when and if they please; there's no problem at all if parents wish to take their children on extended trips or simply keep them home for something that's going on there.

While the children are on the school grounds, they are *absolutely* free to go and do *anything* they wish that does not hurt someone else. They are *free learners.* The italics belong to Will Hawthorne, Kennedy's Principal Educator. The free-learning concept has, of course, been accepted for years all over the U.S. Almost every educator gives it lip service, and the overwhelming majority of them follow it to one degree or another. Will, however, lives and breathes it.

"*Everything* starts there," he tells parents. "Until we had the free learner, we really didn't know *anything* about education. The free learner built Kennedy School." Will is a student of educational history and has created several experiential tapes on the development of the concept. "This feisty old radical named A. S. Neill started a place called Summerhill in England in 1924," Will tells parents. "Children were relatively free, but there was no systematic attempt to create learning environments, to find out what human beings really were capable of. There was no real vision of the human potential. Summerhill was mostly a *reaction* to the incredibly inefficient and cruel teaching system of the day. Unfortunately, too, it was tied to the dogma of the then voguish Freudian psychology, with its static and limiting views of the human personality. Still, there was a remarkable interest in Neill's books that reflected a widespread though unfocused hunger for educational reform.

"It was not until the late 1960s and early 1970s that real free-learning schools began springing up here and there, and it was only then that educators could start learning about education. The first such schools were crude affairs. For one thing, the educators of that day found it very difficult to give up the idea of teacher-led classes at certain periods. So—even though the children were ranging freely all over the building—you had someone walking around at given times ringing a bell to announce the beginning of, say, 'math class' for anyone who cared to attend. If the class was made interesting enough—a heroic endeavor under the circumstances—quite a few kids would come. But the enormous *inefficiency* and the *expense* of the 'class and teacher' situation became more and more apparent. Learning environments could be created, it was discovered, for constant operation and full utilization, always available for children and yet always amenable to modification by educators.

"Among the earliest such environments were simple, paper-and-pencil self-instructional programs, mostly in such basic subjects as reading, spelling, figuring and the like. Most of them were terribly linear, unimaginative and single-tracked. But they did their job in demonstrating that the free-learning situation was feasible, even in terms of the strictly limited training offered in that day. Not only that, they freed some teachers to become educators, and these fledgling educators began asking themselves questions on what education was all about. Free learners were there to help give them the answers.

"At around the same time, another development moved in from an entirely different direction. Several large corporations started pushing Computer-Assisted Instruction (CAI). The computer learning programs were at first even more limited and stereotyped than the paper-and-pencil programs. And the learning consoles were mounted, of all places, in 'classrooms.' Children had to come to them at certain fixed periods and sit there under the 'guidance' of 'teachers.'

"You know, this is one of the most difficult things for our children to recreate experientially. I mean, the whole business of classrooms and teachers. They can conceptualize it. They've seen the historical films. But, during their history-drama sessions, they rarely can truly get the *feeling* we know existed then. When the child playing teacher forces the children playing students to sit still while teacher gives a long blackboard demonstration, the students find it very hard to get the *feeling* of being bored, distracted, or squirming and hoping for time to pass. Many of them simply go into a relaxed, serene state of semimeditation, enjoying the whole situation immensely. The child serving as history-drama coordinator senses this, naturally enough, and stops the drama amid much laughter and confusion. The fact that children once had to get *permission* to go and urinate is even harder for them to understand.

"Anyhow, the computer and the free school were destined for marriage, and it didn't take them long to get together. By the mid-1970s, most of what was called 'Computer-Assisted Instruction' was being applied in free-learning situations. Immediate economies and efficiencies were realized in terms the Systems Engineering people of the time could understand. The system was, in fact, *too* efficient for the educational goals then envisaged. Children could finish everything too fast and too easily. 'Homework' went right out of the window, creating dismay and anxiety, strangely enough, among many parents. The Great National School Debate of the middle and late 1970s concerned what to do with all the extra time gained by the new mode of learning. The question generally was stated in this fashion: 'What is the province of education?' The answer was simple: 'Everything.'

"During the 1970s, most schools spent a great deal of time with encounter groups for children and educators. These served to educate the emotions and to break down the old protective, defensive patterns of relating. They helped open people to all sorts of capacities they barely realized they had. Gradually the encounter mode became a part of everything the learners did, and it was no longer necessary to set up these groups as such.

"At the same time, educators were finding out that computer-mediated programs could be constructed to encourage uniqueness rather than sameness in learners. In fact, by tying to the ongoing program referents from a memory bank consisting of all the learner's past responses, the learner's distinctness from all other learners could be rapidly increased. Too rapidly, it seemed to some educators.

"The programs still were narrow, concerned with one 'subject' at a time—in other words, they were *programs.* Then, gradually, they evolved into what we now call 'dialogues.' It started when programmers began adding novelty and surprise through what they at first termed 'extraneous material.' For example, material about astronomy would pop up in programs on Eastern philosophy. Soon, they began realizing that what they were adding was by no means extraneous. Far from it, cross-matrix learning increased the central nervous system's capability for making connections, as well as enhancing mastery of any given subject. The early 1980s were fascinated with Cross-Matrix Stimulus and Response (CMSR). Naturally enough, the cross-matrix linkage started out quite teleologically, with the dialoguers seeking 'reasons' for their connections. But 'reasons' were found to be unduly limiting. Random retrieval through a central school computer made it possible to bring material up from the general cultural data bank, from the learner's own past responses and from the discontinuous symbolic storage to create displays that were anything but teleological.

"It was about this time, too, that dialoguers began conceiving the displays not only as learning aids, but as artistic creations in their own right. It occurred to them that the two—art and learning —really were one. That was still in the period when the displays were presented on old-fashioned cathode-ray television screens mounted in front of each learner. The art-and-learning movement was given a tremendous push around 1985, when the hologrammatic-conversion problem was solved for mass production. Laser-type projection created images of unimagined brightness and resolution—*moving* images that seemed to hang in midair, in dimensions that somehow outshone reality.

"An even more important development of the 1980s was the application of Ongoing Brain-wave Analysis (OBA) to Computer-Assisted Dialogue (CAD). The experiments of such pioneers as Kamiya and Adey had already shown that it was possible, through computer analysis, to identify the brain-wave patterns not only of certain general states of consciousness but also those associated with effective short-term memory. Certain experimenters began attaching brain-wave sensors to learners' earphones, so that their wave patterns could be fed directly into the computer for ongoing analysis and immediate influence of the dialogue. In this way, the learning process could march along much more swiftly and surely, and the number of overt motor responses—speech or key pressing, for example—required of the learner could be greatly reduced. If the learner was responding neurologically, the dialogue could move on. His general state of consciousness could also influence the dialogue.

"It took a few years for OBA to spread to most of the nation's schools. By that time, of course, musical-rhythmic sound had become a key matrix in CMSR. As the Hindus say, *Nada-Brahma-,* Sound Is God. And with sound responding to a learner's innermost states, a sort of cosmic counterpoint was born. The 1990s were a period of consolidation of the basic techniques, with breathtaking advances in the state of the art not only in Computer-Assisted Dialogue, but in a great number of educational environments."

Will Hawthorne's ebullience turns to caution only when the matter of Direct Brain-wave Manipulation (DBM) comes up. "First of all," he says, "it will be many years before DBM has anywhere near the subtlety and specificity of CAD through the usual sense channels. Then, too, I just don't like the idea of bypassing the senses, the sources of ever-present joy. No, if I have anything to say about it, there won't be any Kennedy children wearing those cumbersome DBM electrode helmets until I've seen a lot more data, especially concerning sensory side effects."

Some parents and children consider Will hopelessly conservative in this matter. But one visit to the Basics Dome explains why he is reluctant to "go inside." My wife and I find our pace quickening as we approach the most active and spectacular learning environment at Kennedy. We go in through one of three tunnel-like entrances and emerge near the center of a great dome lit only by the glow of laser learning displays that completely surround us on the dome's periphery. Sitting or sprawled on cushions scattered on the floor are other parents and older children who have come just for the experience, in addition to the little children waiting their turns at the learning consoles. We settle down and open our senses.

No matter how many times you visit the Basics Dome, its initial effect is literally stunning. It takes a while for the nervous system to begin processing; first, you have to surrender to the overwhelming sensory bombardment that comes from every side. There are, around us, forty learning consoles, at each of which is seated a child between the ages of three and seven, facing outward toward the learning displays. Each child sits at a keyboard, essentially less complex than that of an old-fashioned typewriter, but fitted with a number of shifts so that almost every symbol known to human cultures can be produced. The child's learning display, about ten feet square, is reflected from the hologram-conversion screen that runs all the way around the inner surface of the dome. The image appears to stand out from the screen in sometimes startling colors and dimensions. The screen is slightly elevated above the child's horizontal eye level so that everyone in the dome, by turning all the way around, can view all of the learning displays. Each display joins the one on either side of it, so that the total effect is panoramic. And each has its own set of stereo speakers, joining in a panorama of sound.

There are almost always children waiting for each console. A small electronic tablet on the back of each chair shows the name of the child in the chair and the number of minutes he has left in his learning session. The amount of time allowed for each session varies; it is calculated electronically according to the total number of children waiting in the dome, but it is never less than twenty minutes. Young children entering the dome shop around for consoles that have few or no other children waiting and that have the shortest time to go. The child assures his waiting place simply by touching the tablet with his electronic identification device (EID); a receiver picks up the information and the child's name appears at the bottom of the list on the tablet.

When a child takes the chair to begin learning, another radio receiver senses his presence through his EID and signals the central learning computer to plug in that particular child's learning history. The child puts on his combination earphones and brain-wave sensors, so that OBA can become an element in the dialogue. (Some schools use the brain-wave pattern, much in the manner of a fingerprint, to identify the learner.) Once the computer picks up the child's ongoing brain-waves, it immediately begins reiterating (in drastically foreshortened form) his last learning session. The child watches his most recent lesson reeling by on his display. If he wants to continue where he left off last time, he holds down his "yes" key until the reiteration is finished. If not, he presses "no," and the computer begins searching for other material appropriate to the child's level of learning, material which is flashed onto the display until the child presses "yes." The "select" process generally takes less than two minutes. The dialogue then begins.

At any given time during the dialogue, five variables are at hand:

1. A full bank of the basic, commonly agreed-upon cultural knowledge, arranged in dialogue form. Most children go through the entire basics bank in the four years from age three through age six.

2. Basic material arranged in Cross-Matrix Stimulus and Response form. This material appears at random intervals along with the dialogued material, to provide novelty and surprise and to help the child learn to make those unexpected leaps which are so much a part of discovery.

3. The child's brain-wave pattern, analyzed in terms of general consciousness state and short-term memory strength.

4. The child's overt motor responses as typed on the keyboard or spoken into a directional microphone mounted on the console.

5. Communal Interconnect (CI). This is one of the very latest educational developments. Only a few of the nation's schools have it. Through CI, the material on one learning display sometimes influences and is influenced by the material on nearby displays. This makes the learning process far more communal. It also helps tie together all forty displays into a single learning-art object, enhancing learning and appreciation, not only for the children at the consoles, but for the many spectators in the dome as well.

As soon as our senses become accustomed to the sounds and sights and smells in the dome, we look around for Sally. We are pleased to find her at one of the consoles. We move over to the side of the circle of spectators nearest her.

Sally, we notice on the electronic tablet on her chair, is only five minutes into her learning session. There is a Negro boy, probably six, on her left who is deep into a simple calculus session. On Sally's right, a girl of four or five is dialoguing about primitive cultures. Sally herself, as in her last several sessions, is concerned with simple language skills. It quickly becomes apparent that she has launched into a session on breaking her linguistic set. Standard spelling and syntax are generally learned during the first half of a child's third year of age. During the second half (where Sally is now) an equal or greater amount of time is spent trying out alternate forms. This leads eventually, after the basics are finished, to a key project: almost every child, working with friends, creates an entire new language before leaving Kennedy School.

We watch Sally's display, which now seems to be billowing with pink and lavender clouds. Gradually, the clouds take the shape of some kind of animal's face. Before I can make out what it is, I hear Sally saying "Cat" into her microphone. Almost instantly, a huge, grinning cat's face gathers form and the word "cat" appears at the bottom of the display. Then a written conversation begins between Sally and the Computer-Assisted Dialogue, with the words of each appearing on the display:

Cad: Can you think of an alternate spelling?
Sally *[Typing]*: kat.

On the display, the giant cat face recedes and is transformed into a white Angora cat, surrounded by vibrating, jagged radial lines of many colors. A purring sound comes from the display.

Cad: How about another?
Sally *[Pausing a moment]*: katte.

The purring becomes louder.

Cad: A cat is a kat is a katte.
Sally *[Quickly]*: A katte is a kat is a cat.
Cad: Copy cat.
Sally: Koppy kat.

There is a pause as the cat image gradually fades and the purring mingles with sweeping electronic music coming from the display on the left. As the dialogue goes on there between boy and CAD in the lovely visual symbols of calculus, a spinning wheel fills most of the display. Through its spokes, slender and glistening like the spokes of a bicycle wheel, may be viewed the rush of its motion—across grassy fields, deserts, down winding mountain roads. A ghostly image of the wheel appears on Sally's display, too, along with multicolored, dancing wave forms, related somehow to her brain waves. On the display at the right, an African pygmy with a blowgun stalks an unseen prey through dense jungle as the girl at the console carries on a voice-only dialogue with CAD. Suddenly Sally begins to type again:

Sally: A cat hiss a kat hiss a katte.
Cad: WILD!!!

Sally's display explodes for a moment with dazzling bursts of color, then becomes the jungle of the girl at the right, in which may be seen the prey of the hunter, a leopard. A tentative, suspenseful drumming echoes back and forth between the two displays. The two girls turn to each other smiling, then Sally quickly starts typing:

Sally: A tiger is a tigger./ A gunne has a trigger.

A moment after the last letter of Sally's couplet appears on her display, the jungle remains the same, but the leopard becomes a tiger and the pygmy becomes a white hunter of the early twentieth century, carrying a gun. The girl at the right snaps her head around at Sally, smiling, and Sally laughs delightedly.

Cad: Why not "leopard"?
Sally: "Leopard" doesn't rime with "trigger."
Cad: Okay. How about some alternate spellings for "leopard"?
Sally: That's easy. Leppurd.

Meanwhile, the girl at the right keeps talking to CAD and suddenly the tiger becomes a leopard, the white hunter, a pygmy again. The pygmy lifts his blowgun and with a sharp, explosive exhalation that echoes through the dome, sends a dart into the air. The display becomes a closeup of the dart coursing in slow motion across the girl's display, across Sally's and into the boy's at the left, disappearing in the hub of the spinning wheel. Another dart arches across the three displays, then another and another, sailing, soaring, starting always from different angles but ending invariably in the center of the boy's spinning wheel.

"Beautiful CI!" I hear my wife exclaim, and I notice that several people are watching the sequence and listening to the rise and fall of the accompanying electronic music. I also see that the flight of the darts is beginning to influence displays even farther along the line. But the boy continues his calculus dialogue and Sally goes on, too:

Cad: "Leppurd" is good, but you don't have to stay with sound correspondence. Would you like to try something farther out?

Sally presses her "yes" key, then pauses before beginning to type:

Sally: Leap-heart.
Cad: Nice. Do you want to do another?
Sally: No.

The flying darts begin to fade. Gradually, Sally's display takes on the deep, rich, undulating plum purple that often characterizes the brain's alpha-wave pattern. Some of the gorgeous richness spills over onto the displays at either side. We know her eyes are closed. She is serene. It is one of education's more valuable moments. We, too, are serene. It is easy, in this setting, to share Sally's feelings. We also share the sheer delight of the educators who set up and constantly modify this learning environment. It is a kind of delight that was unknown to lecturers.

When Sally's session is finished, we walk with her out of the Basics Dome. We talk for a while, but soon she sees some of her friends and leaves us. They run off toward the thickest grove of trees to continue an animal game that may take them the rest of the day.

So we stroll from one place to another, looking (but not too strenuously) for Johnny, our nine-year-old. If we were in a hurry to find him, it would be easy enough. We would merely go to the Central Dome and present one of our electronic identification devices to the ongoing scan, then read out Johnny's approximate present location. Every child wears an EID whenever he is on the school grounds, and the central computer continually tabulates how much time he spends in each educational environment. In addition, whenever the child is in dialogue with a CAD, his learning experience is stored in the computer. This allows Kennedy's educators, not only to keep track of each child's educational development with a minimum of effort, but also to evaluate the drawing power and effectiveness of each environment. The first principle of free learning is that if an environment fails to draw or to educate, it is the environment's, not the learner's, fault.

Visiting educators from educationally underdeveloped nations sometimes find it hard to understand that EID tracking serves not to enforce conformity, but just the opposite. In fact, "asymmetry" is highly valued. Will Hawthorne becomes quite excited when a young child resists the enticements of the Basics Dome for a year or two. Such a child may turn out to be so unique that much can be learned from him. And individual uniqueness is itself one of the main goals of the educational process.

Anyway, learning the basics, the commonly agreed-upon cultural stuff, is so sure and easy that there's never any worry about delay in starting it. It seems incredible to today's children that there ever was.

"I still find it hard to believe," Johnny sometimes says, "that people of Grandpa's generation spent *most* of their time in school learning just what the little kids learn in Basics."

"It's really true," my wife tells him. "They learned *much less.* And they did spend almost all their school time working at it."

"Working?" Sally asks in amazement.

"Yes. *Really.* And there were all sorts of discussions and arguments about how to do it and every kind of agony you can imagine."

in my opinion...

After one reads the article he stops to ponder the possibility of such an environment in terms of practicality and expansion of proposed ideas. Both the technical and human aspects of such a proposal must be examined.

Leonard makes use of technology to the utmost degree. He sees technology not as a dehumanizing element in our society, but as one which can bring human beings to a fuller understanding of themselves and others by means of a cybernated learning atmosphere. One of the most unique examples expounded upon was the event which occurred in the Basics Dome involving a small child and his discussion with the master computer. The possibility of a computer directing a child through a learning process seems impersonal when thought of in terms of today's learning process, but why—if a computer can accomplish more and create, in addition to learning, an urge to progress deeper into the problem—should this concept in learning be discredited? Many educators feel that computers have no place on a person-to-person level; but where in our system today is there a direct relationship between teacher and student? With structured classrooms there is neither the time, the convenience, nor the desire to establish a rapport between teacher and student. Leonard's suggestion of an environment in which there is the time and the ability to supply the necessary stimulation and guidance for a child seems much more beneficial. To extend this idea further, the computer is capable of evaluating the progress made and of using its influence to direct, but not force, the student into deeper, more involved areas of thought and study. It will never push too hard and stops when it comes upon even slight resistance. If one objects to this advancement, one need only look at a child who cannot learn arithmetic because he was pushed too hard and too quickly by a teacher whose only desire was that he not lag behind his peers and thus require individual attention.

Again, the technical side has evolved first, but one must look at Leonard's work on the human level also. Leonard stresses the fact that education must evolve from a process to a way-of-life. His whole theory revolves around this concept, and this perhaps is the outstanding feature of his work. Education is not something which is used for purely extrinsic goals but, in contrast, should provide intrinsic satisfactions. Education should not be the means to a desired end but should be the means and the end combined. The child should grasp in his formative years what Leonard calls the "ecstasy" of learning a new concept, of finding a solution to a problem he has worked on; or even the pleasure of being by himself with his own thoughts. This joy of learning would carry over into his life and become one with it—each new act and experience would be added to his knowledge of himself and the world and put to use to enhance himself beneficially.

Equally as important as the experiences which school-age children have and share together will be the opportunity for adults to fuse their living with learning. No longer will they feel pressured to stop "going to school" (which in most instances brings an end to education) and put their knowledge to work for them for financial security. It has been suggested that in the very near future it will not be necessary for every individual to work, but the economic security will be provided by a small percentage of the population. Lack of time will no longer be a valid excuse for allowing the mind to stagnate. A complete new concept of living may be beginning and education could fill the gap between yesterday and tomorrow. The need for "something" to take the place of working might become the new thrust in education.

A problem arises when considering the applicability of Leonard's theory. It is hard to visualize the described environment becoming a reality. The ideas presented are in most cases the exact reversal of the established norm, and man, being the creature of habit that he is, is unwilling to accept even a slight change. One wonders if for each change, a battle must be fought.

Is it worth it? The answer is most definitely "yes", but how long can one wait to put these or similar theories into practice? Is one willing to be content with a minimal amount of knowledge acquired through archaic methods of instruction, or will something be done to change the structure and make it one with life?

gayle shanks

questions

1. From what you have seen, what would you say is the fundamental purpose of education as it exists today? What changes would you suggest?

2. What practical indication is there, if any, that education is being affected by the cybernetic revolution?

3. Given the right atmosphere and instructional materials, what possibilities exist for "free-learning"?

4. What are the dangers involved in computer-centered learning?

5. Compare the educational techniques described by Leonard in this chapter with those of B. F. Skinner in Chapter 15.

20.

can we afford affluence? the challenge of tomorrow

CAN WE COPE WITH TOMORROW?

alvin toffler

introduction and comment by margaret l. sampley

Our research, class discussions, newspaper headlines all have made us more aware of the surging changes that have become so vital a part of the dynamic society in which we live. Caught up as we are in the tensions of today, it is often difficult to become involved with the mysteries of tomorrow.

But much as we would like to consider 2000 A.D. to be remote and unpredictable, it is rapidly approaching. The twenty-first century could offer luxurious living not only for a few but for millions. Adequately prepared, we could be the authors of a new epic poem entitled "The Garden of Eden—Regained." Unprepared, we might be on a one-way road to disaster.

The history of man has been characterized by a striving for perfection. The twenty-first century might well be the climax of that struggle. The next few decades may well see man make great steps toward becoming truly human, or it may bring the total denigration of humanity.

Classroom discussions covered extensive areas of investigation. We became aware of the promises of technology, and even more aware of the changes in attitudes that every man will have to make in order to profit from those changes. With scientific discoveries—those which now exist, those yet to be unveiled—every human being may be affected, physically, mentally, morally. In such a fast-moving environment, man needs a stabilizing force in order to maintain his sanity. If he has confidence in his abilities, change will present no threat; on the contrary, exciting and rewarding challenges will be offered. Above all, change, per se, must be viewed without fear.

The potential of the future is exhilarating. Physical toil may be almost nonexistent; human intelligence could soar. War as an instrument of problem-solving might disappear; the dignity of man could truly become our most sought-after goal. Humanity—all human beings—might truly move toward freedom from tyranny, economic depression and disease. With the time to think and the desire to live fully, man may become more aware of himself, and, eventually more aware of others.

Life in the twenty-first century may include opportunities for a guaranteed international annual income, huge advances in technology, science, new understandings in social relationships, the humanities and philosophy. How man utilizes these opportunities may determine whether Eden is regained—or lost forever. Controls must be established, not to be decided, perhaps by a rule of the majority, but, as Helvetiius said, by "considering the greatest good of the greatest number".

Our discussions were certainly not without skepticism. We did not have to look far to find endless instances of human activities that made the possibility of true advances seem to be dubious, at least. But man has an infinite power within himself to create, as well as to destroy. If man's selfishness overpowers him, and he misuses or ignores the fantastic possibilities of the future, then he is as backward and barbaric as his ancient cave-dwelling ancestors.

We choose to believe that, given the opportunities that technology and science promise, man will choose the good life. The road to Utopia has more barriers than speedways, but the barriers are not impregnable. Men, we believe, are rational: given a choice between a full life and total destruction, we do not doubt—we dare not doubt—that man will opt for life.

If we are to have the chance to exercise that option, we must learn to cope with change rather than to fear it. In the article that follows, Alvin Toffler details many of the questions that we must face today in order to handle progress toward tomorrow.

m.l.s.

CAN WE COPE WITH TOMORROW?

Alvin Toffler was born on October 28, 1928, in New York City. He received his B.A. from New York University. He was a Washington correspondent during 1957–1959, and associate editor of Fortune *magazine in 1959–1961. Since then, Mr. Toffler has worked as a full-time free-lance writer. He has been a member of the Board of Directors of Sulzberg Seminar in American Studies, a member of the Society of Magazine Writers (vice president in 1964) and the Society for the History of Technology. In addition to contributing to* Fortune, Life, The Nation, New Republic, New York Review of Books, Saturday Review, Think, Horizon, Show *and other publications, Mr. Toffler is the author of* The Culture Consumers, *1954, and* Future Shock, *1970.*

The year 2000 seems as remote in time as the stars. Yet the end of the 20th century is already closer than the Wall Street crash of 1929, closer than Einstein's formulation of the theory of relativity, closer than Picasso's early cubism, closer than the introduction of cellophane, Technicolor movies and radar.

As I began to write this, indeed, it came as a bit of a jolt to realize that—barring catastrophe—many of you reading this page will be only in your middle years when man takes time out to celebrate the arrival of the next millennium.

No one can tell in detail what life will be in A.D. 2000. But we do know that more social and scientific changes will be compressed within the years intervening than have occurred in any similar span in history. This will impart a special quality to our lives, a quality we must learn to live with and understand. It can best be described as "transience"; and whatever may lie on the other side of the year 2000, transience will set the dominant tone of our lives until then.

Transience is a new "temporariness" in everyday life. Change is occurring so rapidly now that things, values, even people, pass through our lives at a faster rate than before. Thus each individual's relationships with the world outside himself are foreshortened, telescoped in time. They become transient.

This process, occurring in every cranny of our existence, introduces into our lives a powerfully upsetting new psychological force. For while man until now has been accustomed to long-lasting links with his environment, he is entering a period in which he will be limited increasingly to short-term relationships. It is this that gives rise to the sense of transience in our lives, the almost tangible feeling that we live, rootless and uncertain, among shifting dunes.

Philosophers and theologians, of course, have always been aware that man is ephemeral. In this grand sense, transience has always been a part of life. But today the feeling of impermanence is qualitatively more acute and more intimate. We are citizens of the Age of Transience, for as the rate of change in science and society accelerates, the feeling of transience permeates everything.

For example, Americans are among the most mobile people who ever lived. We move from street to street or city to city with incredible frequency. Pick any date in 1965. By the same date in 1966 one American in five will have moved, bag and baggage, to a new residence, leaving behind neighbors, friends, family members, tradespeople, his church congregation, union local or other associations.

This perpetual geographical motion is matched by movement up and down the economic and social scale. Each time we move, up, down or laterally, we slough off some of our friends and acquaintances and form a new circle of human relationships. Each of us today becomes acquainted with more people in a year than a feudal serf met in his lifetime. But our ties with most people are increasingly transient and perishable.

The same is true of our relationship with objects. We live in what has been called a "disposable" society. We use a napkin once and throw it away. We replace our automobiles every few years. We raze landmarks. We tear down whole streets and cities and put up new ones at a mind-numbing rate.

"The average age of dwellings has steadily declined," writes

E. F. Carter, of the Stanford Research Institute, "from being virtually infinite in the days of caves to . . . approximately 100 years for houses built in U.S. colonial days, to about 40 years at present." He might have added that much contemporary architecture relies on the "modular principle"—the arrangement of interior space so that walls and partitions can be shifted at will from place to place. The highly mobile partition might almost serve as a symbol of the impermanence of contemporary society.

Recently my wife sent our daughter, who is 12, to a supermarket a few blocks from our apartment. Our little girl had been there only once or twice before. Half an hour later she returned, perplexed. "It must have been torn down," she said. "I couldn't find it." It hadn't been. Karen had merely looked on the wrong street. But she is a child of the Age of Transience, and her immediate assumption—that the building had been razed and replaced—was a natural one for a 12-year-old growing up in the United States in 1965. Such an idea probably would never have occurred to a child faced with the same predicament half a century ago. One's physical environment was far less transient.

Values, too, pass into and out of our lives at high speed nowadays. There were periods of history during which attitudes toward the worth or worthlessness of things remained fixed for a long time. Notions of "good" and "bad," "better" and "worse," stayed put, unchanged and unchallenged for longer than the lifetime of a man.

This is no longer true, for the value landscape is changing right along with the physical landscape. In recent decades, for example, refrigerators, vacuum cleaners, automatic washers and dryers and other such products of technology have reduced the number of hours needed to run a home. Automobiles have given the housewife new independence; education has expanded her intellectual horizons. As a result, a job outside the home has become socially acceptable, perhaps even enviable. Its value has risen, whereas the value of housework as such has declined.

In the 1920s and 1930s the typical Hollywood hero asked his sweetheart's mother whether the bride-to-be knew how to cook. Today, more often than not, such a question, if it is asked at all, is facetious. And if a husband dislikes his supper, he is more likely to ask his wife to switch brands than to study the art of cooking, for the value placed on this particular skill has declined. (Gourmet cooking, on the other hand, has risen in value. It is seen as a leisuretime skill, rather than a household chore.)

Simultaneously, by shortening a man's working hours, technology has given the husband more time to spend at home. Today the man who dons an apron to help with the dishes is no longer scorned as a sissy; the man who doesn't is increasingly regarded as old-fashioned and unfair. The value of equality between men and women has risen; the value of male dominance has declined.

Even more striking are the changes in our sexual morality. Today young people can buy books like *Tropic of Cancer* or *Lady Chatterley's Lover* that were forbidden to adults five or ten years ago. The problem of abortion is discussed openly on television. Even the Catholic Church, that most enduring of institutions, debates changing its age-old strictures against contraception. However one may feel about these matters, it is clear that our long-standing notions about the goodness or badness of chastity, obscenity, birth control, abortion and extramarital sexual relations are shifting rapidly and violently. The same may be said of our attitudes toward crime, mental illness, race, nationalism, thrift—all similarly in flux.

In short, whether we observe our relationship with things (our physical environment), with people (our psychological environment) or with values (our moral environment), we find an extremely high rate of turnover. The things that we used to think of as enduring are turning out to be painfully impermanent.

Yet today we are only at the beginning of the Age of Transience. The [few] years between now and A.D. 2000 will be marked by scientific, technical and social changes of such extreme sweep and power that they will force us to abandon all our accustomed ways of doing, thinking and even feeling. A few examples show why.

Put aside for a moment the extraordinary changes that automation will introduce into our lives in the coming decades. Pretend that there will be no new political upheavals in the world. Forget the likelihood that we shall be developing new sources of power, such as solar energy. Ignore the potential control of human behavior through the use of drugs or the electrical stimulation of the brain. Even if we are able to imagine that none of these probabilities and possibilities exist, one cannot think about the next [few decades] without being staggered by the fantastic changes that will touch our lives.

The work being done in biology alone will be enough to transform our physical, psychological and moral environments.

Dr. Charles C. Price, president of the American Chemical Society, recently declared: "The synthesis of life is now within reach. It seems to me that we may be no further today from at least a partial synthesis of living systems than we were in the 1920s from the release of nuclear energy or in the 1940s from putting a man in space. The political, social, biological and economic consequences of the ability to synthesize living organisms in the test tube, however, will dwarf those of either atomic energy or the space programs."

Among the consequences will be seismic tremors in schools of theology all over the world. I can remember as a boy listening to an evangelist prove the existence of God by pointing out that no matter what man could do, he would never be able to create life from inanimate substance. I wonder where that evangelist is now. Wherever he is, he will be compelled to do some deep thinking, for theological arguments too are suffering rapid obsolescence.

If the synthesis of life is not sufficiently impressive, consider the advances in genetics, which suggest that, among other things, it may become possible before long to manipulate the general level of intelligence of the human race.

Physicist-writer Ralph E. Lapp has speculated on the implications of intelligence control. "Suppose," he writes, ". . . it is found possible to upgrade human intelligence by 20 points on the IQ scale. How would a society such as ours exploit such a triumph of modern bioscience? Would the federal government subsidize prenatal treatment for all children? Or would this mental uplift be applied only to those who might be suspected to turn out to be otherwise mentally retarded? Or would such tinkering with the embryonic brain be outlawed through federal legislation? If so, how would our legislators contemplate the application of such a discovery in totalitarian countries? I suppose it is possible that if an American science team makes the initial breakthrough, it might be held top secret. So to speak, the biologists would have their own 'A-bomb.' "

Any such breakthrough would revolutionize all human institutions based on the expectation that a substantial part of the human race is unintelligent. Television programs and political speeches would have to be upgraded—and what could be more revolutionary than that? More seriously, the way we organize governments, our notions about leadership, our methods for teaching and child rearing, all would be deeply influenced by any such change. Native intelligence, for centuries thought to be a God-given and unchanging human attribute, may thus turn out before long to be quite as susceptible to change as anything else.

The day also approaches when we may come to look upon the very parts of our body as transient. Professor R. M. Kenedi, writing in *The New Scientist* about "bioengineering," predicts that "artificial replacements for tissues and organs may well have become commonplace" by 1984. Already thousands of cardiac patients are alive because they carry, surgically implanted in the abdomen, a tiny device that send pulses of electricity to activate the heart. A vast industry eventually may be built to serve the need for artificial organs and replacement parts. Indeed, our concept of what a human being is may be shaken. How much wire and plastic can there be in a human body before it becomes more machine than man? Where is the dividing line?

Events in biology thus outrace the imagination. Similarly, if we turn from biology to the conquest of space, we can predict that our adventure in the skies will change the behavior and psychology of millions. It will increase our ability to predict, and ultimately control, the weather. It will introduce as by-products new plastics, fibers and other materials into everyday use. We have developed strange and novel foods for astronauts, and researchers are already at work attempting to adapt these to the consumer market.

On another level entirely, the drive into space can be expected to have a powerful effect on our art, our architecture, our literature, our concept of time, space and beauty, our belief about man's place in the universe. Just as the discovery of America touched off a cultural and intellectual explosion in Western Europe roughly 500 years ago, just as the existence of the frontier helped shape the American mentality, the opening of the skies will have a profound psychological impact on all of us.

Nor will all the changes between now and A.D. 2000 be scientific. A broad range of social changes will occur as well. A single example is the movement toward urbanization surging across the globe.

The city and its way of life are conquering all. According to such investigators as E. de Vries and J. P. Thijsse, of the Netherlands, world urban population may rise at an annual rate of 6.5 per cent in the years ahead. This single stark statistic means nothing less than a doubling of the earth's urban population within 11 years.

One way to grasp the meaning of change on so phenomenal a scale is to imagine what would happen if all existing cities, instead of expanding, retained their present size. If this were so, in order to accommodate the new urban millions we would have to build a duplicate city for each of the hundreds of cities that already dot the surface of the globe. A new Tokyo, a new Hamburg, a new Rome and Rangoon—and all within 11 years!

Of course, we shall not only build new cities. We shall also jam new millions of people into those that already exist, thereby forcing changes in the way we travel to and from work, the way we shop, the way we relax.

To say that we are changing the face of the earth is no mere figure of speech. But it is only part of the story. We also are changing how people think and feel, and we are doing so at a rate that sends the mind careening.

All this has direct bearing on the problem of impermanence in our lives. Moreover, it raises a provocative question: Just how much change, how much transience, can an individual take? Can we as individuals, or can society as a whole, function rationally in a world in which everything is so terribly temporary?

Unfortunately, no one has the answer to this psychological question. Very little scientific work has been done to study the impact of transience on personality, for example. But there are disturbing hints to suggest that we had better begin to devote some serious research to it.

Sensory-deprivation experiments, in which subjects are kept in a dark room or under water or in any environment that severely limits sensory stimulation, suggest that if one's environment is too unstimulating, too unchanging and featureless, one's ability to function becomes impaired. In other words, some transience in the environment is essential to healthy psychological functioning.

But at the same time there also is evidence that too much transience may affect the individual's ability to understand, and hence cope with, his environment. An environment convulsing with change bombards the individual with stimulation. Impulses race through the brain and neural network—signals, as it were, jamming a busy switchboard. Thus if too little "input" can be damaging, so, it would appear, can too much. In the words of Dr. James G. Miller, Director, Mental Health Research Institute, University of Michigan: "Glutting a person with more information than he can process may also lead to disturbance."

Dr. Herbert Gerjuoy, a psychologist on the staff of the Educational Testing Service in Princeton, New Jersey, explains that: "In a stable society your decisions become 'routinized.' Situations repeat themselves. The number of new decisions we are called upon to make is limited. But when a society changes as fast as ours, the problems no longer repeat themselves. We are constantly confronted with novel problems. This may prove stimulating or arousing, but arousal is itself a form of stress. It involves activation of the adrenals and the sequence of biochemical events that have been found to cause psychosomatic illness and perhaps even aging. Too much excitement and novelty—too much change—can undermine one's ability to make decisions rationally."

Similarly, the World Federation for Mental Health, in discussing difficulties faced by underdeveloped nations on the path to industrialism, has pointed out that rapid change "makes it difficult for individuals to pattern their lives as adults on the lives which, as children, they watched their parents live. . . . Technical change involves new learning, after adulthood, and changing types of behavior which have been heavily reinforced by childhood experiences of reward and punishment." When technical change is introduced into such a society, the federation says, "we can assume that various types of psychological disturbances will occur."

There is every reason to believe that this warning is just as applicable to our own society as it is to the societies of underdeveloped countries.

Sanity, after all, depends upon comprehension of one's surroundings. Yet the degree of transience is already such that by the time most people come to understand the underlying order of their corner of society, that order has already changed into something else.

It is as if the entire human race were sitting in a darkened movie theater. On the screen one scene after another slides by. We laugh, we cry, we throb in response to the filmed action. But imperceptibly the pace quickens. Scenes begin to swim by so swiftly that we can barely comprehend what is happening. Soon the screen is just a blur of racing images and all meaning is lost.

This is a close analogy with reality, except that in the real world we are not mere observers. Despite confusion we must act. But the more rapid the change and the more intense the transience, the more difficult it becomes to remain oriented. This progressive inability to comprehend, this disorientation produced by too-rapid change, is what I have elsewhere called "future shock." It is as if the individual were plunged into a state of shock by the premature arrival of the future.

"Future shock" is more than a figure of speech. It may turn out to be the single most important problem of the coming years. For as the rate of transience around us increases, more and more people will be driven either to vegetablelike passivity or to irrational violence by the frustration of their attempts to cope with an environment they can no longer keep up with.

It is not too much, I think, to view the crimes in the subways of New York and the terrorism committed by motorcycle-mounted hoodlums in California and the senseless battles between "Mods" and "Rockers" in England as expressions, at least in part, of "future shock." I fear that we shall see more of this kind of irrationality rather than less unless we take intelligent preventive steps now.

How to live with high transience—that is our problem. And there is no simple solution. But man has always shown a spectacular ability to survive and he now has powerful weapons to help him. Even as the turnover rate rises in our lives, we shall witness advances in the behavioral sciences, in our general understanding of the mind and the mechanisms that underlie rationality. These advances will in turn help us to cope with the increase in transience.

It is at least reasonable to suppose that we shall learn, before many more decades pass, to control social change much more sensitively than we can at present; that we shall learn to channel it, to regulate its speed. Our more sophisticated understanding not only of man but of the structure of society will make it possible for us to grasp more clearly than at present the implications of any proposed change.

Yet we have a long way to go and a dangerous heritage to overcome. On every level—intellectual, emotional and moral—we must get used to the idea that nothing is fixed or permanent, that everything is transient. This idea is extraordinarily difficult for many of us to accept. For most of us have been educated to believe quite the opposite. We have come out of our schools admiring the solid, safe and secure. We automatically mistrust change. And to the extent that we do, we have been dangerously miseducated.

This is not because of any "conspiracy," but because our educational institutions were designed originally to prepare individuals for life in a relatively static environment. These institutions haven't caught up with the needs of today, let alone those of tomorrow.

It is true that a revolution is already sweeping through our schools and colleges. Much, though not all, of what is happening is excellent. Yet there are three changes that, in my opinion, must be part of any program of educational reform to make education suitable for the Age of Transience. The first of these changes has begun to win serious attention from educators. The second, however, is almost always neglected or misunderstood. And the third is so unorthodox that it so far has received no serious attention at all.

I don't pretend that these three proposed changes are a panacea. They are only a small part of what needs to be done. Nor are they simple or easy to accomplish. But they are important; moreover, they are the kind of changes that those of us who are parents can help bring about.

In the Age of Transience we must first stop thinking of education as something that happens during a fixed period early in a person's lifetime. Traditionally we have conceived of education as a 12- or 16-year process during which young people are taught a number of facts about the world and equipped with certain attitudes toward those facts. The assumption has been that once processed in this way, a human being could live as a rational member of society until he died.

This notion, of dubious value to begin with, must now be revised. Can we expect, in a highly transient society, that an education pumped into a person in the first 20 years of his life will hold good for half a century after that?

It may be that we shall have to give every individual a 15- or 20-year "down payment" on education, but then require him to return to school for fixed intervals every five years or every other year or, for that matter, every other month for as long as he lives. The exact pattern or timing is beside the point. But some variant of this idea is necessary and inevitable. In a transient society education will have to continue throughout one's lifetime. This idea is already gaining currency among educators.

Unfortunately, the same is not true of the second proposal. There is much heated discussion of the place of science in the curriculum. Frequently this takes the form of asking how much more math or physics or biology can be crammed into an already overcrowded syllabus.

Science *should* form the core of the curriculum in a transient society. Yet not everyone can or should be a scientist, and there is only so much room in any curriculum. I would like to suggest that while we may wish to increase the number of hours devoted to mathematics and other scientific subjects, we shall never succeed in preparing the mass of students for life in a transient and science-oriented world simply by adding a course in this or that specialty.

Science is not a body of hard-to-understand fact. It does not consist of test tubes and cyclotrons. It is, stripped to its essence, simply a way of looking at the world, a method for determining what is relatively true and what is relatively false.

It is this method, this way of looking at the world, that needs to be taught. Whether this means more courses in physics or more courses in logic, probability and the philosophy of science instead, it is the *method* that must be communicated.

This method, as the English biologist Thomas Huxley never tired of pointing out, is simply a way of solving problems. It can be applied as easily to figuring out something as concrete and homely as whether or not Johnny ate the missing piece of apple pie as to the more complex and ethereal mysteries of antimatter, mesons and Mars.

This is not the place for an extended essay on scientific method, but it is important to note its dependence on what might be termed the "principle of tentativity." For science tolerates no absolutes; its findings are always presented as tentative. This means that even the most heavily substantiated and familiar scientific generalizations are considered no more than highly probable.

The scientist in this respect is not only responsible for triggering many of the forces of change in the world; he is also the leading prototype of the man of the future, for the true scientist stands constantly ready to scrap his most cherished theories should the facts run against him.

It is this willingness to view every conclusion as "subject to change on short notice," this tentativity, that makes the scientific method so appropriate a system of thought for a transient world.

The method of science takes whatever is new into account. And the scientist knows that when verified fact fails either to confirm or to disprove a theory, he must hold his opinions in abeyance. He refuses to judge theories for which there is no evidence.

It is this open-minded spirit, this respect for fact, this willingness to adapt and to reserve judgment, that is the strength of scientific method. And it is this spirit, along with the method, that the children of transience can learn and apply without necessarily becoming professional scientists. To teach this method and to instill this outlook is in my opinion a primary responsibility of parents and schools.

Third and, it seems to me, most important, the new education must shift its accent from yesterday to tomorrow. The only way to cushion individuals against future shock is to prepare them for the future, to offer them in advance some idea of what they may expect as tomorrow unrolls. We need, in other words, to teach them the habit of anticipation.

When the world is standing still it may be possible to live one's life without ever looking further ahead than a few hours or days. One can be sure, even without thinking about it, that the environment will still be there, essentially unchanged. But in a society of high transience, when change descends upon us like an avalanche, it is difficult but necessary to look further ahead.

Though nobody can predict the future in detail, the sciences— natural and social—are improving their techniques for forecasting at least the broad outlines of future developments. We may not be able to teach students what *will* be, but we can and must teach them what is *possible* and what seems most *probable*. We need to provide them with an image of the future.

Yet while every student today at some point in his education must take courses in history, no one takes a course in "future." Our education system looks backward but not forward. Odd though it may seem to those of us brought up under the old system, a proper education for life in a transient society must include courses in which our young people can explore the possibilities of tomorrow quite as systematically as they are now expected to learn about Rome, the Magna Carta and the American Revolution. The study of history has value, but only if it is balanced by attention to the fascinating probabilities of the future. A course in "future" should be required in every curriculum.

In this course students ought to be encouraged to speculate. They should be encouraged to read the Utopias, from Samuel Butler's *Erewhon* to Bellamy's *Looking Backward,* as well as the anti-Utopias, such as Aldous Huxley's *Brave New World* and Orwell's *1984.* They should read H. G. Wells and Jules Verne. Some of this is already being done. But the schools must also take a new look at the best contemporary science fiction. Despised as a literary form—and perhaps justly so—science fiction nevertheless is important in the education of every person growing up into the transient society because it not only opens one's eyes and mind to the potentials of the future but also raises provocative questions about philosophy, ethics, politics and sociology—questions that are seldom, if ever, encountered in the conventional reading lists and textbooks of today.

The best science fiction writers—such men as Arthur Clarke, Robert Heinlein and William Tenn—should be required reading for the course in "future."

There is a growing body too of important, future-oriented non-fiction, not merely about the hardware of tomorrow but also about the philosophical and moral issues with which our children probably will have to live. An excellent example of this is a brilliant, intellectually thrusting book almost totally neglected in this country, called *Yestermorrow*, by Kurt Marek, who under his pen name, C. W. Ceram, is better known as the author of *Gods, Graves and Scholars.*

Such books freshen one's sense of the future and prepare the mind for the fascinating journey that lies before us.

This journey, despite the harrowing ridges and windswept reaches that lie along the way, should not be feared. Man has survived problems far more difficult than those associated with high transience. But his way will be made more difficult if we glorify the past and fill our children with ignorance or despair about the future, if we teach them that man is doomed, that reason is useless, that individual effort is absurd or futile.

Contemporary literature, drama and art are saturated with a sense of impending doom. They wallow in despair and misery, presenting this as if it were the natural and universal state of man, the so-called human condition. There may be a tragic aspect to man, but it is hardly the only aspect; and if we are heading into a society that will be difficult and dangerous, it also will be filled with marvels and delights. For we live at one of the climactic moments of history. We who are alive today are privileged to live through an astonishing intellectual renaissance, a flick of time during which all shibboleths and superstitions, all the old solutions, all the traditions, are once more open to question.

Horizons expand on every side, and we rob and imperil our children if we fail to build into them—the young citizens of the Age of Transience—a sense of wonder and hope and questing curiosity about its potentials.

in my opinion...

Transience, change, temporariness, impermanence . . . these are the words Alvin Toffler uses to describe the condition of man until the year 2000, and beyond. Uncertainty will be the governing mood of living, many age-old verities will disintegrate. Change is not new; the difference today is the astounding acceleration of the rate of change. How people will cope with change is an important and relevant question.

Many aspects of transience have already been accepted by society. The "itinerant family" is commonplace. One new product after another is advertised as "disposable." But the idea of the perishable transcends material objects. Attitudes and values are in a state of flux. Women's groups vigorously press for independence and equality; accepted attitudes on sexual morality are in violent upheaval.

Living organisms created in a test tube, a population with an intelligence rating of genius—are these predictions just science fiction folly? "No," say researchers, "they could be realities in the twenty-first century". A re-evaluation of man's physical, psychological and moral environments must be made. And we won't be able to thumb through history books to find answers. Novel questions will have to be confronted almost daily. We cannot be sure that even religion will play a part in supplying the answers.

As man explores space, our beliefs with regard to our preeminence in the universe may be threatened. Throughout past millenia, our earth was thought to be the center of the universe. When man inhabits new planets and discovers new worlds, will his self-esteem drop to a feeling of insignificance or heighten to that of a courageous, successful explorer? Today's young adults must learn to contend with these occurrences in tomorrow's world.

Man by his nature is a conservative creature, resisting change. A reeducation or a renaissance in thinking must take place in order for him to make decisions rationally. Mr. Toffler very aptly describes the dangers as being a "vegetablelike passivity" and an "irrational violence". He presupposes that we will learn "to control social change much more sensitively than we can at present". Advanced study in psychology and sociology may achieve this. Each individual holds the answer within himself.

The idea of nothing being fixed or permanent is difficult to adjust to. Today people are set in their ways of thinking and doing things. They pretend to know all the answers because of having lived through similar circumstances or just having lived longer than someone else. But in the decades to come, no one will really know the answers. This does not have to be an alarming fact but rather an exciting opportunity. A revamping of education will be used to combat the many doubts. Education will be utilized in solving problems. By accepting and practising the principle of "tentativity", not absolutism, man will experience a new-found freedom, openness, and search for truth that will revitalize his entire being.

The core of Mr. Toffler's message lies in preparing for "future shock", to incorporate into every curriculum a course that teaches students "the habit of anticipation". Mr. Toffler cites examples of fiction reading material that will provide an image of the future.

It is the hope of the student editors of the preceding articles that some insight has been relayed to the reader about the twenty-first century. Most of us will be alive at that time to experience the full impact of change. If we prepare ourselves now for the coming events, we should not be submerged in the swift currents of discoveries. To be in control of ourselves and knowledgeable about the occurring events may more likely result in peace and happiness. To develop a renaissance of wonder will enable us to experience the vast potentials of life in the twenty-first century.

margaret l. sampley

questions

1.   Toffler strongly emphasizes the short-term relationships prevalent in society today. How will transience be affected by the diminished importance of the work ethic?

2.   Suppose a drug for upgrading human intelligence were discovered tomorrow. Should it be used? For all people, or for a select few? Under whose control?

3.   Both Thoreau and Rousseau proclaimed that living close to nature would save mankind. If an almost total urbanization of people exists, will man be doomed?

4. Let's suppose that the idea of lifelong education is enthusiastically supported. What will the continuous "state of studenthood" do to even out the generation gap?

5. Is the following statement illogical and dangerous to the welfare of mankind ". . . willingness to view every conclusion as 'subject to change on short notice' "? Explain.

21.
on a lighter vein...

**THE DAY THE COMPUTERS GOT
WALDON ASHENFELTER**

bob elliott and ray goulding

THE DAY THE COMPUTERS GOT
WALDON ASHENFELTER

*The writers whose works make up the readings for this book
were, without exception, seriously concerned with the impact
of change on society. Our staff of editors, too, became deeply
involved in the endless number of earth-shaking questions
which their research unearthed. Our involvement is with the
future of mankind.*

*In a satirical vein, and with biting humor, Bob Elliott and
Ray Goulding, internationally-known television and radio
humorists, examine the zaniness of computermania. Jerry
Campbell (Cybernetics) felt this "laughter through tears"
article was important. And we agreed.*

A presidential commission has recommended approval of plans
for establishing a computerized data center where all personal
information on individual Americans compiled by some twenty
scattered agencies would be assembled in one place and made
available to the federal government as a whole.

Backers of the proposal contend that it would lead to greater
efficiency, and insist that the cradle-to-grave dossiers on the
nation's citizens would be used only in a generalized way to help
deal with broad issues. Opponents argue that the ready availability of so much confidential data at the push of a computer
button could pose a dangerous threat to the privacy of the individual by enabling the federal bureaucracy to become a
monstrous, snooping Big Brother.

Obviously, the plan elicits reactions that are emotional, and
cooler heads are needed to envision the aura of quiet, uneventful

routine certain to pervade the Central Data Bank once it becomes accepted as just another minor government agency.

Fade in:

Interior—Basement GHQ of the Central Data Bank—Night. (At stage right, 950 sophisticated third-generation computers may be seen stretching off into the distance. At stage left, the CDB grave-yard-shift charge d'affaires, Nimrod Gippard, is seated behind a desk. He is thirty-five-ish and attired in socks that don't match. At the open, Gippard is efficiently stuffing mimeographed extortion letters to Omaha's 3277 suspected sex deviates into envelopes. He glances up as Waldon Ashenfelter, an indoorsy type of questionable ancestry, enters.)

Gippard: Yes, sir?

Ashenfelter (flashing ID card): Ashenfelter. Bureau of Indian Affairs. Like to have you run a check on a key figure named Y. Claude Garfunkel.

Gippard (reaching for pad and pencil): Sure thing. What's his Social Security number?

Ashenfelter: I dunno.

Gippard: Hmmm. How about his zip code? Or maybe a cross-reference to some banks where he may have been turned down for a loan. Just any clue at all to his identity.

Ashenfelter: Well, as I say, his name is Y. Claude Garfunkel.

Gippard (after a weary sigh): It's not much to go on, but I'll see what I can do.

(Gippard rises and crosses to the master data-recall panel. Ashenfelter strolls to a nearby computer and casually begins checking the confidential reports on his four small children to learn how many are known extremists.)

Ashenfelter: You're new here, aren't you?

Gippard: No. Just my first week on the night shift. Everybody got moved around after we lost McElhenny.

Ashenfelter: Wasn't he that heavy-set fellow with beady eyes who drove the Hudson?

Gippard: Yeah. Terrible thing. Pulled his own dossier one night when things were quiet and found out he was a swish. Kind of made him go all to pieces.

Ashenfelter: That's a shame. And now I suppose he's gone into analysis and gotten himself cross-filed as a loony.

Gippard: No. He blew his brains out right away. But having a suicide on your record can make things tough, too.

Ashenfelter: Yeah. Shows a strong trend toward instability.

(The computer informs Ashenfelter that his oldest boy was detained by police in 1963 for roller-skating on municipal property, and that the five-year-old probably founded the Farmer-Labor Party in Minnesota.)

Ashenfelter (cont.) (mutters in despair): Where did I fail them as a father?

Gippard: Didn't you tell me you're with Indian Affairs?

Ashenfelter: Yeah. Why?

Gippard: I think I'm onto something hot. Is that like India Indians or whoop-it-up Indians?

Ashenfelter: I guess you'd say whoop-it-up.

Gippard: Well, either way, no Indian named Garfunkel has ever complied with the Alien Registration Law.

Ashenfelter: I never said he was an Indian. He's Jewish, and I think he's playing around with my wife.

Gippard: Gee, that's too bad.

Ashenfelter (dramatically): Oh, I blame myself really. I guess I'd started taking LaVerne for granted and—

Gippard: No. I mean it's too bad he's only Jewish. The computers aren't programmed to feed back home-wreckers by religious affiliation.

Ashenfelter: Oh.

Gippard: Can you think of anything kinky that's traditional with Jews? You know. Like draft dodging . . . smoking pot . . . something a computer could really hang its hat on.

Ashenfelter: No. They just seem to feed each other a lot of chicken soup. And they do something around Christmastime with candles. But I'm not sure any of it's illegal.

Gippard: We'll soon see. If the curve on known poultry processors correlates geographically with a year-end upswing in tallow rendering—Well, you can appreciate what that kind of data would mean to the bird dogs at the ICC and the FDA. They'd be able to pinpoint exactly where it was all happening and when.

Ashenfelter: Uh-huh—Where and when what?

Gippard: That's exactly what I intend to find out.

(Gippard turns back to the panel and resumes work with a sense of destiny. Ashenfelter, whistling softly to himself, absently begins plunking the basic melody of "Mexicali Rose" on the keyboard of a nearby computer. The machine responds by furnishing him with Howard Hughes's 1965 income tax return and the unlisted phone numbers of eight members of a New Orleans wife-swapping club who may have known Lee Harvey Oswald. As Ashenfelter pockets the information, Major General Courtney ("Old Napalm

and Guts") Nimshaw enters. He has a riding crop but no mustache.)

Nimshaw: Yoohoo! Anybody home?

Gippard: Back here at the main console.

(Nimshaw moves to join Gippard, then sees Ashenfelter for the first time and freezes. The two stand eyeing each other suspiciously as Gippard re-enters the scene.)

Gippard: Oh, forgive me. General Nimshaw, I'd like for you to meet Ashenfelter from Indian Affairs.

(Nimshaw and Ashenfelter ad-lib warm greetings as they shake hands. Then each rushes off to pull the dossier of the other. Ashenfelter learns that Nimshaw was a notorious bed wetter during his days at West Point and that his heavy drinking later caused an entire airborne division to be parachuted into Ireland on D-Day. Nimshaw learns that Ashenfelter owns 200 shares of stock in a Canadian steel mill that trades with Communist China and that he has been considered a bad credit risk since 1949, when he refused to pay a Cincinnati dance studio for $5500 worth of tango lessons. Apparently satisfied, both men return to join Gippard, who has been checking out a possible similarity in the patterns of poultry-buying by key Jewish housewives and reported sightings of Soviet fishing trawlers off the Alaskan coast.)

Ashenfelter: Working late tonight, eh, General?

Nimshaw (nervously): Well, I just stumbled across a little military hardware transport thing. We seem to have mislaid an eighty-six-car trainload of munitions between here and the West Coast. Can't very well write it off as normal pilferage. So I thought maybe Gippard could run a check for me on the engineer and brakeman. You know. Where they hang out in their spare time. Whether they might take a freight train with them. What do you think, Gipp?

Gippard: Sure. Just have a few more things to run through for Ashenfelter first. He's seeking a final solution to the Jewish problem.

Ashenfelter (blanching): Well, not exactly the whole—

Nimshaw: Oh, has all that come up again?

(Two janitors carrying lunch pails enter and cross directly to the computer programmed for medical case histories of nymphomaniacs. They pull several dossiers at random and then cross directly to a far corner, unwrapping bacon, lettuce, and tomato sandwiches as they go. They spread a picnic cloth on the floor and begin reading the dossiers as they eat. They emit occasional guffaws, but the others pay no attention to them.)

Gippard (as he compares graph curves): No doubt about it.

Whatever those Russian trawlers are up to, it's good for the delicatessen business. This could be the break we've been hoping for.

Nimshaw: Hating Jews been a big thing with you for quite a while, Ashenfelter?

Ashenfelter (coldly): About as long as you've been losing government property by the trainload, I imagine.

(Nimshaw and Ashenfelter eye each other uneasily for a moment. Then they quickly exchange hush money in the form of drafts drawn against secret Swiss bank accounts as Gippard's assistant, Llewelyn Fordyce, enters. Fordyce is a typical brilliant young career civil servant who has been lost for several hours trying to find his way back from the men's room. He appears haggard, but is in satisfactory condition otherwise.)

Fordyce: Are you gentlemen being taken care of?

(Ashenfelter and Nimshaw nod affirmatively. Fordyce hurriedly roots through the desk drawers, pausing only to take a quick, compulsive inventory of paper clips and map pins as he does so.)

Fordyce (cont.) (shouts): Hey, Gipp! I can't find the registry cards for these two idiots out here.

Gippard (faintly, from a distance): I've been too busy to sign 'em in yet. Take care of it, will you?

(Fordyce gives a curt, efficient nod, inefficiently failing to realize that Gippard is too far away to see him nodding. Fordyce then brings forth two large pink cards and hands them to Nimshaw and Ashenfelter.)

Fordyce: If you'd just fill these out please. We're trying to accumulate data on everybody who uses the data bank so we can eventually tie it all in with something or other.

(Nimshaw studies the section of his card dealing with maximum fines and imprisonment for giving false information, while Ashenfelter skips over the hard part and goes directly to the multiple-choice questions.)

Fordyce (cont.): And try to be as specific as you can about religious beliefs and your affiliation with subversive groups. We're beginning to think there's more to this business of Quakers denying they belong to the Minutemen than meets the eye.

(Nimshaw and Ashenfelter squirm uneasily as they sense the implication. Ashenfelter hurriedly changes his answer regarding prayer in public schools from "undecided" to "not necessarily" as Nimshaw perjures himself by listing the principal activity at the Forest Hills Tennis Club as tennis. Meantime, Gippard has rejoined

the group, carrying four rolls of computer tape carefully stacked in no particular sequence.)

Gippard: I know I'm onto something here, Fordyce, but I'm not sure what to make of it. Surveillance reports on kosher poultry dealers indicate that most of them don't even show up for work on Saturday. And that timing correlates with an unexplained increase in activity at golf courses near key military installations. But the big thing is that drunken drivers tend to get nabbed most often on Saturday night, and that's exactly when organized groups are endangering national security by deliberately staying up late with their lights turned on to overload public power plants.

Fordyce (whistles softly in amazement): We're really going to catch a covey of them in this net. How'd you happen to stumble across it all?

Gippard: Well, it seemed pretty innocent at first. This clown from Indian Affairs just asked me to dig up what I could so he'd have some excuse for exterminating the Jews.

(Ashenfelter emits a burbling throat noise as an apparent prelude to something more coherent, but he is quickly shushed.)

Gippard (cont.): But you know how one correlation always leads to another. Now we've got a grizzly by the tail, Fordyce, and I can see "organized conspiracy" written all over it.

Fordyce: Beyond question. And somewhere among those 192 million dossiers is the ID number of the Mister Big we're after. Do the machines compute a cause-and-effect relationship that might help narrow things down?

Gippard: Well, frankly, the computers have gotten into a pretty nasty argument among themselves over that. Most of them see how golf could lead to drunken driving. But the one that's programmed to chart moral decay and leisure time fun is pretty sure that drunken driving causes golf.

(Nimshaw glances up from the job of filling out his registry card.)

Nimshaw: That's the most ridiculous thing I ever heard in my life.

Fordyce (with forced restraint): General, would you please stick to whatever people like you are supposed to know about and leave computer-finding interpretation to analysts who are trained for the job?

(Nimshaw starts to reply, but then recalls the fate of a fellow officer who was broken to corporal for insubordination. He meekly resumes pondering question No. 153, unable to decide whether

admitting or denying the purchase of Girl Scout cookies will weigh most heavily against him in years to come.)

Fordyce (cont.): Any other cause-and-effect computations that we ought to consider in depth, Gipp?

Gippard: Not really. Of course, Number 327's been out of step with the others ever since it had that circuitry trouble. It just keeps saying, "Malcolm W. Biggs causes kosher poultry." Types out the same damned thing over and over: "Malcolm W. Biggs causes kosher poultry."

Fordyce: Who's Malcolm W. Biggs?

Gippard: I think he was a juror at one of the Jimmy Hoffa trials. Number 327 was running a check on him when the circuits blew, and it's had kind of an obsession about him ever since.

Fordyce: Mmmm. Well, personally, I've never paid much attention to the opinions of paranoids. They can get your thinking as screwed up as theirs is.

(Fordyce notices Ashenfelter making an erasure on his card to change the data regarding his shoe size from 9½ C to something less likely to pinch across the instep.)

Fordyce (cont.) (shrieks at Ashenfelter): What do you think you're doing there? You're trying to hide something from me. I've met your kind before.

(Ashenfelter wearily goes back to a 9½ C, even though they make his feet hurt, and Fordyce reacts with a look of smug satisfaction.)

Gippard: Maybe if I fed this junk back into the machine, it could name some people who fit the pattern.

Fordyce: Why don't you just reprocess the computations in an effort to gain individualized data that correlates?

(Gippard stares thoughtfully at Fordyce for a long moment and then exits to nail the ringleaders through incriminating association with the key words "drunk," "poultry," "golf," and "kilowatt.")

Nimshaw: I think maybe I'd better come back sometime when you're not so busy.

(He slips his registry card into his pocket and starts toward the door, but Fordyce grabs him firmly by the wrist.)

Fordyce: Just a minute. You can't take that card out of here with you. It may contain classified information you shouldn't even have access to.

Nimshaw: But it's about me. I'm the one who just filled it out.

Fordyce: Don't try to muddy up the issue. Nobody walks out of this department with government property. Let's have it.

(Nimshaw reluctantly surrenders the card. Fordyce glances at it and reacts with a look of horror.)

Fordyce (cont.): You've filled this whole thing out in longhand! The instructions clearly state, "Type or print legibly." You'll have to do it over again.

(Fordyce tears up the card and hands Nimshaw a new one. Nimshaw, suddenly aware that a display of bad conduct could cost him his good conduct medal, goes back to work, sobbing quietly to himself.)

Gippard (faintly, from a distance): Eureka! Hot damn!

Fordyce (happily): He's hit paydirt. I know old Gippard, and he hasn't cut loose like that since he linked Ralph Nader with the trouble at Berkeley.

(Gippard enters on the dead run, unmindful of the computer tape streaming out behind him.)

Gippard: It all correlates beautifully (ticks off points on his fingers). A chicken plucker. Three arrests for common drunk. FBI's observed him playing golf with a known Cuban. Psychiatric report shows he sleeps with all the lights on.

Fordyce: All wrapped up in one neat bundle. Who is he?

Gippard: A virtual unknown. Never been tagged as anything worse than possibly disloyal until I found him. He uses the name Y. Claude Garfunkel.

Ashenfelter: Y. Claude Garfunkel!

Fordyce (menacingly): Touch a raw nerve, Ashenfelter?

(The two janitors, who are really undercover sophomores majoring in forestry at Kansas State on CIA scholarships, rise and slowly converge on Ashenfelter.)

Gippard: Want to tell us about it, Ashenfelter? We have our own methods of computing the truth out of you anyway, you know.

Fordyce: No point in stalling. What's the connection? The two of you conspired to give false opinions to the Harris Poll, didn't you?

Ashenfelter (pitifully): No! Nothing like that. I swear.

Gippard: Then what, man? What? Have you tried to sabotage the Data Bank by forging each other's Social Security numbers?

Ashenfelter (a barely audible whisper): No. Please don't build a treason case against me. I'll tell. A neighbor saw him with my wife at a luau in Baltimore.

(The CIA men posing as college students posing as janitors react intuitively to jab Ashenfelter with a sodiumpentathol injection. Gippard rushes to a computer, where he begins cross-checking Garfunkel and Ashenfelter in the Urban Affairs file on "Polynesian

power" advocates in Baltimore's Hawaiian ghetto and Interstate Commerce Commission reports on suspected participants in interstate hanky-panky. Fordyce grabs the red "hot line" telephone on his desk and reacts with annoyance as he gets a busy signal. General Nimshaw, sensing himself caught up in a tide of events which he can neither turn back nor understand, hastily erases the computer tape containing his own dossier and then slashes his wrists under an assumed name.)

Fade Out.